DATE DUE

Prosecutors and Politics:
A Comparative Perspective

Prosecutors and Politics: A Comparative Perspective

Edited by Michael Tonry

Crime and Justice
A Review of Research
Edited by Michael Tonry

VOLUME 41

The University of Chicago Press, Chicago and London

The University of Chicago Press, Chicago 60637
The University of Chicago Press, Ltd., London

© 2012 by The University of Chicago
All rights reserved.
Printed in the United States of America

ISSN: 0192-3234

ISBN: 978-0-226-00967-4

LCN: 80-642217

Library of Congress Cataloging-in-Publication Data

Prosecutors and politics : a comparative perspective / edited by Michael Tonry.
    p. cm.—(Crime and justice : a review of research; v. 41)
    Includes indexes. 77—
    ISBN 978-0-226-00967-4 (cloth)—ISBN 978-0-226-00970-4 (pbk.)—ISBN (invalid)
978-0-226-01018-2 (ebook) 1. Public prosecutors. 2. Justice, Administration of.
3. Public prosecutors—United States. I. Tonry, Michael H. II. Series: Crime and justice
(Chicago, Ill.) ; v. 41.
K5425.P78 2012
345′.01262—dc23

                                                                2012022640

Contents

Preface

Prosecutors are not everywhere the same. In every developed country except the United States, they are nonpartisan, apolitical civil servants. In most countries, they are specialized judges or like judges are expected to be evenhanded, dispassionate, and objective. Decisions about individual cases are to be made on their merits, without regard to public attitudes, opinions, and emotions or to politicians' preferences or priorities.

In the United States, things are different. Chief prosecutors are almost always elected, usually at the county level, and sometimes after elections in which more attention was paid to toughness than to justice. In the federal system, US attorneys are appointed on the basis of partisan and sometimes ideological criteria. Because local prosecutors are elected members of the executive branch of government, the US Supreme Court in *Bordenkircher v. Hayes* (434 U.S. 357 [1978]) ruled on separation-of-powers grounds that their decisions are unreviewable by the courts except in cases of alleged corruption or other illegality. American prosecutors are in that sense lawless; they exercise their enormous powers over citizens' lives without being accountable to anyone but the electorate.

In some countries, prosecutors are judges and sometimes switch roles during their careers. In other countries, they work for ministries of justice or, in a few countries, in police departments. In some countries, prosecutors are guided by a "legality" principle that requires them to pursue every case for which available evidence would justify a conviction. In other countries, an "expediency" principle empowers them to exercise discretion in deciding which cases to prosecute.

It would be reasonable to expect there to be a vast literature on how prosecution systems work in individual countries or within the United

States and on the different properties and outcomes of different systems. Any such expectation would be disappointed. Empirical studies of prosecutorial processes, decision making, and outcomes based on original empirical research are almost nonexistent. Almost all current knowledge comes from the personal experiences of individuals, from anecdotal information, and from descriptions of statutory powers, procedural rules, and bureaucratic organization. Knowing about laws and rules in books, however, is not the same as knowing how they are applied and misapplied in action.

Citizens should want to know how such powerful officials exercise their discretion; whether and how personal ideology, political beliefs, or partisan affiliation affects the decisions made; whether the gender, race, or ethnicity of prosecutors, defendants, and victims affects decisions; and whether prosecutors behave more justly and consistently in some types of systems than in others. The existing empirical literature can answer none of these questions.

It is not obvious why prosecution is so understudied. In the United States at least, police departments, courts, probation and parole agencies, and prison systems have permitted observational and other qualitative studies of their operations, have allowed offenders and suspects under their control to participate in surveys, and have made official data available for quantitative analyses. Prosecutors' offices generally have not.

There are good reasons to want to know more. One is to understand better the strengths and weaknesses of particular systems in order to be able to identify and ameliorate the weaknesses. Another is to learn which kinds of systems better promote values of equality, justice, and rationality so that policy makers can look across national boundaries to find ways to improve their own national systems.

The United States is the country most in need of improvement. It is also, because of the entrenched constitutional bases of its prosecution systems, the most resistant to change. That is a great pity because it means that injustice and unequal treatment are inevitable. Local prosecutors proudly declaim the importance of local cultural values, public attitudes, and public opinion. Practices, policies, and priorities necessarily vary widely between counties and thus within a state. Even the best prosecutors sometimes find political implications impossible to ignore in setting policies and priorities and in making decisions about individual cases. The worst give free rein to partisan and ideological considerations. That's no way to do justice.

This volume represents one small effort to begin to build an empirical literature within the United States and cross-nationally. People who are intimately familiar with particular systems were asked to write rich case studies about the system in their state or country. Similar articles have been written before this on individual countries, though usually with greater emphasis on how things are organized and supposed to work than on how they do work. Nothing like the case studies on Arizona, North Carolina, and Washington is available elsewhere on any American state.

Books like this one require lots of work. A conference was held in Minneapolis in April 2011 to discuss initial drafts of the commissioned essays. That conference was attended by the writers and also by Stephanos Bibas (University of Pennsylvania), Frank Bowman (University of Missouri), John Chisholm (District Attorney, Milwaukee), Pat Diamond (Deputy County Attorney, Hennepin County, Minnesota), Anthony Doob (University of Toronto), Antony Duff (University of Minnesota), Richard Frase (University of Minnesota), James Hamilton (Director of Public Prosecutions, Ireland), Robert M. A. Johnson (Anoka County Attorney Emeritus, Minnesota), Wayne Logan (Florida State University), Erik Luna (Washington and Lee University), Ross Macmillan (Bocconi University, Italy), Alan Manson (Queen's University, Ontario), Yann Marguet (University of Lausanne, Switzerland), Sandra Marshall (University of Minnesota), David Nelken (University of Macerata, Italy), Michael O'Hear (Marquette University), Joshua Page (University of Minnesota), Kevin Reitz (University of Minnesota), Kate Stith (Yale University), and Thomas Weigend (University of Cologne, Germany). Fourteen people from a variety of countries served as anonymous reviewers of the initial drafts. Adepeju Solarin, with help from then law students Reece Almond, Colleen Chambers, Karen Nelson, and Nick Wunder, organized the conference. Su Smallen and Robbi Strandemo prepared the manuscripts for publication and coordinated the handling of edited copy and proofs. Su did the onerous and painstaking job of preparing the cumulative indices of the 41 *Crime and Justice* volumes published to date that appear at the back of this volume. Funding for the conference and the volume was provided by University of Minnesota Law School Dean David Wippman from funds provided by the Robina Foundation and by the Law School's Institute on Crime and Public Policy. I am grateful to them all.

Many people and several organizations helped out. Readers will decide for themselves whether the effort was worthwhile.

Michael Tonry
Bologna, Italy, August 2012

Michael Tonry

Prosecutors and Politics in Comparative Perspective

Prosecutors are potentially the most powerful figures in any country's criminal justice system. They decide what crimes to prosecute; whom to charge; what to charge; whether to plea-bargain, offer concessions, or divert a case; how aggressively to seek a conviction; and what sentence to propose. Police arrest people, but prosecutors decide whether those arrests lead to charges. Judges preside over trials and sentence convicted offenders, but only those whom prosecutors bring before them.

Police, courts, and corrections systems are much the same in all developed countries, but prosecutors differ radically. Police everywhere mostly wear uniforms, operate within paramilitary organizations, and devote most of their time to directing traffic, patrolling streets, responding to calls, investigating crimes, and apprehending offenders. Local police cultures vary a bit from place to place, as do uniforms, technologies, and organizational structures, but their functions do not.

Courts process cases, act as impartial fact finders and adjudicators, and decide on dispositions. Organizational charts vary, lay judges or juries may or may not be involved, and trial procedures differ, but the core functions and responsibilities are everywhere the same.

Probation, prison, and parole systems likewise are much the same everywhere. They may be well or poorly managed, brutal or humane, and more or less committed to rehabilitative aspirations, but their responsibilities are the same: to manage people convicted of crimes safely and securely, to supervise performance of conditions, to coordinate delivery of services, and to react appropriately when people under their control misbehave.

Michael Tonry is grateful to Richard Frase, Erik Luna, Perry Moriearty, and Kevin Reitz for helpful comments on an earlier draft of this essay.

1

Individual police officers, judges, and correctional workers may be corrupt or incompetent or insensitive or biased, and institutions may be run poorly, but all those things are palpably undesirable and are everywhere seen as individual or institutional failings. In principle, all these officials and institutions, in every country, are expected to be apolitical, unbiased, and honest processors of offenses and offenders. They are expected to be neutral agents of the state, charged with even-handed enforcement of law and processing of criminal cases.

Prosecutors are different. They are not everywhere the same. One fundamental difference concerns their relations to partisan politics and public opinion. In most developed countries, particularly in continental Western Europe, Canada, and Japan, prosecutors are resolutely non-political and nonpartisan. They are expected to make decisions about individual cases on their merits, without regard to public attitudes, opinions, and emotions or to politicians' preferences or priorities. In the United States, however, local chief prosecutors in 45 states are elected (Perry 2006).[1] In the federal system, US attorneys are appointed on the basis of partisan and sometimes ideological criteria. American prosecutors sometimes openly and unashamedly take media reactions, public opinion, and political considerations into account when deciding what cases to prosecute and how to handle them. In England and Wales, the director of public prosecutions and her senior advisors are political appointees. Lesser-ranking prosecutors are not elected or selected on partisan political grounds, but political appointees set priorities on the basis of government policy preferences and political interests.

Transparently political prosecutions occur in some places. In some Eastern and Central European countries, justice ministers use the prosecution service to settle political scores. This happened regularly in recent years in Poland (Krajewski, in this volume). Western governments repeatedly condemned politically motivated prosecutions in Ukraine of former prime minister Yulia V. Tymoshenko (Barry 2011) and in Russia of Kremlin opponent Mikhail B. Khodorkovsky (Schwirtz 2012). Political prosecutions are less common in traditionally democratic countries but not unheard of. The American presidential administration of George W. Bush initiated politically motivated pros-

---

[1] They are appointed in Alaska, Connecticut, and New Jersey. Attorneys general in Delaware and Rhode Island are responsible for prosecution throughout their states and appoint local prosecutors from within their offices (Perry 2006).

ecutions of Democratic state officials, most notoriously of former Alabama governor Don Siegelman (Nossiter 2008), and fired Republican US attorney David Iglesias in New Mexico and other US attorneys because they refused to initiate politically motivated prosecutions (Lichtblau and Otterman 2008; US Department of Justice 2008).[2]

In most developed countries prosecutors are career civil servants, but they are not everywhere the same. In some countries, for example, in Sweden, Finland, and Germany, legal and professional norms predispose prosecutors to be evenhanded, reactive, case processors. In theory and to a considerable extent in practice, they base their decisions in individual cases solely on whether they believe that a crime has been committed, a particular individual committed it, and sufficient admissible evidence is available to justify a conviction. In others (the Netherlands, Japan, and the United States are well-known examples), prosecutors openly exercise discretion over what kinds of cases and which individuals to prosecute.

There are other important structural differences. In some countries, prosecutors are members of the judiciary. Individuals may serve as prosecutors and judges at different times in their careers. In some, they are part of the executive branch of government. In a few, including Norway and Denmark and until 1986 England and Wales, they are (or were) members of police departments. In most countries, prosecutors, although based in particular cities or towns, work for national (or state or provincial) agencies. In a few places, most notably throughout the United States, prosecutors work for local—city or county—governments.[3] Local prosecution agencies in 47 of the 50 American states are headed by elected officials (Wright 2009), as are a few (e.g., Geneva) in Switzerland.[4]

---

[2] A small political science literature shows that Republican national administrations over the last 30 years have regularly targeted Democratic officeholders in politically motivated prosecutions (e.g., Gordon and Huber 2009, pp. 151–52).

[3] Early postindependence local prosecutors were not elected. They were appointed, mostly by state governors (Jacoby 1980). Beginning in the 1830s, American states enacted constitutional changes and statutes providing for elections. By the 1860s, when the Tammany Machine in New York City controlled the local prosecutors, the dangers of political influence were widely recognized (Ellis 2012).

[4] Swiss prosecutors are organized at the level of cantons. Switzerland is a federal state, making the cantons equivalent to American states. However, the national population in 2010 was 7.6 million people; Swiss cantons range in size from the equivalents of middle-sized to tiny US counties. In 2010, the largest of the 26 cantons had populations near 500,000 people; five had populations under 40,000.

Those organizational differences make a huge practical difference in what prosecutors do and in the roles they play. In most of the developed world, prosecutors project an image of impartiality, objectivity, and insulation from political influence. Many US prosecutors proudly claim to reflect local political and cultural values—as the Boerner, Wright, and Miller and Caplinger essays in this volume make clear. That these vary widely, and therefore lead to stark differences within a state in how similar cases are dealt with, is seen as inevitable. Local prosecutors in recent decades often openly subscribed to "law and order" values, and many ran for office promising they would be tougher than their opponents (Gordon and Huber 2002). In contested prosecutorial elections, candidates tend to focus on prominent criminal trials and conviction rates rather than on less emotive issues (Wright 2009). An accumulating literature shows that impending elections sometimes cause changes in the behavior of elected judges and prosecutors. Research in Pennsylvania showed that elected trial judges became more punitive in their sentencing decisions as elections approached (Huber and Gordon 2004). Trial judges in some judicial districts in Kansas run in unopposed retention elections; judges in other districts run for reelection in partisan contests. Gordon and Huber (2007) showed that judges elected in partisan districts were more punitive than those in nonpartisan districts.

If judges, whose professional ethos includes impartiality, become more severe before elections, it would be astonishing if prosecutors did not. Bandyopadhyay and McCannon (2011) found in North Carolina that prosecutors' offices conducted five times as many jury trials (which in the United States are associated with harsher sentences than plea bargains or bench trials) in election years as in other years.

By contrast, prosecutors in many countries, for example, in Scandinavia, strongly believe that similarly situated offenders should be treated equally, or as close to equally as is humanly possible, no matter where within a country or by whom they are prosecuted. Petter Asp (in this volume) reports that Swedish judges, prosecutors, and newspapers would consider the existence of different sentencing patterns in Malmo and Stockholm to be fundamentally unjust: a principle of equal treatment requires that the state treat similarly situated citizens in the same way.

Remarkably little research is done on public prosecution within single countries, or on jurisdictions within them, or on differences between systems in different places. The European Commission for the Efficiency of Justice biennially publishes statistics for the Council of Europe on judicial and prosecutorial caseloads, case flows, and budgets and summarizes information on a variety of subjects (CEPEJ 2010). With the exception of a few book-length case studies of one or a few countries (e.g., Fionda 1995; Johnson 2002; Hodgson 2005) and a number of collections containing articles providing descriptions of different national systems (e.g., vander Beken and Kilchling 2000; Tak 2004; Jehle and Wade 2006; Jehle, Wade, and Elsner 2008), comparative knowledge about prosecution systems is largely anecdotal.[5]

Despite its scantiness, the comparative literature makes it clear that the American system of public prosecution is unique in the world and in an important sense lawless. Discretionary prosecutorial decisions are for all practical purposes immune from judicial review. The existence in most states and the federal system of mandatory minimum sentence, three-strikes, and "repeat offender" laws means that prosecutors can routinely file or threaten criminal charges that would subject defendants to sentences that are disproportionately severe relative to the offenses for which they were arrested. Offers to dismiss such charges as a condition of a guilty plea to a different charge often are too good to be refused (e.g., Knapp 1991). Partly as a result, 95 percent or more of convictions result from plea bargains.

This means that a prosecutor, not a judge, determines which defendants, if any, warrant special consideration and which should serve disproportionately long prison sentences. Federal Court of Appeals Judge (and Columbia Law School professor) Gerald Lynch observed:

> The prosecutor, rather than a judge or jury, is the central adjudicator of facts (as well as replacing the judge as arbiter of most legal issues and of the appropriate sentence to be imposed). Potential defenses are presented by the defendant and his counsel not in a court, but to a prosecutor, who assesses their factual accuracy and likely persuasiveness to a hypothetical judge or jury, and then decides the charge of which the defendant should be adjudged guilty. Mitigating information, similarly, is argued not to the judge, but to the prosecutor, who decides what sentence the defendant should be given in exchange for his plea. (Lynch 2003, pp. 1403–4)

[5] Worrall and Nugent-Borakove (2008) and Luna and Wade (2012) are collections that solely or mostly discuss American issues and developments.

Lynch suggests that the American criminal justice system now resembles the inquisitorial judicial systems of continental Europe, with the crucial difference that an adversary prosecutor rather than an impartial judge acts as fact finder and assessor of guilt and punishment for most cases.

The system Lynch describes is relatively recent. Before 1975, every American state and the federal system had an indeterminate sentencing system in which judges set maximum and sometimes minimum sentences but parole boards decided when prisoners were released (Rothman 1971; Blumstein et al. 1983, chap. 1). Mandatory minimum sentence laws were few in number and typically required either a minimum 1-year sentence or the addition of a 1-year increment if, for example, a gun was used (Tonry 2009). Plea bargaining was common, but the stakes were not high. If the judge had little control over the lengths of prison sentences, the prosecutor could not have much influence either.

All that changed after 1975 (Fisher 2003). Some states and the federal government abolished their parole boards, which meant that the sentences judges announced in those jurisdictions ceased to be nominal; less predictable reductions for good time (time off for good behavior), the sentence imposed determined the time spent in prison. Every American jurisdiction enacted new mandatory minimum sentence laws, more than half enacted three-strikes laws, more than half enacted "truth-in-sentencing" laws requiring that some offenders serve at least 85 percent of announced prison terms, and many enacted "career criminal" or "repeat offender" laws requiring lengthy minimum sentences for repeat offenders. A few jurisdictions, preeminently the federal system acting through the US Sentencing Commission, enacted "mandatory" sentencing guidelines (Tonry 2011, chap. 1).

Those changes tied judges' hands and shifted enormous power to prosecutors, as Albert Alschuler (1978) quickly recognized and predicted. The power to charge a provable offense subject to a mandatory minimum 10-year sentence or to a three-strikes law requiring a minimum sentence of 25 years to life is tantamount to the power unilaterally to sentence offenders. The power under the federal sentencing guidelines to select the cell in a guidelines matrix that will determine an offender's sentence is tantamount to unilateral power over sentencing.

The statutory changes were part of the "law and order" movement that sought to tie judges' hands and make sentencing harsher. David Boerner (1995), formerly deputy district attorney of King County (Seattle), Washington, pointed out that the transfer of power from judges to prosecutors was not inadvertent. Legislatures had much less worry that elected prosecutors would be "lenient" than that judges would be. Elected prosecutors are much more likely to pay attention to public attitudes and opinions, and the directions the political winds are blowing, than judges are.

Lynch (2003) is right in his description of the power of the prosecutor in many cases to determine both charge and sentence. The implications for the rule of law in American criminal courts are dire. European judges are nonpolitical, nonpartisan, nonadversary, and acculturated into professional values of neutrality, objectivity, and independence; their legal and sentencing decisions are subject to review by higher courts. None of those things is true of American prosecutors (K. Davis 1968; A. Davis 2007).

If prosecutors possess enormous power, as they do everywhere, and if they differ more greatly between jurisdictions than other criminal justice officials and agencies, as they do, we should want to know what differences those differences make. We don't. This essay surveys the intellectual topography of what we do know about prosecution systems and studies. Section I summarizes fundamental structural, normative, and policy characteristics and differences between national systems. Section II discusses important effects of those differences. Any rational, well-informed defendant facing prosecution somewhere would prefer that it happen anywhere except in the United States. Section III discusses explanations for the major differences and proposes ways in which more can be learned.

I. The Differences

There are formal differences between prosecution systems, and there are normative differences that influence day-to-day operations and decisions. Both are important.

A. Foundational Differences

Important differences derive from foundational characteristics of national legal systems. The most important are contrasts between continental European civil-law and Anglo-Saxon common-law systems, between systems characterized by the "legality principle" and the "expediency principle," and between countries in which political influence on criminal justice system operations is and is not considered legitimate. In legality principle jurisdictions, prosecutors officially have limited or no discretion in the handling of individual cases. In expediency principle jurisdictions, they do. These three contrasts move in parallel, but only partly. All common-law systems, for example, follow the expediency principle, but they differ over the legitimacy of political influence on prosecutorial decisions: Australia and Canada celebrate its absence, the English allow it, and Americans celebrate it.

1. *Adversarial and Inquisitorial Systems.* The civil law/common law contrast is exemplified by competing images of "adversarial" and "inquisitorial" processes (e.g., Damaška 1975, 1986). In adversarial systems, the judge and jury in theory have no knowledge of the case. Competing counsel are legal gladiators. They present evidence and offer legal arguments favorable to their clients' interests, constrained only by evidentiary rules and injunctions against dishonest and unethical behavior. Detailed rules govern the admissibility of evidence in order to lessen the likelihood that lay jurors will be influenced by improper emotional considerations or unreliable evidence. The judge resolves legal issues and the judge or jury decides what happened and whether and of what the defendant is guilty.

In most inquisitorial systems, the judge or panel of judges, in some countries including lay members, aim to learn what really happened and whether the defendant is guilty of a crime. Pretrial investigations by the police, the prosecutor, and sometimes an investigating magistrate aim to collect evidence that will show whether a suspect is or is not guilty. The prosecutor is as concerned to exculpate the innocent as to convict the guilty and in many countries makes no recommendations about sentencing; that is solely the judge's responsibility. If the prosecutor decides a crime has occurred, the suspect did it, and sufficient evidence exists to support a conviction, the evidence is usually presented to the court in a dossier containing detailed descriptions of the crime and the evidence.[6] Counsel is present at the trial and sen-

---

[6] The broad picture painted in this paragraph applies to most continental European countries (Tak 2004, vol. 1, p. 13). Italy (Illuminati 2004; Caianiello 2012), Portugal (Barona-Vilar 2004), and Spain (Salreu 2004; Aebi and Balcells 2008), which adopted some elements of adversarial systems including in minor cases joint recommendations about sentences, and the Scandinavian countries, which share a "Scandinavian model"

tencing and may ask questions and make statements, but the judge actively participates and dominates. The judge assesses the evidence; asks questions of the defendant, any witnesses, and sometimes the lawyers; and decides whether the suspect is guilty of a crime. This must be done whether or not the defendant acknowledges guilt. The defendant cannot simply plead guilty and terminate the proceeding. The judge decides the sentence.[7]

The preceding stylized descriptions of course oversimplify (Weigend 2012). In the United States, trials are comparatively rare. Upwards of 95 percent of defendants plead guilty in most courts, usually in response to inducements offered by the prosecutor. English defendants are offered sentence discounts up to one-third depending on whether and when they plead guilty (Ashworth 2010; Lewis 2012). In most civil-law countries, prosecutors have authority, discussed below, to dispose of less serious cases by means of "transactions" (the Netherlands and Belgium), "conditional dismissals" (Germany), and "penal orders" (many countries including France, the Netherlands, and Sweden). The first two involve performance of a financial or equivalent penalty but no conviction. The penal order involves a penalty offered by the prosecutor, results in a conviction, and must be approved by a judge. Some observers, mainly Americans, claim that these dispositions are equivalent to plea bargains. Others, mainly Europeans, disagree, arguing that most such dispositions do not result in convictions, are offered on a take-it-or-leave-it basis, hew closely to established rules, and are even-handedly offered to eligible suspects.[8] They argue that free-ranging negotiations—as in American plea bargaining—would violate the legality principle, or its normative equivalent in expediency principle jurisdictions, that requires that cases be handled consistently.

2. *The Legality and Expediency Principles.* The legality/expediency distinction provides a second fundamental divide (e.g., Pifferi 2011).

---

that combines adversarial and inquisitorial features (Lappi-Seppälä 2001; Lappi-Seppälä and Tonry 2011), are partial exceptions.

[7] Although for less serious cases, prosecutors may allow some defendants to agree to accept financial and equivalent penalties in lieu of prosecution, in which case the charges are dismissed without entry of a conviction. Such diversions are discussed in the following section.

[8] Both sides of the issue are canvassed in Turner (2009) and Thaman (2010), two law-teaching books that somewhat oddly treat the debate over the existence of plea bargaining in countries other than the United States as the principal comparative law question of interest concerning prosecution systems. The only recent history of US prosecution has also focused primarily on plea bargaining (Fisher 2003).

The legality principle, also sometimes called the equality principle, derives from a simple but basic conception of the liberal state. A state governed by the Rule of Law, generally referred to in shorthand by reference to the German term *Rechtsstaat*, should treat comparably situated people in the same or closely comparable ways. In theory, police and prosecutors must follow applicable rules,[9] or their underlying principles, in deciding how to handle particular cases and do not exercise discretion over whether and how to proceed. The aims of the criminal process are to determine whether a suspect has committed a particular offense and, if so, to impose a sanction commensurate with those received by others who have committed the same offense.

The expediency principle, by contrast, justifies discretionary police and prosecutorial decisions in individual decisions. In any legal system, including legality principle systems, prosecutors may decide not to proceed with a case because a crime is *de minimis*, the victim opposes prosecution, or there is insufficient evidence to prove it.[10] In expediency principle systems, however, prosecutors are authorized to dispose of cases for any good-faith reason, such as extenuating circumstances, victim compensation, or conflict with other prosecution priorities.

Whether a legal system gives primacy to the legality principle has important implications. Plea bargaining that resulted in reduced sentences or dismissal of provable charges necessarily would result in unequal treatment of comparably culpable people. That violates the legality principle and cannot be justified. Imposition of exemplary punishments on some defendants in order to send deterrent messages, reassure the public, or take account of public opinion necessarily would result in unequal treatment compared with punishments of comparable defendants. That likewise could not be justified.

Differing views on the importance of the legality principle underlie major differences between countries in punishment policies and practices. In the early twentieth century, American intellectual elites and policy makers, influenced by utilitarian and positivist ideas, came to believe that prevention and rehabilitation, rather than imposition of

---

[9] In Germany, the rules provide that police and other justice system officials may not lie to suspects and defendants as in "Your accomplice in the next room has confessed; it's in your interest to do so" or "The other officer is much harsher than I am; if you know what's good for you, you'll talk to me" (Ross 2008).

[10] Asp (in this volume) describes the detailed Swedish rules governing such decisions not to prosecute.

deserved punishments, should be the primary aims of sentencing (Tonry 2011, chap. 1). Sentences, they believed, should be individualized to take account of rehabilitative and incapacitative considerations (Michael and Adler 1933). Jerome Michael and Herbert Wechsler explained that retribution may represent "the unstudied belief of most men" but concluded that "no legal provision can be justified merely because it calls for the punishment of the morally guilty by penalties proportioned to their guilt, or criticized merely because it fails to do so" (1940, pp. 7, 11). By 1930, every state had established an indeterminate sentencing system; the systems endured everywhere until the mid-1970s (Rothman 1971, 1980) and continued in 2012 to exist in a majority of American states. European intellectuals and policy makers, by contrast, though influenced by the same ideas, rejected indeterminate sentencing as incompatible with the legality principle (Pifferi 2011).[11]

The legality/expediency principle distinction is not congruent with

---

[11] As a historical matter, differing views on the importance of the legality principle underlay major differences between legal systems. From the 1890s through the 1920s, most scholars and many practitioners in North America and Europe described themselves as utilitarians or positivists and believed that most crime is attributable to environmental influences and psychological characteristics. Prevention and rehabilitation, they believed, not imposition of proportionate punishments, should be the primary aim of sentencing. The implications were stark for the traditional "Classical School" view that punishments must be closely apportioned to the seriousness of the crime. Punishments instead should not be predicated on crime seriousness but should be individualized to take account of rehabilitative and incapacitative considerations and should be indeterminate so that prisoners could be released when deemed rehabilitated or no longer dangerous. Michael and Wechsler (1937) discuss these issues and the prevailing ways of thinking in detail.

Debates over the proposed change began on both sides of the Atlantic in the 1890s. By the late 1920s, continental European countries had rejected indeterminate sentencing because of widespread concern that adopting it would violate the legality principle mandate that like-situated citizens be treated equally by the state (Pifferi 2011). In the United States, however, the legality principle was not seen as a fundamental requirement of justice. By 1930, every state had adopted indeterminate sentencing (Rothman 1971). It survived everywhere until the 1970s. Prison sentences imposed by judges had little meaning since parole boards set release dates. The sentences judges announced were usually much longer than prisoners served. One unhappy, unforeseeable consequence is that, when political and normative support for indeterminate sentencing collapsed in the 1970s, new sentencing laws were often based not on the sentences prisoners served before they were released on parole but on the much longer ones judges announced. That is an important structural explanation for why most prison sentences in other developed countries are usually expressed in months or low single-digit years rather than, as in the United States, years and decades. Under indeterminate sentencing, the American numbers were nominal and symbolic. That difference in nominal sentence lengths was a major contributor to the rapid and steep rise in US imprisonment that began in 1973.

the adversarial/inquisitorial distinction. The Anglo-Saxon countries all operate under the expediency principle, but so do some European countries including the Netherlands, Norway, and Denmark. England and Wales, like the continental Europeans, rejected indeterminate sentencing because of concern about the legality principle and established a parole board only in 1968. More recently, however, England has come to resemble the United States much more closely in giving comparatively little weight to ideas about equal treatment in sentencing (Tonry 2004*a*).

3. *Democratic Accountability.* The third important foundational distinction concerns the role of public opinion or, some would say, "democratic accountability." This is to me puzzling since it seems self-evident that external considerations should be irrelevant to decisions in individual cases. In most countries' legal systems, for example, in the Scandinavian countries and Germany, public attitudes, emotions, and preferences are regarded as fundamentally inappropriate considerations in making prosecutorial or judicial decisions about individuals. Fifty years ago that was also true in the United States, as can be seen in the transcripts of 12 years' proceedings of the American Law Institute working group that drafted the Model Penal Code. Participants several times referred to public emotions provoked by notorious crimes, but no one suggested that they should influence decisions. The discussions centered instead on how best to assure that they did not (Tonry 2004*b*). In the contemporary United States, it is otherwise. Elected prosecutors regularly adjust their decisions to take account of public opinion and emotion and admit doing so in order to respond to community values and democratic accountability (Boerner, in this volume; Miller and Caplinger, in this volume; Wright, in this volume).

English policy makers and judges have repeatedly asserted that public opinion is a relevant consideration. Lord Chief Justice Bingham (1997), for example, noted that he "did not consider it would be right, even if it were possible, for judges to ignore the opinion of the public" (p. 1). Similarly, in Australia, an appellate court opinion observed, "the courts must show that they are responsive to public criticism of the outcome of sentencing practices" (Bagaric 2001, p. 23).

The notorious English case of 2-year-old William Bulger offers an extreme instance. His two 10-year-old killers were convicted of murder, which under English law requires imposition of a nominal life sentence. The trial judge set the tariff, or the minimum term to be served before consideration for parole release, at 8 years. Lord Taylor, the Lord Chief Justice, increased the tariff to 10 years. The home secretary, Michael Howard, raised it again to 15 years, taking into account "the judicial recommendations as well as all other relevant factors including the circumstances of the case, public concern about the case, and the need to maintain public confidence in the criminal justice system" (Home Office 1994).[12] Howard had received a petition with 278,300 signatures, demanding the two boys never be released under any circumstances (Green 2008).

The three foundational distinctions between prosecution systems do not line up perfectly, but they cluster. In general, inquisitorial systems are more likely than accusatorial systems to operate under the legality principle and to try to insulate decisions about individuals from influence by elected politicians, public opinion, and emotion.

This is not surprising. Even though the distinctions are not pure ones and every system is affected by budgetary constraints and high-volume caseloads, governing values matter. Most systems attempt to reduce costs and volume by diverting some cases from adjudication and by creating mechanisms for consensual dispositions of less serious cases. For these reasons, some observers argue that the differences between different kinds of legal systems are dissolving and that the implications of subscribing to different governing principles are becoming insignificant. That argument, however, overlooks the fundamental point that structures and values interact. For practitioners working within inquisitorial systems governed by the legality principle, the ultimately important questions are what the suspect did and what punishment he or she deserves. Public opinions and political interests are irrelevant to those judgments, are likely to be seen as normatively inappropriate, and are likely to be resisted or ignored. People working in adversarial systems governed by the expediency principle, especially in countries such as the United States and England, in which politically

---

[12] In 1997 the English Court of Appeal ([1997] 2 WLR 67) and the House of Lords ([1997] 3 All ER 97) quashed the home secretary's decision on the grounds that a government minister should be barred from the inherently judicial function of deciding sentences in individual cases. The European Court of Human Rights ([1999] *T and V v. UK*, December 16) ruled that it was unlawful for government ministers to set tariffs because that is a judicial function. On October 26, 2000, Lord Chief Justice Woolf set the tariff to expire on February 21, 2001, reflecting the trial judge's initial decision (Green 2008).

chosen or elected officials direct prosecution systems, are less likely to consider extraneous considerations inappropriate.

B. Structural Location

The structural question is whether prosecutors are located in the judicial or executive branch of government.[13] In many civil-law countries, prosecutors are magistrates. In Sweden (Asp, in this volume), France (Hodgson 2012), and Italy (Caianiello 2012), for example, they are formally part of the judiciary and can at different times in their careers work as prosecutors or as judges. In other countries, such as the Netherlands (Tak 2012) and Poland (Bojańczyk 2012; Krajewski, in this volume), prosecutors work for independent agencies and typically remain prosecutors throughout their careers but are deemed to be equivalent to judges. This professional identification is important because it allows for a clear distinction between prosecutors' roles and functions. The role may be to prepare charges and process cases, but the functions are to convict the guilty and exculpate the innocent. No doubt sometimes the thrill of the chase, identification with victims, or emotional overreaction to crimes undermines the dispassionate stance the judicial label implies and leads to more aggressive prosecution than the facts warrant, but when that happens it is clearly wrong.

In other countries, prosecutors are members of the executive branch of government. This takes different forms, which have different implications. In England and Wales, prosecutors work for the Crown Prosecution Service, headed by a politically appointed director of public prosecutions. Line prosecutors are civil servants and are members of a national bureaucracy; though assigned to work in a specific district or the central headquarters, they can be transferred between districts. As members of the executive branch, prosecutors' priorities are set by political officials who take public opinion and political considerations into account (Lewis 2012). All Canadian prosecutors are civil servants in the attorneys general departments of a province or the federal government. In Norway and Denmark, prosecutors work within divisions of police departments that are local geographically based units of national police bureaucracies but nonetheless are operationally independent. In Japan, they work directly for the Ministry of Justice. In the

---

[13] Separation of powers is not formally part of Swedish constitutional law, but traditions of complete separation of prosecutorial and judicial decision making from political influence achieve at least equivalent separation.

United States, state prosecutors typically work in county-level offices headed by an elected chief prosecutor (usually called the district or county attorney). US federal prosecutors work in specialized units of the Department of Justice or in offices attached to federal district courts and headed by a US attorney who is a political appointee selected by the government of the day. Under recent Republican administrations, they have often been selected according to ideological and partisan political criteria (e.g., Lichtblau 2008).

The branch-of-government distinction, like the others discussed, is not watertight. The implications of working for an executive branch prosecutor vary between countries. In most countries, day-to-day work is not much affected. Danish and Norwegian prosecutors working in police departments in expediency principle countries do not operate significantly differently from Swedish and Finnish prosecutors working in the judiciary in legality principle countries (Lappi-Seppälä and Tonry 2011). Scandinavian cultural and legal values predominate in all four countries. Polish prosecutors are in theory like judges, though their institutional home is separate from the judiciary, and their work is governed by the legality principle. However, politically motivated prosecutions are not unknown (Krajewski, in this volume). Japanese prosecutors are risk averse, eager to dispose of cases informally, and more likely to drop meritorious cases because of slight doubts than to prosecute weak cases (Johnson, in this volume).

The United States is where the executive branch placement matters. Prosecution policies and priorities vary widely between counties and in the federal system between US attorneys' offices.[14] Local district attorneys are elected at the county level and are as a practical matter, except in relation to their own criminal or otherwise unlawful conduct, answerable to no one but the electorate. In *Bordenkircher v. Hayes* (434 U.S. 357 [1978]), the US Supreme Court made most prosecutorial decisions—whether to prosecute, to offer or enter into plea bargains, to dismiss charges—nonjusticiable as a matter of constitutional law in large part for the separation of powers reason that prosecutors are elected officials in the executive branch. The courts, so reasoned the

---

[14] Successive US attorneys general have issued formal policies on prosecution practices (see, e.g., Podgor 2012), but as a practical matter the individual US attorneys, who are separately nominated by the president and confirmed by the Senate, are highly autonomous.

Supreme Court, have no constitutional authority to second-guess the prosecutor's discretionary decisions. Only the electorate can do that.

The extreme consequences of the American system include use of ideological and partisan political criteria in civil service hiring, spurious federal criminal charges against Democratic Party politicians during the George W. Bush administration, and prosecutions in state courts on the basis of media coverage and electoral implications. Extreme abuses of power for political reasons are clearly wrong, but their origins cannot be attributed only to individuals' bad characters and bad values. The problems are at least partly structural and influence mundane day-to-day operations. Many Arizona prosecutors, for example, as Marc Miller and Samantha Caplinger's essay in this volume makes clear, are unconcerned whether offenders they prosecute are treated the same way as like-situated offenders in other counties. Ron Wright and David Boerner (in this volume) report that most prosecutors in North Carolina and Washington State are more sensitive than their Arizona peers to concerns about unequal treatment. Even in those more cosmopolitan places, though, prosecutors justify their policies and practices in terms of democratic accountability; if voters in county X are especially concerned about drug crimes, then prosecutors feel justified in prosecuting them more severely than elsewhere. If voters are especially concerned about violence or even about a particular notorious case, some prosecutors feel justified processing those cases especially aggressively, selectively seeking especially severe punishments, and in various ways being unusually punitive.

C. Selection, Recruitment, and Training

Recruitment and career structure together constitute a third fundamental differentiation. There are three broad patterns. They have important ramifications for career structure and professional socialization. In some countries, for example, in France, Germany, and the Scandinavian countries, aspiring prosecutors and judges begin to specialize in law school or immediately thereafter, effectively choosing a judicial or quasi-judicial career at an early age. This means among other things that they are socialized into a professional judicial culture that values impartiality and objectivity.

In a second set of countries, including England and Wales and Japan, most prosecutors begin their careers immediately or shortly after completing their legal training, undergo extensive professional training before starting work, and become career civil servants. Later lateral entry after more extended practice experience is possible but not common. In these countries, career officials are socialized into a prosecutorial rather than a primarily judicial professional culture.

In the third set of countries, assistant prosecutors do not have specialized university training and do not undergo lengthy professional training: they learn on the job and are typically recruited early in their careers. Chief prosecutors can be elected or selected at any stage but typically after considerable practice experience. The United States and Canada are examples, but with important differences. Canadian Crown prosecutors, including chief prosecutors, are civil servants who apply for open, advertised posts and are vetted on meritocratic grounds.

Most chief US prosecutors are elected in partisan elections.[15] Assistants are hired by chief prosecutors and in many states are "employees at will."[16] They lack civil service protections and can be fired if the chief prosecutor so wishes (wholesale firings of line staff are uncommon; dismissals of more senior staff are more common when a new elected prosecutor takes office). The internal professional cultures of American prosecutors' offices no doubt vary, and some resemble those in places where prosecutors are career civil servants. Nonetheless, in many or most, the local professional culture is imbued with political awareness and affected by the psychology of adversariness.

These differences have consequences. Prosecutors who are career employees in judicial roles (e.g., in France, Italy, Sweden) typically see themselves as judges or as judge-equivalents. This means that, as Peter Tak (2012) writes of the Netherlands, "both judges and public prosecutors, however, are required to properly apply the law in the manner of a magistrate. This means that the prosecution decision has to be independent of political influence, unbiased and without prejudice" (p. 136). Their primary aims are not to win cases, obtain convictions, or maximize sentence severity but to achieve just results, including dis-

---

[15] Ronald Wright (2009) has shown that contested prosecutorial elections are relatively uncommon and that incumbents are seldom defeated when they seek reelection. Even so, as the essays in this volume by Miller and Caplinger, Boerner, and Wright make clear, most elected prosecutors are highly aware of media and public opinion and loath to disregard them.

[16] The National Prosecution Standards of the National District Attorneys Association (NDAA) provide in sec. 1-5.2 that "assistant and deputy prosecutors, by whatever title, should be selected by the chief prosecutor and should serve at the chief prosecutor's pleasure, unless otherwise provided by law or contract."

missals and acquittals when that seems right, and to achieve sentences that are just and appropriate. Their professional values and ideologies tend to be much more those of impartial, dispassionate judges than those of adversary practitioners: an acquittal is as good as a conviction if that is the right result. In some such systems, prosecutors do not make representations about sentencing.

Patterns of recruitment and career structure interact with the functional and structural distinctions discussed above. Prosecutors working in adversary systems with expediency values are likely to be more psychologically disposed to be moralistic and self-righteous, to stereotype defendants in negative ways, to identify with victims, to care more about convictions than exonerations, and to seek harsh punishments. Working for an elected prosecutor, who often will have run for office declaiming his or her toughness, and may celebrate the office's conviction rates and the severe punishments it obtains, probably exacerbates those tendencies. They appear to be more prevalent in the American system than elsewhere.

Conversely, prosecutors working in inquisitorial systems as judges or near-judges, and subscribing to legality values, are much better insulated from public emotion and political pressures. They are likely to be dispassionate and unemotional and to attach high importance to consistency in processing cases and to equality in punishments. How some of these differences play out in practice is discussed in the next section.

II. Differences the Differences Make

Reading or writing about organizational and structural issues can be less than utterly exciting. Those differences, however, have important implications for how systems work. To show this, I discuss four major settings in which prosecution systems differ in operation—diversion, charging, bargaining, and sentencing. I discuss these differences from the perspective of a hypothetical well-informed person who contemplated the possibility of being prosecuted for a serious crime. Most people are especially sensitive to matters of fairness or consistency when they themselves are affected. Letting chips fall where they may is an easier stance to adopt when the chips will hit someone else. I assume that such a person would want procedures to be fair and even-handed, not coercive, and to take account of the unique circumstances of the alleged crime and of their personal characteristics. By those criteria, the United States is the last place in the developed world where an informed, rational, and self-interested person would choose to be prosecuted.

Because the American system is an outlier but the one familiar to most of the likely readers of this essay, I compare it with a composite continental Western European inquisitorial system in which prosecutors are judges or civil servants.[17] The composite is, of course, an oversimplification, and important differences between continental systems are noted. In describing American prosecution systems, I sometimes draw on "best practices" set out in the American Bar Association (ABA) *Standards for Criminal Justice: Prosecution Function [and] Defense Function* (1993) and the NDAA *National Prosecution Standards* (n.d.).

A. Diversion

Assuming that criminal charges could appropriately be prosecuted, a defendant's natural first interest is in having the charges diverted or altogether dismissed. From the perspective of diversion, most defendants should prefer their cases to be dealt with in Western Europe. Many European countries have long had well-established and frequently used diversion programs that in many cases result in nonincarcerative penalties, usually financial, but not in criminal convictions. Among the best known are German conditional dismissals under section 153a of the German Criminal Procedure Code and "transactions" in the Netherlands; in both, prosecutions are deferred and eventually lapse in cases in which the defendant agrees to and pays or performs a proposed financial or equivalent penalty. In 2008, more than one-third of cases handled by the Dutch prosecution service, 68,000, were resolved by means of transactions (Tak 2012). Many countries also operate broad-based mediation programs in which successfully mediated cases are dismissed (e.g., in Scandinavia: Lappi-Seppälä 2007, 2011). No American jurisdiction has comparable large-scale, jurisdiction-wide, prosecutorial diversion programs. Many local courts operate drug and other problem-solving courts to which prosecutors can refer cases,

---

[17] "Western" because much less has been written about Eastern European systems and because some of them at least are still struggling to put traditions of political and governmental influence behind them (e.g., concerning Poland, Miskolci [2004]; Bojańczyk [2012]; and Krajewski [in this volume]). Accounts of the Hungarian (Lach 2004; Roth 2008) and Czech Republic (Fenyk and Koné-Krél 2005) prosecution systems are also available.

and some prosecutors operate ad hoc diversion programs, but they are not comparable in scale or finality to those in Europe.

In addition, both legality principle and expediency principle jurisdictions in Europe are committed to ideas of equal treatment. As a result, referrals to diversionary programs are usually made on the basis of established rules that specify both the kinds of cases that are eligible and the amount of any financial penalties that should be paid. Dutch transactions are governed by the POLARIS Guidelines, a numerical classification system that takes account of offense seriousness and circumstances, and the transaction is not individually negotiated but offered by a clerk on a take-it-or-leave-it basis (Tak 2012; van de Bunt and van Gelder, in this volume). Diversion from prosecution in US systems, by contrast, depends on ad hoc decisions by individual assistant prosecutors. Section 3-3.8 of the ABA standards says only that "the prosecutor should consider in appropriate cases the availability of non-criminal disposition, formal or informal." The NDAA standards, however, provide that the process must include "appropriate mechanisms to safeguard the prosecution of the case, such as admissions of guilt, stipulations of facts, and depositions of witnesses" (sec. 4-3.6). In other words, the defendant must admit guilt in a form that will make a subsequent conviction inevitable. This is not a condition in the European programs.

Finally, European diversions can be used in moderately serious cases. In the Netherlands, for example, transactions are available for any offense punishable by a prison sentence of 6 years or fewer. Such offenses constitute over 90 percent of Dutch criminal cases (Tak 2012). In Germany, section 153a dismissals for more serious offenses require approval from a judge, but it is almost always forthcoming (Weigend 2001, 2012).

People suspected of very minor offenses might prefer to be dealt with in the United States rather than in a European country that follows the legality principle. American prosecutors have no difficulty in deciding not to prosecute minor offenses (nor in deciding to do so). Nor would prosecutors in an expediency principle jurisdiction such as the Netherlands (Tak 2012). In some legality principle countries, however, there might be problems. Although established rules in Sweden, for example, authorize prosecutors to decline to prosecute very minor offenses (Asp, in this volume), Polish prosecutors lack such authority and often prosecute trivial cases rather than risk criticism for exercising

discretion (Krajewski, in this volume). Italian prosecutors also are unlikely to dismiss cases but may assign them such low priority that as a
practical matter the limitations period lapses before the case can be
acted on (Caianiello 2012).

B. Charging

A rational self-interested defendant would prefer to face criminal
charges in Europe, for two reasons.[18] First, as a matter of principle in
legality principle countries and as a matter of professionalism in all,
prosecutors are expected to file charges that they believe can be proven
in court. Erik Luna and Marianne Wade (2012, p. 429), in the conclusion to a recent comparative book on prosecution, observe that "the
legal culture, the education and training, and the expectations placed
upon prosecutors all shape their self-perception and practice. In continental Europe, these factors contribute to a particular profile: prosecutors as judicial professionals." Like judges, prosecutors are expected
to be impartial and objective. Pursuing charges that cannot be proven
is unprofessional and potentially embarrassing.

Second, European prosecutors are seldom likely to engage in systematic overcharging. Overcharging in its simplest form, in bad faith—
purposely charging a more serious offense than can be proven—would
be unwise and unlikely for reasons just mentioned but also because
prosecutors would necessarily be put to their proof. Defendants cannot, as in the United States, simply plead guilty as part of a plea bargain
and give rote replies to pro forma judicial questions about guilt and
the voluntariness of the plea. In civil-law systems, cases resulting in
court adjudication require judicial fact-finding.[19] The judge must independently decide that an offense occurred and that sufficient evidence proves the defendant's responsibility.

Bad-faith overcharging, however, is not the primary form of coercive

---

[18] There is a third reason but one related to penalties rather than processes. Prison
sentences are vastly longer in the United States than in Europe other than the United
Kingdom. In most countries, sentences longer than a year are rare. In Scandinavian
countries, the longest penalty for an offense other than murder ranges between 12 and
20 years, and sentences to life without possibility of release are not possible or are
rarely imposed.

[19] With the limited exception that recent changes to the criminal procedure codes
of Italy, Portugal, and Spain allow pretrial settlements of cases, with the consent of
the accused, in which the judge does not independently try the case and imposes the
agreed sentence. This is the closest Europe comes to American-style plea bargaining
(Tak 2004, vol. 1, p. 13).

overcharging in the United States.[20] It no doubt sometimes occurs, but it clearly violates both the ABA and NDAA standards. NDAA standard 4-2.2, for example, provides that a prosecutor should file charges only "which he or she reasonably believes can be substantiated by admissible evidence at trial."

Another form of widely countenanced charging, however, is at least as coercive as bad-faith overcharging. This is to file charges under either of two kinds of statutes that prescribe such severe penalties that most defendants given the opportunity will plead guilty to some other offense in order to avoid them. Two kinds of laws are used in this way.

First, American criminal laws abound in offenses carrying mandatory minimum prison sentences ranging from 1 year to life. For many drug and violent crimes, 5-, 10-, and 20-year minimums are common; mandatory 25-year and life sentences are not uncommon. Second, most states have three-strikes or repeat offender laws that require specified minimum sentences following conviction of a particular number of qualifying offenses. Such laws in effect supersede the penalty provisions otherwise applicable. The applicable statute may specify no minimum prison sentence for simple robbery, for example, but a three-strikes law may require a 25-year minimum if the defendant has previously twice been convicted of a felony. Prosecutors may decide whether or not to invoke the three-strikes law. If they do not, it is irrelevant. If they do, it can later be dismissed.

American prosecutors can charge defendants with offenses subject to lengthy mandatory minimums, or trigger the potential application of three-strikes or similar laws, but then offer to dismiss those charges if the defendant pleads guilty. Often this will involve a plea to a lesser included offense (e.g., possession of drugs rather than trafficking; simple rather than aggravated robbery) or to a related inchoate offense not covered by the statutory minimum (e.g., attempt or conspiracy).

This common practice[21] cannot literally be described as being done

---

[20] The ABA standards (sec. 3-3.9[f]) prescribe a good-faith reasonableness standard for the determination of the number and gravity of charges filed. Supporting commentary would forbid the common practice described in the text: "the line separating overcharging from the sound exercise of prosecutorial discretion is necessarily a subjective one, but the key consideration is the prosecutor's commitment to the interests of justice, fairly bringing those charges he or she believes are supported by the facts without 'piling on' charges in order to unduly leverage an accused to forgo his or her right to trial" (p. 77).

[21] Because little empirical work is done on internal prosecution office operations, it is difficult to estimate how common this practice is. One Arizona study (Knapp 1991)

in bad faith under the ABA or NDAA standards as long as the prosecutor reasonably believes that evidence exists to convict the defendant of the offense originally charged. ABA standard 3-3.9(a), for example, provides that "a prosecutor should not institute, cause to be instituted, or permit the continued pendency of criminal charges in the absence of sufficient admissible evidence to support a conviction." Filing legally applicable charges or applicability of a three-strikes law strategically with the intention to dismiss them as part of a plea bargain does not violate that standard. After all, applicable statutes provide for the threatened punishments, and if the defendant is convicted of them at trial, the judge is legally required to impose them.

In many cases, an offer to dismiss a three-strikes provision or a charge subject to a mandatory minimum will be an offer that is too good for most defendants to refuse. Given the choice of either a minimum 25-year three-strikes sentence or a 10-year mandatory minimum, or a guilty plea to an offense not subject to a mandatory penalty, even an innocent defendant will feel pressure to accept a proposed plea bargain. This is often why prosecutors file such charges. Potential loss of that plea bargaining leverage is a major reason why prosecutors typically oppose repeal of mandatory minimum sentence laws.[22]

This form of strategic charging, meant to place substantial pressures on defendants to plead guilty and waive trial and other rights, is not possible in European countries. Laws comparable to American three-strikes, repeat offender, and lengthy mandatory minimum laws do not exist, and for serious crimes prosecutors do not possess unilateral authority to dismiss some charges and elicit guilty pleas to others.

C. Bargaining

Nothing like no-holds-barred American plea bargaining exists in Europe. Consensual dispositions such as German conditional dismissals and Dutch transactions have long been possible, but they are subject to management controls and guidelines, do not result in convictions, and cannot include prison sentences. Penal orders in Sweden

---

showed that 57.3 percent of offenders who were initially charged with felonies were subject to mandatory minimum penalties, but only 8.3 percent of the offenses to which defendants eventually pleaded guilty were subject to mandatories.

[22] For example, Barkow (2005, p. 728, n. 25) gives examples of prosecutors' requests before Congress to have tougher sentencing laws so that those laws can be used to provide incentives for defendants to cooperate.

(Asp, in this volume), the Netherlands (van de Bunt and van Gelder, in this volume), France (Hodgson 2012), and some other countries do involve convictions but cannot provide for prison sentences.[23] Italian prosecutors and defense lawyers can propose negotiated settlements including agreed sentences, which the judge may accept or reject (Caianiello 2012), but the settlements are subject both to the legality principle and to limitations on sentences associated with proportionality principles.

More important, they cannot obligate defendants to do or not do things other than agree to the terms of the dismissal, transaction, or agreed sentence. American plea bargaining is different, not only in the ways described above but because bargains can cover extraneous subjects. For example, American plea bargains can require that the defendant provide assistance to the state in the prosecution of other people. In fiscal year 2010, for example, 25 percent of persons sentenced in US federal courts received sentence discounts because prosecutors requested them on the basis that defendants had provided assistance to the government in the prosecution of someone else (Saris 2011).

Similarly, consensual dispositions in Europe cannot require defendants to waive procedural rights other than the right to trial. The only question is whether in exchange for dismissal of charges the defendant will agree to a designated penalty. In the United States, by contrast, defendants offered plea bargains can be required to waive many more rights. NDAA standard 5-1.3, for example, provides:

> Prior to reaching a plea agreement . . . , the prosecutor may set conditions on a plea agreement offer, such as:
>
> a. The defendant's acceptance of the offer within a specified time period that would obviate the need for extensive trial preparation;
> b. The defendant's waiver of certain pre-trial rights, such as the right to discovery;
> c. The defendant's waiver of certain pre-trial motions such as a motion to suppress or dismiss; or
> d. The defendant's waiver of certain trial or post-trial rights, such as the right to pursue an appeal.

---

[23] Although—a qualified partial exception—Swedish penal orders may include suspended prison sentences of very short duration.

In other words, defendants may be required to waive all procedural and substantive rights associated with being a criminal defendant. These include, among others, claims that evidence was obtained unlawfully, that the prosecution wrongly withheld exculpatory evidence, and that the defendant's lawyer was incompetent. King and O'Neill (2005) found in a random sample of 971 written plea agreements submitted to the US Sentencing Commission between October 2003 and June 2004 that 63 percent contained provisions in which the defendant waived the right to appeal against legal errors in his or her conviction or sentence. American state prosecutors also sometimes require defendants to agree to waive their appeal rights as a condition to a plea bargain (LaFave et al. 2009).

D. Sentencing

Only in America is sentencing an adversary process in which plea bargains sometimes specify particular sentences and prosecutors make charging and bargaining decisions aimed at assuring specific minimum sentences. In England, for a contrary example, prosecutors were until recently ethically proscribed from making any representations about sentencing. English law expressly authorizes sentencing discounts as incentives for guilty pleas, but the ultimate decision is understood to be uniquely judicial in nature (Ashworth 2010). In most continental European countries, sentencing is understood to be an inherently judicial function in which impartiality and objectivity are essential elements. There are a few exceptions, including a Dutch prosecutorial practice of making sentencing recommendations and an Italian practice of proposing sentences agreed on between the parties, but they do not begin to approach American practices. Many American prosecutors believe that they are entitled to influence the sentence offenders receive—their strong support for mandatory minimum sentences is one sign of this—rather than that, like American defense counsel, they are entitled merely to express their views.

III. Learning More about the Differences

Efforts to learn about prosecution in a single country or cross-nationally are handicapped by the absence of a significant empirical literature in any country. Almost all current knowledge comes from the personal experiences of individuals; from anecdotal knowledge; from descriptions of statutory powers, procedural rules, and bureaucratic organization (e.g., Tak 2004); and from a small but growing number of articles based mostly on these sources (e.g., Luna and Wade 2012). Empirical studies of prosecutorial processes, decision making, and outcomes based on original empirical research are almost nonexistent.

Citizens should want to know how so powerful an official exercises his discretion; whether and how personal ideology, political beliefs, or affiliation affects the decisions made; whether the gender, race, or ethnicity of prosecutors, defendants, and victims affects decisions; and whether prosecutors behave more justly and consistently in some types of prosecution systems than in others. The existing empirical literature can answer none of these questions.

It is not obvious why prosecution is so understudied. In the United States at least, police departments, courts, probation and parole agencies, and prison systems have permitted observation and other qualitative studies of their operations; have allowed offenders and suspects under their control to participate in surveys; and have made official data available for quantitative analyses. Prosecutors' offices by and large have not. Outside the United States, observation and other empirical research on criminal justice agencies is less common but focuses on the same agencies. Sizable empirical literatures on police and corrections agencies exist in Australia, Canada, and England and Wales, but work on courts and prosecutors is rare. Courts in England and Wales have been notoriously unwilling to allow researchers to study internal court processes (e.g., Ashworth et al. 1984). I am handicapped by a lack of detailed personal knowledge of research in non-English-speaking countries, but if the reference lists of relevant published works in English are any indication, little empirical work has been done in any developed country.

Nor has there been significant comparative work. A few books based on empirical research compare two or three countries (e.g., Fionda 1995; Hodgson 2005), but that's about it. Fascinating comparative questions exist for which there are no answers. Here are three examples. First, in only two countries are prosecutors elected by popular vote: Switzerland (a few) and the United States (many). Why is it that elected Swiss prosecutors behave as if they were impartial civil servants or judges (Gilliéron and Killias 2008) while American prosecutors behave and campaign like any other partisan politicians and openly take public opinion, media attentions, and political implications into account in their work? Second, prosecutors in Germany and the Netherlands, adjacent countries speaking Germanic languages, are career civil servants and have pioneered model forms of large-scale pretrial diversion that result in proportionate penalties without criminal convictions. Why have Dutch prosecutors long been the most powerful figures in the country's criminal justice system while German prosecutors have behaved in much more restrained ways? In the Netherlands, for example, the primary device aimed at preventing unwarranted sentencing disparities is a set of guidelines for prosecutors' sentencing recommendations, premised on the view that judges will give the recommendations serious consideration (Tak 2012). Third, prosecutors in Finland and Sweden are judges in legality principle legal systems while Danish and Norwegian prosecutors are executive branch officials in expediency principle systems. Why, then, do they behave indistinguishably?

There are two reasons to want to have more and better knowledge. The first is to understand better the strengths and weaknesses of particular systems in order to be able to ameliorate the weaknesses. The second, potentially much more important, is to learn which kinds of systems better promote values of equality, justice, and rationality so that policy makers can look across national boundaries to find ways to improve their own national systems.

Countries have changed their prosecution systems, often with the aim of incorporating features from elsewhere. The Italians, Spanish, and Portuguese through legislation attempted to graft significant features of adversary processes onto their inquisitorial systems. The Poles several times after 1990 enacted legislation to reorganize their prosecution system. The Italians and Germans through legislation abandoned the institution of the separate investigating magistrate. The English in 1985 enacted legislation that fundamentally reorganized prosecution, removing it from the police and creating an independent Crown Prosecution Service.

The United States is, as in so many things involving the criminal justice system, the country most in need of change. It is also, because of the entrenched constitutional bases of its prosecution systems, probably the most resistant to change. That is a great pity because it means that injustice and unequal treatment are inevitable. Most state prosecutors are locally elected and proudly declaim the importance of local cultural values and public opinion. That inexorably means that practices, policies, and priorities differ widely between counties and thus within a state. The prevailing understanding in the rest of the developed world that prosecutors, like judges, should be apolitical, impartial, and unemotional does not exist. Many chief prosecutors are as much politicians as they are prosecutors. Even the best sometimes find political implications impossible to ignore in setting policies and priorities and in making decisions about individual cases. The worst give free rein to partisan and ideological considerations and to considerations about implications for their personal careers. That is no way to do justice.

REFERENCES

Aebi, Marcelo, and M. Balcells. 2008. "The Prosecution Service Function within the Spanish Criminal Justice System." *European Journal on Criminal Policy and Research* 14(2–3):311–31.

Alschuler, Albert. 1978. "Sentencing Reform and Prosecutorial Power." *University of Pennsylvania Law Review* 126:550–77.

American Bar Association. 1993. *Standards for Criminal Justice: Prosecution Function [and] Defense Function*, 3rd. ed. Washington, DC: American Bar Association.

Ashworth, Andrew. 2010. *Sentencing and Criminal Justice*, 5th ed. Cambridge: Cambridge University Press.

Ashworth, Andrew, Elaine Genders, G. Mansfield, Jill Peay, and Elaine Player. 1984. *Sentencing in the Crown Court: Report of an Exploratory Study*. Oxford: University of Oxford, Centre for Criminological Research.

Asp, Petter. In this volume. "The Prosecutor in Swedish Law."

Bagaric, Mirko. 2001. *Punishment and Sentencing: A Rational Approach*. London: Cavendish.

Bandyopadhyay, Siddhartha, and Bryan C. McCannon. 2011. *The Effect of Reelections on Prosecutors*. http://www.ssrn.com.

Barkow, Rachel E. 2005. "Administering Crime." *UCLA Law Review* 52:715–814.

Barona-Vilar, Silvia. 2004. "Law, Policy, and Practice of Prosecution in Spain." In *Tasks and Powers of the Prosecution Services in the EU Member States*, vol. 1, edited by Peter J. P. Tak. Nijmegen, Netherlands: Wolf Legal Publishers.

Barry, Ellen. 2011. "Former Ukraine Premier Is Jailed for 7 Years." *New York Times*, October 11. http://www.nytimes.com/2011/10/12/world/europe/yulia-tymoshenko-sentenced-to-seven-years-in-prison.html?pagewanted=all.

Bingham, Lord Chief Justice. 1997. "The Sentence of the Court." Police Foundation Lecture, July 1997. London: Police Foundation.

Blumstein, Alfred, Jacqueline Cohen, Susan Martin, and Michael Tonry, eds. 1983. *Research on Sentencing: The Search for Reform*. Washington, DC: National Academy Press.

Boerner, David. 1995. "Sentencing Guidelines and Prosecutorial Discretion." *Judicature* 78:196–200.

———. In this volume. "Prosecution in Washington State."

Bojańczyk, Antoni. 2012. "Obsolete Procedural Actors? Polish Prosecutors and Their Evidence Gathering Duty before and during Trial in an Inquisitorial Environment." In *The Prosecutor in Transnational Perspective*, edited by Erik Luna and Marianne Wade. New York: Oxford University Press.

Caianiello, Michele. 2012. "The Italian Public Prosecutor: An Inquisitorial Figure in Adversarial Proceedings?" In *The Prosecutor in Transnational Perspective*, edited by Erik Luna and Marianne Wade. New York: Oxford University Press.

CEPEJ (European Commission for the Efficiency of Justice). 2010. *European Judicial Systems: Efficiency and Quality of Justice*, 2010 ed. (data 2008). Strasbourg: Council of Europe Publishing.

Damaška, Mirjan. 1975. "Structures of Authority and Comparative Criminal Procedure." *Yale Law Journal* 84:480–543.

———. 1986. *The Faces of Justice and State Authority: A Comparative Approach to the Legal Process*. New Haven, CT: Yale University Press.

Davis, Angela J. 2007. *Arbitrary Justice: The Power of the American Prosecutor*. New York: Oxford University Press.

Davis, Kenneth Culp. 1968. *Discretionary Justice*. Baton Rouge: Louisiana State University Press.

Ellis, Michael J. 2012. "The Origins of the Elected Prosecutor." *Yale Law Journal* 121:1528–69.

Fenyk, Jaroslav, and Danuta Koné-Krél. 2005. "The Public Prosecution Service of the Czech Republic." In *Tasks and Powers of the Prosecution Services in the EU Member States*, vol. 2, edited by Peter J. P. Tak. Nijmegen, Netherlands: Wolf Legal Publishers.

Fionda, J. 1995. *Public Prosecutors and Discretion: A Comparative Study*. Oxford: Clarendon.

Fisher, George. 2003. *Plea Bargaining's Triumph: A History of Plea Bargaining in America*. Stanford, CA: Stanford University Press.

Gilliéron, Gwladys, and Martin Killias. 2008. "The Prosecution Service Function within the Swiss Criminal Justice System." *European Journal on Criminal Policy and Research* 14(2–3):333–52.

Gordon, Sanford C., and Gregory A. Huber. 2002. "Citizen Oversight and the Electoral Incentives of Criminal Prosecutors." *American Journal of Political Science* 46:334–51.

———. 2007. "The Effect of Electoral Competitiveness on Incumbent Behavior." *Quarterly Journal of Political Science* 2:107–38.

———. 2009. "The Political Economy of Prosecution." *Annual Review of Law and Social Science* 5:135–56.

Green, David A. 2008. *When Children Kill Children—Penal Populism and Political Culture.* Oxford: Oxford University Press.

Hodgson, Jacqueline. 2005. *French Criminal Justice: A Comparative Account of the Investigation and Prosecution of Crime in France.* Oxford: Hart.

———. 2012. "Guilty Pleas and the Changing Role of the Prosecutor in French Criminal Justice." In *The Prosecutor in Transnational Perspective,* edited by Erik Luna and Marianne Wade. New York: Oxford University Press.

Home Office. 1994. "The James Bulger Murder." News release (July 22). London: Home Office.

Huber, Gregory A., and Sanford C. Gordon. 2004. "Accountability and Coercion: Is Justice Blind When It Runs for Office?" *American Journal of Political Science* 48:247–63.

Illuminati, Giulio. 2004. "The Role of the Public Prosecutor in the Italian System." In *Tasks and Powers of the Prosecution Services in the EU Member States,* vol. 1, edited by Peter J. P. Tak. Nijmegen, Netherlands: Wolf Legal Publishers.

Jacoby, Joan E. 1980. *The American Prosecutor: A Search for Identity.* Lexington, MA: Lexington.

Jehle, Jörg-Martin, and Marianne Wade, eds. 2006. *Coping with Overloaded Criminal Justice Systems: The Rise of Prosecutorial Power across Europe.* Berlin: Springer.

Jehle, Jörg-Martin, Marianne Wade, and Beatrix Elsner, eds. 2008. "Prosecution and Diversion within Criminal Justice Systems in Europe." Special issue, *European Journal on Criminal Policy and Research* 14(2–3).

Johnson, David. 2002. *The Japanese Way of Justice: Prosecuting Crime in Japan.* New York: Oxford University Press.

———. In this volume. "Japan's Prosecution System."

King, Nancy J., and Michael O'Neill. 2005. "Appeal Waivers and the Future of Sentencing Policy." *Duke Law Journal* 55:209–61.

Knapp, Kay A. 1991. "Arizona: Unprincipled Sentencing, Mandatory Minimums, and Prison Crowding." *Overcrowded Times* 2(5):10–12.

Krajewski, Krsysztof. In this volume. "Prosecution and Prosecutors in Poland: In Quest of Independence."

Lach, Arkadiusz. 2004. "The Prosecution Service of Poland." In *Tasks and Powers of the Prosecution Services in the EU Member States,* vol. 2, edited by Peter J. P. Tak. Nijmegen, Netherlands: Wolf Legal Publishers.

LaFave, Wayne, Jerold Israel, Nancy King, and Orin Kerr. 2009. *Hornbook on Criminal Procedure,* 5th ed. St. Paul, MN: West.

Lappi-Seppälä, Tapio. 2001. "Sentencing and Punishment in Finland: The Decline of the Repressive Ideal." In *Sentencing and Sanctions in Western Countries,* edited by Michael Tonry and Richard S. Frase. New York: Oxford University Press.

———. 2007. "Penal Policy in Scandinavia." In *Crime, Punishment, and Politics in Comparative Perspective,* edited by Michael Tonry. Vol. 36 of *Crime and Justice: A Review of Research,* edited by Michael Tonry. Chicago: University of Chicago Press.

———. 2011. "Nordic Youth Justice." In *Crime and Punishment in Scandinavia*, edited by Michael Tonry and Tapio Lappi-Seppälä. Vol. 40 of *Crime and Justice: A Review of Research*, edited by Michael Tonry. Chicago: Chicago University Press.

Lappi-Seppälä, Tapio, and Michael Tonry. 2011. "Crime, Criminal Justice, and Criminology in the Nordic Countries." In *Crime and Punishment in Scandinavia*, edited by Michael Tonry and Tapio Lappi-Seppälä. Vol. 40 of *Crime and Justice: A Review of Research*, edited by Michael Tonry. Chicago: Chicago University Press.

Lewis, Chris. 2012. "The Evolving Role of the English Crown Prosecution Service." In *The Prosecutor in Transnational Perspective*, edited by Erik Luna and Marianne Wade. New York: Oxford University Press.

Lichtblau, Eric. 2008. "Report Faults Aides in Hiring at Justice Dept." *New York Times*, July 29. http://www.nytimes.com/2008/07/29/washington/29 justice.html?pagewanted=all.

Lichtblau, Eric, and Sharon Otterman. 2008. "US Appoints Special Prosecutor to Investigate Firings of 9 US Attorneys." *New York Times*, September 29. http://www.nytimes.com/2008/09/29/world/americas/29iht-justice.4 .16565240.html.

Luna, Erik, and Marianne Wade, eds. 2012. *The Prosecutor in Transnational Perspective*. New York: Oxford University Press.

Lynch, Gerard E. 2003. "Screening versus Plea Bargaining: Exactly What Are We Trading Off?" *Stanford Law Review* 55:1399–1408.

Michael, Jerome, and Mortimer Adler. 1933. *Crime, Law, and Social Science*. New York: Harcourt Brace.

Michael, Jerome, and Herbert Wechsler. 1937. "A Rationale of the Law of Homicide." Pts. 1 and 2. *Columbia Law Review* 37:701–61; 1261–1335.

———. 1940. *Criminal Law and Its Administration: Cases, Statutes, and Commentaries*. Chicago: Foundation Press.

Miller, Marc, and Samantha Caplinger. In this volume. "Prosecution in Arizona: Practical Problems, Prosecutorial Accountability, and Local Solutions."

Miskolci, László. 2004. "The Hungarian Prosecution Service." In *Tasks and Powers of the Prosecution Services in the EU Member States*, vol. 2, edited by Peter J. P. Tak. Nijmegen, Netherlands: Wolf Legal Publishers.

National District Attorneys Association. n.d. *National Prosecution Standards*, 3rd ed. Washington, DC: National District Attorneys Association.

Nossiter, Adam. 2008. "Freed Ex-Governor of Alabama Talks of Abuse of Power." *New York Times*, March 29. http://www.nytimes.com/2008/03/29/ us/29alabama.html.

Perry, Steven W. 2006. *Prosecutors in State Courts, 2005*. Washington, DC: Bureau of Justice Statistics.

Pifferi, Michele. 2011. "Individualization of Punishment and the Rule of Law: Reshaping the Legality in the United States and Europe between the 19th and the 20th Century." Unpublished manuscript. http://works.bepress.com/ michele_pifferi/1/.

Podgor, Ellen. 2012. "Prosecution Guidelines in the United States." In *The*

Prosecutor in Transnational Perspective, edited by Erik Luna and Marianne Wade. New York: Oxford University Press.

Ross, Jacqueline. 2008. "Do Rules of Evidence Apply (Only) in the Courtroom? Deceptive Interrogation in the United States and Germany." *Oxford Journal of Legal Studies* 28(3):443–74.

Roth, E. 2008. "The Prosecution Service Function within the Hungarian Criminal Justice System." *European Journal on Criminal Policy and Research* 14(2–3):289–309.

Rothman, David J. 1971. *The Discovery of the Asylum: Social Order and Disorder in the New Republic*. Boston: Little, Brown.

———. 1980. *Conscience and Convenience*. Boston: Little, Brown.

Salreu, Pedro. 2004. "The Prosecution Service in Spain." In *Tasks and Powers of the Prosecution Services in the EU Member States*, vol. 1, edited by Peter J. P. Tak. Nijmegen, Netherlands: Wolf Legal Publishers.

Saris, Patti B. 2011. *Prepared Testimony of Patti B. Saris, Chair, United States Sentencing Commission before the Subcommittee on Crime, Terrorism, and Homeland Security Committee on the Judiciary United States House of Representatives, October 12, 2011*. Washington, DC: US Sentencing Commission.

Schwirtz, Michael. 2012. "Russian Leader Orders Review of Oil Tycoon's Conviction." *New York Times*, March 5. http://www.nytimes.com/2012/03/06/world/europe/medvedev-orders-review-of-mikhail-khodorkovskys-conviction.html.

Tak, Peter J. P., ed. 2004. *Tasks and Powers of the Prosecution Services in the EU Member States*, 2 vols. Nijmegen, Netherlands: Wolf Legal Publishers.

———. 2012. "The Dutch Prosecutor: A Prosecuting and Sentencing Officer." In *The Prosecutor in Transnational Perspective*, edited by Erik Luna and Marianne Wade. New York: Oxford University Press.

Thaman, Stephen C. 2010. *World Plea Bargaining: Consensual Procedures and the Avoidance of the Full Criminal Trial*. Durham, NC: Carolina Academic Press.

Tonry, Michael. 2004a. *Punishment and Politics: Evidence and Emulation in the Making of English Crime Control Policy*. Cullompton, Devon, UK: Willan.

———. 2004b. *Thinking about Crime: Sense and Sensibility in American Penal Culture*. New York: Oxford University Press.

———. 2009 "The Mostly Unintended Effects of Mandatory Penalties: Two Centuries of Consistent Findings." In *Crime and Justice: A Review of Research*, vol. 38, edited by Michael Tonry. Chicago: University of Chicago Press.

———, ed. 2011. *Why Punish? How Much?* New York: Oxford University Press.

Turner, Jenia I. 2009. *Plea Bargaining across Borders*. New York: Aspen.

US Department of Justice, Office of the Inspector General and Office of Professional Responsibility. 2008. *An Investigation into the Removal of Nine US Attorneys in 2006*. Washington, DC: US Department of Justice.

van de Bunt, Henk, and Jean-Louis van Gelder. In this volume. "The Dutch Prosecution Service."

vander Beken, Tom, and Michael Kilchling, eds. 2000. *The Role of the Public Prosecutor in the European Criminal Justice Systems*. Brussels: Koninklijke Vlaamse Academie van Belgie voor Wetenschappen en Kunsten.

Weigend, Thomas. 2001. "Sentencing and Punishment in Germany." In *Sentencing and Sanctions in Western Countries*, edited by Michael Tonry and Richard S. Frase. New York: Oxford University Press.

———. 2012. "A Judge by Another Name? Comparative Perspectives on the Role of the Public Prosecutor." In *The Prosecutor in Transnational Perspective*, edited by Erik Luna and Marianne Wade. New York: Oxford University Press.

Worrall, John, and M. Elaine Nugent-Borakove, eds. 2008. *The Changing Role of the American Prosecutor*. Albany: SUNY–Albany Press.

Wright, Ronald F. 2009. "How Prosecutor Elections Fail Us." *Ohio State Journal of Criminal Law* 6:581–610.

———. In this volume. "Persistent Localism in the Prosecutor Services of North Carolina."

David T. Johnson

Japan's Prosecution System

ABSTRACT

Criminal justice in Japan is strongly shaped by the way prosecutors organize their activities and perform their jobs. Their discretion is so great that analysts call the criminal process one of "prosecutor justice." Prosecutors exercise this discretion within three overlapping ambits: their own organization, which is centralized and hierarchical and has a division of labor between operators, managers, and executives; a criminal court community that includes police, judges, and defense lawyers; and the broader contexts of economy, polity, and culture. For most of the postwar period there was considerable continuity in Japanese criminal justice, especially in the central roles played by prosecutors and police, the strong reliance on confessions, and a conviction rate that approached 100 percent. But significant changes started in the 1990s. Punishments became harsher, victims were more empowered, revelations of wrongful convictions and official misconduct started to stimulate increased transparency, and the advent of a lay judge system for trying serious cases provoked change in other parts of the process, from bail and discovery to interrogations and defense lawyering. Japan's lay judge system is in its infancy. Time will tell how much reform this fundamental change will arouse. What is clear is that Japanese prosecutors will continue to adapt to the shifting contexts of criminal justice.

> The rationalization and bureaucratization of the penal process has undoubtedly been the most important development to have taken place in penality in the nineteenth and twentieth centuries. (David Garland, *Punishment and Modern Society*, 1990, p. 180)

Prosecutors have more control over life, liberty, and reputation than any other officials in Japan. Their discretion is so great that many

David T. Johnson is professor of sociology, University of Hawaii.

commentators call the country's criminal process a system of "prosecutor justice." Prosecutors exercise this discretion in the context of three overlapping ambits: their own organization, which is highly centralized, hierarchical, and integrated; a criminal court community that includes judges, police, and defense lawyers but is largely controlled by prosecutors; and the political and cultural contexts of Japan's nation-state.

For much of the postwar period Japan was "heaven for a cop" (Bayley 1991) and "paradise for a prosecutor" (Johnson 2002a, p. 21). These law enforcement officials confronted little serious crime, few firearms or illicit drugs, and an impressive quality of public order, all of which made their work less demanding and vastly less dangerous than law enforcement work in many other nations. Five contexts were especially crucial for prosecutors: low crime rates, light caseloads, insulation from public demands and political pressure, criminal procedure laws that conferred extensive powers to obtain confessions and convictions, and a trial system in which professional judges decided guilt and sentence in ways that were more predictable than decision making by jury or other forms of adjudication that involve civilian participants (Johnson 2002a, pp. 21–49).

In some ways Japan remains a propitious place to prosecute crime, but the "paradise" fits less well today than it did in the past because the contexts of prosecution have been changing.[1] Crime rates increased in the 1990s and 2000s, especially in the less serious property crime categories. Caseloads rose because personnel increases did not keep pace with the crime increases. Crime scares (including the lethal gas attacks on the Tokyo subway in 1995—Japan's 9/11), penal populism, and a punitive victims' rights movement have reduced the insulation from public demands and political pressure that prosecutors used to enjoy, and revelations of prosecutor misconduct and miscarriages of justice have intensified public and political scrutiny of the procuracy (Johnson 2007, 2011d). The Code of Criminal Procedure still gives prosecutors many tools with which to investigate, charge, and try cases, but this critical context is changing too as prosecutors (and police) have been pushed to record interrogations electronically and as the rules of discovery were reformed to require more disclosure of evidence to the

---

[1] Law in many fields has been changing in Japan in response to changes in economic, political, and social context (Foote 2007).

defense (Johnson 2011b). The most fundamental change took effect in 2009, when Japan introduced a lay judge system for adjudicating guilt and determining sentence in serious criminal cases (Johnson 2009). These panels of three professional and six lay judges hear only about 3 percent of all criminal cases, but their advent has stimulated reform in many parts of the process.[2] The recording and discovery reforms would not have occurred but for the introduction of lay judges, and trials have become less reliant on dossiers written by prosecutors during the pretrial period and more reliant on oral testimony in open court. Defense lawyers are becoming more aggressive and adversarial. Bail has become somewhat easier to obtain. Sentences for sex crimes have become more severe, whereas for most other categories of crime, lay judge panels are more likely than professional judges to suspend sentences and impose probation as a condition of freedom. Prosecutors are also less likely than they used to be to appeal sentencing decisions made by courts of original jurisdiction. In all of these ways (and more), the change in Japan's system of adjudication has spurred change in other parts of the criminal process (Shinomiya 2010). What has not changed is Japan's famously high conviction rate, which 2 years after the introduction of the new system remains well above 99 percent for lay judge trials, even though almost one-third of defendants tried by the mixed tribunals deny some or all of the facts alleged in the indictment (Kyodo Tsushin Shakaibu 2010).

In short, prosecutors remain a powerful presence in Japan's criminal justice system, but their role is being changed and challenged in several significant ways. This essay describes some of the key dimensions of continuity and change. Section I briefly summarizes some of the changes that occurred in Japanese criminal justice after the country opened its doors to the world in the middle of the nineteenth century. Section II provides an overview of criminal justice in Japan. Section III explains how Japanese prosecutors are recruited and promoted. Section IV describes the structure of Japan's procuracy and two principles—prosecutor unity and prosecutor independence—that shape be-

---

[2] Lay judge courts hear two types of cases: those punishable by death, imprisonment for an indefinite period, or with hard labor and those in which the victim has died as a result of an intentional criminal act (Anderson and Johnson 2009). The law does not give defendants the right to waive a lay judge panel, but it does grant discretion to the court to determine that a case that qualifies for a lay judge trial can be heard by a panel of professional judges if circumstances require (as when lay judges might fear retribution from a defendant who belongs to the yakuza).

havior in the organization. Section V analyzes the three major roles played by prosecutors in Japan: as operators who work on the front line investigating, charging, and trying cases; as managers who monitor and coordinate operators; and as executives who try to secure organizational autonomy and public and political support. Sections VI and VII identify strengths and weaknesses in the Japanese way of prosecution, and Section VIII explores the future of prosecution in Japan by reviewing how prosecutors are responding to changes in their environment.

I. History

Until the Meiji Restoration of 1868, Japan's criminal justice system was mainly controlled by hundreds of local lords (*daimyo*) who wielded authority in their respective domains. The subjects who lived in these domains had many obligations and few real rights (Hiramatsu 1989).[3] Since there were no central penal codes, law and its enforcement varied from domain to domain. Justice could be harsh, with the severity of punishment often depending on the status of the victim and the accused (Botsman 2005, p. 59). Flogging (*tataki*)—50 or 100 blows with a cane across the back—was the most common of all Tokugawa punishments, with 800–1,000 men flogged in Edo (Tokyo) every year between 1862 and 1865. Flogging was usually carried out in front of the main gate of the jailhouse. Often it was combined with tattooing (*irezumi*), which caused even more physical pain and permanently marked the subject as criminal (p. 27). The most severe Tokugawa punishment involved "pulling the saw" on or near the neck of a condemned person who was confined in a wooden box that was buried in the earth with only the head and neck exposed above ground level. Onlookers were permitted to pull the bamboo saw but few ever did. On the third day of this protracted penal performance, the condemned was taken to an execution ground and crucified (p. 26). Torture was frequently used to obtain confessions in Tokugawa Japan, usually by

[3] One obligation concerned ownership of firearms. Noel Perrin (1979) argued that Tokugawa Japan "gave up the gun" by 1696 after firearms first arrived from Portugal in 1543 and flourished for a half century or so thereafter. Perrin's causal account has been criticized as "simplistically cultural" (author's interview on March 3, 1999, with Paul Varley, history professor at the University of Hawaii at Manoa), but Perrin believes that this case teaches much about "the general question of how one unlearns the use of a weapon" (1979, p. xii).

beating suspects with a wooden stick (p. 35). These and other brutal procedures and penalties were combined with "strategies of benevolence" designed to maintain the reputation of the warrior regime (p. 45). Children, women, and the sick and the weak were commonly treated with lenience, and the value of stolen goods or money was sometimes understated in order to avoid the sanction of death.

Japan's modern prosecution system was established when the country was forced to open its doors by Western powers after some two centuries of self-imposed isolation (Storry 1985, p. 45). In order to appear "civilized" and thereby avoid the colonial fates that befell other Asian nations, the oligarchs who ruled Japan in the late nineteenth century encouraged a wide variety of reforms, from the building of prisons, the banning of torture, and the softening of execution methods to the drafting of formal legal codes and the construction of legal institutions such as police, prosecution, and courts (Westney 1987). These changes were intended to administer justice and also to win the respect of the West (Beasley 1990, p. 91).

Japan's first modern penal code and code of criminal procedure were based on French models and promulgated in 1880. The new laws abolished collective guilt and treated all persons as equal while still reflecting traditional attitudes toward authority, as by permitting prosecutors to sit with judges on a raised platform in the courtroom, above the defendant and his or her attorney, who were seated at ground level. In criminal trials, the judge possessed primary responsibility for questioning witnesses, and defense lawyers were allowed to ask questions only through an intermediary. Cases came to trial through a preliminary investigation controlled by the judge, and suspects had no right to silence or counsel in this all-important proceeding. For defendants formally charged with a crime, the presumption of innocence was weak, and there were few possibilities for a vigorous defense because law restricted the evidence lawyers could obtain from the prosecution and because informal norms discouraged aggressive tactics in the courtroom. Before the Lawyer's Law was reformed in 1949, it placed control over the private bar in the hands of the procuracy (Rabinowitz 1956, p. 70). Until this change, the defense lawyer's traditional role "was to humbly point out extenuating circumstances, beg leniency, and promise no future violations" (Mitchell 1992, p. 71).

Japan's Penal Code was revised in 1907 to reflect the growing influence of German law. It has remained much the same ever since.[4] Whereas the old law allowed limited discretion in sentencing, the new one gives judges great latitude to choose sentences within a wide statutory range: from 5 years to death for homicide, for example, and from 0 to 10 years for theft. Prosecutors in Japan also have vast discretion to decide whether and what to charge. Unlike Italy and Germany and like the United States and the Netherlands, there is no rule of "obligatory prosecution." Regardless of the strength of evidence or the crime in question, prosecutors in Japan do not have to file formal charges.

After Japan's defeat in the Pacific War, occupation authorities imposed major reforms in Japanese law, from land redistribution, equality of the sexes, and the downsizing of the emperor from "god" to a mere "symbol of the State and of the unity of the people," to the power of judicial review and the renunciation of the right to wage war. But the Penal Code of 1947 remained much the same as the 1907 version except for omission of offenses related to war, the imperial family, and adultery. By contrast, the new postwar Code of Criminal Procedure incorporated many rules guaranteeing the rights of the accused; judges frequently circumscribed them in the decades that followed (Foote 2010). For example, criminal suspects have the right to remain silent, but judicial interpretation of this right holds that they also have the duty to endure questioning, even after they have stated their desire to remain silent (Foote 1991).

Formally, Japan's postwar system is adversarial, and the judge, while still able to question witnesses at trial, is required to decide cases on the basis of evidence presented by both parties. In practice, while the judge's role in the pretrial process has been reduced and the prosecution and defense now sit below the bench at trial, Japan's postwar system of criminal justice maintains many continuities with the prewar system, especially with respect to the central roles played by prosecutors and police.

---

[4] German and French connections with Japan predated the opening of Japan to the West in the middle of the nineteenth century and accelerated thereafter during the Meiji Restoration, as many advisors from France and Germany came to work in Japan and help modernize the country, especially in the fields of law, education, medicine, and military affairs (Beasley 1990).

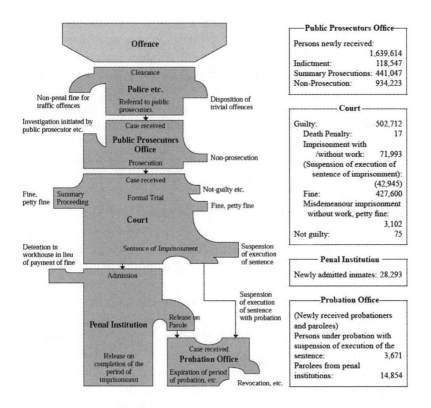

FIG. 1.—Criminal justice flow chart. Source: Ukawa (2011).

II. Overview of Criminal Justice in Japan

Figure 1 summarizes the flow of cases in 2009. Police are the primary investigative agency, and most police duties are carried out by prefectural organizations, while the National Police Agency is in charge of most policy making and coordination (Ames 1981). Police and prosecutors hold similar expectations for each other in Japan and the United States. In both nations, prosecutors want police to provide sufficient evidence to convict offenders and with sufficient conformity to law to keep the state's case uncontaminated by problems with due process. Conversely, police want prosecutors to charge offenders who deserve to be charged. Police everywhere, it seems, disdain prosecutors too timorous to charge anything but clear winners (or "layups," as some American police scornfully put it). These similarities are significant, but three differences are equally striking. First, Japanese prosecutors participate much more actively in investigations than do their American counterparts. As a result, they are less reliant on the police for case information. Second, Japanese prosecutors strongly and frequently direct police investigations—much more so than do prosecutors in the United States. Third, prosecutors in Japan interact more frequently with police during the precharge investigation, not least because charge decisions in Japan are often made 10–20 days after arrest, not 2 or 3 days after as in many American jurisdictions. Together, these differences constitute two important patterns in the Japanese way of justice: prosecutors are often proactive, not passively reactive, in their dealings with the police (Johnson 2002a, p. 51), and they are more independent of the police than are their American counterparts (p. 54). These assertions do need to be qualified, for prosecutors in Japan are not completely independent of police influence, nor do they dominate all encounters with police. In minor cases, prosecutors often *delegate* decision making to the police, and in some serious cases—such as when police have been accused of misconduct—prosecutors *defer* to a police organization that is much bigger than the procuracy in both budget and personnel and is more influential in the spheres of lawmaking and electoral politics (p. 55). Still, what stands out in comparative perspective is how active prosecutors in Japan are in many investigations and how much control they exercise over police in serious investigations.

Police arrest fewer than 20 percent of all suspected Penal Code offenders in Japan; the rest of the cases are sent to prosecutors without arrest. The infrequency of arrest arises from three related sources: concerns about caseload pressure and jail capacity, the desire to protect suspects from the stigma of arrest, and the belief that the failure to charge an arrested suspect is impermissible (Johnson 2002a, p. 13). Once a suspect is arrested, police have 48 hours to transfer the case to prosecutors if further detention is considered necessary. If a suspect is not arrested and detained, investigations face no formal time constraints, though police must refer all cases above the "trivial" (*bizai*) level to prosecutors. If prosecutors believe that a suspect should be detained further, they must ask a judge within 24 hours of receiving the case to approve up to 10 days of additional detention. They may later ask for another 10-day extension. Judges seldom reject these requests. In total, police and prosecutors can detain a suspect for up to 3 days before the suspect appears before a judge and for up to 20 days thereafter (25 days for the crime of insurrection). During this pre-charge period, interrogations are long, thorough, and intense. Police and prosecutors routinely interrogate suspects several times each for several hours each time. Suspects have no right to bail until after indictment, when they may apply to a local court for release. Judges must grant bail as a matter of legal right, but the Code of Criminal Procedure carves out broad exceptions to this rule. In practice, bail is granted only to suspects who are expected to hold to their confession through trial. In the large majority of cases, suspects who do not confess are not released on bail (Johnson 2002a, p. 14).

In contrast to the United States and some other jurisdictions, in Japan there are no "initial" charge decisions, no arraignments, and no preliminary or grand jury hearings in which charge decisions are screened and approved. In Japan, the decision to charge is made at one time solely by prosecutors. Prosecutors institute *summary prosecution* against most suspects accused of minor crimes, though the suspect must consent to use of this purely paper procedure. More serious cases are *formally prosecuted* and then tried in district or summary court. Even if there is sufficient evidence to indict and convict, prosecutors may *suspend prosecution* for any crime if indictment "is deemed unnecessary owing to the character, age, environment, gravity of the offense, circumstances or situation after the offense" (Code of Criminal Procedure, art. 248). Out of 1,648,700 suspects processed by prosecutors in 2009, 52.1 percent were disposed of through suspended prosecution, 26.8 percent were summarily prosecuted, and only 7.2 percent were indicted for formal trials (Ukawa 2011, p. 22). The remaining suspects (13.9 percent) were not charged because prosecutors concluded that no crime had occurred or that there was insufficient evidence to convict.

About 97 percent of suspects who have been formally prosecuted are adjudicated by a trial court consisting of one or three judges; the verdict and sentence are decided at the same time: they are not bifurcated as in the United States. Bench trials convene discontinuously at a pace of about one session per month, and more than 90 percent finish in 6 months or less. The remaining 3 percent of formally charged suspects are adjudicated by a tribunal consisting of three professional judges and six lay citizens. These trials proceed more continuously (meeting every day or almost every day), and the large majority finish in four sessions or fewer (*Kanagawa Shimbun*, May 21, 2011). Prosecutors can appeal all first-instance court decisions, including acquittals.

Japanese prosecutors perform four major roles that American prosecutors either do not play or perform in a more attenuated manner. First, Japanese prosecutors conduct precharge investigations and interrogations, both on their own and in conjunction with the police. Second, Japanese prosecutors have monopoly power to dispose of cases by making charge decisions, and they are permitted to drop any charge, no matter how serious the crime or strong the evidence. Third, Japanese prosecutors present the state's case at trial, recommend a proper judgment to the court, and appeal acquittals and sentencing decisions. Finally, Japanese prosecutors supervise the execution of sentences, ensuring that fines are paid and that correctional officers carry out all other punishments—including death sentences—that courts have imposed (Johnson 2002*a*, p. 15).

Although the powers of Japanese prosecutors are considerable, they are not unlimited. For example, plea bargaining is illegal, though occasionally it occurs sub rosa (Johnson 2002*b*). Hence, prosecutors in Japan cannot concentrate in their own hands the powers to charge, convict, and sentence, as American prosecutors do by using plea bargaining to dispose of more than 90 percent of their caseloads.

Japanese law has two distinct faces. For ordinary crimes such as larceny and assault, the law is highly enabling of prosecutor (Johnson 2002*a*, pp. 35–42) and police (Miyazawa 1992) interests, whereas for corruption and other white-collar and organizational crimes, the law disables law enforcement interests by forbidding or restricting practices that prosecutors in many other countries consider essential. The most important are wiretapping, undercover operations, grants of immunity, and plea bargaining. Restricting these practices may be tantamount to tolerating the kinds of offenses (such as corruption) that they are designed to uncover and that seem to constitute one of Japan's biggest crime problems (Ukawa 1997). These restrictions illustrate a well-known proposition that "downward law is greater than upward law" in the sense that more governmental social control gets directed at low-ranking persons (natural and corporate) than at high-ranking persons (Black 1976, p. 21). This adage apparently applies at all times and in all societies, but Japan may be distinctive in the degree to which downward law is greater than upward law: law's enforcers—police and prosecutors especially—work in a deeply dualistic environment (Johnson

2002*a*, p. 160). One may say, following Jonathan Swift's aphorism, that Japanese law is like a cobweb, highly enabling efforts to indict and convict "small flies" (run-of-the-mill offenders) but simultaneously disabling efforts to bring "wasps and hornets" to justice (Johnson 1999).

The outcomes in Japanese criminal justice also merit mention. Conviction rates exceed 99 percent when the denominator includes all cases, whether contested by the defense or not. Even when analysis is restricted to cases in which defendants deny some or all of the charges against them, the conviction rate in courts of first instance remains above 95 percent. This hallmark of the Japanese way of justice has not changed under the lay judge system. Criminal justice in Japan has also been called "benevolent" because it often aims to achieve "reformation and reintegration into society through lenient sanctions tailored to the offender's particular circumstances" (Foote 1992, p. 317). This characterization has been contested (Peters 1992; Miyazawa 1995; Hamai and Ellis 2008; Herber 2011), and the truth is more complicated than a single-minded stress on "benevolence" would suggest, especially for consensually defined serious crimes such as gun and drug use, acts of violence against strangers, offenses committed by *yakuza* (gangsters) and other incorrigibles, and capital crimes (Johnson 2002*a*, p. 201). Nonetheless, in terms of overall sentencing severity, Japanese criminal justice must be included among the world's least harsh systems. Japan's incarceration rate of 62 persons per 100,000 population in 2009 was 70 percent higher than the national rate of 36 in 1992 but still 50 percent lower than Germany's rate (92), less than half the United Kingdom's rate (146), and only one-twelfth the American rate of 743 (Johnson 2008). In 2009, courts of first instance adjudicated 75,128 defendants who had been formally prosecuted. Of these, 74,733 were convicted, for a conviction rate of 99.89 percent. Of the 71,871 defendants sentenced to imprisonment, 42,569 (59.3 percent) received a suspended sentence (Ukawa 2011, p. 32). Table 1 describes the distribution of sentences in 2009. It shows that only 7.3 percent of all convicted offenders received a sentence exceeding 3 years.

On the other end of the severity spectrum, courts of original jurisdiction sentenced nine offenders to death in 2009. It is sometimes said that Japan employs death as a criminal sanction much less often than America—the only other industrialized democracy that continues to retain capital punishment and carry out executions on a regular basis. This view is mistaken. In per capita terms, Japan's rate is lower than

TABLE 1

Trial Outcomes in Japan, 2009

Defendants adjudicated	75,128
Defendants convicted	74,733
Defendants acquitted	85
Other	310
Defendants sentenced	74,733
Death sentence	9
Imprisoned with work	68,519 (100%)
Life sentence	69 (.1%)
20–30 years	53 (.1%)
10–20 years	276 (.4%)
5–10 years	1,345 (2.0%)
3–5 years	3,191 (4.7%)
1–3 years	48,420 (70.7%)
6 months to 1 year	12,777 (18.7%)
Less than 6 months	2,386 (3.5%)
Imprisonment with work	3,352
Fine	2,836
Misdemeanor imprison- ment without work and with petty fine	17

SOURCE.—Ukawa (2011), p. 32.

that for the United States, and it is much lower than rates in high-rate American states such as Texas and Virginia. But the per capita rate of execution is a highly imperfect measure of frequency of use because (Stalinist nightmares aside) persons are not selected randomly for death; they are condemned and executed from a larger pool of death-eligible cases. In the United States and Japan, this pool consists entirely of homicide crimes. Hence, to determine the scale of capital punishment, one must consider the number of people eligible for it. Relative to their respective murder numbers, the probability of a known murderer being sentenced to death in Japan is not much different than in many American death penalty jurisdictions. For example, from 1994 through 2003, the chance of a Japanese murderer being sentenced to death was 1.3 percent—about the same as in California and Virginia. And in 2007, when Japan had 14 death sentences in courts of original jurisdiction and the United States had 110, the ratio of death sentences to homicides was substantially higher in Japan than in the United States. By these measures, Japan is not cautious in its use of capital punishment; it is a vigorous killing state (Johnson 2011c, p. 283).

III. Recruitment and Promotion

Until 2004, the government-run Legal Research and Training Institute (LRTI) was Japan's only law school. To study there, prospective prosecutors, lawyers, and judges had to pass a notoriously difficult bar exam, a feat that only 2 or 3 percent accomplished in any given year. Bar passers then underwent additional instruction for 18–24 months at the LRTI, much of which involved training as "legal apprentices" (*shiho shushusei*) in local courts and law and prosecutors' offices. In response to demands from businesses and citizens to increase the supply of legal services and to relax government control over legal education, a new system of professional law schools was established in 2004 (*Asahi Shimbun*, June 14, 2011). Since then, almost all prosecutors, lawyers, and judges have had to earn a degree from one of Japan's 74 law schools; they have also had to pass a new bar exam, which was accomplished by 25 percent of those who tried in 2010.[5] After passing the bar exam, graduates are required to study at the LRTI for a year before entering one of the legal professions. During this apprenticeship, veteran prosecutors recruit students who seem well suited for law enforcement, a courtship that involves careful screening for grades, personality, and ideology. Japan's procuracy—like its judiciary—expects new recruits to be cooperative conformists who respect the status quo and avoid political activism (West 2011, p. 16). One result is that there are few leftist or maverick prosecutors. People become prosecutors for many different reasons, but my own survey of 235 of them in the mid-1990s found five main motivations: the desire to do justice, the appeal of investigations, the fit between job and personality, the influence of "significant others," and the attraction to authority (Johnson 2002*a*, pp. 94–97).

After joining the organization, prosecutors are transferred to new positions around the country every 2–3 years. In addition to the executive positions at the top of the organizational hierarchy, the most coveted posts tend to be administrative assignments in the Ministry of Justice (where policies are made) and investigative assignments in one

---

[5] As of 2011, Japan's new law school system is in crisis. The number of applications for admission is declining because tuition is expensive and because the 25 percent bar pass rate in 2010 is much lower than the 70–80 percent rate that was said to be the target when the law school reform was enacted (the pass rate for some schools is in single digits). Moreover, some bar passers are having a hard time finding employment, and many attorneys oppose making the bar exam easier to pass because they fear increased competition (*Asahi Shimbun*, June 14, 2011).

of the Special Investigation Divisions (*tokusobu*) that focus on corruption and white-collar crimes in Tokyo, Osaka, Nagoya, and other large cities.[6] The criteria for transfers are opaque, but college of origin, ideology,[7] age and seniority (including how many attempts it took to pass the bar exam), and previous job performance matter. So does the avoidance of mistakes, for Japan's procuracy has long operated according to a "demerit principle" (*shittenshugi*); the absence of mistakes is esteemed more highly than the accomplishment of excellence. The surest way to get ahead is not by performing one's duties brilliantly—by winning big cases or making bold policy innovations—but by scrupulously avoiding mistakes that might sully one's reputation or that of the organization. Young prosecutors quickly learn the importance of this principle and what mistakes to avoid. Chief among the demerits are acquitted cases that are deemed to have been negligently charged. This institutionalized caution toward acquittals helps explain Japan's 99 percent conviction rate. Even for contested cases, the conviction rate ranges from 93 to 98 percent, depending on the court and the year (Johnson 2002*a*, p. 228).

IV. Structure

On the surface, the organizations of prosecution in the United States and Japan look a lot alike. Both are bureaucratic; both function as criminal justice gatekeepers; both distinguish between frontline, managerial, and executive roles; both promote workers on the basis of some combination of merit and seniority; and both confront the challenges of obtaining worker compliance, adequate resources, and autonomy. However, these similarities must not be allowed to obscure deep differences in how relationships are structured, core tasks are defined, mission is cultivated, frontline prosecutors are controlled, and autonomy is gained and maintained. There is also a significant difference in career trajectories. Few Japanese prosecutors use their posts as launching pads for work in electoral politics or the judiciary (Flemming, Nardulli, and Eisenstein 1992). The large majority of prosecutors in Japan

---

[6] Prosecutors in these Special Investigation Divisions constitute less than 2 percent of the procuracy's workforce (Johnson 2002*a*, p. 8).

[7] In deciding whom to transfer where, partisan political and party affiliation do not play a major role, but the prosecutor executives who make these decisions do look for ideologically reliable people to fill key positions in the organization (Johnson 2002*a*, p. 132).

who leave the organization before or at retirement go to work as private attorneys (Johnson 2006*b*).

The United States has approximately 3,000 distinct prosecutors offices, each with its own structure, chief, policy, and practice. Japan has one: a national, centralized, hierarchical, career procuracy whose structure corresponds to that of the judiciary. Formally, the prosecutors office is just one organ among many in the Ministry of Justice, but in reality prosecutors run the ministry and direct almost all of its principal activities. Although their titular head (the minister of justice) is a cabinet member and usually an elected politician, many prosecutors acknowledge that they cannot recall their nominal boss's name. Some dismiss the minister as "irrelevant" in all but extraordinary cases involving political corruption or other high-profile crimes. In the vast majority of ordinary cases, prosecutors in Japan enjoy significant independence from external authority. Within their organization, however, the discretion of individual prosecutors is significantly constrained by internal controls.

As of 2008, Japan had 1,680 prosecutors (*kenji*) who had passed the bar exam and been educated at the LRTI and 900 assistant prosecutors (*fuku-kenji*), most of whom were appointed from the ranks of clerical workers (*jimukan*) who are not trained as lawyers but who made it through a selection process in the Ministry of Justice.[8] The Supreme Prosecutors Office stands at the apex of the organization, above eight high, 50 district, and 438 local offices (Kamiya 2009).[9] These office levels are tied together, in theory and in reality, by "the principle of prosecutor unity," one of the most important facts about the organization of prosecution in Japan. This precept holds that "the procuracy is a national, united, hierarchical organization in which superiors command and subordinates obey and all prosecutors form one body" (Nomura 1978, p. 126). The principle is rooted in provisions of the Public Prosecutors Office Law that give various office heads, and all prose-

[8] In comparison to these 2,580 prosecutors, Japan (in 2010) had about 3,400 full-time judges and nearly 30,000 private attorneys. The number of attorneys has doubled since 1990 (*Asahi Shimbun*, June 14, 2011), but per capita Japan still has only about one-tenth as many licensed lawyers as Germany and one-twentieth as many as the United States (Kamiya 2008). About 16 percent of lawyers and 15 percent of judges are women; the percentage of female prosecutors is a little lower, though it has risen in recent years (West 2011, pp. 16, 223).

[9] Most local prosecutors offices are staffed by a single prosecutor or assistant prosecutor.

cutor managers, authority to direct their subordinates in any work-related area, whether investigation, indictment, or trial. And while the minister of justice is the formal head of the procuracy, the same law restricts his or her ability to control prosecutors by conferring power to direct only to the prosecutor general—Japan's top prosecutor—in "particular cases." In practice this means that the prosecutor general is expected to shield subordinates from political meddling, though in principle it also enables the minister of justice to intervene in investigations by directing the prosecutor general in specific cases. Most observers believe that a minister of justice has exercised this right only once, in 1954, when Takeru Inukai, at the request of Prime Minister Shigeru Yoshida, ordered the prosecutor general to refrain from arresting Eisaku Sato, the secretary general of the ruling Liberal Party, for allegedly taking bribes. In the face of widespread public and media criticism, Inukai resigned soon afterward. Since then, ministers of justice have exercised their supervisory powers much more circumspectly.

The "principle of prosecutor unity" stands in tension with another provision of the Public Prosecutors Office Law, the "principle of prosecutor independence." Under this tenet, each individual prosecutor is an "independent government agency" with power to institute prosecution and perform other functions as authorized by law. This independence is protected in two main ways. First, no prosecutor can be fired, suspended, or given a pay cut except in narrowly defined circumstances and through specific legal procedures. Second, the minister of justice (and politicians more generally) has limited authority to direct and manage prosecutors. Within the procuracy, the principle of prosecutor independence is usually subordinated to the principle of prosecutor unity and the corollary requirement of obedience to superiors. As elite prosecutor Kawai Nobutaro noted in 1954, "the iron rule" of Japan's procuracy is that "those above command and those below obey." His aphorism is as apt today as when he penned it:

I am sorry to employ such a plebeian example but, if we compare a criminal investigation to basic construction work, then the front-line investigating prosecutor is like a human wheelbarrow used for flattening the earth. The managing prosecutor wields a stick to direct the frontline prosecutor to "carry mud here" and "place a brick there," and then he goes off to the next construction site to do more of the same. The human wheelbarrow works very hard to carry dirt and pound cement as directed. The only job for the human wheelbarrow is to decide how to pound the concrete and to what depth. (Quoted in Kubo 1989, p. 134)

V. Roles and Tasks

Prosecutors in Japan play three main roles, as operators, managers, and executives. Operators (*hira kenji*) investigate, indict, and try cases. These frontline workers perform the organization's core tasks: processing suspects by "clarifying the truth" about alleged bad acts, determining legal guilt and innocence, and deciding appropriate sanctions. Managers (*joshi*) monitor and coordinate the work of operators in order to attain organizational goals. Executives (*kanbu*) are responsible for securing organizational autonomy and maintaining public support.

A. Operators: Uncovering and Constructing the Truth

Operators do the work that justifies the procuracy's existence. They perform its core task, the work that enables the organization to manage its most critical problem. For prosecutors, the central problem is the historian's challenge: determining who did what to whom, and why. The bad acts from which most crimes are constructed consist of events that have already occurred. Since the past does not exist and cannot be directly perceived, prosecutors come to know it not through immediate observation but by collecting and interpreting evidence. Thus, the prosecutor's main task is to clarify and construct the truth about conduct in the past—to recover acts from their ambiguous past by finding a coherent story in them or imposing one on them so that sound charge decisions can be made.

Of course, operators perform many other tasks, such as deciding whether and what to charge and presenting the state's case at trial. But their central task, the fundamental work on which all other work depends and the job prosecutors regard as their primary duty, is to establish the facts of cases by acquiring and interpreting evidence during the preindictment investigation. To put it simply, prosecutors believe that their core task is to "clarify the truth" about alleged criminal acts. In a survey I conducted in 1994–95, 216 out of 235 prosecutors (92 percent) ranked "explicating the truth about a case" a "very important objective." Of the remaining 19 respondents, 18 ranked this objective as "important" and only one as "not very important." Thus, 99.6 percent of 235 prosecutors regarded "explicating the truth" as either important or very important, making this the organization's cardinal objective. In California, Washington, Minnesota, and other American prosecutors offices, the salience of truth-finding is significantly lower, not only in surveys and interviews but also in routine prosecutor practices such as plea bargaining and in the commitment American prosecutors make to the assumption that "truth" is not so much something they "find" through investigation as something that emerges as a result of the adversarial clash of interests (Johnson 2002*a*, pp. 98, 123).

Japanese prosecutors agree not only about what their core task is but also how to perform it. For the most part, prosecutors clarify the truth by preparing written statements (*chosho*) during the investigation that precedes indictment. The most crucial part of these dossiers is usually the suspect's confession, which remains "the king of evidence," "the decisive element of proof sought by every prosecutor before he takes a case into court and the single most important item determining the reception his efforts are likely to receive from most Japanese judges when he gets there" (Johnson 1972, p. 149). But Japan's reliance on confessions is sometimes taken too far. Indeed, many of the most serious miscarriages of justice in Japan have occurred because of false and coerced confessions. In the 1980s, four condemned men were acquitted on retrial and released from death row; in each case the court ruled that their confessions had been coerced. There have been no death row exonerations since then, but there have been revelations of other miscarriages of justice that were rooted in false confessions. In 2008 Hiroshi Yanagihara was released from prison after serving 2 years for a rape in Toyama prefecture that he did not commit (Buerk 2009). In 2010 Toshikazu Sugaya was released from prison after serving 17 years for a rape and murder in Ashikaga that he did not commit (Fackler 2010). And in 2011 Shoji Sakurai and Takao Sugiyama were acquitted on retrial after serving 29 years in prison for a murder in Fukawa that they did not commit (*Japan Times*, March 15, 2011). These and other miscarriages of justice have been sufficiently numerous that in 2008 the Qbrick Company started publishing a magazine called *Enzai File* (Falsely Accused File) to explore wrongful convictions and other potentially false arrests and charges (Ito 2008).[10]

---

[10] The prevailing conception of a "miscarriage of justice" in Japan seems to be broader than the prevailing conception in the United States, for the former includes not only wrongful convictions but also arrests that do not lead to charges and charges

At present, prosecutors and police do not record confessions verbatim; they prepare summary statements that abridge and organize the suspect's statements. These statements synthesize testimony given over several sessions or days of interrogation. They are the prosecutor's reconstruction of the truth or, as many defense lawyers see it, "the prosecutor's essay" (Johnson 2002a, p. 248). This method of constructing "truth" enables prosecutors to generate logically consistent and coherent accounts, which courts often find compelling. Large and liberally interpreted exceptions to the hearsay rule also allow many dossiers to be entered as evidence, even when the defense wants them excluded. The judge's role, in practice if not principle, is to review the results of the investigation as recorded in these dossiers, though reliance on written documents has declined since the advent of Japan's lay judge system in 2009, because lay judges cannot spend weeks or months reading files, as professional judges routinely did in the past and as they still do in cases that are not tried by a mixed panel of professionals and lay persons. Thus, the truth that prevails at trial— and the truth that judges authoritatively pronounce—tends to be the version that prosecutors have uncovered and constructed. In many cases, claims about the status of "truth" depend on perceptions about the legitimacy of the process (and the actors in the process, police and prosecutors especially) for construing and constructing the truth. Some lawyers believe that the process is deeply problematic,[11] and others believe that lawyers themselves are a large part of the problem.

---

that do not lead to conviction (Johnson 2002a, p. 238). Two recent films skillfully explore miscarriages in Japanese criminal justice: *Sore demo Boku wa Yatte Inai* (Even so, I didn't do it), a dramatic depiction of a wrongfully accused groper (directed by Masayuki Suo and released in 2007); and *Shoji and Takao*, a documentary of the lives of two convicted murderers who were released on parole in 1996 and acquitted in the "Fukawa case" retrial of 2011 (directed by Yoko Ide and released in 2011).

[11] A survey about prosecutors' interrogation practices that was sent to all of Japan's 28,870 private attorneys in 2010 generated only 257 replies (an 8.9 percent response rate), but the results are interesting and instructive. Respondents identified six main categories of interrogation abuse: threats (such as "if you do not confess you will not be released on bail"), inducements ("if you confess we will not charge you"), violence (hitting, kicking, throwing things, and so on), attempts to undermine a suspect's relationship with defense counsel ("your young lawyer is lousy!"), long interrogations that overbear a suspect's will (some respondents reported interrogations of 8 hours or more each day for many days in a row), and "other" problems (such as prosecutors telling a suspect "you are the worst kind of human being" or not reading a dossier aloud before asking a suspect to sign it). For more details, see Nihon Bengoshi Rengokai (2011b), and for related analysis of interrogation problems, see Johnson (2002a, pp. 243–75).

There are problems in Japanese defense lawyering. The public defender system is underdeveloped, and few private attorneys spend much time on criminal defense (*Asahi Shimbun*, June 9, 2011). Attorneys who do criminal defense are often passive about protecting and asserting their clients' rights. A survey of more than 1,000 lawyers in 1991 found that over 60 percent had never recommended that a suspect or defendant exercise his or her right to remain silent—not a single time. Sixty-six percent of lawyers had never asked a court to have a witness testify in court when prosecutors sought to rely on written statements, and 75 percent had never requested a court order compelling disclosure of evidence from the prosecution. Criminal defense has improved in the two decades since this survey was done, but many problems remain, including a reluctance to aggressively challenge the state's version of the "truth" (Johnson 2011*a*).[12]

One way to improve Japan's commitment to the truth and to mitigate the problems that arise from overreliance on confessions would be to require the videotaping of the entire interrogation process. This reform is rapidly spreading in many parts of the world, and Japan is slowly moving in this direction too, pushed by the interaction of three causal forces: the revelation of false confessions and public pressure to prevent them, the need in the new lay judge system to assess evidence in open court rather than in chambers or the judge's residence, and the imitation effects that follow from recording reforms in other nations (Johnson 2006*a*). Prosecutors in Japan first recorded some interrogations on a trial basis in 2006 (usually just the final scene), and police reluctantly started to follow suit in 2009. In the years to come, recording seems likely to become a standard operating procedure, especially in serious cases (Ibusuki 2010*a*).

B. *Managers: Cultivating Mission and Controlling Operators*

If Japanese prosecutors believe that uncovering and constructing the truth is their core task, how is this sense of mission inculcated, and how are operators coordinated and controlled so as to accomplish it? The answer has a lot to do with managers, who perform two key functions. First, managers cultivate widespread endorsement of the way the operators' critical task is defined (Johnson 2002*a*, p. 127). Second,

---

[12] For a report by the Japan Federation of Bar Associations on the role of incompetent defense lawyers in the case that resulted in the wrongful murder conviction and 17-year incarceration of Toshikazu Sugaya, see Nihon Bengoshi Rengokai (2011*a*).

managers coordinate and control operators in order to attain organizational and jurisprudential objectives such as the correction of individual offenders and the treatment of similar cases similarly (p. 128).

Japanese prosecutors are educated to believe in the crucial importance of truth through confessions. The instruction they receive is both formal and informal. Formally, legal apprentices listen to many lectures that emphasize the "truth through confession" theme, and in-career training further helps to inculcate this sense of mission. But the most important settings for instruction may be informal and after-hours gatherings in the office and at restaurants, bars, and karaoke clubs. There, young prosecutors are instructed in the organization's traditions and implored to carry them on. Like workers in other large Japanese organizations in business and bureaucracy, prosecutors spend much time together. Their organization so envelops them that it sometimes resembles a "total institution"—a place where the usual barriers between work, play, and sleep disappear (Goffman 1961, p. 5). Most prosecutors routinely spend 12 hours or more in the same place, under the same authorities, and in the company of the same people (other prosecutors). A common subtext of their interactions is that their main task is to determine the truth by obtaining full and detailed confessions. The cumulative effect of these countless conversations is a strongly shared sense of occupational mission.[13]

Managing prosecutors in Japan coordinate and control operators' activities to an extent unseen in American prosecution offices. Most American prosecutor organizations have "virtually no instruments by which to enforce" office policies (Abrams 1971, p. 53), and some American scholars have even argued that "a bureaucratic, rule-oriented, administrative model of management does not fit the nature of the job of criminal prosecution" (Carter 1974, p. 117). Even in federal prosecution, coordination and control are so weak and inconspicuous that one commentator calls it an "adhocracy" (Burnham 1996, p. 83). Some improvement has occurred in some jurisdictions in recent years, but for the most part the discretion exercised by individual prosecutors in America goes largely unchecked within the office (Bach 2009; Davis 2009; Stuntz 2011).

Here, too, Japan is different. Japanese managers employ three mech-

---

[13] On the sociology of work in Japan more generally, see Mauer and Kawanishi (2005).

anisms to ensure that office policies are properly implemented by frontline prosecutors. First, managers articulate specific criteria in written manuals, guidelines, and standards, such as the "disposition and sentencing guidelines" (*shori kyukei kijunshu*) that operators frequently consult. Unlike their American counterparts, prosecutors in Japan work in an organization that is saturated with policy directives. More than 99 percent of the Japanese prosecutors I surveyed said that such directives are indispensable guides to action (Johnson 2002*a*, p. 128). In contrast, a similar survey conducted in California found that more than 80 percent of American prosecutors believed that formal manuals and rules were unimportant (Carter 1974). Manuals and rules are almost always within arm's reach of Japanese prosecutors—and they frequently refer to them.

Second, managers in Japan require frontline prosecutors to clear their decisions with supervisors, chiefly through the *kessai* system of consultation and approval. In order to make charge decisions and sentencing recommendations, operators must consult with and obtain the approval of two or three managers, depending on the seriousness of the case. In serious cases, operators must also obtain approval to arrest and detain suspects and extend their detention, unless arrest must be made on an emergency basis (Miyazawa 1992). Throughout these consultation processes, managers perform major functions. As judges, they review the adequacy of the evidence. As teammates, they provide support in difficult cases. As teachers, they educate young prosecutors about how to do their jobs. And as supervisors, they ensure that like cases are treated alike.

Third, managers control and coordinate operators through audits (*kansa*) of past decisions—especially noncharge decisions. When they come across a dubious noncharge disposition, they require the responsible prosecutors to produce written and oral explanations, which is an onerous obligation. Like audits in the business world, these after-the-fact checks are one more way of ensuring the integrity of prosecutorial decision making.[14]

---

[14] External checks on noncharge decisions are made by Japan's 207 Prosecution Review Commissions (*kensatsu shinsakai*), which are lay advisory bodies composed of 11 private citizens. A law reform in 2004 gave PRCs the legally binding authority to demand explanations for nonprosecution decisions and made indictment mandatory if a PRC recommends prosecution twice for the same case (Fukurai 2011). As of October 2011, reformed PRCs have mandated indictment of six persons in four separate cases, and several of the targets have been high-profile, including Ichiro Ozawa, one of Japan's

In sum, managers in Japan's procuracy wield strong control over their subordinates' behavior—much more control than managers do in American prosecution offices. While these controls go a long way toward explaining some of the achievements of Japanese criminal justice, they also open the door to inappropriate conduct in high-profile cases. Pervasive bureaucratic controls are also reported to be a significant source of dissatisfaction among people who quit the procuracy in order to enjoy more freedom working as private attorneys (Johnson 2002*a*, p. 135).

C. Executives: Securing Autonomy and Maintaining the Organization

The chief concern of executive prosecutors is acquiring sufficient freedom of action so that operators can perform their critical tasks and so that managers can infuse the definition of those tasks with a sense of mission. Executives also maintain the organization by acquiring the resources (money, labor, and political support) it needs to survive and prosper. Both tasks are easier to accomplish in Japan than in the United States.

Organizations need autonomy, which means minimizing rivals and securing freedom from political constraints (Wilson 1989). Since prosecutors in Japan almost monopolize the power to charge people with crimes, they face little competition concerning the critical indictment decision.[15] Police duties, however, do overlap with those of prosecutors, especially with respect to investigations and "clarifying and constructing the truth." As a result, prosecutor relations with the police are more complicated than relations with judges and defense lawyers, the other main actors in the criminal court community. Executive prosecutors spend much time and energy managing this sensitive relationship. Conflict between police and prosecutors tends to occur around three interrelated issues: trust, turf, and timidity. Some police feel that prosecutors try too hard to control the course of investigations, even in

---

most powerful politicians, who was charged with filing misleading financial reports in 2010 and was being tried by a panel of three professional judges in 2011 (*Daily Yomiuri*, October 8, 2011).

[15] In addition to PRCs, which review noncharge decisions, the "analogical institution of prosecution" (*fushimpan seikyu*) provides an external check on prosecutor decisions by empowering private attorneys to file charges for a very narrow range of offenses—mostly police brutality and other abuses of official authority. But this check is so rarely used that in the aggregate it "stands a short step away from utter irrelevance" (Johnson 2002*a*, p. 223).

run-of-the-mill cases, and they complain that this reflects a lack of trust in police. A related concern is the police perception that prosecutors try to own white-collar and other high-profile investigations and that this reflects a lack of confidence in the capacity and integrity of police to handle complicated and politically sensitive cases. The most common source of discontent seems to be the police perception that prosecutors are too timid about charging cases and that many cases are not charged out of an inappropriate preoccupation with maintaining a high conviction rate. Prosecutors seldom compromise on the charging issue, but because they rely on police to do the bulk of investigating in ordinary cases, they are sensitive to the trust and turf issues, and they tend to be soft on police crimes too (Miyazawa 1989; Terasawa 2009).

As for political constraints, crime and criminal justice were quiescent issues in Japan until the 1990s, and politicians routinely deferred to prosecutors on most crime issues. As mentioned earlier, a minister of justice has openly used "the power to direct and manage" the top prosecutor in only one case (the shipbuilding scandal of 1954), though it is difficult to discern how often subsequent ministers have used their authority to influence decision making behind the scenes (the frequency of use is certainly not zero). What is clear, however, is that since the 1990s, as crime and criminal justice became increasingly politicized and politicians began to engage more directly in criminal justice policy making, executive prosecutors have had to spend more energy securing this aspect of organizational autonomy by directly engaging in conversations and consultations with the public, the media, and victims' organizations (Johnson 2007; Miyazawa 2008).

The second major concern for prosecutor executives is organizational maintenance, which requires obtaining adequate resources. Money, labor, and political support are especially crucial inputs.

Obtaining adequate financial appropriations has seldom been a major problem for prosecutor executives. The procuracy's share of the national budget has changed little since 1980. At about 0.12 percent (¥12 per 10,000), the procuracy's budget remains approximately one-third that of the courts but is much larger than that for public defending. Around 90 percent of the budget goes for personnel expenses such as salaries, which compare favorably to prosecutors' salaries in the US Department of Justice (Ministry of Justice, http://www.moj.go.jp).

Acquiring an adequate supply of labor has sometimes been a more difficult task, but executive prosecutors have usually managed to do so satisfactorily. The so-called personnel problem—a shortage of new recruits and an increase in the number of *yameken*, or "prosecutor-quitters"—was most acute from the mid-1980s through the early 1990s, when many real and potential prosecutors expressed frustration about the ubiquitous bureaucratic controls described above and the frequent transfers to new office and job assignments (one purpose of these transfers is to discourage friendships that might breed corruption). Since the mid-1990s, the personnel problem has abated, partly because the number of bar passers—and therefore the number of potential prosecutors—has increased substantially. In 2010, 2,133 people passed the bar exam, compared with 1,000 in 2000 and 500 in 1990. One goal of Japan's justice reform movement is to increase the number of bar passers to 3,000 per year (Jones 2009).

The third way that prosecutor executives maintain their organization is by securing sufficient political support to enable operators and managers to perform their jobs effectively. The key constituency is the public. Executives care about this relationship for several reasons. They need to recruit qualified personnel to fill the organization's ranks, and the people they recruit participate in the general culture and are influenced by popular perceptions. Article 4 of the Public Prosecutors Office Law imposes a duty to "represent the public interest"—an obligation most prosecutors take seriously, not least because public trust helps prevent political intervention in prosecutorial decision making (Haley 1998, pp. 58, 122). Finally, in order to investigate, charge, and try cases, prosecutors must secure citizens' cooperation—as victims, complainants, witnesses, suspects, and defendants and (under the new trial system that started in 2009) as lay judges.

VI. Strengths

The Japanese way of organizing prosecution works well in at least three ways. First, it enables prosecutors to manage the tension between two imperatives that Americans regard as often incompatible and always in tension: the need to individualize case decisions and the need to treat like cases alike so as to achieve a tolerable level of consistency. To an extent inconceivable to many American researchers (Abrams 1971; Carter 1974; Burnham 1996; Davis 2009), the Japanese way of prosecution achieves concord between the values of individualization and consistency. This is one of the most impressive achievements in the Japanese way of justice (Johnson 2002*a*, pp. 160, 181).[16]

Second, the collective and hierarchical features of Japan's procuracy such as *kessai*—the system of consultation with superiors about case dispositions—help explain Japan's high conviction rates. These rates, which average about 97 percent in contested cases, are often criticized as a sign that Japan's criminal process is biased against criminal suspects and offenders and in favor of state interests. There are many pro-state biases in Japanese criminal justice (Miyazawa 1992; Feeley and Miyazawa 2002; Johnson 2002*a*; Foote 2010), but the main proximate cause of the high conviction rates is the "cautious" (*shincho*) and conservative charging policy.[17] That policy is not an accidental achievement; it is the product of conscious planning and well-designed mechanisms (such as *kessai*) for turning aims into accomplishments. It also needs to be noted that the main beneficiary of this cautious charging policy is not the Japanese state (as many critics contend) but rather suspects and offenders who do not get charged in the Japanese system but who would get charged in similar situations in countries such as the United States and United Kingdom, where prosecution is organized differently. In this sense, a system that convicts almost all defendants may actually be more protective of the liberty interests of criminal suspects than a system that acquits 10–20 percent of defendants (as in the United States and United Kingdom) or 50 percent or more (as in India and Pakistan). This possibility is overlooked by many critics who contend that Japan's high conviction rate reflects an "Iron Hand" of justice (Johnson 2002*a*, p. 215) or claim that it is "extremely, and abnormally, high" (Hirano 1989, p. 130). The conservative charging policy does have negative effects. It causes some victims to feel abandoned and frustrated that offenders "got away with it." It short-circuits the com-

---

[16] For a more detailed account of the mechanisms and causes of individualization in Japanese criminal justice, see Foote (1992*a*, pp. 342–59). And for a more detailed account of the mechanisms and causes of consistency in Japanese criminal justice, see Johnson (2002*a*, pp. 161–73).

[17] A survey of 40 prosecutors by a national newspaper in 2011 found an almost even split between those who believe that Japan's high conviction rate should be maintained and those who feel that it should decline. The same survey revealed that all prosecutors believe that the main reasons for the country's high conviction rate are the quality of their own investigations and their own cautious charging policies; not a single prosecutor said that judges or defense lawyers are also responsible for the high conviction rate (*Mainichi Shimbun*, March 9, 2011). For an argument that deferent judges and passive defense lawyers do contribute to Japan's high conviction rate, see Johnson (2011*a*).

municative and pedagogical functions that public trials perform. It suppresses the supply of skilled and vigorous defense lawyers (who wants to defend criminal cases if the outcomes are all but certain?). And it may undermine the deterrent effect of the criminal sanction. These effects are significant and complicated, and they do not fit well with facile conclusions about the meaning of a conviction rate that comes close to 100 percent (Johnson 2002a, pp. 237–42).

Third, Japan's prosecutor organization is highly cohesive. Although some individual prosecutors chafe at the internal controls that constrain their behavior—and some end up leaving the organization for this reason—most accept these office realities as necessary and desirable, and many regard close kinship with their colleagues as a welcome feature of the job. The high level of cohesion also helps explain something that is otherwise hard to comprehend: the seriousness with which Japanese prosecutors perform their roles. Compared to their American counterparts, prosecutors in Japan are extremely earnest (*majime*) about their work. This is evident in many ways: the amount of time they spend in the office, the thoroughness with which they conduct interrogations and interviews, and the diligence with which they approach their duties (Johnson 2002a, p. 88). Since the values at stake—life, liberty, dignity, property, and reputation—are important, Japanese prosecutors should be commended for the seriousness with which they perform their roles. Their commitment to role obligations also reflects high levels of job satisfaction (p. 49). In procuracies no less than in other organizations, "satisfied workers usually work harder and better than frustrated ones" (Etzioni 1964, p. 2).

VII. Problems
The achievements of Japanese prosecution are considerable, and the foregoing summary is hardly exhaustive. As I have written elsewhere,

> The Japanese way of justice is in large part determined by the way prosecutors perform their jobs. If justice means taking into account the needs and circumstances of individual suspects, then prosecutors in Japan must receive higher marks than their American counterparts. If justice implies treating like cases alike, then the capacity of prosecutors to do so is impressive indeed. If justice should promote healing, not just punishment, then Japanese prosecutors must be reckoned more restorative than prosecutors in the

United States. And if justice depends on uncovering and clarifying the truth, then readers will see how fundamental this maxim is deemed to be in Japan. In these ways and more, the Japanese way of justice is uncommonly just. (Johnson 2002*a*, p. vii)

But the Japanese way of organizing prosecution also produces some significant problems. Here I highlight two of the most important: defects in truth finding and deficiencies in accountability.

A. Truth and Justice

The first problem concerns *truth*, the clarification of which prosecutors regard as their cardinal objective. What happens in the interrogation room is especially critical because it is there that truth through confessions is construed and constructed. Confessions are the heart of Japan's criminal process—the pump that keeps cases circulating in the system. Confessions are also the precondition for many of the achievements of Japanese criminal justice. Indeed, here is the primary postulate of Japan's criminal process and the premise that animates much prosecutor behavior: If there is no confession, then there will be no truth, no consistency, no correction, no conviction, and—at the end of the day—no justice (Johnson 2002*a*, p. 268).

Confessions, however, can be difficult to obtain. The biggest truth-finding problems occur when a case is serious, the level of suspicion is high, and the suspect refuses to confess. In these circumstances, dropping a case is seldom considered an option, and the prosecution's extreme reliance on confessions can lead to extreme efforts to obtain them (Johnson 2002*a*, p. 243). Much problematic prosecutor behavior—and many if not most miscarriages of justice—stems from two connected facts: the criminal justice system's deep dependence on admissions of guilt and the absence of checks on official power in the interrogation room.[18] The conditions of interrogation—the duration

[18] It is impossible to know how many persons have been wrongfully convicted. Since 1945, only eight persons have been sentenced to death or life imprisonment and subsequently acquitted at retrial—an average of one exoneration every 8 years (*Asahi Shimbun*, May 25, 2011). By comparison, in the United States between 1973 and 2010, 138 people were released from death row with evidence of their innocence—an average of 3.6 persons per year (Death Penalty Information Center, http://www.death penaltyinfo.org/innocence-and-death-penalty). Japan's low number allows for at least two interpretations. First, Japan has few institutions that aggressively search for miscarriages of justice: the defense bar is small and passive (Johnson 2011*a*), judges often defer to prosecutors (Foote 2010), the press is compliant and tends to rely on government pronouncements in their reporting (Terasawa 2009), there is no Innocence

and intensity of questioning (often many hours a day for many days in a row), the "duty to endure questioning" even after the right to silence has been invoked, and the absence of defense lawyers in the interrogation room—mean that some wills are overborne (Hamada 1992). Japanese courts have been reluctant to acknowledge this problem, but the United Nations has repeatedly rebuked Japan for violating international protocols about the length, location, and methods of interrogation; for relying too much on confessions for evidence; for the "tunnel vision" of police and prosecutors during investigations; and for inadequate disclosure of evidence to the defense (Repeta 2009). In the words of one of the country's preeminent legal scholars, Japan "cannot go on forever ignoring the UN's counsel" (Hirano 1999, p. 4).[19]

Some commentators contend that the solution to the interrogation problem is to relax the long-standing reliance on confessions. This is easier said than done. Norms this deeply embedded are difficult to change; reform will take time. But the advent of Japan's lay judge system in 2009 means that trials and related proceedings—at least in the thin slice of cases tried by lay judge panels—are becoming less dependent on written confessions and more reliant on testimony presented in open court, for lay judges cannot take dossiers home to read as professional judges often did in the past.

Proposals have been made to institute alternatives such as plea bargaining and immunity as alternatives to the standard practice of confession-through-interrogation (Ukawa 1997). Some of these initiatives come from police and prosecutors who believe that it is getting harder

---

Project like those in the United States that have produced more than 270 postconviction DNA exonerations since 1989 (Ibusuki 2010a), and there is no Criminal Cases Review Commission such as the one established in Britain, which has, since 1997, retried 453 cases and set aside sentences in 316 of them—an average of about 20 abandoned decisions per year (Kaneko 2011). Because the number of wrongful convictions revealed depends (among other things) on how hard and how effectively one looks for them, these institutional weaknesses suggest that Japan's miscarriage problem may be much larger than has come to light so far. Second, however, Japan's prosecution system generally prefers the risk that an uncharged offender will reoffend over the risk that a charged suspect will be acquitted (Johnson 2002a, pp. 105–7). This preference, institutionalized and enforced through the organizational mechanisms (pp. 218–30), suggests that Japan's prosecutor-gatekeepers may send fewer miscarriage-risky cases to trial than do their counterparts in some other countries (pp. 238–39). For studies of wrongful conviction in 10 Western nations, see Huff and Killias (2008).

[19] A survey of 1,300 Japanese prosecutors in 2011 found that 26 percent had been told by a superior to compose a written statement (chosho) that differed from what a suspect or witness actually said (Asahi Shimbun, March 11, 2011).

to obtain confessions.[20] Japanese criminal procedure stands out for its reliance on confessions and its banning of investigative methods that are taken for granted in other democracies. Among eight democratic nations—Japan, England, America, France, Australia, Italy, Germany, and Holland—only Japan forbids plea bargaining, immunity, undercover operations, and the presence of defense lawyers during interrogation (*Sankei Shimbun*, May 21, 2011). Japan does allow wiretapping, but on a much more limited basis than these other nations (wiretaps can be used only in organized crime and drug cases). Moreover, in contrast to the United States and England, perjury by defendants is not a crime.

But if Japan stands apart in its dependence on interrogations and in its reluctance to use investigative methods that are routinely used elsewhere,[21] solving this problem faces two serious obstacles. Culturally, many Japanese people resist the notion that justice can be "bargained" (Sato 1974; Sasaki 2000). And politically, giving prosecutors and police more legal levers—to plea-bargain, offer immunity, conduct undercover stings, and so on—is opposed by many liberals and lawyers because those reforms would exacerbate the imbalance of power between the state and the defense that already exist—unless the powers that prosecutors now possess are simultaneously curtailed (*Asahi Shimbun*, August 9, 2011).[22]

Curtailing prosecutor power is one of the main aims of the Japanese movement to record custodial interrogations (*torishirabe no kashika*). Since recording is also a medium for preserving the truth of the interrogation process, it would also seem to serve the central objective of Japanese criminal justice (Ibusuki 2010*a*). More broadly, recording serves the interests of many parties in the criminal process. It benefits suspects and defense attorneys by deterring impermissible interrogation techniques and preventing false confessions and wrongful convictions. Police and prosecutors also benefit because recording protects them against false accusations of abuse. Perhaps most important, re-

---

[20] A nationwide survey of 1,444 prosecutors found that 82 percent believe "it has become more difficult to obtain statements from suspects and witnesses" (*Tokyo Shimbun*, March 11, 2011, p. 1).

[21] As explained in Sec. II, the reluctance to use these investigative methods helps explain why Japanese law enforcement is weak vis-à-vis corporate, white-collar, and other powerful offenders (Johnson 1999).

[22] For summaries of the main developments in prosecution reform between 2009 and 2011, see *Daily Yomiuri*, August 13, 2011, and *Japan Times*, August 2, 2011.

cording helps prosecutors, judges, and lay judges by giving them an empirical basis for assessing the voluntariness and veracity of statements composed in the interrogation room (Johnson 2006*a*). Prosecutors and police have started to experiment with recording on a trial basis, but mostly by taping just the final stage of interrogation. In the first 2 years of the lay judge system (May 2009 to May 2011), prosecutors introduced electronically recorded statements as evidence in 35 trials. In every case the court found the confession voluntary and reliable (*Mainichi Shimbun*, May 21, 2011).

Recording interrogations promotes the goals of fact-finding, due process, transparency, accountability, and public respect for the criminal justice system. And America's experience with recording interrogations reveals that the vast majority of police departments believe it improves police practice and that few want to return to the days when they did not record (Sullivan 2004; Johnson 2006*a*). Because of these many benefits—including benefits for law enforcement—taping has become a mandatory or common practice in England, Italy, France, Australia, Canada, and many American jurisdictions. Among comparable democracies, only Germany rivals Japan in resisting recording reforms. Even the developing nations of South Korea and Taiwan record more frequently and more completely than Asia's richest democracy does. The Japan Federation of Bar Associations has been pushing hard for several years to make this reform a reality. Many prosecutors and police continue to resist—or to insist that they be given additional investigative powers if their freedom in the interrogation room is curtailed by cameras and microphones.[23] Nonetheless, recording seems likely to become an increasingly prominent feature of Japan's prosecution future, not least because of the country's outlier status among comparable nations (Ibusuki 2010*a*).[24] It is difficult to imagine a more beneficial reform for Japanese criminal justice.

---

[23] A survey by Japan's Ministry of Justice of 1,100 prosecutors in 2011 found some ambivalence about recording reforms. Seventy-seven percent of respondents said that recording would help assure the "appropriateness" of interrogations, while 91 percent said that recording would make it "more difficult for prosecutors to obtain truthful statements from criminal suspects" (*Asahi Shimbun*, August 9, 2011). Similarly, a study by the National Police Agency of the 717 cases in which interrogations were partially recorded between April 2009 and March 2011 found that 97 percent of police involved in these interrogations believed that partial recording was "effective" (*koka aru*), yet 91 percent opposed recording interrogations in their entirety (*Sankei Shimbun*, July 1, 2011).

[24] Hitotsubashi University Professor of Law Goto Akira (2011), who was a member

B. Accountability

The most striking symptom of Japan's second prosecution problem is the secrecy that shrouds much prosecutor behavior (Johnson 2011*b*). In some ways this is an extension of the "truth" problem, for interrogation abuses and excessive secrecy both reflect that prosecutors are largely unaccountable to external organs of authority, including courts, which have displayed remarkable deference toward prosecutors in the postwar period (Foote 2010). In the interrogation room, where truth can be fabricated, corrupted, and concealed, it is all but impossible to identify and expose problems if prosecutors are reluctant to do so themselves. Many prosecutors are reluctant, not least because the autonomy and solidarity of their organization insulate them from scrutiny and criticism. The institutional autonomy of Japan's procuracy allows for freedom of action that bureaucrats everywhere crave, but the cost is a loss in accountability to external organs of authority such as politicians, the press, and the public. At the same time, prosecutors on the front lines are constrained to react to internal controls in two main ways: by complying with directives and thereby remaining loyal to the organization or by exiting the role—and the organization. In many instances, "voice" (dissent) is not an option for prosecutors in Japan (Hirschman 1970).

When prosecutors do try to protest, the consequences can be severe. A dissenting prosecutor named Abe Haruo was pressured to quit the organization in the early 1980s after expressing his grievances too directly, and later he was charged with criminal extortion for his behavior as a private attorney (Kubo 1989, p. 97). Some 20 years later, prosecutor Mitsui Tamaki was arrested by his colleagues on the eve of a press conference that he had scheduled to tell the nation what he knew about the embezzlement of slush funds (*uragane*) by executive prosecutors. Tachibana Takashi, one of Japan's premiere investigative reporters, called Mitsui's arrest "absolutely ridiculous," and Uozumi Akira, another respected writer, said that "there are almost no previous examples of exercises of authority as arbitrary as this one" (quoted in Mitsui 2003, pp. 15–19). In 2010, when prosecutors in the Special Investigation Division of the Osaka District Prosecutors Office learned that a colleague named Maeda Tsunehiko had forged a floppy disk in

---

of the Deliberation Committee on the State of Prosecution in Japan (*Kensatsu no Arikata Kento Kaigi* 2011), believes that recording interrogations in their entirety will become standard practice by 2016.

order to increase the odds of convicting an elite bureaucrat (Muraki Atsuko) of fraud, a few of them tried to tell their superiors and were told in turn to approve a cover story that would hide Maeda's crime (Otake 2011).[25] In these and other cases, executive prosecutors in Japan often prefer to ignore or punish subordinates who call for greater accountability (Johnson 2011*d*). Executive prosecutors also tend to dismiss prosecutor deviance as the behavior of "bad apples," even when the evidence suggests systemic problems in their organization (*Asahi Shimbun*, March 11, 2011).

Without more meaningful mechanisms of external accountability, prosecutors in Japan will continue concealing actions that ought to be subject to public scrutiny. This includes their almost complete control over the inputs in the country's death penalty system (who gets charged with a capital crime) and the outputs (who gets hanged). Indeed, capital punishment in Japan is shrouded in secrecy to an extent seldom seen in other nations. If there is no government power greater than the power of life and death and no government intrusion more invasive than the death penalty, then there is no government power in greater need of public oversight. In Japan this oversight is missing. Albert Camus (1960, p. 178) argued that "instead of saying that the death penalty is first of all necessary and then adding that it is better not to talk about it, it is essential to say what it really is and then say whether, being what it is, it is to be considered as necessary." With respect to capital punishment and other criminal justice issues, officials in Japan— and prosecutors in particular—frequently practice a "better not to talk about it" strategy (Johnson 2006*c*). The nation's new lay judge system is helping to shed a little more light on the capital and criminal processes (Anderson and Johnson 2010; Johnson 2010*a*), but whatever change occurs is likely to be evolutionary, not revolutionary. At present, Japan's prosecutor organization is so cohesive, so unaccountable, and

---

[25] In what turned out to be the biggest scandal in the history of Japanese criminal justice, Muraki was acquitted at trial, Maeda was convicted and sentenced to 18 months in prison, and two of Maeda's managing prosecutors (Hiromichi Otsubo and Motoaki Saga) were indicted for trying to cover up Maeda's misconduct (*Japan Times*, April 13, 2011). As of October 2011, the trials of Otsubo and Saga are ongoing. Retired prosecutors and judges have called Maeda's behavior "incredible," "abominable," "deplorable," "suicidal," and "almost unbelievable" (*Daily Yomiuri*, October 6, 2010), but the procuracy's own investigation of this case fell well short of identifying the systemic and organizational factors that enabled misconduct and its cover-up to occur (*Asahi Shimbun*, December 25, 2010; Johnson 2011*d*).

so wary of outside scrutiny that it remains difficult to see or say what many of the problems are.[26]

VIII. The Future

In the years to come prosecutors in Japan will continue to adapt to the changing contexts of criminal justice. Four changes seem especially notable. First, criminal justice in Japan has become considerably harsher since 1990, with longer sentences for a wide variety of offenses and especially sharp increases in the use of life imprisonment and death as a criminal sanction (Johnson 2007).[27] In some respects, prosecutors have led this push toward "harsher punishment" (*genbatsuka*). Second, a punitive victims' rights movement has given victims greater voice in criminal justice decision making and thereby fueled the rise in severity of sanctions while simultaneously politicizing policy making (Miyazawa 2008). Crime and punishment in Japan are no longer the "politically quiescent" issues they were a decade or two ago (Johnson 2002*a*, p. 30). Third, revelations of prosecutor misconduct have undermined public trust in the procuracy[28] and prompted the central government to review some of the standard operating procedures that have characterized Japanese criminal justice in the postwar period (Egawa 2011*b*). The most intense reform efforts have focused on the need to make interrogations more transparent, which the media have supported with unprecedented ardor but which police and prosecutors have strongly resisted.

Finally, Japan's new lay judge system is accelerating change in many parts of the criminal process. One basic innovation is a formal pretrial procedure that aims to clarify points in dispute before adjudication begins. Bail has also become easier to obtain, and defendants' discovery

[26] In many ways, the United States is not a good role model for prosecutor reform in Japan (Johnson 2010*b*).

[27] Japan's incarceration rate has risen by more than 60 percent in the last two decades, from 36 inmates per 100,000 population in 1992 to 58 in 2011, but it still remains lower than the rates in other democracies such as Norway (73), Germany (87), France (109), and the United Kingdom (156)—to say nothing of the United States (743); see International Centre for Prison Studies, http://www.prisonstudies.org/info/worldbrief.

[28] A Nippon Hoso Kyokai (2010) survey of 1,082 citizens carried out at the peak of the forged floppy disk scandal found that 57 percent of Japanese adults mistrusted prosecutors, 38 percent trusted them, and 5 percent could not say. The same survey revealed that seven times more adults supported the electronic recording of interrogations (52 percent) than opposed it (7 percent); the remaining 41 percent could not say either way.

rights have expanded and seem likely to expand even more in the years to come (Ibusuki 2010*b*). Trials are more adversarial than they used to be and less reliant on dossiers constructed behind the closed doors of the interrogation room (Johnson 2011*b*). And defense lawyers are training to become more effective advocates for persons suspected and accused of crimes (Kyodo Tsushin Shakaibu 2010*a*, 2010*b*). These changes began before the lay judge system started, they have accelerated since, and they will continue to transform Japanese criminal justice in the years to come (*Asahi Shimbun*, April 5, 2011). They also are being pushed along by social forces described elsewhere in this essay, including the "scandal and reform" dynamic that sometimes follows the revelation of wrongful convictions and other miscarriages of justice and the general movement in Japanese society toward greater transparency and freedom of information (Ginsburg 2007).

How courts find facts may be the most fundamental feature of any criminal justice system. Legal systems will "do almost anything, tolerate almost anything" before they will admit the need for reform in their systems of proof and trial, because change in those systems frequently stimulates change everywhere else in the criminal process (Langbein 1978, p. 18). Japan has reformed its system of proof and trial for some serious cases. About 2,100 defendants were tried in the first 2 years of the lay judge system, and eight were acquitted. Some analysts regard this—a 99.6 conviction rate—as evidence that the more things change in Japanese criminal justice, the more they stay the same. They also point out that in the first 2 years of the lay judge system, prosecutors appealed only three trial outcomes (verdict or sentence) in every 1,000, whereas defendants appealed 300. On this view, prosecutors appear to be far more satisfied with the way the new system is working than are the people they charge and the lawyers who represent them (Saibanin Netto 2011). Some observers believe, however, that the lay judge reform is altering the behavior of prosecutors more than the behavior of all the other actors in the criminal court community (Egawa 2011*a*) and that the fundamental nature of this reform will have far-reaching effects throughout the criminal process in the years to come. As Kokugakuin University Professor of Law Shinomiya Satoru (2010, p. 13) has observed, the new system of adjudication "has thrown a stone into the pond" of Japanese criminal justice, and "the ripples are gradually spreading."

Japan's lay judge system is still in its infancy, and time will have to tell how far the ripples will spread. For now—and for better and for worse—the Japanese way of justice is strongly shaped by the way prosecutors organize their activities and perform their jobs.

REFERENCES

Abrams, Norman. 1971. "Internal Policy: Guiding the Exercise of Prosecutorial Discretion." *UCLA Law Review* 29:1–58.

Ames, Walter L. 1981. *Police and Community in Japan*. Berkeley: University of California Press.

Anderson, Kent, and David T. Johnson. 2010. "Japan's New Criminal Trials: Origins, Operations, and Implications." In *New Courts in Asia*, edited by Andrew Harding and Penelope Nicholson. London: Routledge.

Bach, Amy. 2009. *Ordinary Injustice: How America Holds Court*. New York: Metropolitan Books.

Bayley, David H. 1991. *Forces of Order: Policing Modern Japan*. Berkeley: University of California Press.

Beasley, W. G. 1990. *The Rise of Modern Japan*. New York: St. Martin's.

Black, Donald. 1976. *The Behavior of Law*. New York: Academic Press.

Botsman, Daniel V. 2005. *Punishment and Power in the Making of Modern Japan*. Princeton, NJ: Princeton University Press.

Buerk, Roland. 2009. "Japan Urged to End 'False Confessions.'" *BBC News*, October 5.

Burnham, David. 1996. *Above the Law: Secret Deals, Political Fixes, and Other Misadventures of the U.S. Department of Justice*. New York: Scribner's.

Camus, Albert. 1960. *Resistance, Rebellion, and Death: Essays*. New York: Vintage.

Carter, Lief H. 1974. *The Limits of Order*. Lexington, MA: Lexington.

Davis, Angela. 2009. *Arbitrary Justice: The Power of the American Prosecutor*. New York: Oxford University Press.

Egawa, Shoko. 2011a. "Hotei no Funiki Yawaragu" [The court atmosphere has calmed down]. *Kumamoto Nichi-Nichi Shimbun*, May 21.

———, ed. 2011b. *Tokuso Kensatsu wa Hitsuyo ka* [Are special prosecutors necessary?]. Tokyo: Iwanami Shoten.

Etzioni, Amitai. 1964. *Modern Organizations*. Englewood Cliffs, NJ: Prentice-Hall.

Fackler, Martin. 2010. "Falsely Convicted, Freed and No Longer Quiet." *New York Times*, August 13.

Feeley, Malcolm M., and Setsuo Miyazawa. 2002. *The Japanese Adversary System in Context: Controversies and Comparisons*. London: Macmillan.

Flemming, Roy B., Peter F. Nardulli, and James Eisenstein. 1992. *The Craft of Justice: Politics and Work in Court Communities*. Philadelphia: University of Pennsylvania Press.

Foote, Daniel H. 1991. "Confessions and the Right to Silence in Japan." *Georgia Journal of International and Comparative Law* 21:415–88.

———. 1992. "The Benevolent Paternalism of Japanese Criminal Justice." *California Law Review* 80(2):317–90.

———, ed. 2007. *Law in Japan: A Turning Point.* Seattle: University of Washington Press.

———. 2010. "Policymaking by the Japanese Judiciary in the Criminal Justice Field." *Hoshakaigaku* 72:6–45.

Fukurai, Hiroshi. 2011. "Japan's Prosecutorial Review Commissions: Lay Oversight of the Government's Discretion of Prosecution." *University of Pennsylvania East Asia Law Review* 6:1–42. http://www.pennealr.com/archive/issues/vol6/EALR%281%29_Fukurai.pdf.

Garland, David. 1990. *Punishment and Modern Society: A Study in Social Theory.* Chicago: University of Chicago Press.

Ginsburg, Tom. 2007. "The Politics of Transparency in Japanese Administrative Law." In *Law in Japan: A Turning Point,* edited by Daniel H. Foote. Seattle: University of Washington Press.

Goffman, Erving. 1961. *Asylums: Essays on the Social Situation of Mental Patients and Other Inmates.* Garden City, NY: Anchor.

Goto, Akira. 2011. *Sore de Ii no ka, Nihon no Kashika': Goto Hatsugen Memo.* Tokyo: Upper House of the Diet.

Haley, John O. 1998. *The Spirit of Japanese Law.* Athens: University of Georgia Press.

Hamada, Sumio. 1992. *Jihaku no Kenkyu.* Tokyo: 31 Shobo.

Hamai, Koichi, and Thomas Ellis. 2008. "Japanese Criminal Justice: Was Reintegrative Shaming a Chimera?" *Punishment and Society* 10(1):25–46.

Herber, Erik. 2011. "From 'Benevolent Paternalism' to *Genbatsuka*: A Changed Way of Japanese Justice?" Paper presented at the meetings of the International Society of Criminology, Kobe, Japan, August 5.

Hiramatsu, Yoshiro. 1989. "Summary of Tokugawa Criminal Justice" (trans. Daniel H. Foote). *Law in Japan* 22:105–28.

Hirano, Ryuichi. 1989. "Diagnosis of the Current Code of Criminal Procedure" (trans. Daniel H. Foote). *Law in Japan* 22:129–42.

———. 1999. "Sanshinsei no Saiyo ni yoru 'Kakushin Shiho' o: Keiji Shiho Kaikaku no Ugoki to Hoko." *Jurisuto* 1148(January 1–15):2–15.

Hirschman, Albert O. 1970. *Exit, Voice, and Loyalty: Responses to Decline in Firms, Organizations, and States.* Cambridge, MA: Harvard University Press.

Huff, C. Ronald, and Martin Killias. 2008. *Wrongful Conviction: International Perspectives on Miscarriages of Justice.* Philadelphia: Temple University Press.

Ibusuki, Makoto. 2010a. *Higisha Torishirabe to Rokuga Seido: Torishirabe no Rokuga ga Nihon no Keiji Shiho o Kaeru.* Tokyo: Shojihomu.

———. 2010b. "Shoko wa Dare no Mono: Shinjitsu o Hakken Suru Kokyo Zaisan." *Asahi Shimbun,* November 20, p. 19.

Ito, Masami. 2008. "New Magazine Takes Aim at Wrongful Convictions: Plenty of Cases to Explore." *Japan Times,* February 1. http://www.japantimes.co.jp/text/nn20080201f2.html.

Johnson, Chalmers. 1972. *Conspiracy at Matsukawa*. Berkeley: University of California Press.

Johnson, David T. 1999. "Kumo no Su ni Shocho Sareru Nihonho no Toku-shoku" [Japan's legal cobweb]. *Jurisuto* 1148(January 1–15):185–89.

———. 2002*a*. *The Japanese Way of Justice: Prosecuting Crime in Japan*. New York: Oxford University Press. Translated into Japanese as *Amerikajin no Mita Nihon no Kensatsu Seido*. Tokyo: Springer, 2004.

———. 2002*b*. "Plea Bargaining in Japan." In *The Japanese Adversary System in Context: Controversies and Comparisons*, edited by Malcolm M. Feeley and Setsuo Miyazawa. New York: Palgrave Macmillan.

———. 2006*a*. "Kazemuki o Shiru no ni Otenki Kyasta wa Iranai: Nihon ni okeru Torishirabe Rokuon-Rokuga ni tsuite Gasshukoku to Kankoku kara Manabu koto." *Ho to Shinri* [Journal of law and psychology] 5(1):57–83. Translated into English as "You Don't Need a Weather Man to Know Which Way the Wind Blows: Lessons from the United States and Korea for Recording Interrogations in Japan." *Ritsumeikan Law Review*, no. 24(2007):1–34; no. 25(2008):141–75.

———. 2006*b*. "Nihon no Kensatsu Soshiki" [The organization of prosecution in Japan]. In *Shakai no Naka no Keiji Shiho to Hanzaisha* [Criminals and criminal justice in Japanese society], edited by Koichi Kikuta, Haruo Nishimura, and Setsuo Miyazawa. Tokyo: Nihon Hyoronsha.

———. 2006*c*. "Where the State Kills in Secret: Capital Punishment in Japan." *Punishment and Society* 8(3):251–85.

———. 2007. "Crime and Punishment in Contemporary Japan." In *Crime, Punishment, and Politics in Comparative Perspective*, edited by Michael Tonry. Vol. 36 of *Crime and Justice: A Review of Research*, edited by Michael Tonry. Chicago: University of Chicago Press.

———. 2008. "Japanese Punishment in Comparative Perspective." *Japanese Journal of Sociological Criminology* [Hanzaishakaigaku Kenkyu] 33(October): 46–66.

———. 2009. "Early Returns from Japan's New Criminal Trials." *Asia-Pacific Journal* 36(3):1–17. http://www.japanfocus.org/-David_T_-Johnson/3212.

———. 2010*a*. "Capital Punishment without Capital Trials in Japan's Lay Judge System." *Asia-Pacific Journal* 8(52):1–38. http://www.japanfocus.org/-David_T_-Johnson/3461.

———. 2010*b*. "U.S. Is No Role Model for Prosecutor Reform." *Japan Times*, October 20, p. 15.

———. 2011*a*. "Keiji Bengoshi to Saibanin Seido: Henkaku no Naka no Toso" [War in a season of slow revolution: Defense lawyers and Japan's lay judge system]. *Sekai* 819(July):255–65.

———. 2011*b*. "Kensatsu Kaikaku o Shinken ni Kangaeru" [Taking prosecutor reform seriously]. *Jiyu to Seigi* [Liberty and justice] 62(4):79–87.

———. 2011*c*. "Shikei wa Tokubetsu ka? Amerika no Shippai kara Erareru Kyokun" [Is death different? Capital punishment in the United States and Japan]. *Sekai* 823(November):280–91.

———. 2011*d*. "Tokuso Mondai no Kokusai Hikaku" [Special prosecutors in comparative perspective]. In *Tokuso Kensatsu wa Hitsuyo ka* [Are special prosecutors necessary?], edited by Shoko Egawa. Tokyo: Iwanami Shoten.

Jones, Colin P. A. 2009. "Japan's New Law Schools: The Story So Far." *Journal of Japanese Law* 27:248–56. http://sydney.edu.au/law/anjel/documents/ZJapanR/ZJapanR27/ZJapanR27_21_Jones.pdf.

Kamiya, Setsuko. 2008. "Scales of Justice: Legal System Looks for Right Balance of Lawyers." *Japan Times*, March 18. http://www.japantimes.co.jp/text/nn20080318i1.html.

———. 2009. "Prosecutors Boast Clout, Success." *Japan Times*, April 7. http://www.japantimes.co.jp/text/nn20090407i1.html.

Kaneko, Yasushi. 2011. "Nations Differ in Their Handling of Wrongful Conviction Cases." *Daily Yomiuri*, May 26, p. 3.

Kensatsu no Arikata Kento Kaigi. 2011. *Kensatsu no Saisei ni Mukete* [Recommendations for the rebirth of prosecutors]. Tokyo: Ministry of Justice.

Kubo, Hiroshi. 1989. *Nippon no Kensatsu*. Tokyo: Kodansha.

Kyodo Tsushin Shakaibu. 2010*a*. *Saibanin Shiho: Kanren Kiji-Tokushu Keisaishi, 5/2007–8/2010*. Kyodo: Kyodo Tsushin Shakaibu.

———. 2010*b*. *Saibanin Shiho: Rensai Kikaku Keisaishi, 11/2007–3/2010*. Kyodo: Kyodo Tsushin Shakaibu.

Langbein, John H. 1978. "Torture and Plea Bargaining." *University of Chicago Law Review* 46:3–22.

Mauer, Ross, and Hirosuke Kawanishi. 2005. *A Sociology of Work in Japan*. London: Cambridge University Press.

Mitchell, Richard H. 1992. *Janus-Faced Justice: Political Criminals in Imperial Japan*. Honolulu: University of Hawaii Press.

Mitsui, Tamaki. 2003. *Kokuhatsu! Kensatsu "Uragane Zukuri."* Tokyo: Kobunsha.

Miyazawa, Setsuo. 1989. "Scandal and Hard Reform: Implications of a Wiretapping Case to the Control of Organizational Police Crimes in Japan." *Kobe University Law Review* 23:13–27.

———. 1992. *Policing in Japan: A Study on Making Crime*. Albany: State University of New York Press.

———. 1995. "Is Japanese Criminal Justice Reintegrative and Benevolent?" Paper presented at Stanford Law School, Stanford, CA, October 6.

———. 2008. "The Policy of Increasing Punitiveness and the Rising Populism in Japanese Criminal Justice Policy." *Punishment and Society* 10(1):47–77.

Nihon Bengoshi Rengokai. 2011*a*. *Ashikaga Jiken' Chosa Hokokusho*. Report on the investigation into the "Ashikaga Case." Tokyo: Japan Federation of Bar Associations.

———. 2011*b*. *Kensatsukan no Torishirabe ni tsuite no Zenkai'in Ankeeto Shukei Kekka* [Results from a survey to all members of the Japan Federation of Bar Associations on interrogations by prosecutors]. Tokyo: Japan Federation of Bar Associations.

Nippon Hoso Kyokai. 2010. "Yocho: Kensatsu Shinrai Shite Inai 57 percent" [Survey: 57 percent do not trust prosecutors]. http://www.nhk.or.jp.

Nomura, Jiro. 1978. *Kenji: Kenryoku to Jinken*. Tokyo: Kyoikusha.

Otake, Tomoko. 2011. "Close-Up: Fighter for Justice." *Japan Times*, May 1, pp. 7–8.

Perrin, Noel. 1979. *Giving Up the Gun: Japan's Reversion to the Sword, 1543–1879*. Boston: Godine.

Peters, Antonie. 1992. "Some Comparative Observations on the Criminal Justice Process in Holland and Japan." *Journal of the Japan Netherlands Institute* 4:247–94.

Rabinowitz, Richard W. 1956. "The Historical Development of the Japanese Bar." *Harvard Law Review* 70:61–81.

Repeta, Lawrence. 2009. "United Nations Committee Faults Japan Human Rights Performance, Demands Progress Report on Key Issues." *Asia-Pacific Journal* 20(5). http://japanfocus.org/-Lawrence-Repeta/3147.

Saibanin Netto. 2011. "Saibanin Seido: Shimin kara no Teigen" [The lay judge system: Proposals from citizens]. http://www.saibabin.net.

Sasaki, Tomoko. 2000. *Nihon no Shiho Bunka*. Tokyo: Bungei Shunju.

Sato, Kinko. 1974. *Torihiki no Shakai: Amerika no Keiji Shiho*. Tokyo: Chuo Koronsha.

Shinomiya Satoru. 2010. "Defying Experts' Predictions, Identifying Themselves as Sovereign: Citizens' Responses to Their Service as Lay Judges in Japan." *Social Science Japan* 43(September):8–13.

Storry, Richard. 1985. *A History of Modern Japan*. New York: Penguin.

Stuntz, William. 2011. *The Collapse of American Criminal Justice*. Cambridge, MA: Belknap/Harvard University Press.

Sullivan, Thomas P. 2004. "Police Experiences with Recording Custodial Interrogations." Center on Wrongful Convictions, Northwestern University. http://www.law.northwestern.edu/depts/clinic/wrongful/Causes/Custodial Interrogations.htm.

Terasawa, Yu, ed. 2009. *Hodo Sarenai Keisatsu to Masukomi no Fuhai: Eiga "Pochi no Kokuhaku" ga Abaita Mono*. Tokyo: Inshidentsu.

Ukawa, Haruhiko. 1997. "Shiho Torihiki o Kangaeru." *Hanrei Jiho* 1583:31–47.

———, ed. 2011. *Criminal Justice in Japan*. Tokyo: United Nations Asia and Far East Institute for the Prevention of Crime and the Treatment of Offenders. http://www.unafei.or.jp/english/pages/CriminalJusticeJapan.htm.

West, Mark D. 2011. *Lovesick Japan: Sex, Marriage, Romance, Law*. Ithaca, NY: Cornell University Press.

Westney, D. Eleanor. 1987. *Imitation and Innovation: The Transfer of Western Organizational Patterns to Meiji Japan*. Cambridge, MA: Harvard University Press.

Wilson, James Q. 1989. *Bureaucracy: What Government Agencies Do and Why They Do It*. New York: Basic Books.

Krzysztof Krajewski

Prosecution and Prosecutors in Poland: In Quest of Independence

ABSTRACT

The Polish procuracy has developed only since the nation regained statehood in 1918. Before World War II, following the French model, it was subordinate to the Ministry of Justice. Under the communist system, although theoretically independent, it was organized according to the Soviet example and subservient to the Communist Party. After the fall of communism, the procuracy partly returned to its prewar structure; however, it is haunted by ghosts from its communist past. One crucial problem concerns political independence. Although in theory procurators are career professionals appointed on merit, the procuracy has never obtained real independence from political influence and has been plagued by the consequences of being subordinate to the Ministry of Justice. This was reinforced by the mentality of individual procurators "socialized" into the values of the communist procuracy and transmitting their professional ideology to younger generations. Recent reforms aim to provide greater independence. A second problem relates to the particularities of the continental system of criminal procedure, in which the procuracy is both an investigating and a prosecuting agency subject to a "principle of mandatory prosecution" that produces mechanical and sometimes perverse results.

Continental systems like Poland's are generally described as inquisitorial, in contrast with the adversarial systems of the common-law countries (Ehrmann 1976, pp. 13–15; Langbein and Weinreb 1978; Pakes 2010, p. 87). The Polish prosecution system is thus similar in

Krzysztof Krajewski is associate professor in the Department of Criminology, Jagiellonian University.

some respects to those of Germany (Herrmann 1987), France (Pakes 2010), Italy (Caianello 2011), and other countries in Europe (Tak 2004, 2005).

Understanding of the current prosecution system and its problems is impossible without some historical background. The system is a relatively recent invention, going back less than 100 years, and has experienced momentous changes. The evolution of the traditional legal system of the Commonwealth of Poland and Lithuania stopped at the end of the eighteenth century as a result of three successive partitions of the country among Russia, Prussia, and Austria in the years 1772, 1791, and 1794 (Davies 2005a, pp. 386–411; Lukowski and Zawadzki 2006, pp. 83–130). Poland ceased to exist as an independent nation for 130 years. It regained independence in 1918 when the three partitioning powers collapsed after World War I and had to rebuild its legal system. Independence lasted, however, only for 20 years (Davies 2005b, pp. 279–365; Lukowski and Zawadzki 2006, pp. 217–80). After the outbreak of World War II and 5 years of German occupation, Poland came under Soviet and communist control, which had profound and continuing consequences for the legal system and its institutions. This ended only 20 years ago, but its legacy endures. The criminal justice and prosecution systems are among the areas of Polish life and government that most suffer the consequences of 45 years of communist rule.

Prosecution of criminal offenses is the responsibility of the *prokuratura*, or procuracy. It performs two main tasks. First, it is in charge of investigating offenses or supervising their investigation by the police. Because of the formal character of the investigative phase of criminal proceedings in continental legal systems (Langbein and Weinreb 1978), this means that the procurator's investigative activities have significant consequences for the trial and its outcome. Second, for most offenses the procuracy brings cases to court and supports those charges during trial. The procuracy also has broad authority to appeal not only acquittals but also convictions if the court's decision is deemed incorrect or the punishment too lenient.

The prosecution process in Poland, as elsewhere in Europe (e.g., Germany, Austria), is governed by the "legality principle" of mandatory prosecution (Jescheck 1970b). The procurator has very little discretionary authority; if he or she concludes during the investigation that an offense has occurred, in principle a prosecution must ensue. The legality principle is meant to assure evenhanded, unbiased treatment of defendants, prevent abuses of prosecutorial discretion, and insulate procurators from pressures to favor particular defendants. This, however, comes at the cost of leading procurators to bring charges in the pettiest cases and creating serious problems of "overprosecuting."

The procuracy is organized hierarchically. There are three levels: county, regional, and appellate, which parallel the three levels of the court system. The procurator general, or chief public prosecutor, is appointed by the president from among the ranks of procurators or judges. Procurators are career civil servants. To be appointed, they must meet designated criteria, including completion of a legal education, an apprenticeship, and a state exam. Once appointed at the lowest level (usually at a young age), procurators are promoted to higher posts throughout their careers and cannot be removed except for cause. Although they enjoy guarantees of independence, procurators are not independent in the sense that judges are, and in contrast to prosecution in other countries, such as France or Italy, and in Poland before World War II, they are not included along with judges in the category of "magistrates." Procurators are expected to be independent from external influences, including the executive branch, individuals, and public opinion. Otherwise, however, they are members of a hierarchically organized agency and are expected to obey instructions and orders from their superiors.

This results from two basic organizational principles, the "principle of hierarchical subordination" and the "principle of uniformity." The first, and more important, refers to the authority of higher-ranking procurators to order subordinates to take certain actions or make certain decisions or to do it themselves. The second means—with certain limitations—that any decision at any level may be made by any procurator in the country. These organizational principles make the procuracy into a rigid hierarchy subject to strict discipline.

Procurators are in reality not autonomous in their decision making and are supposed primarily to implement policies developed by their superiors. The two organizational principles primarily reflect Poland's communist past. Principles of hierarchical subordination and uniformity are at the core of the Leninist conception of the procuracy, which was implemented in the Soviet Union after the October Revolution. Before World War II, the Polish procuracy was patterned on the French model, with procuracies being attached to the courts at a given

level (Vouin 1970). The prewar procuracy was constituted as a hierarchy, subordinate to the minister of justice, who (as in France) was
simultaneously the procurator general; however, the hierarchy in
France was less rigid and procurators enjoyed greater autonomy.

The Leninist model of procuracy was imposed on Poland in 1945–
48 during the communist takeover. The goal was the political subordination of the prosecution system as a means to enforce the policies
of the Communist Party. Prosecution agencies in Poland and other
communist-ruled countries, like many other state agencies, were not
intended to serve the public interest. They were expected to serve the
interests of the Communist Party and the communist elite. The procuracy became subject to an almost military discipline. It also became
highly politicized; in practice, membership in the Communist Party
was a prerequisite for career success. This, together with the hierarchical and uniformity principles, provided the party powerful tools to
steer everyday work and decisions in individual cases. It created a professional culture of political subservience. Rank-and-file procurators
often made decisions not on the merits of the case but to satisfy real
or imagined wishes of their superiors. All this was exacerbated because
the procuracy was headed by procurator generals, who were nominally
elected by the rubber-stamp Parliament. But in fact they were chosen
by the politburo of the Communist Party and always were high-ranking members of the communist *nomenklatura* (Voslensky 1984).

In 1989–90, when the communist system was crumbling in Poland
and throughout Central and Eastern Europe, reforming the criminal
justice system, including the procuracy, was one of the highest priorities of the new government. Under a power-sharing deal struck in
Poland in 1989 between the anticommunist opposition and the Communist Party, a decision was made to return to the prewar system in
which the justice minister was also procurator general. The opposition
hoped in that way to deprive the Communist Party of its direct influence over the procuracy. Otherwise the procuracy remained practically
unchanged: a rigid, hierarchically organized structure governed by requirements of obedience to superiors' commands. Additionally and importantly, with only a few exceptions, most procurators from the communist era retained their positions. There was probably no alternative
to this, but as a consequence the new procuracy continued to be run
by people who were in many cases deeply socialized into the old working culture of subservience.

This had profound consequences. As a hierarchical organization subordinated to the minister of justice, the procuracy became easy prey to political influence and manipulation. And this met little resistance from the rank and file. The history of the last 20 years provides many examples of politicians influencing decisions in individual cases on the basis of political considerations. This did substantial damage to public perceptions of the legitimacy and independence of the procuracy.

Reforms introduced in 2010 finally separated the posts of the minister of justice and the procurator general. The main purposes were to protect the procuracy from direct political influence and to make it more independent. The new approach has been in force only for a short time, but some aspects of the procuracy's functioning have already changed. Whether these positive changes will have lasting effect remains to be seen. The quest for institutional independence is by no means over.

This essay analyzes and discusses the developments and problems just sketched. Section I provides a brief description of the system as it existed before the Second World War and its roots in the French model of a procuracy headed by the minister of justice but attached to the courts. In Section II, the remodeling of the procuracy by the communist regime following the Soviet example is discussed. It followed basic organizational principles of a highly hierarchical, disciplined communist procuracy. Particular attention is paid to the procuracy's role in preserving the Communist Party's grip on power and the consequences that experience had for the professional ideology of procurators. Section III discusses developments since the fall of the communist system. This includes discussion of dilemmas faced by new, democratic governments in dealing with the communist past of its criminal justice system and its officials. The procuracy was again remodeled, with a return to the prewar model of a procuracy headed by the minister of justice, although without a return to the internal structure of the prewar procuracy. The main reasons for and the unhappy consequences of this incomplete reform are presented, the main one being an enormous politicization of the public prosecution system and individual procurators. Sections IV and V discuss organizational changes in 2010; these included the separation of the procuracy from the Ministry of Justice, a system of appointment of the procurator general on the basis of merit and without political interference, and various changes meant to insulate the procuracy from political influence and to permit individual procurators to function more independently. Finally, Section VI provides information on the role of the procurator as public prosecutor under the current system. Particular attention is paid to the consequences of the inquisitorial mode of criminal process and the principle of mandatory prosecution.

I. Prosecution before World War II

One of the most important and difficult tasks facing the reborn Polish state after 1918 was legal unification of a country in which three separate legal systems remained in force in the parts of its territory formerly belonging to Russia, Germany, and Austria. New, unified systems of courts and other criminal justice agencies were quickly established. For several years, however, the courts continued to apply the old laws of the partitioning powers, depending on the part of the country. In some areas—notably private law—unification was not completed until the outbreak of World War II. Progress regarding criminal law and procedure was faster. The new code of criminal procedure took effect in 1928 and the new criminal code in 1932.

The new system did not attempt to recreate institutions and traditions of the historic legal system that preceded partition; it had included many adversarial features. At least in cases involving noblemen, judges played a passive role, and parties were primarily responsible for collecting, introducing, and presenting evidence (Pakes 2010, pp. 86–94). The decision was made instead to draw on features of contemporaneous European legal systems. In the cases of the court, the prosecution system, and criminal procedure, the French example exerted greatest influence. The new court system had four levels: county, district, and appellate courts and a supreme court. Depending on the seriousness of an offense, the courts of original jurisdiction were county courts (in most cases) or district courts (for serious offenses). The three-tier system of trying and appealing cases (both criminal and civil) was similar to that in France. Judgments of county courts could be appealed to district courts. Those of the district courts, as courts of original jurisdiction, were appealed to appellate courts using an appellate measure called *apelacja*, a regular appeal that could raise issues of fact and of law. Under this mixed system, appellate courts could partly retry cases and change the decisions of the lower courts or quash their decisions and remand cases for retrial. All appellate court decisions could be brought to the Supreme Court by the means of *kasacja*, a special appeal that could raise only points of law. The Supreme Court did not retry cases but confirmed decisions or quashed them and remanded them for retrial.

Criminal procedure was based on principles characteristic of inquisitorial continental legal systems. It consisted of a formal investigative phase referred to as "preparatory proceedings," followed by the trial. The trial was dominated by the presiding judge (or judicial panel), who played an active role and was responsible for taking evidence. Cases were tried exclusively by professional judges without the participation of lay assessors. In some instances the code of criminal procedure provided for a trial by jury, but this provision was never fully implemented.[1]

Prosecution was always initiated, and the state was represented in court during the trial, by a special representative called the public prosecutor.[2] But this was then—and is today—only a description of a procedural role that can be played by various actors. Most commonly this role was played by a state official called the procurator (*prokurator*), a representative of an agency called the procuracy (*prokuratura*). But it could also be played by the police or, in certain types of cases (petty offenses such as contraventions or misdemeanors, fiscal offenses, etc.), by various state agencies.

Under the prewar system the work of the public prosecutor was the main, practically the exclusive, task of the procuracy, although it also played some part in investigating cases. The reverse was true of the police, which was the investigating agency but also sometimes performed as public prosecutor. For serious offenses to be decided by the district court as a court of original jurisdiction, pretrial proceedings were called investigations (French *instruction criminelle*) and had to be conducted by an investigating judge, usually in close cooperation with

---

[1] The 1928 code provided for a trial by jury for the most serious offenses (e.g., murder) and political offenses. But these provisions were effectively implemented only in southern Poland, or Galicja, which in the nineteenth century was under Austrian rule, and where jury trial was known under Austrian law. It was unknown in former Prussian and Russian areas (although trial by jury functioned in Russia proper) and was never implemented in practice. In southern Poland it was abolished in 1936, after a jury acquitted a group of notorious nationalist activists accused of instigating anti-Jewish riots in a small town near Krakow.

[2] For a limited number of offenses, private prosecution was possible, which meant that the case could be brought to court directly by the victim or injured person, usually represented by a professional lawyer. This dual system exists today.

the police. The investigating judge examined witnesses and took all other evidence and preserved it for future use in a special form of judicial protocol. The judicial position was meant to guarantee a neutral and objective approach to investigation. The procurator could not directly influence the investigation but could always request the investigating judge to conduct activities he or she deemed necessary. Otherwise the procurator's role was limited to being the public prosecutor. After receiving a dossier of investigation from the judge, the procurator made the final decision whether the evidence collected was sufficient. The procurator could also terminate the case if formal obstacles to prosecution existed. If not, the procurator prepared the charge sheet and attempted to prove the charges during the trial. For lesser offenses, the preparatory proceedings took the form of an inquiry (French *enquete*), conducted usually by the police under some supervision by the procurator. In such cases the police usually performed as public prosecutor in court, although the procurator could always take over this role. In practice that happened only for more serious offenses.

The system—as under current law—was based on the principle of mandatory prosecution; the public prosecutor had very little discretionary authority to discontinue a case because of its petty character or because of a lack of public interest in prosecution. He or she was also not allowed to enter into plea negotiations or to offer concessions. If the preparatory proceedings established a basis for prosecution and there were no other, primarily formal, obstacles to prosecution, the procurator or the police had a duty to prosecute.

French influence is evident in the sole function of the procuracy being to prosecute offenders on behalf of the state (Frankowski 1987*b*). Likewise, the procuracy was part of the judicial system, and procurators had the status of judges (Vouin 1970, p. 484). The organization of the courts and the procuracy was regulated by one piece of legislation. Procuracies and procurators, as in France, were "attached" to courts of different levels. Accordingly the procuracy consisted of the Supreme Court Procuracy and procuracies of the appellate and district courts. Procuracies could be established by the county courts, but it was not mandatory. At the top of the system was the chief or head procurator (*naczelny prokurator*). Not a magistrate like the other procurators, the chief procurator was a political office occupied by the minister of justice. In practice the minister of justice's primary duty was to provide general oversight, with authority to direct prosecution policy in a general way. In principle he or she lacked authority to influence decisions in ongoing cases. Procurators on each level thus remained relatively independent in their decisions, both from the head procurator and from other procurators of higher rank, as was also the case in France (Marguery 2007).

II. Prosecution under the Communist System

All this changed radically immediately after World War II. The communist takeover, which occurred step-by-step during the years 1945–48, had profound and enduring consequences for the entire system of government. It replaced a flawed prewar governmental system that had many authoritarian elements but still respected some principles of the rule of law, with a system of government by one political party that had an absolute monopoly of power and tolerated no opposition or dissent. This monopoly was originally achieved and maintained (through 1956) by use of raw terror. Later on communist rule softened, but the system remained authoritarian in its essence, disregarding basic principles of the rule of law, civil liberties, and liberal democratic values.

Such a government, concentrated on retaining a monopoly of power, could not tolerate an independent judiciary or a purely professional prosecution system. As a consequence, the justice system in Poland underwent profound changes, usually in the shape of new institutions modeled on Soviet ideas and principles and ostensibly "progressive," "proletarian," and "revolutionary" in character.

Even so, some things in Poland developed somewhat differently than in other countries in the region. Complete sovietization of the legal system was never achieved (Frankowski 1987a). For example, the prewar criminal codes remained in force until 1969, although the code of criminal procedure was substantially modified, and the criminal code was "supplemented" by various special bills.[3] In neighboring countries,

---

[3] In criminal procedure it meant abolition of the investigating judge, more powers to the police, reorganization of the procuracy, introduction for serious offenses of summary trials without a possibility of appeal, and jurisdiction of military courts over many political offenses. Many of these restrictions eased after 1956, but some survived until the end of the communist regime. In substantive criminal law, the changes primarily involved adoption of special laws that introduced new offenses protecting political and economic interests of the "socialist state." These included various forms of sabotage, subversion, etc., as well as special protection of state or "socialist" property. The latter offenses usually carried much higher punishments than equivalent offenses against private property.

communist governments immediately replaced the prewar legislation with their own (Pomorski 1981).

The court structure was changed ("simplified") by the abolition of the separate appellate courts. Only county and district courts were kept, with district courts taking over most appeals and the rest decided by the Supreme Court. Case processing was reduced to two tiers only: decisions of the courts of original jurisdiction could be appealed only once, either to district courts or to the Supreme Court. Appellate decisions were final, as prewar *kasacja* was abolished.[4] Judges retained formal guarantees of independence, including lifetime appointments (Garlicki 1980), but there was no real independent judiciary. Although the most flagrant violations of judicial independence largely ended after 1956, profound problems remained.[5] In any case, the judicial nomination system was controlled by the Communist Party, which made it easy to fill most judicial posts with "trusted comrades."

The most profound changes concerned the public prosecution system. A major reform of the legal system in 1950 established the new-style procuracy based on the principles governing the Soviet institution of the same name and organized according to "Leninist" concepts, as expressed in the first Soviet regulations of 1922 (Frankowski 1987*b*, p. 1318). The procuracy was expected not only to be responsible for investigating and prosecuting criminal cases but also to be the general guardian of the "socialist rule of law" concerning civil and administrative law. The procuracy became a general watchdog entrusted with supervision of "the observance of the law by the state administration, local government, and all civic, professional, cooperative, and self-governing bodies, as well as by citizens" (Frankowski 1987*b*, p. 1318). The prewar Polish procuracy had some similar responsibilities, but they were very limited. In 1950, the communists created broad new

---

[4] However, the new system had a limited equivalent called extraordinary appeal (*rewizja nadzwyczajna*) heard only by the Supreme Court. In principle, it could raise errors in law, but appeals against punishment only were also possible. The peculiarity of this extraordinary appeal was that it could not be brought directly by the parties. Only the procurator general and—strangely enough—the president of the Supreme Court could file such an appeal. Parties could file only motions requesting appeals. Extraordinary appeal could be brought both in favor of and to the detriment of the accused. The procurator general could appeal in favor of the accused in his or her capacity as a general guardian of the rule of law.

[5] For example, judges were nominally appointed for life but could easily be removed from office if they did not provide guarantees of the "proper execution of the judicial function." This power was seldom used (apart from several cases after martial law was introduced in December 1981), as judicial selection mechanisms made it unnecessary.

powers intended to make it into a general control agency. There may be nothing inherently wrong with such a concept if the institution in question, like, for example, ombudsmen of various sorts in many contemporary countries, is established to protect individual rights against abuse by the state and is given operational independence. The communist procuracy, however, was intended primarily to protect the state, or the Communist Party, against subversion from citizens. Because of this, the procuracy was completely controlled by the Communist Party apparatus. The procuracy was an "avant-garde of class struggle," a tool of the Communist Party used to fight enemies of all kinds, whether they were political dissidents or common criminals. This initiated a procuratorial culture of political subservience that, despite the political changes of the last 20 years, persists today.

Communist changes also ended the earlier system in which procuracies and procurators were part of the judicial system and were linked to the courts. In 1950 the procuracy was detached from the court system and procurators ceased to have status comparable to that of judges. The new procuracy was a separate, hierarchically organized state agency with the procurator general at the top. He or she was appointed for 5 years by the Council of State, a collective head of state typical in the socialist states of Eastern and Central Europe. In theory, this might have guaranteed independence from governmental influence. Such systems are not unknown in other countries. Separation of the public prosecution system from other state and judicial authorities, combined with appointment of the chief public prosecutor by the head of state or election by the parliament for a fixed period, normally serves the purpose of political independence. However, this was not the case in a system in which the Council of State was a rubber stamp that mostly ratified decisions made by the Central Committee of the Polish United Worker's Party (Marguery 2007, pp. 79–80).

The procuracy became one of the most important state agencies. It was watched closely and expected without reservation or hesitation to follow and enforce the policies of the Communist Party. This was easy to achieve given that the positions of the procurator general and the chiefs of district and county procuracies remained within the *nomenklatura* (Voslensky 1984); only party members, and usually the most experienced and trusted among them, could be recommended for these positions. Most rank-and-file procurators were also party members. Although membership was not a formal requirement, procurators who were not members were rare, were often viewed with suspicion, and usually had no chance of promotion.

Political control was reinforced by special rules and principles contained in the Procuracy Act of 1950.[6] The most important is the "principle of hierarchical subordination" (*zasada hierarchicznego podporządkowania*). Subordinate procurators are obliged always to follow instructions from their superiors and to implement their decisions and orders. The principle commands obedience from subordinates. There are two subprinciples. The first, the principle of substitution, means that a superior procurator can delegate any activity or decision to subordinates, unless they are specifically reserved by the law to a procurator at a given level. The second, the principle of devolution, means that a superior procurator can execute any activity or make any decision in place of a subordinate (Waltoś 1979, p. 20; 2009, pp. 171–77).

Decisions, instructions, orders, or interventions of superiors may be general or specific (Marguery 2007, pp. 75–76). There were seldom special problems with general instructions or guidelines, as they were understandable as a tool for directing and unifying national prosecution policy (although there should have been some limits to this). Serious problems were often created by decisions, instructions, or explicit orders concerning individual cases. Subordinates cease to be independent decision makers if their superiors can order them whom to charge and for what offense, how to conduct given activities, and how to end the case. They may—and did—cease to make decisions on merits and instead tried first of all to satisfy their superiors. The problem may be bigger or smaller depending on whether only direct superiors, or any superior procurator, can issue such instructions or orders. Regulations were changing during the period after World War II and resulted in some limitations on the powers of procurators who were not direct superiors. But problems usually remained. Higher-level procurators could still influence decisions made at even the lowest levels by influencing the direct superiors of investigating procurators.

The second important organizational principle is the "principle of uniformity" (*zasada jednolitości*). This means that every procurator represents the procuracy as a whole, and, conversely, the procuracy may

---

[6] The 1950 Procuracy Act was supplemented in 1985, during the final stages of communist rule. Although details changed, the basic model of procuracy remained intact. The 1985 Procuracy Act remains in force in 2012, although since 1990 it has in most parts been amended beyond recognition.

use any procurator to perform its tasks. As a result, a change in the identity of the procurator in a specific proceeding has no legal relevance. Any legal action may be taken by any procurator of any level— unless specifically reserved for a particular level—and in any place.

This means that there is no formal territorial jurisdiction within the procuracy (for practical reasons there are some internal rules, but they are not binding). This makes it possible for a procurator at the district level to give binding instructions to a subordinate on the county level on how to conduct an individual investigation or how to prosecute a given case. They can always, in addition, "appropriate" the case and do everything on their own. Moreover, if a senior procurator does not like the way a case is being investigated or prosecuted by a procurator in town X, the case can be transferred to town Y to be handled by a procurator there.

Operating under such principles, the procuracy became a rigid hierarchy governed and controlled from above and characterized by almost military discipline. Procurators at the lower level had in principle very little independence in deciding what to do in an individual case. Instructions of general and individual character were common. It also became common to move up the chain of command so that more important decisions were discussed and approved by direct superiors or by higher-level superiors. This often resulted in awkward situations during trials. If new or unexpected circumstances arose and had to be dealt with, line procurators did not want to, or even could not, decide what to do on their own. In such situations, the court was usually asked for a short break so that superiors could be consulted about what should be done. Such situations were often the subjects of jokes by judges and defense lawyers.

This produced an atmosphere and a distinctive "professional culture" that permeated the procuracy. It also produced a practice of following instructions from above without question, and a subservient approach and guesswork about the decision superiors would prefer, even in cases about which superiors had no particular preference. The main principle was conformity with expectations, which guaranteed at least "having no trouble" and "survival" and facilitated promotions.

Additional problems resulted from the closeness of the procuracy to the Communist Party. Although procurators were supposed to be career professionals with special training and appointed and promoted according to merit, political loyalty and party membership powerfully influenced the promotion system.[7] Procuratorial apprentices were closely monitored for purely professional skills but also for their political loyalty, or for signs of potential disloyalty, such as sometimes expressing their own, independent opinions. Any procurator could theoretically be promoted to the highest ranks or even became procurator general, as appointees had to satisfy a requirement of having procuratorial experience (though political qualifications had absolute priority). But procurators who were not party members, or were not considered trustworthy and obedient, had little chance of being promoted beyond the lowest ranks.

Such a system had enormous implications for how the justice system functioned. Under the communist regime, the procurator's influence was much more significant than before the war. This resulted from other changes, primarily the abolition of the investigating judge, which made the procurator the sole master of pretrial proceedings (Frankowski and Wąsek 1993, 1995). The procuracy was thus not only the prosecuting agency but also the investigating one. Procurators were supposed primarily to investigate more serious offenses, those that earlier fell within the jurisdiction of investigating magistrates. Lesser offenses remained within the competence of the police (or "civic militia," as police were officially called under communism). In practice, however, most investigations of serious offenses were done by the police, under a procurator's supervision (although some cases were always investigated personally by procurators). Lesser offenses were investigated by the police with much less supervision by procurators. The decision to prosecute was always made by the procurator, and he or she personally prepared the charge sheet[8] and appeared in court.[9]

The postwar system had consequences. The most profound was that the procuracy acquired a double identity, being an investigating and prosecuting agency but also serving as a general guardian of the rule of law. During the investigation, the procurator was supposed to act

[7] It was not unusual to require young procurators, or even apprentices, to become party members.

[8] The term "charge sheet" is equivalent to the Polish *akt oskarżenia* rather, and not a synonym for "indictment." The latter implies notions specific to common-law systems. The Polish term *akt oskarżenia* is comparable to the German term *Anklageschrift* and means a written document containing charges and a summary of evidence to support them. This document initiates prosecution in court.

[9] Except under a simplified procedure, applicable to some petty offenses that the police prosecuted.

primarily in his or her capacity as a general guardian of the rule of law, being impartial just as the investigating judge was expected to be (Krajewski 1985). Unlike the investigating judge, however, the procurator always had a personal stake in the outcome of investigation, as at its end he was supposed to change his role, making decisions to prosecute, and then proving the charges. Most procurators probably considered themselves primarily to be prosecutors and acted accordingly throughout. This was encouraged by their position within the procuracy's rigid hierarchy, which deprived them of real independence.

This system of course had consequences, and not only in purely political cases investigated by especially trustworthy procurators under close supervision of superiors (and the political police). It also had consequences for common criminal cases. The procuracy was an effective enforcement tool in the punitive crime control approach consistently adopted by the communist authorities. It resulted in harsh sentencing policies and high imprisonment rates (Krajewski 2004). Procurators usually requested very stiff sentences and, if they encountered an independent judge, could always appeal the penalty imposed. Such appeals became a common means of implementing punitive sentencing policies preferred by the Communist Party, especially during the 1980s. It became common at that time for the procuracy general to file extraordinary appeals against penalty only to the Supreme Court, whose members were usually ready to grant such appeals.[10]

III. Major Problems during the Past 20 Years

In February 1989 the Polish communist authorities began official negotiations with the political opposition (Davies 2005b, pp. 401–518; Lukowski and Zawadzki 2006, pp. 319–39). The anticommunist opposition groups, usually more or less openly supported by the Catholic Church, were always present in Poland. During the 1970s, they became stronger and more visible than elsewhere in the Eastern Bloc. By the end of the 1980s, despite martial law imposed in 1981 to crush the independent trade union Solidarity (*Solidarność*), the communist authorities under general Wojciech Jaruzelski began to recognize that the

---

[10] Beginning in the 1970s, judges of the Supreme Court were appointed for renewable 5-year terms instead of for life. This made them more susceptible to various forms of pressure than judges of other courts, who were appointed for life (but in cases of disloyalty to the communist system could be removed from office).

growing crisis of political legitimacy and a near total collapse of the centrally planned economy made some sort of a deal with the opposition unavoidable. Additional impulses to talks were provided by changes taking place in the Soviet Union under Mikhail Gorbachev's *perestroika* and *glasnost*.

Negotiations took place in spring 1989 and ended with a formal accord that introduced changes to the communist system of government, including legalization of the independent trade union Solidarity and partly free elections to the Parliament. The Communist Party and two nominally noncommunist satellites were guaranteed half of the seats, but the other half were subject to a completely free ballot. Both sides were cautious and intended a power-sharing arrangement, not a total change of the political system. But even within such a cautious approach the position, organization, and functioning of the procuracy, the police, and the court system became important subjects for negotiation and agreement. The reasons were the special roles played by criminal justice agencies as instruments for securing the Communist Party's grip on power. For the opposition, the main task was to soften the Communist Party's influence over the procuracy. The opposition proposed to return to the prewar system of having the minister of justice also serve as procurator general. The rationale was that the communist procurator general, appointed for a fixed term by the head of state, was beyond anyone's control—apart from the Communist Party. Even if the minister of justice in the future were a member of the Communist Party, he or she would be subject to influence or control by the parliamentary opposition. Activities of the procuracy were expected to become more transparent (Jasiński 1995).

There were also concerns that under the agreement a president could replace the Council of State. Should the presidency be filled by a member of the Communist Party, the procuracy would remain under communist control (Herzog 2009).

The communists accepted this idea. Amendments to the 1985 Procuracy Act were agreed on and implemented in March 1990. Unfortunately, for those who wanted an independent, politically impartial procuracy like, for example, those in Germany or the Scandinavian countries, this proved a pyrrhic victory. The 1990 reforms did not depoliticize the procuracy. The opposite occurred.

The partly free elections took place in June of 1989 and resulted in a complete defeat of the Communist Party, the creation of the first noncommunist government since World War II, and the total collapse of the old system within a few months. The communists did not win a single open seat. The two satellite parties switched alliance and joined a coalition with the opposition, which deprived the communists of their majority. This made it possible to form a government dominated by the anticommunist opposition, with a noncommunist prime minister, the well-known dissident and Catholic activist, Tadeusz Mazowiecki. To appease communist hard-liners and the secret services, the Parliament elected the communist party leader, General Wojciech Jaruzelski, as state president. He served in this post until 1991, when Solidarity leader Lech Wałęsa replaced him after winning national presidential elections.

Poland began to head toward liberal parliamentary democracy. However, the arrangement concerning the procuracy proved to be highly problematic, as the return to the prewar system of "plurality of functions," with the justice minister also serving as procurator general, occurred without substantial changes in the internal structure of the procuracy or in its organizational culture (Marguery 2007). Probably no one thought seriously about this at that time or anticipated the consequences of retaining the old structural arrangements. As a result, the rigid, hierarchical, disciplined structure of the procuracy was detached from exclusive control by the communist authorities but fell prey to the political ambitions of each successive parliamentary majority, as represented by the minister of justice.

In principle the newly created National Procuracy[11] should have been headed by a new national procurator who was a career civil servant designated from among the ranks of procurators. But he or she was supposed to be appointed by the minister of justice in his capacity as procurator general. This could have worked if the ministers had made appointments in good faith and then maintained a hands-off relationship to the procuracy. This did not happen.

The problem was that the minister of justice as procurator general not only enjoyed powers of general oversight (as before World War II) but was legally empowered with all the prerogatives of the procu-

---

[11] The terms National Procuracy and national procurator were introduced as a consequence of amendments enacted in 1996. Before that, there was a Procuracy Department within the Ministry of Justice, which meant that the procurator general had more day-to-day influence over the entire procuracy. The 1996 change was not substantive. It was intended to make the system more efficient and to grant more independence to the procuracy.

rator superior, including the abilities to interfere in ongoing investigations or prosecutions and to issue binding instructions and orders. Possibilities of political abuse of these powers were great because the minister of justice was not required to fulfill the criteria applicable to career procurators (i.e., to have passed a procuratorial or judicial apprenticeship exam). The 1990 Procuracy Act was not clear about this, but the 1996 amendments made it clear that the procurator general was exempt from normal procuratorial qualifications. Most ministers of justice since 1990 have had no such qualifications. Poland wound up, once again, with a highly politicized procuracy. One observer noted that "the intent of the reforms introduced in 1990 was to position the Minister of Justice being also Procurator General, as a sort of a king who reigns but does not govern. . . . [But] successive ministers very quickly got used to governing the procuracy using 'manual controls.' . . . Ministers of Justice as Procurators General comprehended their role as being the most superior procurator influencing the way individual cases are investigated and prosecuted" (Herzog 2009, p. 115).

One additional factor was important. The new authorities faced a serious dilemma: what to do with the people working within the apparatus of the communist state, including policemen, procurators, and judges. Most were party members (especially policemen and procurators), and during the 1970s and 1980s, many were involved in investigating, prosecuting, and convicting opposition activists who became leading politicians in the new government. They had also enforced repressive communist crime control policies concerning "common crime."

What to do with existing police, procurators, and judges? Some proposals called for broad-based purges, with the aim of breaking completely from the communist past. Others argued that many police, procurators, and judges, even if they were Communist Party members, were basically professionals trying their best under difficult circumstances. Some may have been involved in discreditable activities, but, the argument went, unless there was some proof that they had been especially eager in following directives and persecuting opposition activists or had committed offenses under the law in force at that time, they should not be deprived of their jobs and livelihoods.

The second approach prevailed. A completely new beginning was, as a practical matter, not possible. Old communist cadres could not easily on a wholesale basis be replaced with completely new ones, because in Poland, and in other countries of the region except Germany, qualified and experienced people with "clean records"—that is, having no prior involvement with the communist system—were not available in sufficient numbers or were not available at all.

Because of this, only members of the political police (security service) underwent widespread screening by a special parliamentary committee concerning their records during the communist period. Most were fired, with only a few being allowed to continue in the criminal police. Procurators were also screened, but only records of drastic misconduct served as grounds for forced departures. Most procurators from the communist period retained their jobs. Judges were not subjected to screening, apart from those who had committed obvious offenses. Wholesale screening and removal were widely considered a breach of the principle of judicial independence.[12]

Although there was probably no realistic alternative to the approach taken, it has had negative effects. Many procurators were unable to adjust to the new conditions of the democratic state. And the old professional culture of the communist-controlled procuracy partly survived. This had consequences for the training and socialization of new generations of procurators. Some have argued that control of the procuracy by the minister of justice was a necessary evil, in effect a transitory approach that guaranteed democratic control over the old, postcommunist procuracy (e.g., Marguery 2007). Unfortunately, in reality, this control became increasingly political in character.

Many experts recognized these problems soon after the collapse of communism, but political parties valued the powers the system gave them. First, it provided opportunity to influence politically sensitive investigations and prosecutions, either to protect their own or to settle accounts with political foes. Second, it provided a tool for indulging in the "politics of law and order."

Despite repeated proposals for change, the system introduced in 1990 lasted for 20 years. Problems first became visible in cases involving politicians. During the 1990s, a period of rapid political, economic, and social change, offenses frequently occurred that related primarily

[12] However, some observers disagree. Despite formal guarantees of judicial independence under communism, the reality was different. Because of this, until real guarantees and real independence were established by the democratic state, there was no reason not to screen former communist judges and, when justified, remove them from office (Gaberle 2005).

to privatization of state property (involving, e.g., bribes or political favoritism) and other types of economic and fiscal misconduct (often resulting from an initial lack of necessary legislation or from old legislation that was unclear and not adequate in the new conditions). They were perceived as a serious threat to the economy and the state, especially as they often occurred in a triangle involving legal businesses, politicians, and organized crime (Jasiński 1996). Investigating them was inherently difficult because of the complexity of such cases and the lack of experience in economic and white-collar crimes by procurators educated under a legal system regulating a centrally planned economy.

Political interference often made things even more difficult. Selection criteria in such cases often were influenced by political considerations, and investigations primarily targeted politically suitable criminals. The "professional culture of conformity" that permeated the communist procuracy proved often to be useful under the new circumstances. As a consequence, dysfunctional attitudes that were well established among old guard procurators influenced new recruits rather than disappearing with generational change.

Early examples of political influence and pressure on procurators from the ministers of justice occurred during the 1990s, although initially they were primarily passive. They usually involved attempts to protect people, mostly colleagues from governing parties, from being investigated. One well-known example is the "Moscow loan" case. In 1990 the Polish United Workers Party, as the Polish Communist Party was officially called, obtained a loan of US$1.2 million from the Soviet Communist Party. The money was most probably brought into Poland in cash by a prominent party member who later became prime minister. But this violated several financial regulations in force at that time. The case was investigated for several years but was abandoned in 1994 after the postcommunist Left won elections in 1993. As part of a coalition government, a member of the successor party to the Communist Party became minister of justice and procurator general.

Later on political interventions became more active. Investigations were often initiated against political opponents or people somehow connected to opposition parties. In some cases, investigations were started after elections against politicians of a losing party. In February 2002, for example, a procurator cooperating with the internal security agency ordered the arrest of Andrzej Modrzejweski, chief executive officer of the state-owned oil company Orlen; he had been appointed under the preceding conservative-liberal coalition. At the elections, the postcommunist Left regained power and the justice ministry was controlled by that party. The arrest took place in a spectacularly public way, just before a meeting of Orlen's board. It appears to have been arranged to influence the board's decision and to prevent signing of particular pending contracts.

A comparable arrest of Emil Wąsacz occurred in 2005 involving alleged improprieties in privatization of state companies. Wąsacz had been a minister in a previous conservative-liberal government and was investigated for several years under the subsequent postcommunist government. Courts later ruled that his arrest was unlawful. All this echoes an old political tradition under communism: departure from office was often associated with some sort of criminal charges (as there were few other ways to get rid of unwanted comrades).

After the fall of communism, the problem of settling accounts with the communist past was hotly discussed. The choice was either to use the criminal law broadly to achieve some sort of accountability for communist officials or to try to avoid this in the name of national reconciliation. This discussion reinforced perceptions of the criminal law as an instrument to be used for settling accounts with political opponents and today still leads to calls for prosecutions in circumstances that, in better-established democracies, are dealt with by means of political accountability. However, such investigations rarely ended in charges being brought to court, or in convictions, usually because of the vagueness of the allegations. Several such cases produced media headlines but ended with acquittals or with charges being dropped because of a lack of evidence (the Modrzejewski and Wąsacz cases belong in this category).

As a result, the procuracy became politicized in the sense that some procurators were known, or even notorious, for actively supporting particular political parties and options. This occurred even though, since 1990, the Procuracy Act had provided that procurators may not be members of political parties or organizations and have a duty to remain apolitical. Nonetheless, with the ascent to power of a minister of justice from a given political party, certain procurators were quickly appointed to leading positions (and lost them equally quickly when a new minister of justice was designated).

Tony Marguery has claimed that "although the organization of the Polish institutions might leave the door open to abuses, it does not mean that abuses actually happen" (2007, p. 79). This claim is difficult to support. One of the insiders in the Polish procuracy recently observed, "There is no way to deny that during the entire period of the existence of the current model [since 1990] constant and widespread allegations have appeared (especially in the media) that the procuracy as an agency and also individual procurators have been guided by political motivations. Such allegations were made regardless of which political party was at a given moment in power" (Herzog 2009, p.115). This process accelerated after 2000 and reached its peak in 2005–7, under the government of the Law and Justice party of the twin brothers Jarosław and Lech Kaczyński. In the prevailing view expressed in the media and by many experts and insiders, the procuracy under Zbigniew Ziobro, the minister of justice at that time, became an almost openly political tool, searching eagerly everywhere for alleged corruption and similar forms of misconduct. Corruption unquestionably became a serious problem in Poland beginning in the 1990s, and Law and Justice campaigned heavily on anticorruption issues. The problem was that, when in power, the party focused primarily on trying to develop cases involving political opponents and labeling them as corrupt rather than attacking real, systemic corruption.

The activities of the procuracy at that time, usually undertaken in conjunction with the secret services, involved abuses of power, dubious sting operations, and exertion of pressure on investigating procurators. One conspicuous case involved Barbara Blida, construction minister under an earlier postcommunist government. Because Blida had contact with people allegedly involved in various economic offenses (none of them was convicted of an offense), she was seen as an obvious target in efforts to prove the existence of a broad-based criminal conspiracy.

The procurators were never able to produce any convincing evidence. Everything was based on vague suspicions and hopes for a confession. During an attempted arrest in her home in April 2007, Blida committed suicide in ambiguous circumstances. This led to widespread public outrage, especially in her native Silesia, where she was quite popular. Subsequent parliamentary investigations indicated that both the internal security agency and the procuracy may have been involved in a clumsy attempt to cover up the circumstances of her death.

Other problems included obviously uncritical use, or in some cases possibly outright abuse, of uncorroborated testimony by state witnesses—criminals who testified in exchange for concessions in their own cases. Yet another problem concerned use of dubious sting operations to serve as bases for charges against prominent politicians, lawyers, and academics. Well-known defense attorney and former Deputy Interior Minister Jan Widacki, for example, was investigated and tried on charges of obstructing justice by attempting to influence a witness's testimony in a case involving one of his clients. Charges were based on the uncorroborated testimony of a state witness, even though that particular witness was already known to be unreliable. Widacki was acquitted. In another case, in 2007 a special anticorruption agency created by Kaczyński's government targeted dubious sting operations against several people, including Beata Sawicka, a member of Parliament from the opposition party Civic Platform. In 2009, Sawicka was charged with bribery, although there are serious doubts about this case concerning possible entrapment.

The minister of justice Ziobro involved himself and procurators heavily in media campaigns to promote his achievements. Nearly every week he organized major media conferences to present his successes as procurator general in fighting crime, especially corruption and misconduct among his political opponents. Investigations appear to have often been conducted and arranged to produce the best possible media effects and political impact. Some procurators played active roles in these media spectacles.

In one blatant case, a minister during a press conference personally decided to release suspects in a notorious case that had attracted huge media attention; the decision was implemented by subordinates.[13] However, at that time, the procurator general lacked legal authority to interfere in decisions concerning individual cases (Herzog 2009, p. 116; Grzegorczyk 2010, p. 30). This controversy led to changes in the Procuracy Act. In 2007, the minister of justice when acting as procurator general was given explicit authority to participate personally in decisions on individual ongoing cases (Waltoś 2009, p. 175). This was the apogee of political subordination of the procuracy.

Abuses of the procuracy were made easier by the organizational prin-

---

[13] The case regarded the lynching by a group of angry men of an ex-convict who threatened people in a small town. The incident was troubling and was the result primarily of a failure to act by the local police but constituted a clear-cut case of unjustifiable violence. The perpetrators enjoyed full support from the local community and some local and national media. It may be disputed whether preliminary detention was really necessary, but the action of the minister of justice was transparently politically motivated.

ciples discussed above and by an organizational structure that gives superiors enormous power over lower-level procurators, including power to transfer investigations across the country to procuracies having no direct territorial jurisdiction connection with the case. In 2005–7, two district-level procuracies (one in the north, one in the south) enjoyed the full trust of the minister of justice Zbigniew Ziobro; procurators in these districts investigated most cases considered by the government to be especially important. Some suspected offenses allegedly occurred hundreds of kilometers away from the investigating procuracy's location. At the same time some disobedient procurators of high rank were transferred as punishment to posts in small, remote procuracies far from their homes.

It is difficult to estimate how frequent such cases were. Probably most cases during that period, those not considered by the government to be sensitive, were handled without political interference. However, the events of 2005–7 resulted in enormous damage to the procuracy's image. It began to be perceived as deeply politicized, without independence, and unable to resist political pressure. There were three major reasons for this: the procuracy's subordination to the minister of justice as procurator general, its organizational principles (the principles of hierarchical subordination and uniformity), and prevailing staff attitudes (a culture of conformity and survival strategies meant to avoid trouble). Because of this, when a new center-right government coalition came to power in fall 2007, it made major reform of the procuracy a priority.

IV. Recent Reforms

The main idea underlying proposed reforms concerned the procuracy's position within the system of state agencies. It was decided that a basic precondition to any change was to separate the offices of the procurator general and the minister of justice. Ironically, this meant returning to the model that existed under the communist regime and that the opposition had contested during the 1980s. But under the new circumstances this approach seemed to offer better protection against political abuses. The lesson may be that there is no universal solution to the problems of prosecutorial independence and insulation from politically motivated interference. Having prosecutors be career civil servants may in principle protect against politicization of the prosecution system

(Tonry 2007, p. 35), but it does not provide absolute protection. The possibilities and protections of prosecutorial independence depend on particular circumstances of a country's political culture, its political system, and its political traditions.

Some countries that give justice ministers control of the public prosecution system appear not to have experienced such problems as Poland has faced. Illustrations may come from France, where the powers of the minister of justice over the *procureurs* are significant (Roché 2007, pp. 482–86), but the *procureurs* retain a large margin of independence (Marguery 2007, pp. 75–77). The same is true of Germany, where *Staatsanwaltschaft* is also organized hierarchically, and *Generalstaatsanwalt*, the general attorney, is responsible to the minister of justice (Herrmann 1987, p. 112).

Moreover, certain aspects of the communist inheritance, still widely present in Central and Eastern Europe, have made it much more complicated to achieve effective solutions to the problems of political interference. After all, the pre–World War II Polish system, modeled on French patterns, and having the justice minister also serve as procurator general, seemed not to suffer from such profound problems.

Amendments to the Procuracy Act of 1985, as revised in 1996, were adopted in 2008. Implementation was completed in spring 2010. A new post of procurator general, independent of and separate from the Ministry of Justice, was created. The former National Procuracy, subordinated via the national procurator to the minister of justice, became the General Procuracy headed by the procurator general. The procurator general is appointed by the president of the republic for a nonrenewable term of 6 years from among two candidates presented by the National Procurators Council and the National Judicial Council (each is entrusted with various tasks, discussed below, concerning procuratorial and judicial appointments).

The procurator general in principle cannot be removed from his or her office before completion of the term except for cause. Otherwise removal can happen only in cases of resignation, lasting inability to serve, or conviction for an offense. The procurator general may be removed during his or her term by the Parliament in two instances. The first concerns an annual report on the procuracy's activities, which the procurator general must submit to the prime minister. If the prime minister rejects such a report, he or she may seek advice from the National Procurators Council (its advice being nonbinding) and ask the Parliament for removal of the procurator general. This requires a two-thirds majority in Parliament with at least 50 percent of members present. The same procedure may be initiated by the prime minister if the procurator general—as the law formulates it—"betrays his or her oath." This is not necessarily a precise formulation and for that reason has been criticized. Some observers worry that the possibility of removal before expiration of the procurator general's term may seriously undermine the procuracy's independence (Herzog 2009; Grzegorczyk 2010).

The president must select the procurator general from two candidates selected by the National Judicial Council and the National Procurators Council. The procedure for selecting the two candidates is supposed to be based primarily on professional criteria. Anyone can apply. The candidate must have been a procurator with at least 10 years' professional experience or a judge with at least 10 years' experience deciding criminal cases. Candidates are screened by the National Judicial Council and the National Procurators Council. Their involvement should guarantee the independence of the process. The procedure was tested for the first time in 2010, with a district court judge being appointed. Thus ended 20 years of subordination of the public prosecution system to partisan political officials.

It is difficult to predict how this attempt at insulation from political influence will affect the traditional working culture within the procuracy and how procurators function and do their everyday work. This is much more difficult to effect than to change organizational rules. As in 1989, the recent changes do not significantly alter the internal structure of the procuracy or its fundamental organizational principles. The procuracy remains a rigid hierarchy governed by the principle of "hierarchical subordination," with superior procurators having broad powers over subordinates.

However, new provisions are meant to protect procurators from the most troubling forms of interference, by providing guarantees of independence. The current Procuracy Act states, "The procurator is obliged to undertake all his or her activities specified by the law guided by the principle of impartiality" (art. 7) and "the procurator is independent in undertaking actions defined by the law" (art. 8, para. 1).

"Independence" in relation to procurators, however, means something very different from "independence" in relation to judges. This is reflected in the use of different Polish terms: *niezawisłość* and *niezależ-*

ność. Judicial independence (*niezawisłość*) means being subordinated only to law and being protected against external (e.g., the executive) and internal (e.g., from superiors, as judges have no formal superiors) interference. Procuratorial independence (*niezależność*) refers only to external influence (primarily from the executive) but not from internal interference from higher-ranking procurators. A politically independent procurator general may be able to provide better protection against governmental or political influence, even if complete autonomy is not assured.

The Procuracy Act clearly confirms the principle of hierarchical subordination: "The procurator is obliged to execute dispositions, guidelines, and orders of procurator superior." At the same time, however, it provides that "dispositions, guidelines, and orders shall not regard the content of legal action" (art. 8, para. 2).

This formulation is most crucial concerning decisions in individual cases. It suggests that senior procurators may not prescribe specific decisions to be made in individual cases, such as "charge Y with an offense X," "terminate the investigation against Z or release him or her from detention," or "prosecute A."

Under article 8b, senior procurators retain authority to delegate any action to a subordinate or to execute any action of a subordinate themselves. Senior procurators also retain authority to reverse or change any decision of a subordinate (art. 8a). However, such decisions must now be written, and the writing must be included in the dossier of the case.

The 2008 amendments raise constitutional questions, partly because the Polish procuracy, like the German *Staatsanwaltschaft*, has no clear constitutional position and role (Frankowski 2005). The Constitution of 1997 contains provisions on the government, and governmental administration, and provides in detail for courts of various kinds. However, unlike its communist predecessor, it does not mention or regulate the procuracy. It is clear that the procuracy does not belong to the judicial branch of government, but it is not clear whether it is a part of the executive branch or is some sort of special agency. Because of the procuracy's separation from the Ministry of Justice, the latter is true. In any case, the procuracy's position is precarious and constitutionally ambiguous. This has led to proposals to add provisions to the Constitution concerning the procuracy (Stankowski 2009).

Commentaries on the Procuracy Act attempt to delineate the autonomy each procurator possesses (e.g., Mitera, Rojewski, and Rojowska 2011), but they cannot insulate procurators from intrusions by senior procurators into individual investigations. Providing insulation may require changes in fundamental organizational principles. Some observers propose returning to prewar policies that gave independence to procurators at each level, with the procurator general having only general oversight powers (Gaberle 2005, pp. 99–101).

V. Current Organization and Functioning

The modern procuracy is a hierarchical system consisting of four levels: county, district, appellate, and the General Procuracy (Krajewski 2010). With one modification, reintroduction of procuracies at the appellate level, this continues the structure established under the communist government. This results in a return to the prewar four-level court system and the three-tier system of deciding cases with two different kinds of appeals. Nearly every town or city having a court of a given level also has a procuracy at that level. However, in contrast to before the war, the procuracies are not "attached" to the courts but are completely separate.

In 2010, there were 11 appellate procuracies, 45 district procuracies, 342 county procuracies, and the General Procuracy.[14] According to Council of Europe data, in 2008 there were 5,379 procurators in Poland (a country of approximately 38 million inhabitants), an average of 14 per organizational unit (CEPEJ 2010). Of course some city procuracies were much larger, and some small county procuracies consisted of only a few procurators. Relative to its population, Poland had many prosecutors: 14.1 per 100,000 inhabitants. Within Europe, only Lithuania (25.7), Latvia (23.0), and Russia (21.3) had higher ratios. Only one Western European country, Norway (15.4), had a higher ratio. Portugal (12.6) was slightly lower. Central and Eastern European countries typically had much higher ratios than did most Western European countries. In continental Europe, the ratio is usually well below 10: Belgium (7.8), Spain (4.8), the Netherlands (4.6), Italy (3.4), and France (3.0). Why this is, is a question whose answer is well beyond the scope of this essay. But it is natural to wonder whether part of the answer is

---

[14] These numbers parallel the number of courts. In 2009 there were (apart from the Supreme Court) 11 appellate courts, 45 district courts, and 320 county courts. Only on the county level do the numbers differ.

the lingering effect of postwar systems being modeled on the Soviet example.[15]

The average workload of a Central or Eastern European prosecutor in 2008, measured by cases handled in first instance, is not high (CEPEJ 2010). In Poland it was 209.1, but in Latvia it was 27.9, in the Czech Republic 60.1, and in Hungary 92.1. By contrast, in Austria the average was 1,893.3, in Spain 2,048.1, and in France 2,673.1! Poland and most Central and Eastern European countries have a ratio below both European average (507.1) and median (234.7) values, which means that their prosecutors handle many fewer cases. Of course this measure is crude; prosecutors in different countries have different powers, play different roles, and deal with different types of cases in different manners. But even with all those qualifications, the caseload difference suggests that the average workload in Western Europe is much higher than in Central and Eastern Europe. This again raises questions about the residual influences in Europe of the earlier division of the continent between two political and ideological blocks.

As in most European countries, procurators in Poland today are career officials appointed on their merits and in principle are insulated from political influence. Under article 14b, paragraph 1, of the Procuracy Act, anyone satisfying designated criteria may apply for a procurator's post at any level. Candidates must have graduated from law school, completed special training and an apprenticeship (*aplikacja*), and performed satisfactorily on an exam.[16] Later career possibilities include promotion to a higher level or appointment into specialized roles (mainly as chiefs of procuracy units or internal departments at various levels). In principle, people with judicial qualifications can be appointed as procurators, but in practice this is not common.

The procurator general appoints and promotes procurators but does

---

[15] Fairly similar differences were reported at the beginning of the 1990s (Kangaspunta, Joutsen, and Ollus 1998, pp. 62–63). Before World War II, the Polish procuracy had about 500 procurators (Herzog 2009).

[16] Before 2009 Poland had a complicated system for training legal professionals with separate apprenticeships of different durations for future judges, procurators, and defense attorneys; with separate exams; and with limited eligibility to work in other legal specialties (Sitarz 2008). In 2009, the National School of Judiciary and Procuracy was established in which judicial and procuratorial training were partly unified. Training is divided into two phases. The initial general phase lasts 12 months. After that there is a judicial track lasting an additional 54 months and a procuratorial track lasting an additional 30 months. Each ends with a state exam. Defense attorneys have a completely separate training, apprenticeship, and examination system run by the bar association.

not act alone.[17] Appointment is preceded by a review of the candidates' applications and a screening by the National Council of Procurators. It consists of 25 members serving 4-year terms. Members include the minister of justice, the procurator general, a representative of the president of the republic, four members of Parliament, two senators, and 16 procurators designated by procuracies of various levels. This council has a number of functions, but primarily it reviews and evaluates job applications. The council selects candidates for appointments as procurators in county, district, or appellate procuracies or the Procuracy General and proposes them to the procurator general, who makes final decisions.

For appointments to administrative posts such as chief procurators at county, district, or appellate levels, the procurator general proposes a candidate to the procurators working in that county, district, or appellate procuracy. If the proposed candidate is not approved, the procurators in the unit may propose their own candidate. The procurator general does not have to accept him or her and may start again from scratch. This system, in principle, should guarantee that appointments are made on merits without political or other interference.

Procurators are appointed for an unspecified period. They may be dismissed as a consequence of a decision of a disciplinary court. They may also be dismissed by the procurator general but only after having been convicted twice by the disciplinary court—and sentenced to punishment other than dismissal—and subsequently having committed a third disciplinary offense.

Chiefs of appellate and district procuracies are appointed for 6 years and those of county procuracies for 4 years. They cannot be removed except according to narrow criteria laid out in the law. These conditions include such straightforward circumstances as the lasting inability to serve or an offense conviction. However, the law contains a more general and vaguer provision justifying removal for "improper fulfillment of duties." This may be subject to various interpretations.

[17] Procedures described here are regulated by the most recent amendments to the Procuracy Act of 1985, introduced in 2008, simultaneously with the separation, discussed above, of the function of the procurator general from that of the minister of justice.

VI. Prosecution under the Current Criminal Procedure Code

The role of the procurator in the criminal process is regulated in detail by the 1997 criminal procedure code (Krajewski 2010). It does not differ substantially from regulations under the communist system. Of course, there have been some important changes, and some issues are handled significantly differently, especially concerning guarantees of the rights of the accused. The best example concerns pretrial detention and other "protective measures" (Morgenstern 2009). Under the communist system, use of pretrial detention, bail, police supervision, and supervision by a person or organization of trust were controlled by the procurator. Procurators' decisions regarding pretrial detention could be appealed to court, but appeals concerning other measures could be made only to superior procurators. It was common to use pretrial detention not only to guarantee the presence of the accused and prevent obstruction of the investigation but also to pressure the suspect to confess.[18] Since 1991, the procurator must apply to the court to use pretrial detention, and the lower court decisions are subject to appeal. Other protective measures remain within the procurator's discretion. However, decisions about their use may be appealed to the court.

There were other changes based on general concerns regarding the rule of law in a liberal democracy and the requirements of the European Convention of Human Rights. However, many problems remain. For example, pretrial detention seems still to be used too often and in many cases for unacceptably long periods. As a consequence, Poland has repeatedly lost cases concerning pretrial detention in the European Court of Human Rights. In December 2009 in *Jamroży v. Poland* (6093/04), the court suggested that there may be a structural problem. It pointed out that pretrial detention is used too often, that about 90 percent of procuratorial applications for preliminary detention are granted by courts, and that decisions are often made by inexperienced, young judges, and without detailed consideration (Morgenstern 2009). This means that procurators continue to exert significant influence on

---

[18] Handbooks on investigative techniques from that time regularly—and without embarrassment—refer to the "getting out function" of pretrial detention, use of preliminary detention solely to exert psychological pressure on the suspect to obtain a confession and other information. This was often combined with promises of the type "if you confess I will let you out." Unfortunately, these practices, always and still unlawful, did not disappear with the communist system and seem sometimes still to be used.

the use of preliminary detention and, with it, on the national imprisonment rate.

Otherwise the procuratorial system remains fairly similar to the postwar communist system, although it also reflects the principles regulating the prewar system. Proceedings begin with a formal pretrial investigative phase referred to as "preparatory proceedings" (*postępowanie przygotowawcze*). Its goal is to prepare the dossier of the case containing all the relevant evidence and formal protocols of all the activities undertaken during the investigation; this may be used as evidence in court.

Preparatory proceedings take two forms: investigations for more serious cases and inquiries for lesser ones. This is a remnant of the earlier system involving the investigating judge, but under that system the evidence collected by the investigating judge usually had more credibility in court during the trial than evidence collected by the police during an inquiry. Today there is no such difference.

What remains is a simplification of procedural requirements during the inquiry and a difference in the agencies in charge: investigations in principle conducted by the procurator (but with the police playing in practice a large role) and inquiries conducted by the police (with the procurator nominally supervising but sometimes acting on his or her own). Relations between the police and procurator are thus of great practical importance. In principle the procurator is always in charge of pretrial proceedings, with the police being subordinate. This was formally also true during the communist era, but the reality then was often different, with the procurator often being controlled by the police (especially the political police). Today many things have certainly changed, but in practice procurators depend heavily on the police.

As in earlier periods, the procurator is supposed to investigate cases not only for prosecution purposes. He is to collect all the relevant evidence, reveal it to the suspect at the end of pretrial proceedings, and supply it to the court. In other words, the purpose of pretrial proceedings is not only to prepare cases for prosecution but also to establish the truth.

When preparatory proceedings are complete, the procurator decides what to do. If there is no evidence of an offense, the perpetrator cannot be identified, or the evidence is insufficient to obtain a conviction, the procurator terminates the case. However, the victim may, under article 306 of the code, appeal such a decision to the court. If the court decides that the termination was not justified, it may give instructions as to what should be done. This does not mean that the procurator is obliged to prosecute. He or she must supplement the investigation but may terminate it again. However, in that case the victim has a right to initiate a private prosecution (art. 330 of the code of criminal procedure).

If there is sufficient evidence, the procurator is bound by the principle of mandatory prosecution to prepare a charge sheet, an official document indicating the nature of the charges and their justification. After an investigation, the procurator prepares the charge sheet. After an inquiry it may be prepared by the police, although the procurator always has the right to do so. If not, the charge sheet prepared by the police must be accepted and confirmed by the procurator. The charge sheet with the dossier is then sent to the court.

The principle of mandatory prosecution, in Poland as in Germany (Jescheck 1970a, 1970b), means that in principle the procurator has no discretion to drop charges or to take no further action (although the case may be terminated if the procurator considers the evidence to be insufficient). The procurator cannot drop a case because of the petty character of an offense or because there is no valid public interest to be furthered by prosecuting the case. If preparatory proceedings establish that an offense has been committed, that the offender is known, and that there are no formal obstacles, the procurator must prosecute, independently of all other considerations.

That is the theory. Practice sometimes differs. The law provides some exceptions, primarily resulting from the so-called substantive concept of offense contained in article 1, paragraph 2, of the criminal code. It states that an act satisfying the formal definition of an offense but causing negligible social harm is not to be considered a criminal offense. In such a case investigation may be discontinued. Despite the existence of a large amount of literature on this provision, its practical application is inconsistent, and it is sometimes interpreted as giving procurators substantial latitude not to prosecute. Sometimes serious cases are terminated whereas petty ones are vigorously pursued. However, it is necessary to underline that the negligible social harm clause is comparatively seldom invoked to justify discretionary decisions.

The principle of mandatory prosecution, intended to avoid discretionary, unequal, or arbitrary differences in treatment, is increasingly perceived as creating problems no one knows how to handle. Procurators and courts are overwhelmed by petty cases, including cases that make headlines because of their absurdity. Procurators bring such cases to courts both because they are not allowed to drop them and because the cases are easy to investigate and to win. In such a way procurators score easy victories and improve their statistical performance measures. And statistical evaluation (e.g., the number of convictions and cases ended in a month) has been sacrosanct within the procuratorial bureaucracy since communist times.

One example of this problem involves petty drug possession cases. Polish courts regularly deal with cases involving drug amounts that are legally irrelevant in many other European countries or that seldom lead to prosecutions. Polish procurators press charges because they are obliged to do so. They prefer not to discontinue proceedings under the negligible social harm clause because they dread negative reactions by superiors. They also seldom resort to the provisions in Polish drug laws that authorize suspension of investigations of drug-using offenders if the suspect agrees to undergo treatment.[19] Instead they prosecute the pettiest possession cases, secure convictions to suspended sentences, and enjoy the statistical results (Krajewski 2008).[20]

The obsession of Polish procurators with petty offenders can be illustrated by another recent example that has led to tensions between Poland and the United Kingdom. More than half of European arrest warrants (EAWs) from the 27 EU member states handled by British courts come from Poland (*Economist* 2009). The reason is not that many Poles live and work in Britain. Most requests concern petty offenses, infuriating the British government, which must pay for the court proceedings. The explanation, partly, is the rigid understanding of the principle of mandatory prosecution. If the suspect is abroad but there is no way to drop the case, under current regulations the procurator should suspend pretrial investigation until a suspect is apprehended. But having too many suspended cases may mean trouble with

[19] These regulations, which also may be applied by courts during the trial, fulfill tasks similar to those of American drug courts.

[20] This type of procuratorial hyperactivity may be restrained by a recent Supreme Court decision. The court decided that the criminal offense comes into question only in case of an act involving possession of drugs in quantities large enough to result in a psychoactive effect (*Judgment of the Supreme Court from November 4th, 2008*, IV KK 127/08). Earlier it was not uncommon to bring charges when tiny traces of illicit substances were found in containers, bags, or clothing because such cases are extremely easy to win.

superiors, who may interpret this as a sign of inefficiency. The best way to deal with the problem seems to be to issue an EAW. The British can then be blamed for not finding the suspect. This illustrates the fundamental weakness of the rigid, inflexible hierarchical organization of a procuracy, in which justifying decisions to superiors takes precedence over making sensible decisions.

Under the new code of criminal procedure the procurator, under certain conditions, may negotiate with the accused (art. 335 of the code of criminal procedure). This bargaining in principle must concern the punishment and not the charges. In other words, a lesser punishment is negotiable within the limits provided by the penal code for the offense charged but not by reducing or dropping charges.[21] The code does not require the defendant to plead guilty in such situations, although he or she has to agree to such a deal. The code requires only that the circumstances of the case be clear beyond any doubt. If the procurator strikes a deal with the suspect, he or she prepares not a charge sheet but a special motion to the court to convict without trial. If the court accepts the proposed deal, the sentence is imposed and the case—as in the Anglo-American system—is over. These new possibilities are becoming increasingly popular among procurators: they save time and resources.[22] No national statistical data on their use are available. In a study mentioned above concerning drug possession cases, 61 percent of convictions took place after some sort of a deal was reached. This is extremely high, probably because of the nature of such cases, and is not generalizable to other offenses. The use of such techniques is growing (Krajewski 2008).

Setting aside cases involving negotiated sentences, the procurator sends the charge sheet with the dossier to court for trial. From that

---

[21] Despite this, procurators at least in some cases tend to "overcharge," with the intent to stimulate suspects to cooperate. But this means that negotiations must take place within the limits provided by the "overcharged" offense. This may not be a special problem, as statutory minima and maxima are quite broad.

[22] In some cases, the use of these provisions takes strange forms. In a case concerning extradition under the EAW to another EU member state of a suspect charged with murder, the judge was asked by a procurator how long after the court's decision the suspect would remain in Poland. The puzzled judge asked why the procurator wanted to know. The answer was that drugs had been found in the suspect's apartment. He pleaded guilty to the drug charge, and the procurator wanted time to send a motion to the other court concerning the agreed punishment. The current code explicitly contemplates no further action in such circumstances; it is not required to press charges for a petty offense when a more serious charge is pending (this is one of the few permissible exceptions to mandatory prosecution).

moment he ceases being an investigator and becomes the public prosecutor, a party to the proceedings. But this does not mean that Polish procurators are very active during the trial. Usually they are not. Materials collected during the preparatory proceedings may exert very significant effects on the court's decision (as in any inquisitorial system). The trial is dominated by the judge (or judicial panel), who (or which) is responsible for the conduct of the trial, establishment of the facts, and the final decision, which should be based on all the relevant evidence. The court relies heavily on the dossier and tries primarily to verify what was learned during the investigation or inquiry.

Some provisions of the code of criminal procedure make procurators' work easier and safer than elsewhere but effectively discourage active participation in the trial. In most systems if the procurator has failed to collect all relevant evidence during the investigation, his or her position during the trial becomes problematic, and the case may end in acquittal. This makes it essential to assure the quality of the investigation. For a long time this was not the case in Poland. Because the court is responsible for the final judgment and the evidence on which it is based, things neglected during the investigation may or must be dealt with by the court. But even in cases of the most flagrant neglect, until 2003, the procurator's failure need not jeopardize prosecutions. If repairing mistakes would require too much effort for the court, it was possible to return the case for supplementary investigation. The procurator could then abandon the case and discontinue the investigation without again filing a charge sheet. An acquittal, usually perceived by superiors as a black mark, could be avoided. That possibility was limited substantially by a statutory change in 2003. The court may now ask the procurator to provide supplementary evidence, but without formally returning the case to investigation. This precludes the possibility of the procurator terminating the case. The law change was intended to make procurators more responsible for the quality of the investigation and the evidence.

Various attempts have been made in the last 20 years to change this situation, to stimulate involvement of the parties—especially the procurator—during the trial, and to make them more accountable. New laws, for example, specify that evidence for the prosecution be presented first (art. 369 of the code of criminal procedure) and that the parties ask questions first and the judge, or members of the judicial panel, at the end (art. 370 of the code of criminal procedure). These changes do not contemplate real cross-examination but aim to make the parties more active during the trial and to relieve judges of some burdens. Unfortunately, these provisions have not significantly changed the character of the trial.

The Polish procuracy has few prospects of having significant influence on sentencing. Procurators make oral recommendations concerning punishment in their final statements at the ends of trials (only orally; such recommendations are not contained in the charge sheets). Courts need not follow these recommendations. In practice, most sentences are less severe than procurators recommend. Because of this, procurators tend to make harsher recommendations than they believe warranted in the expectation that courts will reduce them. The opposite also happens: courts sometimes impose harsher sentences than procurators propose.

Owing to its hierarchical structure, the procuracy is able to promote its own sanctioning policy, sometimes without much regard to the opinions of the procurators who handled the case. Uniformity often prevails. The real problems occurred under the old model of the procuracy in which the justice minister was also procurator general.

The minister could and sometimes did, for political reasons, steer procuratorial sentencing recommendations as he wished, independent of the merits of the individual case. For example, sometimes such instructions forbade procurators from recommending suspended sentences in cases the public was concerned about. Before the 2009 changes to the Procuracy Act, recommendations regarding punishment were commonly discussed and agreed on with superiors. This may continue to be common practice, but now the individual procurator has authority to deviate from such instructions if the circumstances change during the trial (i.e., superiors need not be consulted). This makes a more flexible approach to sentencing possible.

One extreme example of questionable influence exerted by the procurator general occurred in 2000–2001 when the late President Lech Kaczyński was minister of justice. Portraying himself as "tough on crime" and engaging in the "politics of law and order" to an extent previously unknown in Poland, he indiscriminately used his authority as procurator general for those purposes. Issuing various instructions, he contributed decisively to a rapid increase in the Polish imprisonment rate. Of course, he could not directly influence courts' sentencing decisions. But he did possess authority to instruct procurators to apply to courts for preliminary detention in practically all cases of certain types independently of any other circumstances, including the possibility that the suspect may escape. Procurators had to obey, and this indirectly affected patterns of court decisions. The number of people in preliminary detention soared. In 1997–99, pretrial detainees constituted 30.8 percent of the general prison population; by 2000–2003 this had increased to 40.4 percent, which contributed decisively to a general increase in Polish imprisonment (Morgenstern 2009).

Kaczyński's term in office also had a huge influence on parole or early conditional release. Early conditional release in principle is decided by the judge and for most convicts is possible after serving half of their imprisonment term (for some categories of convicts, the threshold is higher). But the judicial decision may depend on factors the procurator general or the minister of justice could influence at that time. These include recommendations by the prison administration (which is subordinate to the Ministry of Justice) and the recommendation of the procurator (who could be influenced by the procurator general). Procurators can be quite effective at blocking parole decisions. As a consequence of Kaczyński's instructions, the ratio of successful parole applications dropped from about 70 percent at the beginning of the past decade to 40 percent. This also had a significant effect on the imprisonment rate.

Of course, there is nothing wrong with a public prosecution system having policies concerning applications for preliminary detention or early release of convicts. The problem arises when policies result from outside political pressure rather than from professionally informed decisions made within the system. Unfortunately, the previous system made such influences very easy. General procurators in Poland were quite effective in directing subordinate procuracies in the direction of increased punitiveness. But they were, and seem still to be, reluctant to use tools at their disposal to steer policies in the opposite direction such as, for example, doing something about obsessive prosecution of petty cases.

Prosecution in Poland underwent significant changes during the period after World War II and slowly evolved from a tool of the authoritarian communist regime to an agency of a democratic state, governed by the rule of law. But Poland's becoming a liberal parliamentary democracy 20 years ago did not automatically change or improve the prosecution system. For the last 20 years the system was haunted by ghosts of the communist past that proved extremely resistant to exorcism. Despite all reform attempts, politicians have been pleased to have and to exercise significant influence over the prosecution system. So far it has proven impossible to insulate the system from such influences. Whether recent reforms separating the procuracy from the justice ministry, and thus directing political influence through a governing majority, will bring significant changes remains to be seen.

In a period when law and order politics have been considered an important weapon for winning elections, politicians may prove reluctant to give up the control over the prosecution system they have long exercised.[23] Some observers believe lasting damage has been done during the last 20 years, and especially the last 10. Even under the new circumstances and with new statutory protections against direct interference, inertia and resistance to change may cause the procuracy to continue to function according to the old, well-established patterns and principles. Real change may require profound institutional reform. That kind of change is not very likely.

REFERENCES

Caianello, Michele. 2011. "The Italian Public Procurator: An Inquisitorial Figure in Adversarial Proceedings." In *Transnational Perspectives on Prosecutorial Power*, edited by Eric Luna and Marianne Wade. New York: Oxford University Press.

CEPEJ. 2010. *European Judicial Systems: Efficiency and Quality of Justice.* 2010 ed. (2008 data). Strasbourg: Council of Europe.

Davies, Norman. 2005a. *God's Playground: A History of Poland.* Vol. 1, *The Origins to 1795.* Rev. ed. Oxford: Oxford University Press.

———. 2005b. *God's Playground: A History of Poland.* Vol. 2, *1795 to the Present.* Rev. ed. Oxford: Oxford University Press.

Economist. 2009. "Wanted for Chicken Rustling." December 30. http://www.economist.com/node/15179470.

Ehrmann, Henry W. 1976. *Comparative Legal Cultures.* Englewood Cliffs, NJ: Prentice-Hall.

Frankowski, Stanisław. 1987a. "Poland." In *Major Criminal Justice Systems: A*

---

[23] During parliamentary elections in October 2011, the opposition Law and Justice party proposed abolition of that separation and return to the old system as one of its most important priorities. Law and Justice lost the election and remains in opposition.

Comparative Survey, 2nd ed., edited by George F. Cole, Stanisław J. Frankowski, and Marc G. Gertz. London: Sage.

———. 1987*b*. "The Procuracy and the Regular Courts as the Palladium of Individual Rights and Liberties: The Case of Poland." *Tulane Law Review* 61:1307–38.

———. 2005. *Introduction to Polish Law*. Krakow: Kantor Wydawniczy Zakamycze, Kluwer Law International.

Frankowski, Stanisław, and Andrzej Wąsek. 1993. "Evolution of the Polish Criminal Justice System after World War II: An Overview." *European Journal of Crime, Criminal Law and Criminal Justice* 1(2):143–66.

———. 1995. "Polish Criminal Law and Procedure." In *Legal Reform in Post-Communist Europe: The View from Within*, edited by Stanisław Frankowski and Paul B. Stephan III. London: Nijhoff.

Gaberle, Andrzej. 2005. *Rozważania o sądownictwie i prawie* [Deliberations on courts and law]. Krakow: Kantor Wydawniczy Zakamycze.

Garlicki, Leszek. 1980. "Legal Profession in Poland." *St. Louis University Law Journal* 24:486–513.

Grzegorczyk, Tomasz. 2010. "Niezależność prokuratury i prokuratorów w świetle znowelizowanej ustawą z dnia 9 października 2009 r. ustawy o prokuraturze" [Procuracy's and procurator's independence under the Procuracy Act as amended by the Act of October 9, 2009]. *Prokuratura i Prawo* [Procuracy and law] 2010(1–2):27–40.

Herrmann, Joachim. 1987. "Germany." In *Major Criminal Justice Systems: A Comparative Survey*, 2nd ed., edited by George F. Cole, Stanisław J. Frankowski, and Marc G. Gertz. London: Sage.

Herzog, Aleksander. 2009. "Niezależność prokuratury—mit czy nadzieja?" [Independence of procuracy—myth or hope?]. *Prokuratura i Prawo* [Procuracy and law] 2009(1):111–28.

Jasiński, Jerzy. 1995. "Crime Control in Poland: An Overview." In *Crime Control in Poland: Polish Report for the Ninth United Nations Congress on the Prevention of Crime and the Treatment of Offenders*, edited by Jerzy Jasiński and Andrzej Siemaszko. Warsaw: Oficyna Naukowa.

———. 1996. "Crime in Central and East European Countries." *European Journal on Criminal Policy and Research* 56(1):40–50.

Jescheck, Hans-Heinrich. 1970*a*. "The Discretionary Powers of the Prosecuting Attorney in West Germany." *American Journal of Comparative Law* 18: 508–17.

———. 1970*b*. "Principles of German Criminal Procedure in Comparison with American Law." *Virginia Law Review* 56:239–53.

Kangaspunta, Kristina, Matti Joutsen, and Natalia Ollus, eds. 1998. *Crime and Criminal Justice Systems in Europe and North America, 1990–1994*. Helsinki: HEUNI.

Krajewski, Krzysztof. 1985. "Poland: The Procurator and Preparatory Proceedings in Polish Criminal Procedure." *Comparative Law Yearbook* 9:69–82.

———. 2004. "Crime and Criminal Justice in Poland." *European Journal of Criminology* 1(3):377–407.

————. 2008. "Przestępstwo posiadania narkotyków w świetle badań aktowych" [Drug possession offenses—a study using court files]. *Państwo i Prawo* (State and law) 2008(90):31–45.

————. 2010. "Poland." In *Crime and Punishment around the World*, edited by Graeme R. Newman. Vol. 4 of *Europe*, edited by Marcelo F. Aebi and Veronique Jacquier. Oxford: ABC-CLIO.

Langbein, John H., and Lloyd L. Weinreb. 1978. "Continental Criminal Procedure: 'Myth' and Reality." *Yale Law Journal* 87:1549–77.

Lukowski, Jerzy, and Hubert Zawadzki. 2006. *A Concise History of Poland*. 2nd ed. Cambridge: Cambridge University Press.

Marguery, Tony. 2007. "The 'Plurality of Functions' of the Polish Minister of Justice—General Procurator: Paradox or Adaptation?" *European Journal of Crime, Criminal Law, and Criminal Justice* 15(1):67–82.

Mitera, Maciej, Michał Rojewski, and Elżbieta Rojowska. 2011. *Ustawa o prokuraturze: Komentarz* [Procuracy Act: Commentary]. Warsaw: C. H. Beck.

Morgenstern, Christine. 2009. "Poland." In *Pre-trial Detention in the European Union*, edited by Anton van Kalmthout, Marije Knapen, and Christine Morgenstern. Nijmegen, Netherlands: Wolf.

Pakes, Francis. 2010. *Comparative Criminal Justice*. 2nd ed. Cullompton, UK: Willan.

Pomorski, Stanisław. 1981. "Communists and Their Criminal Law: Reflections on Igor Andrejew's 'Outline of the Criminal Law of the Socialist States.'" *Review of Socialist Law* 7:7–34.

Roché, Sebastian. 2007. "Criminal Justice Policy in France: Illusions of Severity." In *Crime, Punishment, and Politics in Comparative Perspective*, edited by Michael Tonry. Vol. 36 of *Crime and Justice: A Review of Research*, edited by Michael Tonry. Chicago: University of Chicago Press.

Sitarz, Julia. 2008. "Recent Changes to the Legal Professions in Central and Eastern Europe: The Case of Poland." *Connecticut Law Review* 40(February): 883–925.

Stankowski, Andrzej. 2009. "Propozycja unormowań prokuratury w Konstytucji RP" [Proposals to regulate procuracy under the constitution of the republic]. *Prokuratura i Prawo* [Procuracy and law] 2009(10):5–15.

Tak, Peter J. P., ed. 2004. *Tasks and Powers of the Prosecution Services in the EU Member States*. Vol. 1. Nijmegen, Netherlands: Wolf.

————. 2005. *Tasks and Powers of the Prosecution Services in the EU Member States*. Vol. 2. Nijmegen, Netherlands: Wolf.

Tonry, Michael. 2007. "Determinants of Penal Policies." In *Crime, Punishment, and Politics in Comparative Perspective*, edited by Michael Tonry. Vol. 36 of *Crime and Justice: A Review of Research*, edited by Michael Tonry. Chicago: University of Chicago Press.

Voslensky, Michael. 1984. *Nomenklatura: The Soviet Ruling Class*. New York: Doubleday.

Vouin, Robert. 1970. "The Role of the Procurator in French Criminal Trials." *American Journal of Comparative Law* 18:483–97.

Waltoś, Stanisław. 1979. "Introduction." In *Code of Criminal Procedure of the*

Polish People's Republic, edited by Stanisław Waltoś. Warsaw: Wydawnictwo Prawnicze.

———. 2009. *Proces karny: Zarys systemu* [Criminal process: Outline of the system]. 9th ed. Warsaw: LexisNexis.

Henk van de Bunt and Jean-Louis van Gelder

The Dutch Prosecution Service

ABSTRACT

The Dutch Public Prosecution Service has undergone major changes in recent decades. Public prosecutors were initially little more than intermediaries who delivered cases from the police to the judge, but the modern-day public prosecutor has many tasks entrusted to him and wide-ranging responsibilities. The case-oriented magistrate who dealt with cases from behind his desk now actively operates outside the confines of his office, developing local crime policy and monitoring criminal investigations. However, in his original judicial role, the Dutch prosecutor remains a powerful player. Only he can bring criminal cases to court and determine the parameters of court proceedings. Prosecutors have gained discretion to settle more cases out of court. Prosecutors can offer settlements to suspects through which further prosecution is averted and, most recently, have gained authority to impose sanctions, so-called penal orders, for designated offenses without the involvement of a judge. Another important change is a computerized decision support system to determine appropriate sentences. The Dutch prosecutor is an increasingly central player in the criminal justice process.

The Dutch Public Prosecution Service (PPS) experienced a series of important changes in recent decades. Changes in tasks and competencies have greatly altered the position of the service with respect to the police force and the judge and also led to important changes in the daily work of prosecutors. Discretionary powers were widened to deal with an increasing caseload, and the PPS as a whole evolved from a

Henk van de Bunt is professor of criminology at the Erasmus School of Law, Erasmus University Rotterdam. Jean-Louis van Gelder is a researcher at the Netherlands Institute for the Study of Crime and Law Enforcement.

117

little-integrated organization that primarily handled cases into a unified entity that shapes and executes criminal justice policy together with local authorities and the police.

Some characteristics of the service have remained constant over time. The PPS remains an intermediary body in the criminal justice process operating between pretrial investigation and the trial itself, and it continues to determine what cases receive priority in criminal investigation. Furthermore, the PPS continues to be the hybrid organization it was when it was established. Formally, Dutch prosecutors are civil servants employed by the Ministry of Justice and are therefore accountable to the minister of justice. Simultaneously, the PPS forms part of the judiciary, and public prosecutors receive in large part the same training as judges. Individual prosecutors operate relatively independently with respect to making decisions in cases. Paradoxically, this independence is at times manifested to a greater extent concerning more serious offenses, as a computerized decision support system now guides decisions in routine low-level cases.

The prosecutor also remains the gatekeeper to the courtroom. Only the prosecutor can bring criminal cases to court, deciding what and who comes before a judge. Under the "expediency principle," the PPS has discretion to decide to prosecute or not. The only option for victims who are unhappy with a decision not to prosecute is to appeal that decision to a court of appeals.

In 1983, the PPS was authorized to resolve cases by offering suspects settlements called "transactions." The suspect can avert prosecution by accepting one or more specified conditions, most commonly—in 60 percent of cases—the payment of a sum of money. If the suspect accepts the offer, the case is dealt with solely by the prosecutor and will not result in a criminal record. More recently, the "penal order" was introduced (Wet OM-afdoening, *Kamerstukken II* 2002/03, 28 600). This is a sanction that is imposed directly by the prosecutor, without court intervention, and is not dependent on the suspect's consent; the suspect's only recourse is to appeal the decision to a judge.

Important changes have occurred in the last four decades. The most important driver of change has been a large increase in caseload that has forced the PPS to operate more efficiently. Crime in the Netherlands started to rise significantly in the second half of the 1970s, and recorded crime doubled between 1980 and 1984. By the mid-1980s, it was widely acknowledged that the increasing caseload could not be dealt with simply by appointing more prosecutors. In response the capacity of the PPS was increased, along with those of the police, the prison services, and the judiciary.

A 1985 white paper, "Society and Crime," laid out new directions in crime prevention and criminal justice policy (Ministry of Justice 1985; van de Bunt 2004). Instead of continuing primarily to process cases brought to its notice, the PPS began to develop policy instructions and guidelines, and through consultation with the regional chief of police and local authorities, it attempted to ensure that the courts did not drown in a flood of cases. Tak (2008) observes that the number of cases tried in court only doubled in this period even though the number of registered crimes increased more than fivefold between 1970 and 2005. While the volume of cases can partly be attributed to a drop in the clearance rate from 41 to 19 percent, the other explanation is that the PPS was granted more powers to deal efficiently with cases out of court (Tak 2008). One of the most important and, from a comparative perspective, probably one of the most unusual of these measures was the introduction of a computerized decision support system in the 1990s. The "BOS-Polaris" system was intended to standardize PPS decision making for a large number of common, high-volume, criminal offenses including shoplifting, domestic violence, and vandalism. A detailed set of decision rules is used to determine appropriate sentences (this is discussed in detail in Sec. III).

The white paper stressed that maintenance of law and order should no longer be seen as a matter solely for the police and the justice system. Local authorities and other ministries of government besides the Ministry of Justice had to be involved. The PPS's limited focus on criminal investigations and prosecutions was abandoned in favor of a broader approach that included prevention and collaboration with other agencies. Preventing crime and dealing with it, even with organized crime, increasingly became a concern of local authorities, particularly mayors of large cities (Fijnaut 2002; van de Bunt 2004; van der Schoot 2006). Through the use of preventive measures such as closed-circuit television and restrictions on the sale of alcohol and the opening hours of bars, they could contribute to surveillance and monitoring and reduce criminal opportunities. Mayors also have shared responsibility with police officials concerning allocation of the police force's financial resources, deployment of personnel (e.g., patrolling or carrying out criminal investigations), and the organization of the force.

The local chief of police, the mayor, and the prosecutor meet on a regular basis during so-called triparty consultations to shape local security policy (see Sec. III for more detail).

We examine recent changes in the Dutch Prosecution Service in this essay. We start in Section I with a brief overview of the organizational structure and operations of the PPS. In Section II we discuss the three main roles Dutch public prosecutors play—as magistrate, worker, and civil servant—and the tensions inherent in the coexistence of these roles. Prosecutors have steadily gained broader authority to dispose of cases without judicial involvement (though subject to appeal to judges) through dismissals, "transactions" in which suspects agree to pay a penalty without pleading guilty, and "penal orders" in which penalties are imposed and convictions are entered. Prosecutors' work has, however, become increasingly bureaucratized; BOS-Polaris, a point-counting set of decision rules, affects many decisions from transactions to sentence recommendations in court. And, at the same time, prosecutors are increasingly called on to monitor police operations and collaborate with municipal and police officials in crime prevention and public order initiatives. Section II continues with further explanation of the BOS-Polaris system, the transaction, and the penal order. We then discuss the relationships of the PPS with the police and local authorities. Section III further discusses relations with and oversight of the police. Section IV discusses the changing ethnic, gender, and political makeup of the prosecution service, with an overview of the political affiliations, beliefs, and the selection and training process of prosecutors. Section V offers brief concluding remarks. Throughout this process, we will particularly focus on those features of the service that are unique to the Dutch situation and make it different from prosecution organizations in other countries.

I. Organization and Operations

The Dutch Public Prosecution Service, founded in 1811 and modeled after its French counterpart, is part of the public administration, a *Ministère Public*, and also part of the judiciary. The PPS to this day continues to be organized according to this dual structure. The PPS is accountable to the courts, which review its conduct, and to the minister of justice. The public prosecutor thus has a peculiar position. He is a civil servant but also shares important characteristics with judges in terms of recruitment, training, mandate, and organizational culture.

The institutional and functional structure of the PPS follows that of the courts. The Netherlands is currently divided into 19 judicial districts, each with its own court and an attached office of the PPS. Each office operates under the authority of a chief public prosecutor who is responsible for the functioning of the prosecutors in his or her district. Appellate jurisdiction is organized into five regions. Appeals against district court judgments are filed in the appropriate court of appeal. The five regional Public Prosecution Offices are headed by chief advocate generals. The appeals are handled by prosecutors in the regional office.

Higher appeals in criminal cases are lodged at the Supreme Court of the Netherlands in The Hague. A procurator general heads a prosecution office attached to the Supreme Court. In the Supreme Court, the prosecutor does not argue for a particular sentence, as prosecutors in lower courts do, but advises on how a case should be dealt with. Importantly, the procurator general's Supreme Court office is not part of the formal PPS and is wholly independent of the minister of justice. The procurator general is appointed by the Crown for life with mandatory retirement at the age of 70.

The current organizational structure differs drastically from a few decades ago. Until the 1960s, there was a procurator general for each regional court of appeal and there was no centrally led organization. The service was said to consist of five rather isolated islands or archipelagos each dealing with cases in its own way and largely oblivious to what happened on the other islands ('t Hart 2006). This is in sharp contrast with the current state of affairs in which the PPS is organized centrally and hierarchically and is headed by a Board of Prosecutors General, which, together with the minister of security and justice, sets priorities for police work and prosecution policy.[1]

The highest authority over investigation and prosecution rests with the Board of Prosecutors General. It supervises the implementation of prosecution policy and police investigation policy by giving directives

[1] In 2013 the current 19 district courts will be reduced to 10 and the five appeals courts regions to four. The new structure is uncontroversial and is aimed at cost reduction and more effective functioning. It will parallel the regional structure of the police organization, which is being restructured and will be reduced from 26 units to 10.

to the police, for example, regarding types of crimes that should receive investigative priority (Tak 2008, pp. 50–51). The board can issue directives concerning investigation, for example, concerning large organized crime cases. Instructions of the Board of Prosecutors General, whether general or specific, are binding for individual prosecutors. The board is also entitled to give specific instructions in individual cases concerning whether or not to prosecute. However, it is generally accepted that individual prosecutors are autonomous in making sentencing proposals in individual cases.

Finally, there are two other offices of the PPS that operate at the national level (van de Bunt 2004; Commissie Toedeling Zaakspakketten 2008). The National Prosecutor's Office, set up in 1995, deals with terrorism and (international) organized crime such as money laundering, human trafficking, and similar offenses. The National Prosecutor's Office also provides services and support to other offices in implementing police infiltration and witness protection initiatives. The National Prosecutor's Office serves as a liaison between the PPS and the national intelligence and security services. Beyond the domestic level, the National Prosecutor's Office facilitates international cooperation and acts as a liaison for foreign prosecution services regarding legal aid requests.

The other national office is the Financial, Environmental, and Food Safety Offenses Office (Functioneel Parket). It was established in 2003 and, besides being a center of specialized expertise, is charged with the responsibility for prosecuting economic, financial, and environmental crimes. These are crimes mainly brought to light by special investigative services, such as the Fiscal Information and Investigation Service and the Economic Investigation Service.

A. The Minister of Justice

The PPS formally operates under the political responsibility of the minister of justice, but it simultaneously forms part of the judiciary. The minister of justice is politically accountable to the PPS. This does not mean, however, that he is responsible vis-à-vis Parliament for the PPS's policies, but only for his own actions or inactions.

The minister of justice is entitled to give instructions to public prosecutors. In general the minister can prescribe priorities for police work or develop guidelines or grids for decision making. He has authority to order that a specific crime be prosecuted or that an alleged offender (not) be indicted. These types of orders about specific cases are required by law to be made public. In practice, issuance of specific instructions and guidelines is exceedingly rare, and the power to order to prosecute or not has never been exercised. There is a common understanding that the minister will exercise great restraint in this respect (van Daele 2003, p. 165). As a practical matter, therefore, the PPS can be considered as part of an independent judiciary.

There is, however, consultation between the minister and the Board of Prosecutors concerning sensitive cases. One recent example concerns a member of Parliament who was accused of discriminating against minorities and engaging in hate speech. Complaints were lodged by individuals in order to have him appear in court. The Board of Prosecutors General did not want to bring the case to court. The minister of justice did but eventually accepted the board's decision. This example illustrates the reluctance of the minister to assert his formal power over the PPS.

B. Discretionary Powers

The Dutch PPS is thus a hierarchical national organization headed by the Board of Prosecutors General. Its members are professionally educated lawyers who are appointed by the Crown. These characteristics seem to imply that the Dutch PPS is a prototypical example of a continental criminal justice service, which guarantees the correct application of legal rules and assures uniformity of decision making, but that view is slightly misleading. Members of the Dutch PPS possess a great deal of discretionary authority to settle felonies out of court and to drop charges "for reasons of public interest." The expediency or opportunity principle, laid down in article 167 sub 2 of the Code of Criminal Procedure, is the only statutory provision regulating the discretionary power of the PPS.

Generally speaking, individualized justice has traditionally been the goal of the Dutch PPS. This implies that prosecutors are expected to pursue an ideal of arriving at charges and punishments that fit the individual circumstances of each offender and offense. In recent decades this ideal has been pushed somewhat into the background and the discretion of the individual prosecutor has been structured and streamlined through adoption of PPS sentencing recommendation guidelines (De Doelder 2002). Even so, the view that the public prosecutor can make his own decisions remains accurate.

It would, however, also be wrong to conclude that the discretionary powers of the Dutch PPS make it more akin to prosecutorial agencies in Anglo-American criminal justice systems. The Dutch system differs fundamentally in that prosecutors do not view themselves as engaged in an adversary process. That is, the PPS expressly does not consider that its primary goal is to achieve the conviction of the accused (van de Bunt 1985; De Doelder 2002; Tak 2008). It regularly happens, for example, that prosecutors recommend acquittal. The role of the victim is small, though it may be increased in the near future (see Groen-huijsen 2008). In general, Dutch prosecutors are reluctant to be re-sponsive to victims. The prosecutor takes the interests of victims into account but is not expected to act as their spokesman. Furthermore, there is no lay participation in criminal cases. These factors imply, exceptions aside, that the Dutch prosecutor does not operate in a highly contentious and emotional legal arena and that he manifests himself neither as an adversary party nor as a spokesman for victims.

The Dutch prosecutor exercises his role as the gatekeeper to the court not by means of plea bargaining, as in the United States or En-gland, but makes decisions about charges and prosecutions indepen-dently. The prosecutor is expected to weigh all interests involved (i.e., those of the public, the victim, and the offender). In complex cases, the prosecutor may at times negotiate with the defense lawyer regard-ing the conditions under which a settlement is offered, but the impor-tance of this negotiation should not be overestimated.

In short, the Dutch public prosecutor operates in a sense like a pre-trial judge, assessing the evidence and merits of each case that lands on his desk by himself. Settlements out of court take place behind closed doors, and the prosecutor is not accountable to the police, vic-tims, the judge, or the defendant and is not required to consult with any of these parties.

The only form of control on the PPS in relation to filing criminal charges is a procedure laid down in article 12 of the Dutch Code of Criminal Procedure that allows a plaintiff to petition a court of appeal to order the PPS to prosecute. The annual number of requests has increased recently, from 1,200 in 2000 to 2,400 in 2010, a period when the number of cases brought to the PPS dropped from 266,859 to 208,596.[2] Roughly 10 percent of appealed cases result in rulings in

---

[2] The drop in recorded cases is partly attributable to changes in how crimes are recorded by the PPS (see Brouwers and Eggen 2011).

favor of the plaintiff (Brouwers and Eggen 2011). The combination of wide-ranging discretionary powers and relatively weak monitoring of their exercise shapes the position of the PPS in the Dutch criminal justice system.

II. One Individual, Three Roles

The Dutch public prosecutor plays three distinct, partly conflicting roles: as magistrate, frontline worker, and civil servant (van de Bunt 1985). In recent decades there have been shifts in emphasis between the roles. Discussing them brings the inherent tensions in the position of the public prosecutor to the surface.

A. The Magistrate

The Dutch public prosecutor's classical role is as a magistrate. He or she is a member of the judiciary who receives much the same training as judges, in terms of both university education and subsequent professional training. The principal responsibility in the role as magistrate is to engage in balanced and impartial weighing of all interests involved in a case. This function is comparable to that of a judge. The magistrate tries to make just decisions through the individualization of cases (e.g., taking into account differences between committed crimes, the background of the offender, circumstances under which the offense was committed, culpability). The main aim is not effectiveness or crime control, but justice. Indicatively, the term "crime fighter" is used mainly in a pejorative sense by most public prosecutors. Tak (2008, p. 54) notes that within the PPS the most appropriate attitude for prosecutors to manifest is to be detached and magisterial as judges are expected to be.

B. The (Frontline) Worker

Another role of the public prosecutor becomes visible on the shop floor: he is a worker who makes many decisions on a daily basis. The central concern is "getting the job done," which means dealing efficiently with a high caseload under time pressure. In order to do that, the worker is oriented toward reducing complexity as much as possible. He relies on his routine knowledge and, instead of individualizing each case, is oriented toward efficiently categorizing cases by stereotyping offenders and offenses (Sudnow 1965). When making speedy decisions, the worker focuses on a few decisive factors in the files in front of him. The magistrate is oriented toward individualizing cases and making just decisions; the worker is more focused on handling cases efficiently and generating output.

C. The Civil Servant

The third role is that of civil servant. The public prosecutor is a member of a hierarchical organization and is accountable to the minister of justice. In this role, the prosecutor is oriented toward executing the directives and policies of his organization. As a member of the state bureaucracy, he must be focused on the state's interests and take into consideration the instrumental goals of its criminal laws. He is expected to participate in developing and implementing governmental policies against crime. He is not primarily case oriented but focused on identifying and tackling crime problems in a larger context and in cooperation with other agencies.

D. Dynamics between the Magistrate and the Worker Roles

In the last four decades the case input into the PPS has increased dramatically. Remarkably, through those years a near-constant percentage of cases brought to the PPS have been settled out of court. The two most common out-of-court dispositions are decisions not to prosecute and transactions (to be explained in detail below). The number of nonprosecutions decreased from 53,290 cases in 1995 to 35,339 in 2008 (the last year for which data are available). Transactions increased from 57,608 in 1995 to 68,290 in 2008 (data from Statistics Netherlands 2012, http://www.cbs.nl/en-GB/menu/home/default.htm ?languageswitch = on). The availability of the transaction to settle cases out of court has essentially replaced the decision not to prosecute in a significant number of cases. Although the PPS started out as an agency responsible for bringing cases before a judge, in approximately 50 percent of all cases in our time, the final decision is made by the PPS itself (see tables 1 and 2).

The Dutch public prosecutor has broad discretion concerning prosecution of crimes. The prosecutor can decide not to prosecute on grounds of public interest. Other grounds for dismissal are that the offense involves minor harm or minor culpability or certain circumstances regarding the perpetrator such as ill health or addiction. Lack of sufficient evidence is a separate ground for dismissal.

TABLE 1

Recorded and Resolved Criminal Cases, 1960–2008

	1960	1970	1980	1990	2000	2008
Total recorded cases	121,318	136,135	229,771	260,844	233,324	260,228
Settled by the PPS	70,185	77,445	129,548	144,758	118,369	122,248
Settled by the courts	50,468	56,431	91,764	82,341	111,033	127,389
Proportion settled by PPS/court	1.4	1.4	1.4	1.8	1.1	1.0

SOURCE.—Data from Statistics Netherlands (2012), http://www.cbs.nl/en-GB/menu/home/default.htm?languageswitch=on.

TABLE 2

Cases Resolved by the Public Prosecution Service, 2005–10

	2005	2006	2007	2008	2009	2010
Total recorded cases	122,999	126,091	122,274	122,248	116,326	83,579
Dismissal	28,362	30,644	30,460	35,339	34,011	25,013
	(23.1%)	(24.3%)	(24.9%)	(28.9%)	(29.2%)	(29.9%)
Transaction	76,062	77,861	74,210	68,290	65,115	42,298
	(61.8%)	(61.7%)	(60.7%)	(55.9%)	(56.0%)	(50.6%)
Penal order	. . .	. . .	. . .	. . .	2,098	6,820
					(1.8%)	(8.2%)
Other	18,575	17,586	17,604	18,619	17,200	16,268
	(15.1%)	(14%)	(14.4%)	(15.2%)	(13%)	(11.3%)

SOURCE.—Brouwers and Eggen (2011).

There have been major changes in the decision-making process. In 1979–80, van de Bunt carried out a yearlong participant observation study inside the PPS (van de Bunt 1985). During this period all criminal cases were examined by public prosecutors and were therefore processed manually. However, a major change was that for the first time in the history of the PPS, nongraduate staff were involved in making decisions. The secretaries' task was to make summaries of files and to examine whether they met formal legal requirements. Secretaries were not allowed to make decisions on their own; at most they could advise the prosecutor on whether or not to prosecute. At the time, prosecutors had wide autonomy because there were few institutional directives and regulations.

Gradually, the emphasis in PPS decision making has shifted from the magistrate's toward the worker's role. All prosecutor's offices currently employ "processing programs," which are separate units that deal with particular kinds of cases: standard cases (such as shoplifting, burglary, violence, fraud), special cases, and sensitive cases. Special cases tend to involve serious crimes involving one or more offenders who have to await the verdict of the judge in custody. Sensitive cases are atypical and tend to attract large media coverage or to involve offenders who are considered to be a threat to society; politically sensitive cases, such as serious organized crime cases; or instances of terrorism and white-collar crime. The public prosecutor is directly involved in handling special and sensitive cases, and decision making is individualized and nonroutine. The prosecutor oversees the police investigation and participates in preparation for court sessions and during the sessions.

However, decision making in standard cases, which amount to about 80 percent of the total caseload, is entirely standardized. Directives have replaced discretion. The directives emanate from the Board of Prosecutors General and leave little room for individualized decisions in which nuances and special facets of a case are weighed. The directives are incorporated in the BOS-Polaris system, which emphasizes a small number of variables, thereby enabling speedy decisions.

BOS-Polaris is a computerized decision support system directed at the standardization of PPS decision making for common, high-volume offenses. These offenses are weighted according to a rule-based system in order to determine appropriate sentences. Bos-Polaris prescribes the decision to be made on the basis of a point score. Each base offense receives a fixed number of points. Bike theft receives 10 points, breaking and entering 60. Some aggravating (e.g., recidivism, discrimination) and alleviating circumstances (e.g., attempted as opposed to successful burglary) can lead to increases or decreases in points.

On the basis of the total number of points, the BOS-Polaris system prescribes the sanction. For scores up to 30 points, a case can be handled with a transaction requiring payment of a sum of money to the state, between 31 and 60 points a community penalty can be ordered (community work as a condition for a transaction), and with 61 points or higher the accused must appear in court. The point score also prescribes the sanction the prosecutor is to propose in court. Up until 120 points, a community penalty may be proposed. Above that, the prosecutor should in principle propose a prison sentence. As a rule of thumb, one point represents 1 day in prison (De Doelder 2011).

The variables weighed in the BOS-Polaris system pertain mostly to the offense, not to the offender. In cases of violence, for example, BOS-Polaris takes into account the location of the offense (e.g., domestic or traffic) and whether there was a relationship between the victim and the offender. The offender himself is hardly considered. Whether the offender is a recidivist or not, or acted alone or with others, is weighed, but other, more personal characteristics that may have influenced his behavior are not.

The BOS-Polaris system is heavily oriented toward efficiency. The system does not involve making decisions as the criteria applied to cases and the ensuing decisions result from ticking boxes. Public prosecutors are consulted only in exceptional cases that do not fit in the BOS-Polaris schemes. The decision makers are semiskilled PPS employees, who in case of uncertainty must consult a secretary of the public prosecutor or the programmers of the BOS-Polaris software.

BOS-Polaris is used in all 19 regional offices and is becoming a routine element of criminal proceedings. Because the system is public, the accused, his lawyer, and judges can calculate the variables in a specific case and check the decision by the prosecutor for errors. For cases serious enough to appear in court, the number of points that follows from the BOS-Polaris calculation has a certain authoritative status. Discussions in the courtroom increasingly center on whether the decision in a particular case should deviate from the standard one suggested by BOS-Polaris.

The standard case-processing program has resulted in greater speed and efficiency. An unforeseen consequence is that the BOS-Polaris system makes it possible to make policy changes quickly. For example, there recently was public outrage about an increase in violence against police officers, ambulance personnel, and other relief workers. After a parliamentary debate on the subject, the minister of justice urged the Board of Public Prosecutors to toughen sentences for the perpetrators of these crimes. By adjusting BOS-Polaris, the PPS implemented the change overnight.

As a result of standardization of the decision-making process, the third role of the public prosecutor, that of a civil servant who executes government policies, has come more to the fore. We examine this role in more detail below. It might be thought from the discussion of BOS-Polaris that the magistrate role of the prosecutor has been absorbed into the worker role, but this is not true. Ironically, thanks to efficiency measures, the role of the PPS has become more judicial. The PPS has gained a number of quasi-judicial powers in the form of transactions and punishment orders and now has authority to impose sanctions without the involvement of a judge. As a result of the new efficiency measures, the PPS has steadily gained adjudicatory powers formerly exclusively within the domain of the judge.

E. The Punishment Order and the Transaction

Transactions are a form of diversion in which offenders are given the opportunity to pay a specified amount of money or fulfill one or more other conditions (e.g., community service) to avoid prosecution and public trial. If the suspect disagrees, the case is taken to court. Transactions are most often used for relatively minor offenses such as shoplifting or minor damage to property. However, the range of offenses for which transactions may be offered has increased since their introduction in 1983 from infractions that were in principle punishable only with a fine to crimes that carry a prison sentence of up to 6 years.

Since 2008, the PPS has also been given authority to impose a punishment order for a number of common offenses. Punishment orders can entail a fine, community service, or entry into a training program. Defendants may appeal an order, after which the case is referred to a judge. A punishment order can be imposed for crimes punishable by a prison sentence up to 6 years. Offenders who do not comply with the conditions will be summoned to appear in court.

The punishment order is a sanction. In a transaction, by contrast, the offense is not punished as such but entails a settlement between the prosecutor and the suspect (Kessler and Keulen 2008). The punishment order thus departs from the basic principle that only criminal courts can impose penalties (De Doelder 2000; Kessler and Keulen 2008). The transaction and the punishment order are prime examples of the fusion of worker role considerations and the magisterial role of prosecutors: they require impartiality and a careful weighing of all interests but have clearly been introduced because of efficiency considerations.

F. The Emergence of the Civil Servant

The emergence of the civil servant role since the 1960s has been an important change. Two factors contributed to this restyling of the PPS.

First, during the 1960s, inconsistencies in decisions of different offices and individual prosecutors became increasingly visible. Differences in decisions to prosecute were highly contested, and the PPS found itself no longer able to credibly justify inconsistencies by referring to differences between individual cases. There was a lack of coordination within the PPS and a lack of internal discussion about directives and policies.

This criticism resulted in major changes. Individual decision making combined with a great deal of discretionary power was replaced by decision making structured through directives. At the end of the 1970s, national guidelines were developed for handling common crimes such as shoplifting and drunk driving. For the first time, the PPS activated its sleeping hierarchical structure to pursue coordinated policies that enabled prosecutors to determine what kind of cases should be brought to court and what sentences the courts should be asked to impose (van de Bunt 1985, pp. 64–113; Steenhuis 1986).

Second, it became increasingly clear that the PPS was powerless in the face of rising crime levels. In the 1960s and 1970s, crime was seen as primarily the responsibility of professionals such as magistrates and the probation services, but the increasing crime rates of the 1980s led to questions about the effectiveness of this approach. It was understood that appointing more magistrates and expanding the police force would not suffice to deal with the rise in crime rates. In 1985 in "Society and Crime," the white paper discussed above, the national government launched its first policy plan to control crime (Ministry of Justice 1985; see also Blankenburg and van de Bunt 1986; van de Bunt 1986).

The PPS was directed to develop a crime control strategy and formulate related policies on local and national levels. The document did not propose more of the same—that is, more judicial and police personnel and increased prison capacity. More money was allocated to these areas, but the most important element of the plan was that the effort to control crime was no longer to be perceived as a matter for the police and the justice system alone. The emphasis was on prevention of crime by mobilizing people and services outside the justice system. This policy plan constitutes an example of what Garland terms the "responsibilization of society" (1996, pp. 445–71). Encouraged and partly funded by the central government, local authorities and the business community started to invest in crime prevention. The PPS was given a key role in implementing the new crime strategies. Public prosecutors were now supposed to focus on responsibilization by entering into a dialogue with local administrators and police in order to set the right priorities and shape a multiagency approach to crime control.

These strategic changes and expectations formed the impetus for restyling the PPS from a loosely integrated organization centered on the prosecutor as a magistrate into an integrated national organization emphasizing the role of the public prosecutor as a "civil servant." The PPS was forced to change its focus. Previously the judge was the main reference point for public prosecutors, and their duties revolved around reaching the right decisions in individual cases. Now the police and public administrators are the prosecutor's main partners in the search for effective strategies to deal with crime.

Prosecutors have become discussion partners of city mayors and chiefs of police working together in shaping criminal policy and defining local police priorities in triparty consultations. When determining priorities, questions may come up as to which types of offenses the police should focus their attention on. For instance, should the emphasis be on investigating human trafficking or on street violence? The management of the police service may also come up in these talks. The head of the local office of the PPS is by law obligated to consult with the mayor of a city and the chief of police in his district, and he has the power of co-decision with respect to the organization, formation, budget, and policy for the regional police force.

The triparty consultations also play an important role in coordinating the approach to major incidents such as serious crimes, terrorist attacks, or gross violations of public order. Apart from such incidents, efforts also are made to coordinate the tackling of other crime problems. For instance, in the approach to illegal street races, human trafficking, or domestic violence, a programmed procedure can be initiated. In these cases the triparty consultation partners agree with each other on their respective shares in dealing with the problem. For instance, the PPS promises to prioritize prosecution of participants in illegal street races, provided that the municipality designates a legal area where such races can take place under controlled conditions. The police, in turn, promise to ensure that future legalized street races will proceed in an orderly fashion (Den Breejen 2011, p. 22).

The police and the public administrators are not the only consultation partners of the PPS. Depending on the nature of the offenses, the public prosecutor will also consult with public notaries, medical specialists, or financial service providers in cases in which professionals are involved in serious crimes. In this way an attempt is made to prevent recidivism.

In sum, during the past decades the policy element has pushed itself increasingly to the foreground. The Board of Prosecutors General and the minister of justice have reshaped the service into a governmental organization in an ambitious attempt to shift its professional emphasis from that of magistrate to that of civil servant. This, however, is not to say that the PPS has become an ordinary state bureaucracy; the main force in developing prosecution policies is still the service itself. Local prosecutors have a broad mandate to enter into arrangements with mayors and local police forces. The national policies of the PPS, that is, the priorities set at the national level, are mainly determined by the Board of Prosecutors General instead of by the minister of justice. Although crime control has become a politically sensitive issue, the PPS itself has not become politicized. There can be little doubt that the PPS has become more hierarchically structured and that public prosecutors are expected to act as civil servants in the implementation of policies and guidelines. Yet, the PPS remains an extraordinary organization. It is still considered to be part of the independent judiciary, even though the prosecutors/magistrates of previous times are now largely operating outside the confines of the judiciary.

III. Monitoring the Police

Authority over criminal investigations resides with the PPS. The police have to account for their actions to a public prosecutor, and all investigations are carried out under the PPS's auspices to ensure that the relevant legal rules and procedures are observed. In case of serious offenses, the public prosecutor is directly in charge of the investigation.[3] In practice, this means that a prosecutor deliberates regularly with police investigators and makes the main strategic decisions regarding the scope of the investigation, such as whether coercive measures will be used and who will be targeted in the investigation.

The police organization and the PPS are separate entities. The prosecutor may be in charge of the investigation, but there is no hierarchical relation between personnel of the two organizations. In practice,

---

[3] The PPS is also responsible for supervising investigations carried out by other investigating authorities, such as the municipal social services, the Fiscal Intelligence and Investigation Service, and the Economic Investigation Service.

prosecutors are relatively dependent on the police because they have to rely on information gathered by them. If the police do not start an investigation or do not share information, a prosecutor is left empty-handed. Many cases never reach the PPS because the police dismiss them (De Doelder 2000, p. 191). The Netherlands Court of Audit recently concluded that 70 percent of all crimes registered by the police are dismissed, that is, not taken into investigation. Only 8 percent of crimes recorded by the police are sent to the PPS (Rekenkamer 2012). Through the use of directives, the PPS attempts to ensure that the priorities they set are leading for the police in selecting cases.

If necessary, the public prosecutor can authorize the police to apply certain coercive measures, such as confiscation of stolen goods or arrest of a suspect. The PPS's powers are not unlimited, however, and measures such as house searches or wiretapping are beyond its mandate. In cases of complicated or serious crimes that require such intrusive measures, the public prosecutor needs permission from an investigating judge (Tak 2008).

Until the 1970s, the general requirement that a public prosecutor direct all police investigations was seldom followed. The police had nearly free rein to conduct criminal investigations unless there was a need for involvement of the public prosecutor or an investigating judge concerning use of intrusive measures. As a result all sorts of miscommunication arose. This affected, first of all, the selection of cases. In a period characterized by an increase in reported crimes (and dwindling police resources), a relatively large number of cases investigated by the police did not result in prosecution. The PPS did not deem these cases serious enough to take them to court or decided that there was not enough evidence for a successful complaint. Both reasons were evidence of a lack of communication between the police and the PPS in a period when the available resources were already insufficient. This prompted the PPS to develop a clearer policy and to set priorities concerning use of police resources.

Second, the distance between the police and the PPS in the 1970s and 1980s resulted in several major blunders in the investigation of complex fraud cases, organized crimes, and white-collar crimes. Some cases took years of police investigation without leading to any significant result in court. Uncontrolled investigative methods were thought out on the shop floor and eventually led to the Interregionaal Recherche Team affair (see Fijnaut et al. 1998). The affair concerned joint investigation teams made up from several regional police forces that had used unacceptable investigation methods. For example, several tons of drugs were imported into the country under the supervision of the authorities (Kleemans 2007). The main conclusions of a Parliamentary Inquiry Committee were that "there was a legal vacuum concerning criminal investigation methods, that the organization of the criminal justice system was inadequate, and that the command and control of criminal investigations should be improved" (Kleemans 2007, p. 165).

Since then, the position of the public prosecutor during police investigations has changed dramatically (van de Bunt 2004, p. 711). A new Special Powers of Investigation Act (2000) prescribed the direct involvement of a prosecutor in complex criminal investigations and reduced the role of the examining judge. Meanwhile, two national offices of the PPS were established with a view to improving the quality and capacity of the PPS in monitoring complex police investigations into organized crime and white-collar crime (see above). At present, public prosecutors are directly involved in serious or sensitive cases in police investigations. This has not resulted in prosecutors developing into crime fighters. Their role and attitude remain magisterial; they are charged with monitoring the application of methods of investigation. Working in the front line of the fight against serious crime, the prosecutor has not turned into a supercop but continues to be a member of the judiciary.

IV. Political Affiliations and Beliefs and Selection and Training

There has been a substantial increase over the past 40 years in the number of public prosecutors and, especially, the number of staff members (see table 3). The PPS has evolved into a large organization.

TABLE 3
Prosecutors and Judges, Selected Years, 1951–2008

	1951	1974	1986	1995	2000
Judges	317	494	694	1,223	1,546
Public prosecutors	94	152	238	391	450
Total	411	646	932	1,614	1,996

SOURCE.—De Groot–van Leeuwen (2006).

A. Joining the PPS

Since 1957, there are two ways of joining the judiciary, which comprises both judges and prosecutors. One way is for people with a university law degree to enter the 6-year Raio training program.[4] Currently, around 30 percent of all magistrates, both judges and prosecutors, come from the Raio training program (van der Kraats et al. 2010). Alternatively, 6 years of working experience as a legal professional allows one to enter the judiciary directly. Here, too, a university law degree is required. The other statutory requirement for becoming a member of the judiciary as a judge or prosecutor is having Dutch nationality.

The Raio training program consists of theoretical and on-the-job training in the form of internships. The first half of the program is identical for aspiring judges and prosecutors, and compulsory internships are done in both a district court and a district prosecution office. After 3 years, a choice is made to become a judge or a prosecutor. The admission criteria mentioned by the Raio education institute include analytical skills, legal insight, decision-making ability, ability to perform under stress, communication skills, and judgment ability.

The selection procedure for outsiders who want to enter the judiciary occurs under the auspices of a special-purpose selection committee. There are several interviews with committee members and a psychological assessment. A third option concerns only internal candidates from the PPS. Legal staff at the district level who have a law degree, Dutch nationality, and 4 years of work experience as a senior secretary can apply to become a public prosecutor in sections of the court presided over by a single judge. After 2 years of work experience, the candidate can apply for a regular prosecutorial position.

B. Demographic Characteristics

A number of polls and surveys have been conducted among members of the judiciary and the PPS. The main results are summarized below. Some polls and surveys were conducted among students of the Raio training program. As the training program is identical for future judges and prosecutors, sometimes no results are available for the groups separately. When this is the case, this is indicated.

The PPS has experienced important changes in composition over

---

[4] Raio stands for "judicial servant in training."

the last four decades. An early study on political preferences and social backgrounds of magistrates showed that in the 1970s there was an overrepresentation of the higher social classes in the Raio training program, but there were no differences in political preferences compared to law students generally (Ten Kate and van Koppen 1977). More recent, large-scale surveys of judges and public prosecutors show that the higher social classes continue to be overrepresented in both (*Vrij Nederland* 1991, 2003). According to De Groot–van Leeuwen (2006), law students generally tend to come from the higher social classes compared with other types of university students.

Greater ethnic diversity is widely considered to be a policy priority in order to make the judiciary more representative of society. The Council for the Judiciary has a "diversity employee," and law students from nonnative Dutch backgrounds are actively approached to encourage interest in working for the judiciary (van der Kraats et al. 2010). In 2010 around 5 percent of respondents in a Raio training program survey had at least one parent who was born in a non-Western country. This indicates underrepresentation compared with law faculties at universities in the Netherlands, where the corresponding percentage is 10.2 percent (van der Kraats et al. 2010). However, the percentage of nonnative applicants for the Raio training program is 10.8 percent, showing that uneven representation of nonnatives does not result from lack of interest. According to van der Kraats et al. (2010), underrepresentation results from lower scores on an analytic aptitude test that aspiring magistrates must take to enroll. Even though bicultural applicants may take an alternative test, this has not led to the "desired results."

There has been a marked gender shift over the last two decades. As recently as the early 1990s, two-thirds of the Dutch judiciary were men; the number of female prosecutors and judges has been increasing rapidly since and is expected to continue to grow. In 2010, 51 percent of judges were women, while 76 percent of students of the Raio training program were (van der Kraats et al. 2010). However, females are still underrepresented in the higher positions in the courts and the PPS.

C. *Political Preferences*

There have been some important changes in recent decades in political preferences among the judiciary. In the early 1970s, the dominant political orientation was conservative (and denominational). As a consequence of pressure from society and opposition groups in Parliament, but also from within the judiciary (Ten Kate and van Koppen 1977), political orientations became more diverse.

In 1970 two-thirds of the judiciary, both judges and PPS, voted either Christian-Democrat or Liberal/Right; this fell to around 30 percent in 1991. In the same period, the group expressing moderate left political preferences grew from 11 to 39 percent, only to fall to around 20 percent in 2003; that was still about twice the national average. There has also been a steady increase in preference for the Social Democratic Party since 1970 from 21 to 29 percent.[5]

De Groot–van Leeuwen (2006) notes that the political preferences of the judiciary have become more diverse since the early 1970s. While in the 1970s almost 90 percent of the judiciary had a preference for one of the three main political parties (Liberal, Social-Democrat, and Christian-Democrat), this had fallen to 65 percent in 2001. During the largely "left" years in Dutch society around 1970, the political preferences of the judiciary were largely right wing. Currently there is a dominance of left-leaning preferences (while the Dutch population has shifted to the right).[6]

V. Conclusions

Within the Public Prosecution System, tensions can be observed among the prosecutor's roles as a magistrate who weighs all interests involved and whose main concern is impartiality, as a worker handling a large caseload under time pressure and whose main concern is efficiency, and as a civil servant who develops and implements policies and whose main concern is the effectiveness of the criminal justice system.

Many of the changes in the Dutch PPS over recent decades play out in this force field. The role of the worker has unmistakably gained prominence at the expense of the role of the magistrate. Minor offenses dealt with manually 15 years ago are now processed automatically. The

---

[5] Christian Democrats and populist parties are represented little or not at all among students of the Raio training program (van der Kraats et al. 2010). This was also the situation in the early 1990s (De Groot–van Leeuwen 1991).

[6] The political profile of candidates is not a criterion for selection. There is no preference for hardliners or crime fighters. Since the selection criteria and procedures are the same for judges and public prosecutors, crime fighters are unlikely to succeed (see also van der Kraats et al. 2010).

reduction in complexity and in the number of factors in the decision equation designed to deal with an increasing caseload has been detrimental to careful and cautious magisterial decision making. The PPS has been transformed from a closed legal culture into an open organization that operates in local and national networks and both develops and executes policy; this implies a greater prominence of the civil servant role. At the same time, and in spite of all the changes, magisterial elements persist within the PPS. Their position has become more judicial in that they now possess power to impose sanctions as if they were judges and they play a judge-like role in complex police investigations.

REFERENCES

Blankenburg, E., and H. G. van de Bunt, eds. 1986. "Samenleving en criminaliteit." *Tijdschrift voor Criminologie* 28(5–6):215–339.

Brouwers, M., and A. Th. J. Eggen. 2011. "Vervolging." In *Criminaliteit en rechtshandhaving 2010*, edited by S. N. Kalidien and N. E. De Heer–de Lange. Meppel: Boom Juridische Uitgevers.

Commissie Toedeling Zaakspakketten. 2008. *Specialisatie, concentratie en kwaliteit van rechtspraak*. The Hague: Raad voor de Rechtspraak.

De Doelder, H. 2000. "The Public Prosecutor Service in the Netherlands." *European Journal of Crime, Criminal Law, and Criminal Justice* 3:187–208.

———. 2002. "Richtlijnen en rechtshandhaving." In *De weging van 't Hart*, edited by K. Boonen. Deventer: Kluwer.

———. 2011. "Computergebruik bij straftoemeting." In *Something Bigger Than Yourself? Essays in Honour of Richard de Mulder*, edited by P. Kleve. Rotterdam: Erasmus School of Law.

De Groot–van Leeuwen, L. E. 1991. *De rechterlijke macht in Nederland: Samenstelling en denkbeelden van de zittende en staande magistratuur*. Arnhem: Gouda Quint.

———. 2006. "De samenstelling van de rechterlijke macht." In *Rechterlijke macht: Studies over rechtspraak en rechtshandhaving in Nederland*, edited by E. R. Muller and C. P. M. Cleiren. Deventer: Wolters Kluwer.

Den Breejen, M. 2011. "Kicken op snelheid." *Blauw* 14:22–25.

Fijnaut, C. J. C. F. 2002. "The Administrative Approach to Organised Crime in Amsterdam: Backgrounds and Developments." In *The Administrative Approach to (Organized) Crime in Amsterdam*, edited by C. J. C. F. Fijnaut. Amsterdam: Public Order and Safety Department.

Fijnaut, C., F. Bovenkerk, G. Bruinsma, and H. van de Bunt. 1998. *Organized Crime in the Netherlands*. The Hague: Kluwer Law International.

Garland, D. 1996. "The Limits of the Sovereign State: Strategies of Crime Control in Contemporary Society." *British Journal of Criminology* 36(4):445–71.

Groenhuijsen, M. S. 2008. "Slachtoffers van misdrijven in het recht en in de victimologie: Verslag van een intellectuele zoektocht." *Delikt en Delinkwent* 38(2):121–45.

't Hart, A. C. 2006. "Het nieuwe OM." In *Rechterlijke macht: Studies over rechtspraak en rechtshandhaving in Nederland*, edited by E. R. Muller and C. P. M. Cleiren. Deventer: Wolters Kluwer.

Kessler, M., and B. F. Keulen. 2008. *De Strafbeschikking*. Deventer: Kluwer.

Kleemans, E. R. 2007. "Organized Crime, Transit Crime, and Racketeering." In *Crime and Justice in the Netherlands*, edited by Michael Tonry and Catrien Bijleveld. Vol. 35 of *Crime and Justice: A Review of Research*, edited by Michael Tonry. Chicago: University of Chicago Press.

Ministry of Justice. 1985. *Samenleving en criminaliteit: Een beleidsplan voor de komende jaren*. The Hague: Research and Documentation Centre.

Rekenkamer, Algemene. 2012. *Prestaties in de strafrechtsketen*. Tweede Kamer, 2011–12 (report), 33 173. The Hague: Staatsuitgeverij.

Steenhuis, D. 1986. "Coherence and Coordination in the Administration of Criminal Justice." In *Criminal Law in Action*, edited by J. van Dijk et al. Arnhem: Gouda Quint.

Sudnow, D. 1965. "Normal Crimes: Sociological Features of the Penal Code in a Public Defender Office." *Social Problems* 12(3):255–76.

Tak, P. J. P. 2008. *The Dutch Criminal Justice System*. Nijmegen: Wolf Legal Publishers.

Ten Kate, J., and P. J. van Koppen. 1977. "Weledelgestrenge selectie: Een onderzoek naar de selectie voor de Raio-opleiding." Unpublished manuscript. Erasmus Universiteit, Juridisch Instituut.

van Daele, D. 2003. *Het openbaar ministerie en de afhandeling van strafzaken in Nederland*. Leuven: Universitaire Pers Leuven.

van de Bunt, H. G. 1985. *Officieren van justitie: Verslag van een participerend observatieonderzoek*. Zwolle: Tjeenk Willink.

———. 1986. "Drift en koers." *Tijdschrift voor Criminologie* 28(5–6):280–302.

———. 2004. "Organised Crime Policies in the Netherlands." In *Organised Crime in Europe: Concepts, Patterns, and Control Policies in the European Union and Beyond*, edited by C. J. C. F. Fijnaut and L. Paoli. Dordrecht: Springer.

van der Kraats, K., M. Croes, A. Klijn, and A. Diephuis. 2010. *Magistrale perspectieven: De Raio's anno 2010*. Zutphen: SSR. http://www.ssr.nl/uploads/Pdf-documenten/Boekjes/SSR_boekje%20enquete.pdf.

van der Schoot, C. R. A. 2006. *Organised Crime Prevention in the Netherlands*. The Hague: Boom Juridische uitgevers.

Vrij Nederland. 1991. "Vrij Nederland. De rechterlijke macht van Nederland: Een geruststellend gezelschap." November 2.

———. 2003. "Grote Vrij Nederland. Rechterlijke macht onder vuur." December 11.

Petter Asp

The Prosecutor in Swedish Law

ABSTRACT

Prosecutors in Sweden are not elected. They are selected meritocratically under procedures that are nonpartisan and nonpolitical. They are career civil servants but of a special—highly autonomous—kind. The Swedish prosecutor has three main tasks: to conduct the investigation of an offense (with the assistance of the police), to decide whether or not to prosecute, and to represent the state once a case comes to court. The main principles that apply to the work of the prosecutor are the principle of legality (i.e., in principle, cases have to be investigated and taken to trial if there is reason to expect a conviction) and the principle of impartiality (the prosecutor should also take into account factors that point in favor of the defendant). High importance is also attached to the value of equality (the result should ideally be the same no matter who the prosecutor is or where in Sweden the case is dealt with).

The Swedish Prosecution Service is formally part of the national government, but in practice it operates as an independent part of the judicial system. The national headquarters is in Stockholm. However, the service is divided into 32 local prosecution offices, in which most of the daily work is carried out.

Under Swedish law, the prosecutor has three main tasks: to investigate offenses (with the assistance of the police), to decide whether to prosecute, and to represent the state once a case comes to court. In performing these tasks, prosecutors are guided by two overriding principles: the prosecutorial principle of legality (the prosecutor is obliged

Petter Asp is a professor of criminal law at Stockholm University. He is grateful to Iain Cameron, Nicklas Englund, Per Lennerbrant, Nils Rekke, and Jenny Ahlner Wetterqvist for various forms of assistance.

to investigate cases and to prosecute them when there is reason to believe that a conviction will result) and the principle of impartiality (the prosecutor should take into account not only facts and circumstances that are incriminating to the defendant but also those that point in his or her favor). Strong emphasis is also given to the achievement of equal treatment, that is, that cases are dealt with in the same manner throughout the country.

There is not much debate about the prosecutorial system as such (though at times there is debate about how particular cases are handled). Insofar as the system is changing, recent developments can probably be described in terms of a trend toward a more flexible and pragmatic system or of a search for ways to deal with a growing number of cases within a prosecutorial system based on the principle of legality; recent changes and proposals concerning delimitation of preliminary investigations to principal offenders are illustrative.

In this essay, I discuss the role and position of the prosecutor under current Swedish law.[1] This includes a description of the powers of the prosecutor and of the general rules and principles that direct the prosecutor's work. In addition, I discuss the general understanding of what a prosecutor is, how prosecutors see themselves, and how one might answer the more general question "who is a prosecutor in Sweden today?"

Section I provides general information about Sweden and about the organization of the prosecution service. Section II offers a very brief historical sketch. In Section III, I describe the role of the Swedish prosecutor and in Section IV discuss basic principles of the Swedish system of criminal procedure that are of special importance to the role of the prosecutor. Section V discusses selection, training, and career structures and provides information on the demographic characteristics of Swedish prosecutors. I conclude by discussing the notorious (and, as this is written, ongoing) case of Julian Assange, the founder of Wikileaks. This is not done for the primary purpose of discussing the case as such but because it provides a concrete illustration of fundamental features of the Swedish system. The Assange case is not exceptional, but it reflects the basic structure of the system.

---

[1] The text discusses basic features of the Swedish system. I have not provided references in all instances in which it would have been possible. Basic books and articles on the Swedish prosecutorial systems are contained in the reference list.

I. Sweden and Its Prosecution System

Sweden is a constitutional monarchy with about 9 million inhabitants. Most people live in the southern part of the country. There is a concentration of people in Sweden's three metropolitan areas: Stockholm in the east, Gothenburg in the west, and Malmo in the south. There are approximately 2 million people in the Stockholm metropolitan area.[2] Sweden is a representative democracy. The king is head of state but has no real power. The Parliament consists of 349 members elected under a system of proportional representation. This assures that any party receiving significant support is represented in Parliament and means that governments are often coalitions. The prime minister is selected by the Parliament and forms the government.

The Swedish constitutional system is not formally based on the doctrine of separation of powers; the fundamental constitutional principle is popular sovereignty. This does not mean, of course, that the power of the people acting through the elected members of Parliament is unlimited. There is, for example, a constitutional prohibition of government interference with the decision making of the courts and judicial authorities in individual cases. The courts have been entrusted with enhanced powers of legal review (a reformed version of the Instrument of Government, the most important constitutional document, took effect in 2011).[3] In practice, the Swedish judicial system is little different from systems in countries whose constitutions are based on a formal separation of powers.

One important element in the public exercise of control over the government and also over politicians generally is the principle of public access to official documents, which was accorded constitutional status in chapter 2, section 1, of the Freedom of the Press Act: "to encourage the free exchange of opinion and availability of comprehensive information, every Swedish citizen shall be entitled to have free access to official documents." This means that officials must almost always (there are exceptions that build on laws on secrecy) expect that their actions and decisions will be scrutinized by individual citizens or the media. The individual's right to see public documents is mirrored in a right

---

[2] For a more detailed description of Sweden and the Swedish criminal justice system, see Cameron et al. (2011).

[3] The Instrument of Government is one of four constitutional documents. The others are the Freedom of the Press Act, the Freedom of Expression Act, and the Act of Succession.

for officials to provide information to the media and to other persons outside the state agency in question. The importance of this principle for the proper exercise of public power can hardly be overestimated.

The Swedish Prosecution Service. The main elements of the Swedish judicial system are the judiciary (*Domstolsväsendet*), the prosecution service (*Åklagarmyndigheten*), the police (*Polizen*), and the Swedish prison and probation service (*Kriminalvården*) (see Zila 2006, p. 285). These authorities are organized under the government but are independent when applying the law and dealing with individual cases. This independence is protected by the Instrument of Government and is respected in practice.

Sweden has slightly more than 900 prosecutors. Around 80 are employed by the Swedish Economic Crimes Bureau and the rest by the National Prosecution Service. It has responsibility for the whole country. The prosecutor general heads the prosecution system. The prosecutor general at the time of writing is Anders Perklev, who has a background in the courts and in government ministries. The prosecutor general is appointed by the government and has enhanced employment protection comparable to that of judges. The goal of such enhanced protection is to guarantee independence and integrity. It is theoretically possible to remove a person appointed as prosecutor general from serving as head of the National Prosecution Service, but he or she would continue to be the prosecutor general. In practice, this has never happened.

The Stockholm office of the prosecutor general houses the organization's basic administrative functions. A legal division deals with, among other things, bringing cases to the Supreme Court, with international questions, and with the development of information and guidelines concerning various legal questions.

Three prosecution development centers, located in Stockholm, Gothenburg, and Malmo, deal with legal and methodological developments. The development center in Stockholm is responsible for theft, fraud, forgery, terrorist offenses, corruption, perjury, and money laundering and also for issues related to sentencing. The development center in Gothenburg is responsible for domestic violence, victims' issues, and questions related to DNA and also for other offenses including violence, trafficking in human beings, and sexual offenses. The development center in Malmo has responsibility for environmental offenses, smuggling of goods, traffic offenses, and questions related to human rights. The development centers produce extensive legal memoranda and instruction manuals on diverse subjects. The development centers also handle appeals against, or reviews of, decisions made by ordinary prosecutors.

Within the National Prosecution Service there are 32 local prosecution offices in which most day-to-day work is done. There are also three international prosecution offices that deal with organized transnational crime, international cooperation, and the like and four national prosecution chambers that deal, respectively, with corruption, environmental offenses, offenses committed by the police, and issues related to security or terrorism. Formally, the National Prosecution Service is an executive agency of the government. In practice, it has great independence and is perceived by the public to be an independent part of the judicial system.

II. Historical Context

Crime and punishment were not initially state concerns but a matter to be resolved between the perpetrator and the injured party. Around 1600, particularly as incarceration and fines became accepted forms of punishment, representatives of the Crown began to initiate charges on behalf of injured parties. Later on, Crown representatives also began to bring charges in cases in which there was no individual victim. Crime and punishment gradually became matters for the state rather than for the individual.

The interest of the state in reacting to and punishing crimes was manifested in three ways. First, the right of the injured party to bring charges was in some instances transformed into a duty. Second, inquisitorial processes were developed under which the court could try a case independently of any indictment. Third, the right and duty to bring charges were given to state officials; this is where the idea of a prosecutor came from.[4]

Only recently, however, was a designated professional prosecution authority established. For centuries, state representatives brought charges against persons suspected of committing crimes. However, until early in the twentieth century, this was but one of many functions

---

[4] For more detailed information about the historical development, see Träskman (1980), Landström (2011), and the website of the National Prosecution Service, http://www.aklagare.se.

of the bailiff (*länsman*), who was simultaneously head of the police, the prosecutor, and the enforcement agency.

Prosecution authorities were created early in the twentieth century, and the *landsfiskal* took over the prosecutorial tasks of the *länsman*. Not until 1948, however, when the new Swedish Code of Judicial Procedure (SCJP) took effect, was the term *åklagare* (prosecutor) introduced into Swedish law, and not until 1965 (when the new Swedish Criminal Code [SCC] took effect) were the prosecution authorities fully separated from the police.

The prosecution service was originally organized at state, regional, and local levels. In 1965 there were 21 regional prosecution authorities with 90 local authorities under them. The number of regional prosecution authorities was reduced during the 1980s and 1990s to six, and a separate authority, the Swedish Economic Crimes Bureau, composed of prosecutors, policemen, and accountants, was created to deal with what was considered in the 1980s to be a serious increase in economic crimes.

Finally, in 2005, the prosecution service became a single authority and the prosecutor general became its head. Since then, except for specialist offices, the prosecution service has been a two-level organization: a central level consisting of the office of the prosecutor general and the three prosecution development centers and a local level consisting of the local prosecution offices.

III. The Role of the Prosecutor

Prosecutorial functions and institutions are not regulated in the constitution of Sweden except for a few rules concerning prosecution of members of specified groups, for example, members of the Parliament. There is, however, a constitutional prohibition against interference with decision making by the courts and other authorities in individual cases.[5] Neither the Parliament nor the government may interfere in cases dealt with by the prosecution service. The prosecutor thus has constitutionally guaranteed independence in making decisions about individual cases. As I discuss below, prosecutors are also independent from direction by their superiors, up to and including the prosecutor general, in making case-level decisions.

---

[5] Concerning the courts, see the Instrument of Government, chap. 11, sec. 3; concerning other authorities, see chap. 12, sec. 2.

Chapter 7 of the SCJP is devoted to the prosecution service. However, it contains only nine paragraphs and lays out only very basic rules, partly of an organizational nature. For example, it explains what a public prosecutor is, indicates that the prosecutor general heads the National Prosecution Service, and prescribes under what circumstances a senior prosecutor can take over a case from a lower prosecutor.

The SCJP rules are supplemented by rules in the ordinance on the prosecution service. This contains more detailed rules on the authority of different categories of prosecutors, on requirements to become a prosecutor, and on similar matters. This ordinance is, in turn, supplemented by government-issued instructions that lay out only organizational rules.

A. Three Primary Tasks

The Swedish prosecutor has three primary responsibilities: to investigate offenses (with the aid of the police), to decide whether to prosecute a case, and to represent the state in court.

1. *The Investigation.* The purpose of the preliminary investigation is to learn whether an offense has been committed and by whom, whether there is sufficient evidence to prosecute the suspect, and whether the case should be prepared for a hearing. With the exception of minor offenses, which the police may investigate on their own, the prosecutor oversees the investigation as soon as there is a suspect. The prosecutor will decide how to conduct the investigation, whether coercive measures should be used, and similar matters. The investigation, however, is conducted by the police. The prosecutor is expected simultaneously to direct the work of the police and control the work of the police, for example, by deciding whether there is reason to use certain coercive measures, such as holding suspects in custody awaiting a decision on detention, authorizing searches of premises, or prohibiting suspects from traveling. Some especially intrusive investigative measures, such as wiretapping, must be authorized by a judge upon application by the prosecutor.

When the preliminary investigation is completed, the prosecutor must decide whether to initiate proceedings. This decision is made by the individual prosecutor responsible for a case on his or her own. The guiding policy is set out in chapter 20, section 6, of the SCJP: "unless otherwise prescribed, prosecutors must prosecute offenses falling within the domain of public prosecution." This is generally understood to mean that the prosecutor is obliged to initiate proceedings whenever he or she—on objective grounds—believes that an indictment will lead to a conviction. This assessment primarily concerns the question of whether there is sufficient evidence that the suspect has committed the offense, but it necessarily also involves questions of law, such as checking that the alleged conduct is actually criminal.[6] There is no system of plea bargaining or plea agreements under Swedish law. However, the prosecutor may end the preliminary investigation without taking the case to trial by issuing a penal order or waiving prosecution. These powers are discussed below.

2. *The Decision to Prosecute.* Not all cases must be taken to trial. For less serious offenses the prosecutor can issue a penal order (which may include a fine or a conditional sentence). For even less serious offenses, punishable only by lump-sum fines, the police have authority to issue a regulatory fine. The main rules concerning penal orders are set out in chapter 48, sections 4–5, of the SCJP:

Section 4. Fines may be ordered by summary penalty orders concerning offenses in respect of which fines are included in the range of penalties.

Conditional sentences or such a sanction coupled with a fine may be ordered by means of a summary penalty order in cases in which it is obvious that the court would order such a sanction. However, this does not apply to offenses committed by a person younger than 18 years if there is reason to combine the conditional sentence with a community service order.

Corporate fines may also be ordered by summary penalty orders in cases where the fine does not exceed 500,000 kr.

Section 5. Orders for summary penalty may not be issued, if the preconditions for public prosecution do not exist, if the order does not include all offenses committed by the suspect that are under consideration according to the knowledge of the prosecutor, or if the aggrieved person has declared that he intends to institute an action for a private claim in consequence of the offense relating to other than an obligation to pay.

The penal order system is a simplified way of dealing with less se-

[6] See Elwing (1960) and Fitger (2012) for commentary on chap. 20, sec. 6, of the SCJP.

TABLE 1

Prosecutorial Case Dispositions by Offense Category and Type of Disposition, Sweden, 2010

| | | | | No Charges | | |
| | | | | --- | --- | |
	Prosecution	Penal Order	Waiver of Prosecution	Not Enough Evidence	Other Reasons	Total
Violence	39,624	1,183	3,880	5,831	1,233	51,751
	(77%)	(2%)	(7%)	(11%)	(2%)	(100%)
Drugs	35,893	8,996	10,940	2,929	1,177	59,935
	(60%)	(15%)	(18%)	(5%)	(2%)	(100%)
Environmental offenses	168	123	11	24	136	462
	(36%)	(27%)	(2%)	(5%)	(29%)	(100%)
Economic offenses	2,156	584	168	358	192	3,458
	(62%)	(17%)	(5%)	(10%)	(6%)	(100%)
Offenses on the level of fines	17,799	14,219	4,112	2,874	1,019	40,023
	(44%)	(36%)	(10%)	(7%)	(3%)	(100%)
Others	113,052	25,815	28,773	14,145	5,253	187,038
	(60%)	(14%)	(15%)	(8%)	(3%)	(100%)
Total	208,692	50,920	47,884	26,161	9,010	342,667
	(61%)	(15%)	(14%)	(8%)	(2%)	(100%)

SOURCE.—2010 annual report of the National Prosecution Service (http://www .aklagare.se), p. 14.

rious offenses. It saves money for the state and ensures that individuals who have committed minor offenses need not bear the burden of a criminal process. The system is not intended to be used for the purpose of negotiating with the suspect and is not used in that way. If the prosecutor neither initiates formal charges nor issues a penal order, the preliminary investigation may be discontinued. Alternatively, the prosecutor may issue a waiver of prosecution under chapter 20, section 7, of the SCJP.

Thus, as a matter of principle, there are four different potential outcomes of a preliminary investigation. The prosecutor may discontinue the investigation, issue a waiver of prosecution, impose a punishment by means of a penal order, or decide to bring the case to court.

Table 1 summarizes prosecutorial decisions in 2010.[7] Among violent offenses investigated, 77 percent resulted in prosecutions, 2 percent in penal orders, 7 percent in waivers of prosecution, and 13 percent in decisions not to charge for other reasons. Nearly a third of drug offenses were resolved with penal orders or waivers. Overall, for all kinds

[7] The pattern was broadly similar in 2008 and 2009 (2010 annual report of the National Prosecution Service, http://www.aklagare.se, p. 14).

of offenses combined, 15 percent were resolved with penal orders and 14 percent by waivers.

3. *Trials.*   The primary responsibilities of the prosecutor during the trial, while having regard to the principle of objectivity, are to present the case and prove that the person accused committed the alleged offense. The trial in Sweden is built on the principles of orality, concentration, and immediacy: all relevant evidence should be presented.

B. Important Features of Swedish Prosecution

A number of general features of the Swedish prosecutorial system need to be understood if the operation of the system in practice is to be understood. These include general understandings about the role of the prosecutor, the heavy weight attached to the value of equality, the relationship between independence of individual prosecutors and guidance within the National Prosecution Service, and the role of the victim in the criminal process.

1. *Selection and Independence.*   Prosecutors are selected meritocratically and are very much seen as civil servants. They are not chosen because of their personal agendas or ideas; they are not to promote interests they believe to be important. Nor is the prosecutor—other than indirectly—supposed to reflect the views of the public or handle a case compatibly with the common understanding of the public, as might be the case in systems in which prosecutors are elected (see Boerner, in this volume; Miller and Caplinger, in this volume; Wright, in this volume). The mission of the prosecutor is to enforce the values and priorities set by the legislature and, within that framework, by the prosecution service.

2. *Equal Treatment.*   The Swedish system is characterized by a very strong emphasis on equality before the law. When considering questions of equality, the relevant frame of reference is the country as a whole. It would, for example, be considered a major problem if the probability of receiving a prison sentence differed between areas of the country or if there were divergences in the length of prison sentences in different parts of the country. As an illustration of this, and also a demonstration of how widely held these views are, some years ago the best-known television magazine for societal journalism (*Uppdrag granskning*, meaning something like *Mission: Scrutinize!*) devoted an entire program to alleged, and probably real, differences in sentencing between Stockholm and Gothenburg.

This emphasis on equality is reflected in chapter 1, section 9, of the Instrument of Government: "courts of law, administrative authorities, and others performing public administration functions shall pay regard in their work to the equality of all before the law and shall observe objectivity and impartiality." Chapter 29, section 1, of the SCC emphasizes equal treatment as a central value in sentencing: "punishments shall, with due regard to the need for consistency in sentencing, be determined within the scale of punishments according to the penal value of the crime or crimes taken." Achievement of equal treatment throughout the country is explicitly made a basic task of the prosecutor general (in sec. 2 of the Ordinance on the Prosecution Service 2004: 1265).

3. *Oversight of Line Prosecutors.* The prosecutor when performing his or her tasks acts independently as a person (i.e., has personal responsibility under the law) and not merely as a representative for the prosecution authority. This means that no one but the prosecutor himself or herself can decide what should be done in an individual case. Thus, neither the prosecutor general nor any other superior prosecutor can decide what another prosecutor should or should not do. Higher-ranking prosecutors can give advice or provide guidance, but instructions concerning decisions in particular cases are not binding on the lower-ranking prosecutor.

However, this independence is balanced with a system of review and with fairly effective means to steer the work of individual prosecutors. Within the National Prosecution Service there is an informal system of administrative review. Decisions made by individual prosecutors can be appealed or a reconsideration can be requested. The review system is built on chapter 7, section 5, of the SCJP, which authorizes senior prosecutors to take over matters initially assigned to lower-ranking prosecutors. As a matter of principle, however, a higher prosecutor may not decide how the subordinate prosecutor should handle a case; he or she will have to assume primary responsibility for it (this does not preclude, however, having the subordinate prosecutor given the task of executing the decisions made).

The prosecution development centers are responsible for operating the review procedure. If the reconsideration leads to another decision and further action is needed—for example, if a decision to close an investigation has been revised—the case will normally be dealt with by a different prosecutor in the local prosecution office. It is possible to ask for a second review in the prosecutor general's office, but that is allowed in only a very small number of cases. Approximately 2,000 reviews are made each year. Of these, some 10 percent lead to a revision of the original decision. Further review at the office of the prosecutor general is allowed in only a limited number of cases.

This system functions mainly as a way to correct decisions in individual cases, but like all hierarchical review systems, it provides a way to give guidance and secure uniformity and equality. It may, of course, also affect the receptiveness of lower-ranking prosecutors to advice and guidance from senior prosecutors (see Fitger [2012], the commentary on chap. 7, sec. 5). My impression is that the review system is not misused to influence decisions in individual cases.

There are several other ways for the prosecutor general to steer the work of line prosecutors. On a general level, the annual operational plan and its follow-up are used to set general aims and priorities. Since the National Prosecution Service is a single national organization, its capacity to steer the work of individual prosecutors, by means of internal guidelines, memoranda, handbooks, and educational programs, is also quite good. The home page of the National Prosecution Authority suggests an agency that consciously uses information for the purpose of steering and leading; it seems clear that recommendations are normally followed (e.g., how to interpret a certain legal provision or deal with a certain issue). One important limitation, of course, is that more information should not be given in this way than its target audience can be expected to absorb.

4. *Victims.*   The aggrieved or injured party holds a strong position under Swedish law. As a general rule, chapter 20, section 8, subsection 2, of the SCJP permits the aggrieved party to support the charge of the prosecutor. The aggrieved party becomes a part of the process and has a right to supplement the investigation. Concerning some offenses, for example, defamation, only the aggrieved party may bring charges. For certain types of offenses, primarily sex offenses and offenses including violence, counsel for the aggrieved person can be appointed with the role of supporting and assisting the aggrieved person.

IV. Swedish Criminal Procedure

The Swedish criminal process is adversarial. The prosecutor presents the case before the court. This means that the prosecutor has the important task of choosing what charges to bring. It is, for example, the prosecutor who decides whether a threat communicated in connection with an assault should be charged separately or should be considered to be encompassed in the assault. This means that many criminal law questions are decided by prosecutors; matters dropped by the prosecutor will not be tried by the court.

The judgment may relate only to an act included in and covered by the description of the act given by the prosecutor when bringing charges. The court is, however, as a matter of principle not bound by the prosecutor's legal characterization of the behavior involved. If, for example, the prosecutor brings assault charges that include a slap in the face causing pain to the victim, the court may recharacterize this as molestation if the description of the act satisfies the relevant statutory requirements (see chap. 30, sec. 3, of the SCJP). To some extent, however, the European Convention on Human Rights—and the right to a fair trial—sets limits on this authority.

If the role of the prosecutor when it comes to the charge as such is very important, the prosecutors' role as regards the punishment or the sanctions is more informal. There is no requirement that prosecutors should propose a specific sanction or a specific quantum of punishment (though they often, or even generally, do so). As a matter of principle it is thus for the court to decide on the punishment. Lately, however, proposals have been put forward by a legislative committee requesting that the role of the prosecutor be increased in this regard, for example, by making it mandatory for the prosecutor to state what he or she considers to be a proper punishment for the crime in question (Statens offentliga utredningar 2008, p. 85).

A. The Prosecutorial Principle of Legality

The Swedish criminal law process is built on the prosecutorial principle of legality (as opposed to the principle of opportunity). In principle, the police and the prosecutors have no discretion over whether to investigate a case, and, correspondingly, the prosecutor has no discretion whether to prosecute (see chap. 23, sec. 1, and chap. 20, sec. 6, of the SCJP; Lindell et al. 2005, p. 186). In practice, the distinction between the principles of legality and opportunity is not as clear as the conceptual dichotomy implies. Systems based on the principle of opportunity normally contain some limits to the discretion of the prosecutor (e.g., general principles of nondiscrimination and of treating like cases alike will normally be applicable), and systems based on the principle of legality normally contain fairly extensive exceptions that give prosecutors some discretion (see Träskman 2007, p. 363).

In the Swedish system, the following qualifications warrant mention: a general exception for cases in which it is obvious that the crime is impossible to investigate (SCJP, chap. 23, sec. 1, subsec. 2); limitation of the preliminary investigation to certain offenses (SCJP, chap. 23, sec. 4a); decisions not to prosecute due to special rules making indictment subject to a special prosecutorial decision (SCC, chap. 5, sec. 5; chap. 8, sec. 13); decisions on a waiver of prosecution (SCJP, chap. 20, sec. 7); discretion that follows from vague rules or standards, such as (i) vagueness in doctrines of concurrence of crime, (ii) the general need to decide whether there is sufficient evidence, and (iii) the general need to decide whether the behavior in question is actually criminalized; and practical limitations.

1. *Cases That Are Practically Impossible to Investigate.* This exception is intended for cases in which it is (or might be) clear that a crime has been committed but there is no practical way to start or continue an investigation. A classic example is when money (which is fungible and usually not possible to identify) has been stolen from a pocket in a crowd in the city and there is no chance of finding the perpetrator. Other examples include cases in which the crime was committed abroad and evidence is not available in Sweden and cases in which the perpetrator has left the country and can neither be expected to return nor be brought back by means of extradition. The rationale behind the exception is, of course, that resources should not be spent on things that cannot lead to a result.

2. *Certain Offenses among Several.* According to chapter 23, section 4a, of the SCJP, a preliminary investigation may be limited to certain offenses among several. Other offenses (possibly committed by the person in question) are not part of the investigation. A decision to delimit a preliminary investigation in this way is possible

1. when there is reason to expect that prosecution will be waived in relation to the offense in question (thus, the rules on waiver of prosecution, discussed below, are important at this earlier stage of the process) and
2. when a continued inquiry would incur costs not in reasonable proportion to the importance of the matter and the offense, if prosecuted, cannot be deemed to have a penal value exceeding

3 months of imprisonment.[8] That is, it is possible to exclude certain offenses on the basis of cost-benefit considerations.

The first situation, relating to a presumptive waiver of prosecution at a later stage, is in practice much more important. In 2009, approximately 41,000 decisions were made to limit a preliminary investigation. Of these, all but 14 concerned waivers (Landström 2011, p. 223). Thus, more than 99 percent of the decisions concerned cases in which there were reasons to expect a waiver of prosecution in relation to the offense not investigated.

In 2010, a public inquiry proposed that the rules on limiting preliminary investigations should be extended to permit not only certain offenses but also certain less central persons to be excluded from a preliminary investigation (Statens offentliga utredningar 2010, p. 43). This would be of special importance in large investigations concerning serious organized crime and would mean that the investigation could focus on the central persons. In this regard, the proposal has not been adopted but at the time of writing remains under consideration by the government.

Those proposals have been criticized from the perspectives both of the aggrieved party and of equal treatment. The Swedish legislator is cruising between Scylla (sticking to the principle of legality even though in practice its effectuation is undermined by practical considerations) and Charybdis (giving prosecutors and police too much discretion, which has potential to undermine equality before the law).

3. *Special Prosecution Rules.* Some laws explicitly state that prosecution is subject to a special decision by the prosecutor. For example, the offenses of defamation and insulting behavior may, as a general rule, be prosecuted only by the injured party. In certain cases, the offense may be prosecuted by a public prosecutor, but only if certain requirements are satisfied (e.g., that prosecution is necessary to the public interest). This means that prosecution is based on the prosecutor's judgment about the public interest in a prosecution. Another example concerns prosecution of theft and other similar offenses against the family. Such offenses may be prosecuted only if reported by the injured party or if prosecution is called for in the public interest.

---

[8] "Penal value" is a conceptual component of Swedish sentencing jurisprudence and relates to the appropriate prison sentence to be imposed should a conviction occur.

Thus if such offenses are not reported, prosecution will depend on the same considerations as defamation and insulting behavior.

Offenses committed abroad or in Sweden on a foreign vessel may generally be prosecuted only following decisions by the government or the prosecutor general. The rationale is to allow room for considerations of foreign policy and international relations (see also chap. 2, secs. 7a–c of the SCC).

4. *Waiver of Prosecution.*   The main rule concerning waivers of prosecution is contained in chapter 20, section 7, of the SCJP. Special waiver rules apply to young offenders. Section 7 provides the following:

> Prosecutors may waive prosecution (waiver of prosecution), provided no compelling public or private interest is disregarded:
>
>   1. if it may be presumed that the offense would not result in a sanction other than a fine;
>   2. if it may be presumed that the sanction would be a conditional sentence and special reasons justify waiver of prosecution;
>   3. if the suspect has committed another offense and no further sanction in addition to the sanction for that offense is needed in respect of the present offense; or
>   4. if psychiatric care or special care in accordance with the Act on Support and Service for Certain Persons with Functional Impairments (1993:387) is rendered. A prosecution may be waived in cases other than those mentioned above if it is evident from special circumstances that no sanction is required to prevent the suspect from engaging in further criminal activity and that, in view of the circumstances, the institution of a prosecution is not required for other reasons.

The general requirement for a waiver of prosecution is that such a measure would not disregard any compelling public or private interest. If that precondition is fulfilled, a waiver is allowed if the presumed punishment will be modest or if the person will be subject to other punishment or certain other measures.

A decision to waive prosecution is considered a sort of conviction. That is, it is a decision by the prosecutor that implies that the suspect has committed the offense in question but should nonetheless not be indicted or punished. The waiver decision has negative consequences. It may, for example, lead to withdrawal of a driver's license, it is recorded in the person's criminal record (Landström 2011, p. 227), and in relation to the application of the rules on previous convictions in sentencing, it is considered a conviction. Waiver of prosecution presupposes that the facts are clear and, in practice, that the person admits the offense in question.

5. *Other Bases for Nonprosecution.* In practice, other factors give prosecutors discretion in deciding if and how charges should be brought. These factors are not intended to provide for discretion on the part of the prosecutor, but in practice they do.

One example concerns the estimation of whether there is enough proof for a conviction. When deciding whether to prosecute, the prosecutor should consider whether there is reason to believe that a conviction should result. This is, of course, a judgment matter. In a similar way, uncertainties about the law may provide the prosecutor with some discretion. For example, when there are diverging opinions as to whether a certain behavior is criminal, the prosecutor has some room to maneuver. He or she should take a stand on the legal question, but when it is open, it is possible to defend both positions.

It is important to note that the Swedish doctrine on concurrence of crime is—as in most legal systems—fairly vague. Thus, when questions arise whether a certain behavior constitutes one or two (or more) offenses, the prosecutor in practice often has some leeway. There are general principles on the concurrence of crime and there is a fairly stable case law and general practice concerning standard situations, but with cases outside the standard there is—in practice—a choice to make.

Last, but not least, decisions will probably always be affected by a sense of priorities and the bottom-of-the-pile principle. If there are not sufficient resources to investigate and prosecute all offenses, priorities set by the police and prosecutors will in practice have considerable effect. If certain offenses are not given priority, they will, with time, eventually become impossible to investigate and be barred by the statutes of limitation. The word "priorities" implies that someone has decided what to prioritize. Selection is also made according to the bottom-of-the-pile principle. Certain offenses are investigated because they happen to be at the top of the pile on the desk of the prosecutor whereas others are not being investigated because they are at the bottom. The proposals mentioned above for widening the rules on limiting preliminary investigations should be seen in this perspective. Resources are limited, and someone will have to decide how they should be used and which cases should receive attention. It may be better in such a situation if basic rules are decided by the legislature rather than leaving decisions to the National Prosecution Service or to individual prosecutors.

B. The Principle of Objectivity (Impartiality)

A second fundamental guide to prosecutors is the principle of objectivity (or impartiality): prosecutors should take into account not only facts and circumstances that are incriminating but also factors that point in the defendant's favor (Lindberg 1997, p. 202). The principle of objectivity in regard to the preliminary investigation is codified in chapter 23, section 4, of the SCJP:

> At the preliminary investigation, not only circumstances that are not in favor of the suspect but also circumstances in his favor shall be considered, and any evidence favorable to the suspect shall be preserved. The investigation should be conducted so that no person is unnecessarily exposed to suspicion, or put to unnecessary cost or inconvenience.
>
> The preliminary investigation shall be conducted as expeditiously as possible. When there is no longer reason for pursuing the investigation, it shall be discontinued.

A more general emphasis on the values of impartiality and equality is expressed in chapter 1, section 9, of the Instrument of Government.

Under the principle of objectivity the prosecutor has a responsibility in relation to the suspect or defendant. The prosecutor should—in principle—intervene if he or she observes the defense counsel to be doing an inadequate job and should not refrain from taking an investigative measure because it might turn out to the advantage of the suspect. Ordinarily the prosecutor is seen as a person responsible for getting people who have committed offenses prosecuted and convicted and as a counterpart to the defense lawyer. If combined with the general role of the prosecutor, the principle of objectivity makes the prosecutorial service a bit Janus-faced: representing the state and the public interest in combating crime but at the same time expected to be neutral.

The objectivity requirement may at times be problematic in light of the prosecutors' obligations to assist the aggrieved party. For example, under SCJP, chapter 22, section 2, the prosecutor is directed to prepare and present the aggrieved person's action for damages in conjunction with the prosecution, provided that no major inconvenience will result and that the claim does not manifestly lack merit. Thus, the prosecutor is obliged to assist the aggrieved person, but this does not mean that the prosecutor can see himself or herself as a representative of the aggrieved person.

V. Who Are the Swedish Prosecutors?

To become a prosecutor in Sweden, one must have a Swedish master of laws. That degree, which requires $4\frac{1}{2}$ years of study, can be obtained at Gothenburg, Lund, Stockholm, Uppsala, Umeå, and Örebro Universities. A Danish, Finnish, Icelandic, or Norwegian degree also satisfies the requirement, unless it did not require at least 4 years of study, in which case additional study is required.

An additional requirement entails 2 years' service as a junior judge in a Swedish district court. One can apply for this trainee position after receiving a law degree. The only factor taken into account in selecting persons for these positions is university grades, which are transformed into points, with the positions given to those having the highest scores. Generally this system functions fairly well (even though grades necessarily give limited and incomplete information about a person), but there are also negatives. For example, grades tell nothing about one's personal qualities. Neither do they do justice to late bloomers who perform much better near the ends of their education and as a result do not rank high overall.

People who want to be judges or prosecutors must satisfy both requirements. This means that judges and prosecutors have a common educational and early-career background. They are seen as career alternatives. The common background provides a shared understanding of the roles and functions of the legal system.

Personal qualities are, of course, taken into account. The work as a prosecutor is independent of personal character, requiring an ability to take a stand on difficult and complex issues, often with quite short notice. The website of the National Prosecution Service provides the following information to potential applicants: "In addition to the formal merits, there are a number of personal qualities that have to be satisfied. A prosecutor should be analytical, logical, and independent, and have a good capacity to cooperate. Prosecutors must also be able to reach their own conclusions and stand by them. They should also have a sound judgment and have a high degree of personal maturity. In order to find out whether or not an applicant satisfies these criteria, use is made of interviews, work psychology tests, and reference taking."

When first employed, those hired become prosecutorial aspirants (trainees). After 9–12 months they become, if accepted, assistant prosecutors, which lasts for 2 years. After this, the prosecution service decides whether to promote assistants into positions as chamber prosecutors, that is, as ordinary prosecutors. In addition to this normal way of becoming a prosecutor, there are other possibilities for individuals with experience in other legal professions (they can be appointed as *extra åklagare*).

There are reliable figures on only a few basic facts about Swedish prosecutors, such as their genders, national backgrounds, and ages. In 2009, 65 percent of employees of the National Prosecution Authority were women. Among prosecutors the percentage is lower, but women were a majority at 54 percent. Of people in chiefs' positions, only 38 percent were women. Among people appointed as prosecutorial assistants or as extra prosecutors, 65 percent were women. Against this background, it seems reasonable to expect that there will be a majority of women at all levels within a short time. The average prosecutor in 2009 was 44 years old (47 years for men and 42 years for women).

Of all prosecutors, 4.8 percent have a non-Swedish background (3 percent were born in another country and 1.8 percent were born in Sweden but both parents were born elsewhere). Since immigration into Sweden is substantial, those numbers also are likely to increase.

It is difficult to say much more about prosecutors as a group. No political considerations are weighed when appointing a prosecutor. I know of no research on prosecutors' social background. It is reasonable to assume, however, that most prosecutors (like most judges) are from middle- or upper-class backgrounds.

VI. The Assange Case

I think it useful to end by commenting on the Julian Assange case. Assange is the founder of Wikileaks, a website that specializes in obtaining and disseminating confidential government documents. Shortly after Wikileaks released large numbers of confidential and embarrassing American government documents, allegations were made that Assange committed sexual offenses against two Swedish women. A Swedish prosecutor reviewed the allegations and decided not to proceed. That decision was reviewed by a more senior prosecutor, who overturned it. Assange was asked to come to Sweden to be interviewed. He declined, and in due course his extradition was sought from the United Kingdom. Assange attempted to resist extradition and lost initial judicial decisions. At the time of writing he has not been extradited. Swedish prosecutors assert that the case has been handled like any other. Assange supporters hypothesize that American or other political pressure has influenced the Swedish prosecutors. The case can be used to illustrate the main features of the Swedish prosecutorial system.

As a background, here is a chronological summary of events that was published on the home page of the Swedish National Prosecution Service (for purposes of reference, I have numbered the different events).

1. August 20, 2010. The duty prosecutor orders the arrest of Julian Assange, suspected of rape and sexual molestation.
2. August 21, 2010. The case is transferred to a prosecutor at the City Public Prosecution Office in Stockholm.
3. August 25, 2010. The prosecutor decides to terminate the preliminary investigation into the rape charge.
4. August 27, 2010. Lawyer Claes Borgström, legal representative of the women who reported Julian Assange, requests a review of the prosecutor's decision to terminate the preliminary investigation concerning the rape charge. The request is sent to the prosecution development center in Gothenburg.
5. September 1, 2010. Marianne Ny, director of public prosecution, decides to resume the preliminary investigation concerning the rape charge. The preliminary investigation on sexual molestation is expanded to cover all the events in the crime reports.
6. September 2010. The investigation is under way.
7. September 2010. The arrest of Julian Assange is requested.
8. November 18, 2010. Marianne Ny orders the arrest of Julian Assange, with probable cause, on suspicion of rape, three cases of sexual molestation, and illegal coercion. This measure is taken as it has been impossible to interview him during the investigation. The Stockholm district court orders the arrest of Julian Assange in accordance with the prosecutor's request. To

execute this decision, the prosecutor issues a European Arrest
Warrant for the arrest of Julian Assange.

9. November 22, 2010. Julian Assange appeals the issuance of the
    district court arrest warrant to Svea Court of Appeal.

10. November 24, 2010. Svea Court of Appeal refuses the appeal
    and decides that the arrest warrant should remain in place, with
    probable cause, on suspicion of rape (less serious crime), un-
    lawful coercion, and two cases of sexual molestation. The in-
    ternational request and the European Arrest Warrant are con-
    firmed in accordance with the decision of the district court.

11. November 30, 2010. Julian Assange appeals the arrest warrant
    issued by Svea Court of Appeal to the Supreme Court.

12. December 2, 2010. The Supreme Court decides not to grant
    Julian Assange leave to appeal. The decision of the Svea Court
    of Appeal stands. On the request of the British police, addi-
    tional information is added to the European Arrest Warrant
    concerning the maximum penalty in Sweden for the crimes of
    sexual molestation and unlawful coercion.

13. December 7, 2010. Julian Assange is arrested by the British
    police. Since then the Westminister magistrates court and High
    Court have decided that Assange should be surrendered. When
    this essay is being finalized (February 2012), a decision is ex-
    pected shortly.

First, it should be noted that one of the charges against Assange is
that he had intercourse with a person who was asleep at the time. This
is a criminal offense in Sweden if the act amounts to an "improper
misuse" of the situation (see SCC, chap. 6, sec. 1, subsec. 2). The
starting point of the law is that sexual acts toward someone who is not
conscious raise a prima facie case of such misuse (the limitation to
improper misuse is more important when it comes to other states of
helplessness than total unconsciousness). It could be argued that one
has to take the relation between the parties into account when deciding
whether sex with someone who is asleep should be considered as "improper misuse," but there is no clear case law and there are no clear
statements in the preparatory documents setting out the rationale for
the law. Thus, the argument that the act amounts to rape under Swedish law is at least not unreasonable (I do not intend to take a clear
position in this essay).

Second, the principle of prosecutorial legality implies that if there is reason to assume that an offense has been committed, a preliminary investigation must be instituted. Thus, if one concludes that the act performed by Assange might amount to an offense, there is effectively no discretion for the prosecutor. He or she is obliged to start a preliminary investigation. Thus, the argument put forward by (among others) Michael Moore (http://www.michaelmoore.com/words/mike-friends-blog/dear-government-of-sweden) that the Swedish National Prosecution Service honors strange priorities when investigating the Assange case, while being unsuccessful in many instances of alleged rapes in bringing charges and gaining convictions, is clearly misleading. If there is reason in this case to believe that an offense has been committed, it should as a matter of principle be investigated.

Third, that the senior prosecutor (September 1) decided differently than the line prosecutor (August 25) is not in itself extraordinary (points 3 and 5 of the chronology). The decision on September 1 was made within the normal review procedure on the initiative of the counsel to one of the aggrieved parties. It may be more common for senior prosecutors to reach the same conclusion as the line prosecutor, but it is not uncommon for reviews to result in a different decision. In 2008, for example, 2,007 decisions were subject to review (i.e., less than 1 percent of all decisions), and 220 of these led to a revision of the decision (i.e., 11 percent of the reviews). Further review by the office of the prosecutor general was allowed in nine cases (eight cases of a similar kind that were decided at the same time and in which the decision was changed, and one additional case in which the decision was not changed; 2008 annual report of National Prosecution Service, http://www.aklagare.se). Thus, the decision by Marianne Ny on September 1 (point 5) was not something extraordinary.

In the international debate it has also been suggested or implied that decisions of the National Prosecution Service were affected by improper pressure from the government (which in turn is supposed to have been affected by improper pressure from, among others, the United States). In this regard it should first be underlined that the decision to prosecute in Sweden is made by civil servants (prosecutors) according to their own responsibility under the applicable laws. Neither the government nor other politicians are involved in the process in any way.[9]

---

[9] Except as noted above, when alleged crimes occurred abroad, etc.

Furthermore, the constitutional documents forbid the government to interfere with the decision making in individual cases by judicial authorities (including the National Prosecution Service). This prohibition is respected. Civil servants are very sensitive toward such involvement. Any attempt to influence National Prosecution Service handling of the Assange case would create a major political scandal.

I have no special knowledge of the case and cannot, of course, vouch that no improper influence has been attempted or used. From my knowledge of and experience with the Swedish system, however, I find it highly unlikely that the government would have tried to influence the behavior of the National Prosecution Service in this case.

It has also been asked whether it is proper to issue a European Arrest Warrant for the purpose of questioning a suspect. There was a court decision on the arrest of Assange. He is accused of minor rape, which is a fairly serious offense under Swedish law. It is not extraordinary that the prosecutor—given that Assange refused to come to Sweden to be questioned—found that the proportionality test, which should always be considered before issuing a European Arrest Warrant, was fulfilled.

Reasonable people, of course, may disagree whether the decisions made in this case were the right ones. One can debate the reasonableness of the Swedish rape legislation or the reasonableness of the international system for surrendering (and extraditing) people between states when they are suspected of having committed offenses. The system can be very burdensome to the individual. However, given the characteristics of the Swedish prosecutorial system and of the European Arrest Warrant system, the decisions in the Assange case are more properly described as an outcome of the system than as something extraordinary. In this respect the case perhaps says more about the Swedish prosecutorial system (and the dynamics of the European Arrest Warrant) than about the particulars of the Assange case.[10]

REFERENCES

Boerner, David. In this volume. "Prosecution in Washington State."

[10] The person in charge of the initial interrogation of Assange knew one of the aggrieved parties; it can be argued that that person should have disqualified himself.

Cameron, Iain, Malin Thunberg Schunke, Karin Påle-Bartes, Christoffer Wong, and Petter Asp. 2011. *International Criminal Law from a Swedish Perspective*. Cambridge: Intersentia.

Elwing, Carl M. 1960. *Tillräckliga skäl: Studier över förutsättningarna för allmänt åtal*. Lund: Gleerupska.

Fitger, Peter. 2012. *Rättegångsbalken*. Stockholm: Norstedts.

Landström, Lena. 2011. *Åklagaren som grindvakt: En rättsvetenskaplig studie av åklagaren befogenheter vid utredning och åtal av brott*. Umeå: Iustus Förlag.

Lindberg, Gunnel. 1997. "Om åklagaretik." *Svensk Juristtidning* 3:197–221.

Lindell, Bengt, Hans Eklund, Petter Asp, and Torbjörn Andersson. 2005. *Straffprocessen*. Uppsala: Iustus Förlag.

Miller, Marc L., and Samantha Caplinger. In this volume. "Prosecution in Arizona: Practical Problems, Prosecutorial Accountability, and Local Solutions."

Statens offentliga utredningar. 2008. *Straff i proportion till brottets allvar, 2008: 85*. Stockholm: Statens offentliga utredningar.

———. 2010. *Förundersökningsbegränsning, 2010:43*. Stockholm: Statens offentliga utredningar.

Träskman, Per Ole. 1980. *Åtalsrätt: De offentliga åklagarna, deras behörighet och uppgifter enligt gällande finsk rätt*. Helsinki: Juridiska föreningens i Finland Publikationsserie.

———. 2007. "Vad duger en åklagare egentligen till?" In *Jurist uden omsvøb: Festskrift til Gorm Toftegaard Nielsen*, edited by Annette Möller-Sörensen and Anette Storgaard. Copenhagen: Aarhus Gyldendal.

Wright, Ronald. In this volume. "Persistent Localism in the Prosecutor Services of North Carolina."

Zila, Josef. 2006. "The Prosecution Service Function within the Swedish Criminal Justice System." In *Coping with Overloaded Criminal Justice Systems: The Rise of Prosecutorial Power across Europe*, edited by Jörg-Martin Jehle and Marianne Wade. Berlin: Springer.

David Boerner

Prosecution in Washington State

ABSTRACT

The prosecution function in Washington State is carried out by 39 locally elected county prosecuting attorneys who operate autonomously both from each other and from any central state authority. The results are in some ways paradoxical. At the state level, policy making is premised on ideas of policy rationality and equal treatment. Washington has long been a leader in development of innovative sentencing and parole initiatives and policies. Prosecutors have played influential roles in their development and have worked to constrain the influence of populist political pressures. Prosecutors long ago developed statewide prosecution guidelines, and local prosecutors' offices have been national leaders in developing internal office policies aiming at consistent and principled handling of criminal cases. At the same time, however, prosecutors have vigorously opposed state initiatives that would limit their discretion. Prosecutors are locally elected and respond to prevailing social and cultural attitudes. As a result, prosecution policies, practices, and patterns vary widely between counties. So do sentencing patterns.

Understanding prosecution in Washington State must begin with the decentralized nature of its criminal justice system. From its origins in territorial days, local government in Washington has been characterized by autonomous, independently elected officials whose ability to establish and implement policies is essentially unconstrained by state-level actors. Law enforcement and prosecution operate wholly at the

David Boerner is emeritus professor of law and faculty fellow at the Fred T. Korematsu Center for Law and Equality, Seattle University School of Law, and was assistant attorney general for the State of Washington and chief criminal deputy in the King County Prosecuting Attorney's Office. Since 1999, he has been chair of the Washington Sentencing Guidelines Commission.

local level. Sentencing policy is established at the state level but is implemented locally. The state operates the prison system but does not fund or operate county jails. Supervision of felons in the community is also a state function. Prosecuting attorneys play a dominant role at the local level and are influential players at the state level. Acting without significant restraint from the state, they, in major part, set criminal justice policy in their jurisdictions.

For at least a century, Washington prosecutors have been major participants in shaping sentencing and other criminal justice policies in Washington. The 1909 criminal code, the existing criminal code and criminal procedure system, the 1981 Sentencing Reform Act, and drug reform initiatives of the past two decades have sometimes been initiated and have always been importantly influenced by prosecutors. Prosecutors have, however, always fought to preserve their authority as elected county officials answerable to a local electorate to set their own priorities and follow their own policies. As a result, practices and policies vary substantially between counties. So far, at least, this has been seen as an acceptable price to be paid to respect local values and protect local autonomy.

This essay describes the development of public prosecution in Washington from its earliest days as the Washington Territory. It contains nine sections. Section I discusses the history and organization of public prosecution. Section II describes the legal autonomy and the organization of county prosecutors' offices. Despite the existence of potential state-level executive branch and judicial controls over prosecutors' offices, in practice they are highly independent. Few of the theoretically available control mechanisms offer practical limitations on prosecutors' discretionary powers. Nonetheless, though prosecutors are in one sense highly political and responsive to local electorates, in practice many elected prosecutors remain in office for long periods. In recent years few have sought higher elected offices, and none have succeeded in winning them, as Section III shows. Section IV describes prosecutors' efforts since the 1970s to establish statewide support systems and political organization. Sections V and VI discuss relations with law enforcement and the judiciary. Section VII, the longest, offers extensive discussions of prosecutors' involvement in state-level law reform initiatives. Section VIII reviews empirical and other evidence on the effects of local autonomy on individual prosecutors' ability to create innovative programs in their own offices and of consequences of that autonomy in terms of substantial differences between counties in how state laws are enforced and how criminal offenders are prosecuted and punished. Section IX reflects on the tensions between state laws premised on ideas of consistent and equal treatment of offenders and local traditions of prosecutorial autonomy.

I. Organization

Prosecuting attorneys have been elected local officials since the Washington Territory was formed in 1854 (An Act Relating to Prosecuting Attorneys, Code of Washington, sec. 1, 1854). The first three in 1854 served a territorial population of 4,000. They were selected by judicial district, served 2-year terms, and were required to live in the district. Each received a fixed salary, payable from the territorial treasury, and also received per-case fees, paid by the county, of variable sums depending on the severity of the potential punishment and whether the prosecution resulted in a conviction or an acquittal.[1] In 1881 prosecuting attorneys were authorized to appoint one or two deputies whose salary was paid by the prosecuting attorney personally. Compensation increased over time, but at a variable rate depending on the judicial district. The formula of a fixed sum payable from the territorial treasury and variable sums paid from the county treasury was retained, as was the limitation of territorial funding for only a portion of the elected prosecuting attorney's salary.

When Washington became a state in 1889, its constitution established the prosecuting attorney as an elected county official and authorized the legislature to "prescribe their duties and fix their terms of office" (Washington Constitution, art. 11, sec. 5). The legislature, in addition to making the prosecuting attorney the lawyer for all components of county government—a significant source of their local influence—provided that the prosecuting attorney shall "prosecute all criminal and civil actions in which the state or the county may be a party" (Revised Code of Washington 36.27.020[4]). Misdemeanors that occur within cities are prosecuted by city attorneys.

Washington, with a population of 6.75 million, contains 39 counties.

---

[1] For example, for a potential penalty of death or life imprisonment, the fee was $25 for a conviction and $12 for an acquittal; for all other felonies, $15 for a conviction and $7 for an acquittal; and for misdemeanors, $10 for a conviction and $5 for an acquittal (sec. 9 of the 1854 act).

They are based on geography, not population, and have widely varying populations. The largest is King County (Seattle) with a population approaching 2 million (larger than 13 states). The smallest, Garfield County, has a population just over 2,200. Each has a locally elected prosecuting attorney. The five largest counties (King, Pierce, Snohomish, Spokane, and Clark) make up 65 percent of the state's population. The 10 smallest make up only 1.6 percent of the state's population. The same issues may arise in small and large counties, but because of difference in scale, resolution of issues can vary widely.

Salaries were initially fixed by the county legislative authority with one-half to be paid by the state and one-half by the county. The state legislature later established minimum salaries, based on county population, and provided that prosecuting attorneys in counties of more than 18,000 inhabitants must serve full-time (Revised Code of Washington 36.27.060). Currently the state contributes one-half the salary of a superior court judge (currently $148,832) to each county as the state share of the prosecuting attorneys' pay and requires the county to contribute an amount that equals or exceeds the amount paid by the county in 2008 (Revised Code of Washington 36.17.020[11]). The effect has been to make most prosecuting attorneys full-time. The term of office is now 4 years (Revised Code of Washington 36.16.020), and the prosecuting attorney's position is designated as a "partisan office" (Revised Code of Washington 29A.040.110).

Prosecuting attorneys are authorized to appoint any number of deputies who serve as at-will employees (Revised Code of Washington 36.27.040). Deputies' salaries are paid entirely by the county. This funding formula reinforces the local nature of prosecuting attorneys. The level of resources they have to carry out their duties is determined by local budget processes; not surprisingly, the resources available to prosecutors vary widely. The number of deputy prosecuting attorneys in the larger counties varies from a high of 11.3 per 100,000 population (Pierce County) to a low of 8.3 (Clark County).

Each prosecuting attorney is responsible for hiring his or her deputies. While there is some movement of deputies between counties, most spend their prosecutorial careers in the same county. Historically, deputy prosecuting attorneys were hired directly from law school, and for many the position served to provide trial experience before they moved to private practice. Over the past two decades, this pattern has changed. Particularly in the larger counties, it is now common for some deputies to serve their entire career as prosecutors. In those offices, a central core of career prosecutors serves along with a rotating group of beginners.

II. Accountability

Washington prosecutors are highly autonomous in how they manage their offices and in their charging decisions. Some judicial review of postcharging decisions exists, but the initial decision to prosecute and the selection of charges are solely the responsibility of the prosecutor. The consequences of this independence are significant.

A. Supervision by the State

With one narrow theoretical exception, prosecuting attorneys are legally free from control by state officials. While they enforce state criminal law in the name of the state, they operate autonomously. The attorney general has no supervisory power over them. Although Washington statutes give the state attorney general the power to "consult with and advise the several prosecuting attorneys" (Revised Code of Washington 43.10.030[4]) and provide that prosecuting attorneys shall "appear for and represent the state . . . subject to the supervisory control and direction of the attorney general in all criminal and civil proceedings in which the state . . . may be a party" (Revised Code of Washington 36.27.030[3]), the Washington Supreme Court in *State ex. Rel Hamilton v. Superior Court* (3 Washington 2d 633 [1940]) held that these provisions do not give the attorney general the power to supersede a prosecuting attorney. Only the governor is formally authorized to request the attorney general to investigate violations of the criminal law (Revised Code of Washington 43.10.090). If so requested, the attorney general is authorized to investigate, and if he or she determines that "the prosecuting attorney has failed or neglected to institute and prosecute violations of such criminal laws," the attorney general may "direct the prosecuting attorney to take such action . . . as the attorney general determines necessary and proper." Only if the prosecuting attorney refuses to do so may the attorney general prosecute. In practice there is no record of any governor ever ordering the attorney general to investigate an alleged crime over the objection of a prosecuting attorney. The attorney general does, however, provide assistance to prosecuting attorneys at their request and maintains a staff of five attorneys who fulfill this role (e.g., *State v. Howard*, 722 Pacific 21 783 [1985]). In practice this assistance is mainly used to assist small counties in major cases and in response to conflicts of interest.

B. *Judicial Supervision*

As a practical matter, courts have little authority over prosecutors' charges, dismissals, or plea negotiations. Courts do have authority to dismiss charges once filed, but appellate courts have interpreted this authority narrowly.

1. *Removal.* The legislature authorizes the superior court to appoint special counsel when "from illness or other cause" the prosecuting attorney is "temporarily unable to perform his duties." The Supreme Court, however, in *State v. Heston*, 56 Pacific 843 (1899), held that this statute does not authorize the superior court to replace the elected prosecuting attorney because it disagrees with his judgment concerning the dismissal of a criminal case. The court observed that "his discretion in the exercise of his duties must not be in any wise controlled by legal consequences unpleasant or unfavorable to himself."

2. *Initial Charging.* Prosecutors in Washington have a de facto monopoly on the initial filing of criminal charges. They may initiate charges by filing an information in superior court (the general jurisdiction trial court) or by filing a complaint in district court. Defendants have no right to indictment by a grand jury, and there is no requirement of a precharging judicial determination of probable cause.[2] All that is legally required is the signature of the prosecutor (Superior Court Criminal Rules 2.1; Superior Court Criminal Rules Limited Jurisdiction 2.1).

The decision not to prosecute is also solely that of the prosecutor.[3] While in territorial days citizens were allowed to file criminal complaints, to present matters to a grand jury, and to function as a private

---

[2] There is a requirement of a judicial determination of probable cause if an arrest warrant is sought (Superior Court Criminal Rules 2.2[a]; Superior Court Criminal Rules Limited Jurisdiction 2.2[a]). This is typically done in an ex parte judicial determination supported by written affidavits. See *Gerstein v. Pugh*, 420 U.S. 103 (1975): "a judicial hearing is not a prerequisite to prosecution by information."

[3] "It remains a prosecutorial duty to determine the extent of society's interest in prosecuting an offense" (*State v. McDowell*, 685 P.2d 595 [1984]). "There is no role for the court at the time the prosecuting attorney files the original charge" (*State v. Haner*, 631 P.2d 381 [1181]).

prosecutor, since statehood, the right to file citizen complaints has been limited to misdemeanors and is very rarely exercised.

Prosecutors have maintained their gatekeeping role as drug courts have expanded across the state. When the legislature authorized drug courts and provided for state funding, it left eligibility criteria for local determination in the belief that allowing local control over eligibility would increase local support for creation of drug courts. The Supreme Court in *State v. DiLuzio*, 90 Pacific 3rd 1141 (2004), held that the decision to refer an offender to a drug court is an "initial referral" whose allocation to a prosecutor "does not constitute an unconstitutional delegation of judicial power to the prosecutor."

The Washington Supreme Court has, however, held that a prosecutor does not have sole authority to determine the eligibility of an offender for a "deferred prosecution" under a statutorily authorized program for offenders facing gross misdemeanor, misdemeanor, or traffic charges, characterizing the program as "essentially a sentencing alternative." The court held that a statutorily authorized veto by the prosecutor was an unconstitutional violation of separation of powers. The court noted that "the court's disposition of the petition followed the prosecutor's decision to charge; once the accused has been charged and is before the court, the charging function ceases" (*State v. Cascade Dist. Ct.*, 621 P.2d 115 [1980]).

This limitation on prosecutorial control over misdemeanor and traffic charges does not apply to felonies. As I discuss below, judges have chafed at the prosecutor's monopoly over diversion of felony charges, but the legislature has not adopted their proposals to give judges authority to divert felony cases.

3. *Postcharging Decisions.* Once formal charges have been filed, subsequent prosecutorial decisions are subject to judicial authority. While prosecutors may not act unilaterally after charges are filed, the power of the court is not unlimited. Dismissal or amendment of charges, once filed, is subject to judicial approval (*State v. Haner*, 631 Pacific 2d 381 [1981]), but the court's power to dismiss over the prosecuting attorney's objection is limited to situations "when there has been prejudice to the rights of the accused which materially affect the accused's right to a fair trial" (Superior Court Criminal Rules 8.3[b]). This power "is designed to protect against arbitrary action or governmental misconduct and not to grant courts the authority to substitute their judgment for that of the prosecutor" (*State v. Cantrell*, 758 Pacific 2d 1 [1988]).

Courts do have the power to dismiss before trial if "there are no material disputed facts and the undisputed facts do not establish a primae facia case of guilt" (Superior Court Criminal Rules 8.3[c][3]).

Most revisions to the initial charges occur in the course of plea bargaining, which occurs in a large majority of cases. Ninety-four percent of all convictions in felony cases in 2010 occurred by plea of guilty. Prosecuting attorneys have collectively developed and supported legislative adoption of standards for the exercise of prosecutorial discretion (Revised Code of Washington 9.94A.401–.470). The standards, however, are voluntary and have not operated to give judges supervisory powers over plea bargaining (*State v. Lee*, 847 P.2d 25 [1993]). When the legislature adopted the Sentencing Reform Act, it expressly directed that courts "at the time of the plea, shall determine if the agreement is consistent with the interests of justice and with the prosecuting standards" (Revised Code of Washington 9.94A.431). In practice, judges have not exercised this power. The standard form on which a plea of guilty is entered and accepted contains a printed recitation that the plea agreement "is consistent with the interests of justice and with the prosecuting standards." No independent judicial review of the plea bargaining process occurs.

The net effect of these provisions and practices is that prosecuting attorneys are not subject to any significant judicial supervision over the exercise of their broad discretionary powers. Prosecutors vary significantly in how they exercise their discretion.

III. Prosecutors and Politics

As locally elected officials, prosecuting attorneys are political actors. While they are not frequently challenged for reelection, they are quite aware of the temporary nature of their tenure in office.

A. Career Patterns

Historically there has been wide variation in length of service by elected prosecuting attorneys. Some counties have been served for decades by a single prosecutor. In others, turnover has been frequent. A survey in 1977 covering the period 1965–77 showed that 13 of Washington's 39 counties had then been served by one prosecuting attorney for 10 years or more, while in 15 counties the prosecuting attorney had served for less than 3 years. The pattern in 2011 is much the same. Fourteen prosecuting attorneys have served 10 years or more. Nine were newly elected in 2010. Nineteen had served for 4 years or less.

The larger offices are mostly led by prosecuting attorneys who have spent all or the major portion of their careers as prosecutors. The prosecuting attorneys of the largest three counties, King, Pierce, and Snohomish, have spent their entire legal careers in the offices they now lead. In nine of the 10 largest counties (constituting 78 percent of the state's population), the prosecuting attorneys have either served as the elected prosecuting attorney for 20 or more uninterrupted years or spent their entire legal career as prosecutors.

B. Partisan Politics

That prosecuting attorneys in Washington are elected on a partisan basis has not had any noticeable effects on how they carry out their duties. Twenty-two prosecuting attorneys in 2011 were Republicans and 17 were Democrats, a small change from 1990 when 19 were Republicans and 20 were Democrats.

Most large counties have been served by prosecutors of the same party for many years. While there is undoubtedly a correlation between the prosecutor's party and the underlying partisan leanings of the county, the correlation is far from perfect. King County, which is heavily Democratic (Barack Obama received 70 percent of the vote in 2008 and John Kerry received 65 percent of the vote in 2004), has elected Republican prosecuting attorneys for the past half century. No Democratic challenger has run in the past four elections.

Pierce County, also strongly Democratic in national races, has consistently elected Democrats for the past quarter century, and Clark County has elected Democrats for the past 30 years. Spokane County after electing Democrats for 30 years has elected a Republican for the past 12 years. Only Snohomish County, a rapidly growing suburban community north of Seattle, has alternated between parties. In none of these counties do partisan politics appear to have played any role. In recent memory, prosecuting attorneys have never divided on party lines with regard to any statewide issue.

C. Higher Office

Prosecuting attorneys in Washington have been remarkably ineffective in seeking higher office. Stuart Scheingold[4] identified King County Prosecuting Attorney Christopher Bayley's ambition for higher office as a reason why policies and practices in the office changed in the mid-1970s, but Bayley did not run for higher office. When he chose not to run for a third term in 1978, he returned to private practice.

Since 1980, only three elected prosecuting attorneys have sought statewide office. None was successful. Norm Maleng, Republican Prosecuting Attorney for King County, sought election as attorney general in 1992. He won the Republican primary but lost to Democrat Christine Gregoire, who now is Washington's current governor. Also in 1992, John Ladenburg, Democratic Prosecuting Attorney for Pierce County, also ran for attorney general. He lost in the Democratic primary to Gregoire. He was subsequently elected Pierce County executive in 2000 and currently serves in that post. Maleng ran for governor in 1996 but lost in the Republican primary.

Jeffrey Sullivan, the Republican Prosecuting Attorney for Yakima County, ran for the US House of Representatives in 1998. He finished third in the Republican primary. In 2000, Sullivan ran for election to the Washington Supreme Court. He lost in the general election to current incumbent Susan Owens.

Political ambition may well influence Washington's prosecutors as they exercise their discretion setting policy and in relation to individual cases, but there is little in recent history to support the thesis that ambition for higher office is a significant factor.[5] More likely it is their desire to retain their offices. Prosecutors would argue that Washington's system of local elections presupposes that prosecutors be responsive to local values and that paying attention to the desires of the local populace is precisely what they should be doing.

---

[4] Stuart Scheingold, a political scientist at the University of Washington, conducted a study of King County from 1964 to 1980. His *The Politics of Street Crime* (1991) is a rich case study of "Park County," which is King County. Christopher T. Bayley is "Whitney Steele." I am "Billy Dorffler."

[5] Senators Warren G. Magnuson and Henry M. Jackson began their political careers in the 1930s as elected prosecuting attorneys of King and Snohomish Counties, respectively. That path has not been followed since.

IV. Collective Action

Prosecuting attorneys in Washington operate independently but have long come together to discuss common issues and formulate joint positions on the issues of the day. The vehicle is the Washington Association of Prosecuting Attorneys (WAPA), a voluntary organization in which all prosecuting attorneys participate. In the early years the organization met twice per year, but with no staff it was largely inactive otherwise.

In the early 1970s, WAPA first acquired staff. In 1972, the Criminal Justice Training Commission, funded by a Law Enforcement Assistance Administration (LEAA) grant, assigned a staff member part-time to serve as staff for WAPA. In 1974, WAPA obtained its first LEAA grant in its own right and employed a "prosecutor coordinator." The position was filled on an annual basis until 1977, when Michael Redman, the former prosecuting attorney of San Juan County, became executive secretary. He served in that post until 1993 and led WAPA to become a stable and productive association.

WAPA was incorporated as a nonprofit corporation in 1977 and obtained a second LEAA grant that funded two attorneys and a secretary for a technical assistance project to produce training manuals. WAPA has also been funded by the Washington Association of Counties, which also provided offices, and by dues from individual prosecuting attorneys.

Permanent staff enabled WAPA to become a continuing presence in the legislature, where it achieved significant influence on criminal justice issues. With funding from the state Criminal Justice Training Commission, it also assumed responsibility for a comprehensive training program for prosecutors. Beginning in 1977 the association offered 2-day training sessions twice each year. Separate programs for criminal and civil deputies are offered, and additional programs addressing specific topics are held periodically. Every 4 years a 2-day training program for newly elected prosecutors is held. All programs are approved by the Washington State Bar Association's Continuing Legal Education program; prosecutors are able to satisfy all their 15 hours per year continuing legal education requirement by attending WAPA training programs.

The larger counties also provide significant internal training programs with emphasis on both newly appointed deputies and specialized programs for the more experienced.

WAPA employs a staff attorney who provides legal advice to local offices on request and keeps prosecutors informed of significant legal developments. It also files amicus briefs in appellate cases of statewide import on its own initiative and occasionally at the request of the Supreme Court.

V. Relations with Law Enforcement

Prosecuting attorneys have traditionally had close working relationships with law enforcement. Each prosecuting attorney is the lawyer for his or her county sheriff, and it is common for prosecutors and sheriffs to work closely together on local criminal justice and budget issues. Because prosecutors decide whether to initiate charges and for what, they necessarily evaluate and pass judgment on the investigative work of law enforcement officers. This inevitably sometimes leads to disagreements and tensions. Nonetheless, there tends to be a commonality of interests that leads prosecutors and law enforcement leaders to act together to further joint goals.

At the state level, WAPA works closely with the Washington Association of Sheriffs and Police Chiefs in formulating their positions on policy issues. When differences do exist, the organizations work together privately to try to come to common positions. When they do, they form a very effective political force before the legislature. They are not always successful at gaining adoption of joint proposals but have been extremely effective at preventing legislation they oppose from being adopted. For example, during the most recent legislative session, they were successful at blocking a proposal to retroactively reduce the lengths of prison sentences in response to the state's budget crisis.

VI. Relations with the Judiciary

The inherent tensions of the adversary system are of course always present in the relationship between prosecutors and judges. That judges pass judgment on prosecutors' work creates continuing tensions. That said, prosecuting attorneys tend to have good working relationships with judges at the local level. They frequently espouse common positions on policy and budget issues. That the prosecuting attorney is the civil legal advisor to the judges undoubtedly furthers this working relationship.

At the state level the relationship is more complex. Washington's judiciary has a strong central administrative body, the Administrative Office of the Courts, which supports the various branches of the judiciary in budget and policy matters. Each level of the judiciary has its own judges' association through which judges express their positions on criminal justice policy issues. The Superior Court Judges' Association has been very active. A strong convention exists among judges that they should express their views collectively rather than individually and that differences should be worked out internally within the judiciary. The Board for Judicial Administration, created by the Supreme Court, represents the judiciary collectively on budget and broad policy issues.

There are recurring tensions between prosecutors and judges. To some extent the tensions are institutional as each group seeks to maximize what it believes is its necessary discretion. Tensions also arise from the nature of the judicial role. Sentencing reform, for example, has been a recurring subject of disagreement. While there are individual exceptions, most judges have not been supporters of legislative efforts to structure judicial discretion. The Superior Court Judges' Association opposed the Sentencing Reform Act when it was initially adopted in 1981. Although judicial members of the initial Washington State Sentencing Guidelines Commission worked effectively to promote and implement the Sentencing Reform Act, many, perhaps most, judges remained opposed on a policy level to presumptive, as opposed to voluntary, sentencing guidelines.

Prosecutors, by contrast, have generally supported the Sentencing Reform Act. Over the years, this has led to times when the two groups took strongly opposed positions. One example arose when Washington formulated its response to the decision of the US Supreme Court in *Blakely v. Washington*, 542 U.S. 296 (2004), that the aggravated sentence provisions of Washington's Sentencing Reform Act were unconstitutional. The Superior Court Judges' Association strongly supported making Washington's sentencing guidelines voluntary whereas the Sentencing Guidelines Commission, supported by the prosecutors, advocated a procedural approach that retained the presumptive nature of the guidelines.

The commission's position prevailed in the legislature, but the dispute left some judges unhappy. For a period of time, the Superior Court Judges' Association adopted the position of opposing every amendment to the Sentencing Reform Act, arguing that until the guidelines were made voluntary, the judges would not support any changes, regardless of their individual merits. This led the judges to oppose a proposal by the Sentencing Guidelines Commission, with the support of prosecutors and law enforcement, to broaden the guidelines' ranges, thus expanding judicial discretion. The proposal also provided for longer presumptive sentences for offenders with very long criminal histories, a provision the prosecutors strongly supported. The judges were successful, and the legislature did not adopt the commission's proposal. Since then, the judges have moved away from their adamant position and have supported reform efforts that do not include voluntary guidelines.

There remains, however, a lingering frustration among judges about the existence of Washington's Sentencing Reform Act. The act, which significantly constrains judicial sentencing discretion, was an initiative sponsored by prosecutors that was adopted over the objection of the judges. Judges, rightly, see their discretion curtailed while prosecutorial discretion remains essentially unchecked. Many judges resent this asymmetry, and it contributes to continuing tensions.

To some extent, the tensions arise from the nature of the judicial role. Judges in adjudicating cases decide legal and factual issues, to be sure after consideration of the arguments of lawyers, but they make the ultimate decisions. The parties accept those decisions.

In political and policy arenas, the dynamic is quite different. Proponents of different interests strongly advocate their positions, but no one group gets to decide the matter. Resolution is frequently the result of compromise and not the imposition of what one party believes is the correct decision. Judges tend to be uncomfortable with a process that resembles Bismarck's sausage factory more than a principled search for the correct decision. This leads, in my experience, to a certain level of frustration on the part of judges that reduces their effectiveness in the political process. Prosecutors tend to see judges in the political arena as rigid and autocratic. Judges see prosecutors as advocates whose goal is to maximize their position rather than to reach a principled resolution. These differences in perspective are deep and enduring but, of course, do not prevent prosecutors and judges from finding common ground in many areas. They are, however, always present and contribute to continuing unease in the relationship.

There have been instances in which prosecutors have come into sharp conflict with the Supreme Court, both institutionally and with individual justices. In 2002, the Supreme Court held in *In Re Andress*, 56 Pacific 3d 981 (2002), a 5–4 decision, that when the legislature adopted Washington's felony murder statute in 1975, it had not intended to include assault as a predicate felony. It had been common for prosecutors to use the underlying felony assault as the predicate felony for felony murder when the assault resulted in death. This allowed conviction for murder in the second degree without proving intent to kill. Intent to assault was legally sufficient until the Supreme Court ruled otherwise.

The prosecutors' response was quick and strong. They accused the court of misreading legislative history and argued that the decision would result in the release from prison of hundreds of murderers. The controversy became a front-page story throughout the state, and it was rekindled again and again as other defendants serving felony murder sentences sought and frequently obtained postconviction relief. In their motion for reconsideration, prosecutors identified 299 other cases as likely to be affected by the court's decision. The Supreme Court granted *Andress*'s motion to strike these submissions as "not relevant."

The *Andress* decision was announced on October 24, 2002. Justice Charles Johnson, who was one of the five justices in the majority, was running for reelection in a contested race. His opponent in the general election was Pamela Loginsky, a staff attorney for WAPA. In the primary in September, Johnson received 41 percent of the vote, Loginsky 37 percent, and a third candidate 22 percent. The *Andress* decision became an issue in the campaign but had no visible effect on the outcome. Johnson won with 55 percent of the vote.

When their motion for reconsideration was denied, the prosecutors turned to the legislature for a curative amendment. The legislature quickly agreed. The bill passed the Senate 49–0 and the House 95–1. An explicit reference to assault was added to the felony murder statute, and the legislature adopted the following findings of its intent:

> The legislature finds that the 1975 legislature clearly and unambiguously stated that any felony, including assault, can be a predicate offense for felony murder. The intent was evident: Punish, under the applicable murder statutes, those who commit a homicide in the course and in furtherance of a felony. This legislature reaffirms that original intent and further intends to honor and reinforce the court's decisions over the past twenty-eight years inter-

preting "in furtherance of" as requiring the death to be sufficiently close in time and proximity to the predicate felony. The legislature does not agree with or accept the court's findings of legislative intent in *State v. Andress* . . . and reasserts that assault has always been and still remains a predicate offense for felony murder in the second degree.

To prevent a miscarriage of the legislature's original intent, the legislature finds in light of *State v. Andress* . . . that it is necessary to amend Revised Code of Washington 9A.32.050. This amendment is intended to be curative in nature. The legislature urges the supreme court to apply this interpretation retroactively to July 1, 1976.

The Supreme Court subsequently in *In Re Hinton*, 100 P.3d 80 (2004), held that retroactive application of the amendment was unconstitutional. The court began its opinion with a pointed rejoinder to prosecutors:

> While the facts of each petitioner's conduct are immaterial to the legal questions we address in this opinion, we are aware that some of these cases involve horrifying conduct, and all involve heartbreaking loss of life. The cost in terms of human anguish is immeasurable. Judges are not immune to these horrors. Yet, to assure lawful and fair treatment of all persons convicted under a statute that did not criminalize their acts as felony murder, all of these petitioners are entitled to relief. Our obligation is to see that the law is carried out uniformly and justly.
>
> We note that the prosecutors in these cases have stressed the nature of the petitioners' conduct and have vigorously argued that their convictions should stand. A public prosecutor is "a *quasi*-judicial officer, representing the People of the state, and presumed to act impartially in the interest only of justice." . . . It is important to remember that such officers "have to deal with all that is . . . criminal, coarse and brutal in human life. But the safeguards which the wisdom of ages has thrown around persons accused of crime cannot be disregarded, and such officers are reminded that a fearless, impartial discharge of public duty, accompanied by a spirit of fairness toward the accused, is the highest commendation they can hope for." (856)

While passions have cooled with the passage of time, memories are long and the relationships between prosecutors and the Supreme Court remain strained.

Just last year a sitting justice was defeated in his bid for reelection in a race in which the prosecutors supported his challenger. Richard B. Sanders was first elected to the Supreme Court in 1995 and promptly become embroiled in a judicial ethics imbroglio. Immediately after being sworn into office in January 1996, Justice Sanders attended and spoke at a rally held by March for Life, an organization opposed to abortion. This resulted in his being admonished for a violation of the Code of Judicial Conduct (*In Re Sanders*, 955 Pacific 2d 369 [1998]). Unbowed, Sanders continued to espouse his libertarian views, on and off the bench. He drew political support from conservative groups and the trial lawyers. Prosecutors, however, found his libertarian philosophy not to their liking when it led him to find a violation of defendants' rights in a number of criminal appeals. In 2003, prosecutors filed a complaint with the Washington Commission on Judicial Conduct alleging unethical action by Sanders while he was on a tour of the Special Commitment Center, the facility where sexually violent predators who had been civilly committed were held. The commission found that Sanders's ex parte conversations with inmates who had pending cases before the Supreme Court created an appearance of partiality that violated the Code of Judicial Conduct. Sanders vigorously defended himself, but the Supreme Court affirmed the admonishment imposed by the Commission on Judicial Conduct (*In Re Sanders*, 145 Pacific 3d 1209 [2006]).

In 2010, when Sanders sought reelection, prosecutors endorsed his opponent, a well-respected appellate lawyer and former Washington Court of Appeals judge. Sanders lost narrowly, receiving 49.66 percent of the vote. The extent to which the prosecutors' endorsement of his opponent made a difference is difficult to assess. The biggest public issue in the campaign was racially insensitive remarks by Sanders during the campaign that received a large media play.[6] This probably played a larger role.

---

[6] Sanders stated that African Americans were overrepresented in the prison system because they commit a disproportionate number of crimes. This led the *Seattle Times*, the state's largest newspaper, to call for his defeat. This controversy led to the publication of a *Preliminary Report on Race and Washington's Criminal Justice System* by an ad hoc Task Force on Race and the Criminal Justice System, which is affiliated with the Fred T. Korematsu Center for Law and Equality at Seattle University School of Law. The report, which includes the newspaper stories, is available at http://www.law.seattleu.edu/x8777.xml.

VII. Prosecutors and Law Reform

Prosecutors have been active participants in the many reforms that have been implemented in Washington over the past half century. Often they were major proponents of proposed changes that were ultimately adopted.

A. Procedural Reform

Beginning in the late 1960s, Washington entered an era of reform throughout the criminal justice system. Prosecutors played an active role. Stimulated by the adoption by the American Bar Association of its *Minimum Standards for Criminal Justice*, the Washington Judicial Council undertook to develop comprehensive court rules for criminal procedure. Previously, criminal procedure had been governed by statute. Funded by a grant from the LEAA, a broadly representative group of judges, prosecutors, and defense attorneys working from 1966 to 1971 proposed a comprehensive set of criminal procedure rules for the superior and district courts. The prosecuting attorneys of Snohomish and Pierce Counties acted as co–vice chairs. The new rules included broad reciprocal pretrial discovery, a strong speedy trial rule, and pretrial release on recognizance in preference to bail. The development process was contentious with major differences asserted by prosecutors and the defense bar, but consensus was finally reached and prosecutors supported the proposals. They were adopted by the Washington Supreme Court and became effective in 1973.

B. Substantive Criminal Law Reform

Revision of Washington's criminal code was undertaken at the same time. Stimulated by the American Law Institute's 1962 promulgation of the *Model Penal Code*, a grant from LEAA was obtained that supported hiring of staff by the Washington Legislative Council. Drafting began in 1969 and produced a proposal to the legislature in 1970. Prosecutors did not support all the proposals, and the proposed code stalled. In 1973 prosecutors proposed their own draft of a revised criminal code. This was the first joint action by prosecuting attorneys, independent of other actors in the criminal justice system. The Washington State Bar Association followed with a proposed draft in 1974. The differences in the various proposals were mainly technical. All groups supported the concept of comprehensive reform based on the

Model Penal Code format. The 1975 legislature resolved the differences and adopted a new criminal code.

C. Plea Bargaining Reform

Beginning in the mid-1970s, the King County Prosecuting Attorney's Office undertook a reexamination and reform of its plea bargaining practices. Influenced by the work of Kenneth Culp Davis (1969) and a national debate about the long-standing practice of extending concessions to defendants in return for guilty pleas, Christopher T. Bayley developed and promulgated a series of policies governing the use of prosecutorial discretion (Bayley 1976*b*).

The initial policies restricted the filing of habitual criminal charges, which potentially could be applied to many offenders, to only a few of the cases to which they were literally applicable. Those policies received judicial approval when the selective enforcement they embodied was challenged as violative of due process and equal protection guarantees (*State v. Nixon*, 517 Pacific 2d 212 [1973]). The Court of Appeals observed that "we find present here no laxity in enforcement but rather an objective approach consistent with pragmatic and due process values" (360).[7] By the late 1970s, written standards had been adopted governing essentially all aspects of the exercise of prosecutorial discretion and the criteria on which it was exercised in King County. These policies drew on the Uniform Crime Charging Standards adopted by the California District Attorneys Association (1974) and the National Prosecution Standards adopted by the National District Attorneys Association in 1972 (National District Attorneys Association 1977). The King County standards were the most detailed in Washington, but a number of other Washington prosecuting attorneys adopted policies governing prosecutors' exercise of discretion.

Washington's prosecutors' experience with written standards has been positive. Apprehensions that had inhibited their development proved to be unfounded. With the exception of those relating to habitual criminal prosecutions, the standards did not become the subject of litigation. In the larger offices the standards significantly increased

---

[7] Subsequent versions of these standards also withstood constitutional attacks (*State v. Lee*, 558 Pacific 2d 236 [1976], appeal dismissed for want of a substantial federal question; 432 U.S. 901 [1977]; *State v. Anderson*, 528 Pacific 2d 1003 [1974]; *State v. Clark*, 572 Pacific 2d 734 [1977]; *State v. Cooper*, 583 Pacific 2d 1225 [1978]; *State v. Rowe*, 609 Pacific 2d 1348 [1980]).

consistency of decision making and provided an effective tool for prosecuting attorneys to use in implementing policy changes. Public reaction was positive, even concerning policies providing for less than full enforcement. In King County, for example, an "expedited crime" policy resulted in essentially all first-offense thefts involving $250–$500 in value being prosecuted as gross misdemeanors rather than as felonies, as they were classified by the Criminal Code. The policy was adopted to conserve limited resources for prosecution of more serious crimes. The public reaction, even within the retail business community, was positive. The policy was seen as a rational exercise of discretion, and rather than provoke public resentment, it furthered a sense of community satisfaction with the performance of the prosecutor.

In 1977 the Washington House of Representatives asked WAPA to propose policies "designed to afford similarly situated defendants equal opportunity with respect to plea bargaining discussions and agreements."[8] The association responded by adopting a resolution "Policies and Guidelines for Plea Bargaining" (1977), which contained an analysis of the reasons for, and an articulation of the factors to be considered in, plea bargaining. In 1980, the Washington Supreme Court in a series of cases held that a uniform prosecutorial policy of always filing habitual criminal charges whenever they could be proven, without regard to the presence or absence of mitigating circumstances, was an unconstitutional abuse of discretion (*State v. Pettitt*, 609 Pacific 2d 1364 [1980]; *State v. Barton*, 609 Pacific 2d 1353 [1980]; *State v. Rinier*, 93 Washington 2d 309, 609 Pacific 2d 1358 [1980]). The Supreme Court reviewed the King County standards at length, finding that their "classification of felonies as 'high impact' and 'expedited' crimes for the purposes of determining whether a habitual criminal charge should be filed is not only reasonable and logical, it permits an objective approach consistent with pragmatic and due process values" and that the criteria and procedures applicable to the use of exceptions provided "protection against arbitrary decisions" (*State v. Rowe*, 609 Pacific 2d 1348 [1980]).

The message was clear. They provided a strong impetus to the development of explicit prosecutorial policies and contributed to the

---

[8] House Floor Resolution 77-57, June 18, 1977. The language was evidently derived from the American Law Institute's (1968) *Model Code of Pre-arraignment Procedure*, which called for "each prosecution office . . . [to] issue regulations . . . setting forth guidelines and procedures with respect to plea discussions and plea agreements designed to afford similarly situated defendants equal opportunities for plea discussion and plea agreements" (sec. 350.3 [2]).

adoption by WAPA of statewide charge and disposition policies in 1980 (Washington Association of Prosecuting Attorneys 1980). While these policies were stated in general terms and expressly permitted local variations, they reflected commitment to the reasoned, consistent, and public exercise of prosecutorial discretion.

By 1981, when the legislature adopted the Sentencing Reform Act, explicit standards governing the exercise of prosecutorial discretion were an accepted practice that the legislature took into account when it directed the Sentencing Guidelines Commission to "give consideration to the existing guidelines adopted by . . . the Washington Association of Prosecuting Attorneys and the experience gained through use of those guidelines" (Revised Code of Washington 9.94A.040[2][b]) in carrying out a statutory directive to "devise recommended prosecuting standards in respect to charging of offenses and plea agreements." The commission's proposal closely tracked the existing guidelines of WAPA and was adopted by the legislature without controversy.

At the urging of prosecutors, the commission prefaced its proposal to the legislature with this limitation: "These standards are intended solely for the guidance of prosecutors in the State of Washington. They are not intended to, do not and may not be relied upon to create a right or benefit, substantive or procedural, enforceable at law by a party in litigation with the state" (Revised Code of Washington 9.94A.401). Not surprisingly, the courts have honored that limitation and held that defendants may not raise issues in court relating to the application of the prosecutorial standards (*State v. Lee*, 847 Pacific 2d 25 [1993]).

The legislature, following a recommendation by the Sentencing Guidelines Commission, did provide for judicial review of the manner in which prosecutors implemented the standards in the plea bargaining process:

> If a plea agreement has been reached by the prosecutor and the defendant pursuant to Revised Code of Washington 9.94A.421, they shall at the time of the defendant's plea state to the court, on the record, the nature of the agreement and the reasons for the agreement. The prosecutor shall inform the court on the record whether the victim or victims of all crimes against persons, as defined in Revised Code of Washington 9.94A.411, covered by the plea agreement have expressed any objection to or comments on

the nature of and reasons for the plea agreement. The court, at the time of the plea, shall determine if the agreement is consistent with the interests of justice and with the prosecuting standards. The court shall, on the record, inform the defendant and the prosecutor that they are not bound by the agreement and that the defendant may withdraw the defendant's plea of guilty, if one has been made, and enter a plea of not guilty. (Revised Code of Washington 9.94A.431[1])

Information concerning plea bargains is routinely submitted to the court at the time of the entry of the guilty plea, but Washington's judges have in form but not in substance exercised the authority given them by the legislature. The statutory requirement that "the court, at the time of the plea, shall determine if the agreement is consistent with the interests of justice and the prosecuting standards" is routinely satisfied by a preprinted judicial finding in the standard sentencing form that "the agreement is consistent with the interests of justice and the prosecuting standards."

The explanation is inherent in the nature of the plea bargaining process. Judges rely on the adversary presentation of issues; when a guilty plea is offered, neither the defense attorney nor the prosecutor has any interest in having it rejected. They have resolved their differences, and both want the judge to accept the plea. In the absence of anyone asking them to review the bargain, it is not surprising that judges do not typically exercise the authority they have been granted. Crowded judicial dockets in any case create an incentive for cases to be disposed of by guilty plea rather than by trial.

That prosecutorial guidelines are not legally enforceable does not mean they are not an effective internal tool in the management of a prosecutor's office. Many of the large prosecutors' offices in Washington employ written policies to implement office policies and to ensure uniformity. They have become a central feature in large and midsized prosecutors' offices.

D. Sentencing Reform

Prosecutorial involvement in sentencing reform in Washington has a long history. In 1909 Washington adopted a comprehensive criminal code drafted by George Vanderveer, then King County Prosecuting Attorney. The Criminal Code of 1909 abolished the insanity defense. The Washington State Supreme Court responded by holding the abolition unconstitutional because it denied a defendant the right to trial by jury and due process. In the course of its opinion the court quoted from Vanderveer's brief:

> The central idea upon which the whole fabric of criminal jurisprudence was formerly built was the idea that every criminal act was the product of a free will possessing a full understanding of the difference between right and wrong and full capacity to choose a right or wrong course of action, and as one error naturally and logically follows another, it was only natural and logical that society should have prescribed punishments as a central feature of its scheme for correction. A better understanding of crime and the science of criminology now convinces us that this theory is wholly wrong—that a dominant percentage of all criminals are not free moral agents, but as a result of hereditary influences or early environments, are either mentally or morally degenerate or their crimes are committed under the degenerating influence of intoxicating liquor. An understanding of this fact has made readily apparent the folly of expecting that punishment could relieve the condition, and accordingly stocks, whipping posts and chain gangs are giving way to workhouses, reformatories and asylums, the purpose of which is to instruct, educate and reform rather than further to debase the individual; and the modern system of criminal classification and segregation are themselves a recognition of the fact that every criminal is a concrete problem. (*State v. Strasberg*, 110 Pacific 1020 [1910])

The court quoted Vanderveer as arguing that the purpose of the sentencing provisions of the code "is to put in operation in this state a scheme of criminal jurisprudence which gives recognition to these ideas." "Learned counsel's premise," said the court, "suggests a noble conception, and may give promise of a condition of things towards which the humanitarian spirit of the age is tending." While sympathetic to Vanderveer's argument, the court concluded, "We cannot shut our eyes to the fact that the element of punishment is still in our criminal laws" and that "as long as this is the spirit of our laws, though it may be mellowed in the treatment of the convicted, as compared with former times, the constitutional rights here invoked must be given full force and effect when an accused person is put upon trial to determine the question of his guilt of crime" (1022). The attempt to abolish the insanity defense was rejected, but the balance of Vanderveer's reform remained intact.[9] It was to remain the basic structure of Washington's sentencing system for three-quarters of a century, until its replacement by the Sentencing Reform Act.

Sentencing reform once again became a public issue in Washington in 1975, with the proposal of a new Sentencing Act by the Governor's Task Force on Decision Making Models in Corrections.[10] The act pushed the rehabilitative ideal to its logical conclusion. It abolished distinctions in potential punishment among crimes, thus severing the proportionality link between crime and punishment. All felonies, regardless of severity, were to be punishable by an indeterminate sentence of not more than 5 years. A category of "dangerous offenders" who would receive an indeterminate life sentence was to be created.

Response was quick and sharp. Christopher T. Bayley, then prosecuting attorney of King County, led a public attack. He argued that sentencing based on the rehabilitative ideal would be unjust because it would sever the link between crime and punishment and be ineffective because it rejected the benefits of deterrence and incapacitation. The controversy evolved into a major public debate on the purposes of sentencing. In December 1975, Bayley sponsored a conference on sentencing at the University of Washington, which brought such national figures as Norval Morris and Robert Martinson into the local debate. In 1976 the *Washington Law Review* published a symposium issue that brought together a number of articles from different perspectives (Talmadge 1976). The intensity of the public debate was demonstrated by the reelection defeats of two superior court judges who were prominently identified with the rehabilitative ideal side of the debate. The election campaigns focused on their views on sentencing.[11]

The guidelines movement was a significant influence on Washing-

---

[9] Vanderveer's life is chronicled in Hawley and Potts (1953). Vanderveer later became a prominent defense attorney representing the International Workers of the World and other labor unions.

[10] The task force was made up of criminal justice professionals and was chaired by the Honorable George Revelle, judge of the King County Superior Court. Judge Revelle had long been active in sentencing reform, served as a member of the Council of Judges of the National Council on Crime and Delinquency, and was the author of *Sentencing and Probation* (1976), which was used as the text for judicial education in sentencing at the National Judicial College.

[11] The Honorable Solie M. Ringold and the Hononorable Donald J. Horowitz of the King County Superior Court were defeated in the judicial elections of September 1976. Both had been public participants in the debate. See Ringold (1976) and Horowitz (1976).

ton's criminal justice system during this period. Beginning in 1975, Washington's Board of Prison Terms and Paroles developed guidelines for fixing minimum terms of imprisonment. The guidelines were based on extensive empirical analysis of past board practices. The final version contained 85 pages of extraordinarily detailed provisions that concerned both the initial fixing of minimum terms and the later reconsideration of the length of confinement (Washington State Board of Prison Terms and Paroles 1978, 1979). The guidelines required written reasons to support a decision not to follow them, but there was no provision for internal or external review of such decisions. A study in 1980 showed that the board complied with its guidelines 66 percent of the time (Washington Legislative Budget Committee 1981).

In 1978 the Superior Court Judges Association began a project to develop sentencing guidelines. Using techniques developed in other states (Kress 1980), the guidelines that were developed (Washington Association of Superior Court Judges 1979) were based on empirical analysis of past judicial practices and were intended to guide but not restrict judicial discretion. Their goal was increased consistency, not any normative change in sentencing patterns. They were purely voluntary; no statute or court rule compelled judges to consider them. A study in 1981 found that judges reported using the guidelines in 70 percent of cases sentenced and that 66 percent of those sentences were within the guidelines (Washington Superior Court Judges Association and Office of Administrator for the Courts 1981). That less than half of sentences were imposed within the guidelines became a powerful argument against voluntary guidelines.

Washington's prosecuting attorneys also developed guidelines governing sentencing recommendations during this period. The effort began in King County, where the Office of the King County Prosecuting Attorney in the early 1970s promulgated policies governing filing and disposition decisions. A number of other offices followed, and in 1980 WAPA adopted uniform charging and disposition policies (Washington Association of Prosecuting Attorneys 1980).

These experiences with guidelines played an important role in the development of sentencing reform proposals in Washington. With the use of the guidelines, judges and other professionals came to understand the benefits of the structuring influence of external standards. The fear that guidelines would produce rigid, mechanistic decisions dissipated with experience. By 1981 the use of guidelines, albeit voluntary, was an accepted fact throughout Washington's criminal justice system. This reduced opposition to the idea of guidelines with legal force and also shaped their content. In the Sentencing Reform Act, the legislature directed the newly created Washington State Sentencing Guidelines Commission to "give consideration" in developing its proposals to the existing judicial and prosecutorial guidelines and to "the experience gained through use of those guidelines" (Revised Code of Washington 9.94A.040[5]).

The first legislative consideration of sentencing reform in Washington occurred in 1977. A sentencing act proposed by the King County Prosecuting Attorney was introduced and passed the House of Representatives (Bayley 1976a). Though the proposal died in the Senate, it provided an important part of the theoretical basis for the Juvenile Justice Reform Act of 1977 (Becker 1978) and for future legislative consideration of sentencing reform. Norm Maleng's replacement of Christopher Bayley in 1979 did not diminish support for sentencing reform by the King County Prosecuting Attorney's Office. Maleng supported Bayley's proposals and assigned Robert Lasnik, a member of his staff, as legislative liaison to push sentencing reform.[12]

Sentencing reform was considered at every subsequent session until the Sentencing Reform Act of 1981 was adopted. It was developed by an interim Select Committee on Corrections of the House of Representatives. This committee, led by Representatives Mary Kay Becker (Democrat, Whatcom) and Gene Struthers (Republican, Walla Walla), spent months considering various proposals and listening to arguments of proponents and opponents of various proposals. The committee considered the experiences of other states that had reformed their sentencing systems in the 1970s and benefited from the theoretical debate that had raged nationally over the preceding decade. The Sentencing Reform Act reflects a uniquely Washingtonian perspective. It represents a consensus of otherwise disparate interests and groups. Becker observed that the fact that she and Struthers reached agreement was like "Jane Fonda and John Wayne coauthoring a book on the Vietnam War." By extending guidelines to all felony sentences, not only those involving prison sentences, and by seeking to regulate both plea bargaining and sentencing, Washington's approach was substantially more

---

[12] Lasnik became Maleng's chief of staff and later a King County superior court judge. He now serves as chief judge of the US District Court for the Western District of Washington.

comprehensive and ambitious than any adopted elsewhere in the United States at the time.

Prosecutors continued their involvement in sentencing reform after the Sentencing Reform Act went into effect in 1984. Norm Maleng and Don Brockett, prosecuting attorney for Spokane County, were appointed as prosecutor representatives on the Sentencing Guidelines Commission and played influential roles as the guidelines were developed. Maleng served as the commission's chair.

E. Citizen Initiatives

Populist politics, in the form of citizen initiatives, strongly influenced sentencing policy in the 1990s although prosecutors were not the proponents of the initiatives. Washington's political system reflects its populist origins. The first provision of Washington's Constitution declares that "all political power is inherent in the people" (Washington Constitution, art. I, sec. 1). The "people's power" has been jealously guarded and frequently exercised. In 1992 and again in 1995, the people of Washington by supporting initiatives brought back mandatory sentences for certain offenders. The Sentencing Reform Act had repealed Washington's habitual criminal and almost all other mandatory sentencing laws. Its premise was that sentences should be presumptive, not mandatory, and that judges should decide what sentences were appropriate in individual cases.

A conservative Washington think tank, headed by a talk show host, promoted legislation in 1992, under the banner "Three Strikes and You're Out," that would impose mandatory life sentences for people receiving a third conviction for certain designated felonies. The Sentencing Guidelines Commission proposed a narrower alternative. The legislature was unable to resolve the differences, and both measures failed. The "three strikes" supporters then turned to the initiative process under which any proposition may be placed on the ballot if petitions to do so have been signed by voters totaling 8 percent of voters in the previous general election.

Initiatives are common in Washington, as in most western states. In 1993, for example, voters adopted measures concerning legislative term limits and freedom of reproductive choice. The three strikes initiative easily qualified for the 1992 ballot and passed with over 75 percent of the state vote, carrying each of Washington's 39 counties. Prosecutors were not major visible proponents.

Encouraged by the success of three strikes, the same sponsors returned in 1994 with an initiative to the legislature concerning weapons used in crimes. Titled "Hard Time for Armed Crime," this initiative proposed a system of mandatory prison sentence enhancements for felons committing crimes while armed with a deadly weapon. The initiative also sought to make criminal justice decisions more transparent. Prosecutors were required to make public their reasons for plea bargains, and the sentencing commission was required to publish sentences imposed by individual judges.

Washington law allows the legislature two choices when initiatives to the legislature gain the necessary signatures: adopt the initiative as proposed or adopt an alternative and place both the initiative and the alternative on the ballot. Legislative leaders believed that a more moderate alternative would be defeated, and none was proposed. With the memory of the people's overwhelming vote on three strikes in mind, the legislature adopted the initiative by strong bipartisan majorities. Again prosecutors were not prominent proponents or opponents. Many prosecutors favored longer sentences and some favored the initiatives, but most believed that they had sufficient authority to achieve sentences they believed appropriate under existing law. WAPA took no position on the initiative.

In recent years, Dan Satterberg, King County Prosecuting Attorney, has successfully supported clemency petitions for a few offenders serving three-strike life sentences. He has also supported legislation to eliminate the least serious predicate felonies and to provide for a "second look" after 15 years with eligibility for release at that point.

The initiative's direction to the sentencing commission regarding judicial sentencing patterns was very specific. The initiative required that the commission record each judge's sentences for all violent crimes and those involving deadly weapons. When the commission had created its original database, it decided not to record judges' names with each sentence. The judicial members had successfully argued that such information could be used to unduly pressure judges who were, after all, operating within discretion granted by the legislature.

The commission first responded to the legislative direction by publishing the total number of standard range sentences imposed by individual judges, with detailed information on each exceptional sentence. The initiative's chief proponents objected strongly, both to the limitations of the information and to its timing, since it was released after elections. Subsequent reports covered each judge's felony sentences, and publication was advanced to before the filing date for judicial elections.

To date the information published on judge's sentences has never been the focus of a contested judicial election, and in recent years the legislature has permitted the commission to suspend publication of this report, along with others, to save funds. Whether the fear that judges expressed has influenced their behavior is difficult to assess, but it seems reasonable to assume that potential public reaction to their sentencing decisions is in judges' minds when they exercise their sentencing discretion.

The initiative's requirement that prosecutors make their reasons for plea bargains public has had no discernible effect. No organized system exists for recording plea bargaining reasons, and judges do not routinely require prosecutors to indicate why they enter into bargains. The sentencing commission's report on sentencing indicates whether the prosecutor agreed with or opposed an exceptional sentence. The non-implementation of this initiative provision has not attracted criticism. For the initiative sponsors at least, concerns about leniency toward criminals were focused on judges, not prosecutors. Although complaints that judges are "soft on crime" are not uncommon, such criticisms are seldom lodged against prosecutors.

F. Sex Offender Sentencing

The Sentencing Reform Act of 1981 provided that sex offenses were to be sentenced in the same way as other crimes. Participation in treatment programs was to be voluntary, not mandatory, and the just-deserts principles that underlay the act called for relatively severe prison sentences in many cases. Both victim advocates and deputy prosecuting attorneys who handle sex offense prosecutions argued that eliminating treatment as an alternative to confinement would cause many victims not to report sex crimes, especially in cases of intrafamilial sexual abuse against children, concerning which victims frequently wanted treatment for the offender more than punishment. The Sentencing Guidelines Commission was persuaded by these arguments and in 1983 recommended the creation of a special sex offender sentencing alternative that allowed mandatory treatment in the community rather than prison sentences for first-time nonforcible sexual offenses. The prosecutors supported this recommendation, and it was adopted by the legislature in 1983.

Over the years, this sentencing option came under attack as "soft" on sex offenders. Prosecutors have consistently supported the crime victim advocates' defense of the alternative, and it remains available today.

When the legislature revisited sex offender sentencing in the late 1980s, prosecutors were again involved, in a supportive role to victim advocates. The major exception involved the official response to the public outrage that followed the rape and mutilation in 1989 of a young boy by a sex offender recently released from prison. In an effort to respond to and calm public calls for a special session of the legislature, which it was feared would rush to adopt ill-considered sentencing proposals, Governor Booth Gardner, a Democrat, appointed a broadly based Task Force on Community Protection and asked King County Prosecuting Attorney Norm Maleng, a Republican, to chair it. Maleng led the task force to reach consensus on a series of proposals, which the legislature unanimously adopted in 1990 and which were widely seen as rational responses to the crisis. The reform included significant increases in the severity of sentences for sex crimes between strangers but preserved treatment-based sentences for sex crimes involving children in family situations.

One aspect of the proposals is interesting for what it reveals about prosecutorial attitudes. The sex offender whose crime provoked the public outcry had been released from prison at the end of his sentence. His release was not discretionary but occurred because his maximum term had expired. Prison officials had recognized his continuing dangerousness but had no legal power to continue to hold him. Ken Eikenberry, the attorney general and a Republican, proposed a return to indeterminate sentencing with all people convicted of Class A sex offenses to receive a life maximum sentence. Maleng and his office crafted a narrower proposal that allowed civil commitment of "sexually violent predators." Part of Maleng's argument was that the attorney general's proposal would result in significantly more defendants being subject to the control of the state for longer periods. Maleng was successful, and the task force and the legislature unanimously adopted his proposal (Boerner 1992). Maleng's proposal was the first in the nation to employ civil commitment in this context and spawned a number of replications throughout the United States.

G. Drug Sentencing

Prosecutors in Washington have been particularly active with regard to drug sentencing. The success of their efforts over time reveals both their political effectiveness and the shifting nature of their goals over time. Drug sentencing in Washington now is quite different from what it had been in recent years. Prosecutors have significantly influenced those changes.

When it became apparent that judges were frequently using "first-time offender" provisions of the Sentencing Reform Act to reduce sentences for first-time drug delivery convictions from a 12–14-month prison sentence to a 0–90-day jail sentence, Norm Maleng led the prosecutors in advocating elimination of this option for cases involving heroin or cocaine. He consistently took the position that those who "deal" hard drugs deserve prison and saw the extensive use of the first-offender option as inconsistent with this goal. The legislature agreed, and the option was eliminated for those offenders.

Prosecutors' concerns about drug offenses did not subside. By 1988, Maleng and Don Brockett, the Spokane County Prosecuting Attorney, convinced the commission to revisit the sentencing ranges for drug crimes. The commission recommended that the 1989 legislature increase seriousness levels (and, thus, presumptive sentence ranges) for certain drug offenses. Its recommendation was incorporated into an omnibus bill developed and supported by a bipartisan group of legislators. When the legislation passed in 1989, the presumptive sentence ranges for first-offense delivery of drugs increased from 12–14 months to 21–27 months, the offender's score points for prior drug convictions were increased, and a 24-month sentence enhancement was added for deliveries occurring within 1,000 feet of a school or a school bus stop or in a public park. The legislation also included a special tax on bottled beverages that funded treatment centers for drug addicts (it was repealed in the next legislative session).

These sentencing charges combined with more aggressive prosecution of drug offenses to double the number of convictions for drug offenses between 1985 and 1987. They doubled again between 1987 and 1989. Prison admissions for drug offenses increased from 143 in 1986 to 1,565 in 1990, becoming 37 percent of all prison admissions (Boerner 1993).

During the early 1990s prosecutors successfully opposed proposals to adopt a sentencing alternative for drug offenders whose crimes were caused by drug addiction. By 1994, however, the prosecutor's position began to change. In 1994 King County began a drug court with Maleng's support. The first drug court judge was Ricardo Martinez, who had previously served as the head of the King County prosecutor's drug unit.[13] Drug courts in Washington proved to be as popular as they are across the United States and have come to be widely supported by prosecutors. An evaluation of drug courts by the Washington State Institute for Public Policy concluded that they reduced recidivism and, though more expensive to operate than regular courts, returned $1.74 in benefits for each dollar of costs (Washington State Institute of Public Policy 2003). Currently there are drug courts in 24 of Washington's 39 counties.

In 1995, Maleng organized a diverse coalition of supporters, including law enforcement officials and the sponsors of the Three Strikes and "Hard Time for Armed Crime" initiatives, to promote a drug sentencing alternative. The proposal for a "Special Drug Offender Sentencing Alternative" combined a drug treatment option for addicted offenders while retaining the concept of "prison sentences for dealers," a consistent feature of Maleng's sentencing priorities. The alternative authorized judges to waive the standard sentence for first-time drug offenders and impose a prison sentence of one-half of the standard range followed by 1 year of community-based drug treatment. Those who violated conditions of the community portion of the sentence could be returned to prison for the remaining one-half of the standard range. In 1999 the legislature expanded eligibility for this sentencing alternative to include all drug offenders who had no prior violent offense convictions (Revised Code of Washington 9.94A.660).

In 1999 prosecutors proposed to relax the strictures of the Sentencing Reform Act on sentences of less than 1 year in confinement (approximately 70 percent of all felony sentences are less than 1 year). The act had always authorized judges to convert any jail sentence (total confinement of 1 year or less) to partial confinement (work or education release) and to convert up to 30 days of total confinement to community service at the rate of 8 hours of community service for 1 day of total confinement. Local officials have long believed that the Sentencing Reform Act caused upward-spiraling jail costs and have

---

[13] Judge Martinez now serves as a US district judge for the Western District of Washington.

argued that meeting those financial obligations leaves them without resources to develop alternative sanctions. At the urging of prosecutors the 1999 legislature added a cryptic but potentially powerful sentence to the provisions of the Sentencing Reform Act governing alternatives to total confinement: "For offenders convicted of non-violent and non-sex offenses, the court may authorize county jails to convert jail confinement to an available county supervised community option and may require the offender to perform affirmative conduct" (Revised Code of Washington 9.94A.680[3]). No definition of "county supervised community option" was provided, but there was a clear intent to maximize local discretion. Correctional resources at the county level are the fiscal responsibility of county government, and no state funding accompanied the expansion of direction. To date, little implementation has occurred.

In 2001 prosecutors worked with the Sentencing Guidelines Commission to develop a series of changes to the drug sentencing laws. The changes reflected an increased commitment to treatment for drug offenders while retaining severe punishments for those whose involvement with drugs was motivated by profit rather than addiction. The proposal included a separate sentencing grid for drug offenses. The legislature adopted the proposal in 2002 stating, "It is the intent of the legislature to increase the use of effective substance abuse treatment" (Laws of 2002, C. 290, sec. 1).

VIII. The Consequences of Autonomy

That prosecutors have worked collectively to reform Washington's criminal justice system does not mean all agree on how that system should operate in their respective jurisdictions. The policies detailed above were all adopted at the state level but are implemented county by county. The legislature presumably intended that the policies be implemented equally throughout the state. For example, the Sentencing Reform Act provides that "the sentencing guidelines and prosecuting standards shall apply equally in all parts of the state, without discrimination as to any element that does not relate to the crime or the previous record of the defendant" (Revised Code of Washington 9.94A.340). It is, of course, well known that prosecutors in Washington enjoy effective autonomy in how they enforce the laws. This creates an inevitable tension between statewide laws and policies and local

TABLE 1

Part I Offenses Reported per
100,000 Population by County
(2010 Population)

County	Offenses/ 100,000
King (1,933,400)	4,454
Pierce (795,225)	4,457
Snohomish (713,335)	3,382
Spokane (471,221)	5,410
Clark (425,363)	3,104
Thurston (252,264)	3,488
Kitsap (251,133)	2,992
Yakima (243,231)	4,952
Whatcom (201,140)	3,590
Benton (175,177)	2,749

SOURCE.—Washington Association of
Sheriffs (2010).

implementation by autonomous prosecutors answerable only to a local electorate.

I have separated drug crimes from other crimes for analysis because the fundamental differences in how they come to the attention of the criminal justice system make them particularly susceptible to the influence of varying enforcement and prosecutorial policies. I first examine what can be discerned from data available by county regarding nondrug crimes and then turn to analysis of how drug enforcement varies county by county.

Washington's counties vary widely not only in population but also demographically and culturally. Comparisons between them are thus fraught with difficulties in whether the counties are truly comparable on the issue in question.

There are significant differences between counties' reported crime rates. Table 1 depicts Part I offenses reported to the police per 100,000 population for Washington's 10 largest counties.

Prosecutors, however, do not deal with reported crimes. They rely on law enforcement agencies to identify suspects and present cases for prosecution. Comparing the number of Part I crimes cleared by arrest by county provides a closer approximation of those cases that prosecutors actually deal with and thus permits analysis of whether prose-

TABLE 2

Part I Offenses Cleared by
Arrest per 100,000 in 2010

County	Offenses/ 100,000
King	701
Pierce	612
Snohomish	744
Spokane	837
Clark	632
Thurston	807
Kitsap	585
Yakima	996
Whatcom	837
Benton	982

SOURCE.—Washington Association of Sheriffs (2010).

cutors in various counties deal with those cases similarly or differently (see table 2).

Comparing the number of felony filings of Part I offenses with the number of Part I offenses cleared by arrest (table 3) gives some indication of how aggressively prosecutors respond to the cases presented to them.

The variations appear significant, and they are unlikely to result solely from the various offices applying different levels of evidentiary sufficiency. King County, for example, has long had an "expedited crime" policy in which less serious felony property crime cases for which the presumptive sentence would be a year or less in jail are prosecuted as gross misdemeanors for which the maximum sentence is 1 year in jail. Those cases thus receive sentences similar to those they would receive if prosecuted as felonies but are disposed of in district court as gross misdemeanors rather than in superior court as felonies. The justification is efficiency, not the inability to prove a felony. Similar policies in other counties may explain their lower felony filing rates.

The amount of resources assigned to the initial filing decision may also make a difference. For example, in King County, filing decisions are made by a filing unit staffed on a rotating basis by experienced prosecutors. The unit seeks to identify problem cases early and to resolve proof problems either by requiring further police investigation or by adjusting the charges to what can be readily proven. In addition,

TABLE 3

Percentage of Part I Offenses
Cleared by Arrest Resulting
in Felony Filings, 2010

County	Offenses (%)
King	32.0
Pierce	42.8
Snohomish	23.2
Spokane	48.3
Clark	45.0
Thurston	47.0
Kitsap	31.5
Yakima	38.4
Whatcom	44.9
Benton	35.3

SOURCE.—Washington Association
of Sheriffs (2010).

it ensures consistent application of the "expedited crime" policy. Thus it is not surprising that prosecutors in King County file felony charges in a lower percentage of the cases presented to them than do those in Pierce and Spokane Counties, where similar policies are not in effect.

The differences between counties in how they exercise their charging discretion is at least a partial explanation of the large differences in the number of felony convictions per capita between counties. Table 4 displays the wide variation in the number of felony convictions per county on a per capita basis.

Turning to drug offenses, which are particularly responsive to differences in prosecutorial policies, provides further basis for assessing county-level differences. An examination of drug sentencing in Washington in 2001 revealed significant differences between counties in how drug offenses were prosecuted and sentenced (Boerner and Lieb 2001). At that time, King County was the outlier, convicting a far higher percentage of drug offenders of dealing offenses, who thus received prison sentences, than did the other counties. King County remains an outlier a decade later, but in the opposite direction.

Table 5 displays the number of felony drug convictions in the 10 largest counties and in the balance of the state and also the percentage of all felony drug convictions that each county represents. Both increases in the 1990s and decreases in the 2000s were not evenly distributed across the state. Overall statewide trends are consistent with

TABLE 4

Nondrug Felony Convictions
per 100,000

County	Convictions/ 100,000
King	160
Pierce	369
Snohomish	161
Spokane	340
Clark	292
Thurston	320
Kitsap	258
Yakima	409
Whatcom	339
Benton	316
State total (39 counties)	261

SOURCE.—Sentencing Guidelines Commission (2010).

legislative changes in drug sentencing policy, but individual counties varied widely. More than one-third of the total statewide increase in convictions from 1990 to 2000 resulted from increases in Pierce County. By contrast, nearly half of the statewide decrease in convictions from 2000 to 2010 resulted from changes in King County. The overall decrease of 621 convictions from 1990 to 2010 is more than accounted for by King County's decrease of 1,476 convictions. If King

TABLE 5

Total Felony Drug Convictions

County	1990	1995	2000	2005	2010
King	1,849 (32%)	1,805 (27%)	2,015 (23%)	1,172 (14%)	373 (7%)
Pierce	1,092 (19%)	1,744 (26%)	2,133 (25%)	1,334 (16%)	985 (19%)
Snohomish	341 (6%)	310 (5%)	505 (6%)	511 (6%)	263 (5%)
Spokane	243 (4%)	318 (5%)	353 (4%)	759 (9%)	477 (9%)
Clark	169 (3%)	347 (5%)	428 (5%)	623 (7.5%)	395 (8%)
Thurston	158 (3%)	183 (3%)	440 (5%)	429 (5%)	230 (4%)
Kitsap	131 (2%)	169 (3%)	275 (3%)	425 (5%)	264 (5%)
Yakima	572 (10%)	345 (5%)	396 (5%)	350 (4%)	267 (5%)
Whatcom	75 (1%)	109 (2%)	156 (2%)	241 (3%)	212 (4%)
Benton	82 (1%)	114 (2%)	287 (3%)	471 (6%)	242 (5%)
Balance of state (29 counties)	1,046 (18%)	1,206 (18%)	1,632 (19%)	2,007 (24%)	1,429 (28%)
Total	5,758	6,650	8,630	8,322	5,137

SOURCE.—Sentencing Guidelines Commission (2010).

NOTE.—Percentage of state total is in parentheses.

County had produced the same percentage of total convictions in 2010 as it had in 1990, there would have been more than 1,200 more drug convictions in 2010. Something other than changes in statewide drug sentencing policy is responsible. Displaying the data on a population basis makes the county-by-county differences stark.

The decreases in felony drug convictions over the past decade are responsive to legislative changes in drug sentencing policy. The legislature authorized and provided funding for drug courts beginning in 1999. In addition, a new sentencing grid for drug offenses that emphasized treatment options for lower-level offenders was adopted in 2002. The legislature stated its intent as follows:

> It is the intent of the legislature to increase the use of effective substance abuse treatment for defendants and offenders in Washington in order to make frugal use of state and local resources, thus reducing recidivism and increasing the likelihood that defendants and offenders will become productive and law-abiding persons. The legislature recognizes that substance abuse treatment can be effective if it is well planned and involves adequate monitoring, and that substance abuse and addiction is a public safety and public health issue that must be more effectively addressed if recidivism is to be reduced. (Laws of 2002, C. 290, sec. 1)

Prosecutors supported these legislative changes. The changes depicted in table 6 reveal that most, but not all, counties had reduced the number of felony drug convictions by 2005. By 2010 all counties were showing decreases in convictions, but again not evenly across the state.

Pierce County continues to be a significant outlier. While the other counties are demographically different in ways that may influence the manner of drug distribution and thus the visibility of drug offenses, King and Pierce Counties are similar. Both contain central cities in which street-level drug dealing is present. Yet the differences in the number of felony drug convictions are enormous. Tip O'Neill's dictum that "all politics is local" applies to local prosecutors' policies as well.

Examining the data year by year over the past 5 years highlights the changes. Table 7 depicts total felony drug convictions year by year from 2005 to 2010. It reveals declines in all of the larger counties; in 2007 King County's decrease was significantly greater than in any other county. Two reasons appear to account for the differences.

First, Dan Satterberg replaced Norm Maleng as King County Pros-

TABLE 6
Felony Drug Convictions per 100,000 Population

County	1990	1995	2000	2005	2010
King	123	112	116	69	19
Pierce	186	264	304	176	124
Snohomish	73	59	83	78	37
Spokane	67	79	84	116	101
Clark	71	119	124	159	86
Thurston	98	97	212	191	91
Kitsap	96	77	119	177	105
Yakima	303	169	178	152	110
Whatcom	59	73	94	133	105
Benton	73	87	201	298	138
Others (29 counties)	80	110	278	178	113
Total	118	122	146	133	76

SOURCE.—Sentencing Guidelines Commission (2010).

TABLE 7
Felony Drug Convictions

	Fiscal Year					
County	2005	2006	2007	2008	2009	2010
King	1,172	1,188	1,427	1,116	618	373
Pierce	1,334	1,352	1,377	1,314	1,004	985
Snohomish	511	507	532	621	472	263
Spokane	759	821	882	944	759	477
Clark	623	681	665	521	493	395
Thurston	429	414	499	354	282	230
Kitsap	425	488	449	290	295	264
Yakima	356	320	367	290	442	267
Whatcom	241	195	296	235	221	212
Benton	471	489	446	280	255	242
Balance (29 counties)	2,001	2,320	2,123	1,889	1,600	1,429
Total	8,322	8,615	9,063	7,854	6,441	5,137

SOURCE.—Sentencing Guidelines Commission (2010).

ecuting Attorney in June 2007. Satterberg had been a deputy prosecuting attorney in King County since 1986 and served as Maleng's chief of staff for 17 years, but he implemented very different drug enforcement policies. The economic downturn that began in 2008, accelerated in 2009–10, and resulted in significant cuts in the resources available to the prosecutor's office was also important. Satterberg managed the reduction in prosecutorial resources not by across-the-board cuts but by reordering his priorities. Many less serious drug cases that earlier would have been prosecuted as felonies were classified as "expedited crimes," which resulted in a gross misdemeanor conviction or were diverted to drug court. This combination of an evolution in drug sentencing policy and resource constraints reduced felony drug convictions from 1,427 in 2007 to 373 in fiscal year 2010.

All other counties experienced budget cuts during this period, but none experienced as great a decrease in drug convictions as King County. The pattern in King County is likely to continue. Just this year, Satterberg announced a new drug crime diversion program LEAD (Law Enforcement Assisted Diversion). Under the program, cosponsored by the Prosecuting Attorney's Office, the Seattle Police Department, the Seattle City Attorney's Office, the Defender Association, and the American Civil Liberties Union, Seattle police officers are authorized to directly divert low-level street drug offenders to treatment without formal arrest and booking in jail. While the program will probably serve as a division from drug court rather than from felony conviction, its establishment, and its planned extension to the King County Sheriff's Office, is a strong indication of the commitment of the current King County Prosecutor's Office to alternative responses to drug crimes.

The cumulative effect of the variations in policies on state resources is obvious. In Washington, the state government bears all the costs of prison sentences whereas all the costs of jail sentences are borne at the county level. Table 8 displays the total number of prison sentences by county in 2010 on a per capita basis.

King, Snohomish, and Clark Counties use prison sentences far less than other counties while Pierce, Thurston, Yakima, and Benton Counties use them far more. The effects are enormous. If, for example, King County were to impose prison sentences at the same rate as Pierce County, there would have been 2,177 more prison sentences from King County in 2010. Conversely, if Pierce County had imposed prison sentences at the same rate as King County, there would have been 900 fewer prison sentences from Pierce County.

Despite the magnitude of these differences and their consequences for prison costs, which fall wholly on the state budget, they have not prompted a response by the state. In contrast to North Carolina (Wright, in this volume), the data presented above are not regularly reported. No analysis highlights the differences county by county. That

TABLE 8

Total Prison Sentences per
100,000 Population, 2010

County	Sentences/100,000
King	82
Pierce	195
Snohomish	73
Spokane	111
Clark	72
Thurston	165
Kitsap	127
Yakima	198
Whatcom	162
Benton	176
Balance (29 counties)	140
Statewide	126

SOURCE.—Sentencing Guidelines Commission (2010).

county prosecution practices vary is generally understood, but their effects have not been central to policy discussions. The long tradition of local prosecutorial autonomy is accepted as a given. That the existence of statewide prosecutorial guidelines has not effectively constrained that local autonomy has not produced any further efforts to address the disparities that result.

IX. Reflections

This survey of Washington's prosecutors presents a paradox. Acting collectively, prosecutors have been a positive force in law reform over the past half century. Their involvement in substantive criminal law, criminal procedure, and sentencing reforms has been a significant factor in the evolution of generally rational criminal justice policies, and they have moderated the populist passions of the times. They have recognized the challenges of regional differences and have worked to develop and adopt policies to promote a commitment to equal treatment of similarly situated offenders.

Simultaneously, however, their individual autonomy has allowed significant differences between counties to exist in a state that professes a commitment to equality. The differences in practice raise issues not just of unequal allocation of state resources by autonomous local actors but also of the injustice inherent in treating offenders differently not on the basis of what they have done but where they have done it.

The problem of territorial inequality is, of course, inherent in sovereignty. Independent nations will resolve issues differently and thus present widely disparate responses to crime and punishment. We accept such disparities as the inevitable consequence of sovereignty. While comparative analyses can draw attention to how disparately different nations respond to crime, accepted notions of sovereignty prevent efforts to eliminate the disparity.

The same issues are present in the United States, where the principles of federalism cede the great majority of criminal justice policy making to the states. While we may criticize states for the wide differences that exist in how they respond to crime and we accept national efforts to stimulate the adoption of enlightened policies, the inherent right of each state to set its own criminal justice policies is not questioned. That Arizona, North Carolina, and Washington, for example, have criminal justice systems that produce quite disparate results is accepted as inherent in the independent authority of each state to determine its own criminal justice policy.

Similar notions of sovereignty underlie Washington's long-standing commitment to local autonomy in prosecution. From its beginning, Washington has allocated significant autonomy to counties. While cities are the creations of the legislature, counties are established in the state constitution. The tradition of deference to local prosecutors is deep and enduring. On a surface level the justification is that autonomy and resulting disparity are the inevitable consequences of the allocation of authority to local authorities just as it is between nations and between states. But prosecutors themselves have recognized the injustice inherent in their adoption of policies that produce disparate results. They have developed policies that promote equal treatment of similarly situated offenders both internally and statewide. Yet their commitment to their own autonomy has led them to work to prevent adoption of any legally binding mechanisms that would enforce uniform treatment.

Thus the paradox. In a state seemingly committed to equal treatment, local prosecutors who work toward equal treatment within their own jurisdictions operate autonomously from their fellow prosecutors and from the state. The result is that the varying belief and interpretations of Washington's 39 independently elected prosecutors determine, day to day and case by case, how Washington's criminal justice policies are actually implemented.

REFERENCES

American Law Institute. 1962. *Model Penal Code—Proposed Official Draft*. Philadelphia: American Law Institute.

———. 1968. *Model Code of Pre-arraignment Procedure*. Philadelphia: American Law Institute.

Bayley, Christopher. 1976*a*. "Good Intentions Gone Awry—a Proposal for Fundamental Change in Criminal Sentencing." *Washington Law Review* 51: 529–63.

———. 1976*b*. "Plea Bargaining: An Offer a Prosecutor Can Refuse." *Judicature* 60:229–32.

Becker, Mary Kay. 1978. "Washington State's New Juvenile Code: An Introduction." *Gonzaga Law Review* 14:289–312.

Boerner, David. 1992. "Confronting Violence: In the Act and in the Word." *University of Puget Sound Law Review* 15:525–77.

———. 1993. "The Role of the Legislature in Guidelines Sentencing in 'the Other Washington.'" *Wake Forest Law Review* 28:381–420.

Boerner, David, and Roxanne Lieb. 2001. "Sentencing Reform in the Other Washington." In *Crime and Justice: A Review of Research*, vol. 28, edited by Michael Tonry. Chicago: University of Chicago Press.

California District Attorneys Association. 1974. *Uniform Crime Charging Standards*. Sacramento: California District Attorneys Association.

Davis, Kenneth Culp. 1969. *Discretionary Justice: A Preliminary Inquiry*. Baton Rouge: Louisiana State University.

Hawley, Lowell Stillwell, and Ralph Bushnell Potts. 1953. *Counsel for the Damned: A Biography of George Francis Vanderveer*. New York: Lippincott

Horowitz, Donald J. 1976. "Improving the Criminal Justice System: The Need for a Commitment." *Washington Law Review* 51:607–16.

Kress, Jack. 1980. *Prescription for Justice: The Theory and Practice of Sentencing Guidelines*. Cambridge, MA: Ballinger.

National District Attorneys Association. 1977. *National Prosecution Standards*. Chicago: National District Attorneys Association.

Revelle, George H. 1976. *Sentencing and Probation*. Bloomington: Indiana University, National College of State Trial Judges.

Ringold, Solie M. 1976. "A Judge's Personal Perspective on Criminal Sentencing." *Washington Law Review* 51:631–42.

Scheingold, Stuart. 1991. *The Politics of Street Crime: Criminal Process and Cultural Obsession*. Philadelphia: Temple University Press.

Sentencing Guidelines Commission. 2010. *Statistical Summary of Adult Felony Sentencing—Annual Reports, from 1990–2010*. Olympia, WA: Sentencing

Guidelines Commission. http://www.sgc.wa.gov/informational/Publications .htm.

Talmadge, Philip, ed. 1976. "Law and the Correctional Process in Washington." Symposium issue, *Washington Law Review* 51(3).

Washington Association of Prosecuting Attorneys. 1977. "Policies and Guidelines for Plea Bargaining." Resolution no. 1-77. Olympia: Washington Association of Prosecuting Attorneys.

———. 1980. "Charging and Disposition Policies." Olympia: Washington Association of Prosecuting Attorneys.

Washington Association of Sheriffs. 2010. *Crime in Washington 2010 Annual Report.* Olympia: Washington Association of Sheriffs and Police Chiefs.

Washington Association of Superior Court Judges. 1979. *Resolution.* Olympia: Washington Association of Superior Court Judges.

Washington Legislative Budget Committee. 1981. *Performance Audit of Washington State Board of Prison Terms and Paroles.* Olympia: Washington Legislative Budget Committee.

Washington State Board of Prison Terms and Paroles. 1978. *Guidelines for Fixing Minimum Terms 1978.* Olympia: Washington State Board of Prison Terms and Paroles.

———. 1979. *Guidelines for Reconsideration of Length of Confinement 1979.* Olympia: Washington State Board of Prison Terms and Paroles.

Washington State Institute of Public Policy. 2003. *Outcome Evaluation and Cost Benefit Analysis 2003.* Olympia: Washington State Institute of Public Policy.

Washington Superior Court Judges' Association and Office of Administrator for the Courts. 1981. *Report of the Sentencing Guidelines Committee.* Olympia: Washington Superior Court Judges' Association and Office of Administrator for the Courts.

Wright, Ronald F. In this voume. "Persistent Localism in the Prosecutor Services of North Carolina."

Ronald F. Wright

Persistent Localism in the Prosecutor Services of North Carolina

ABSTRACT

The distinct flavor of each local prosecutor's office persists in North Carolina despite unusually strong efforts to centralize and unify the prosecution function across the entire state. The 44 offices share a common legal framework, including structured sentencing rules that channel the available punishments in predictable directions. Almost all their operating funds derive from the state rather than from the local level of government. The ties that bind the offices together do not, however, create a single organizational identity. Each office pursues a unique mix of criminal charges, responsive to the priorities of local voters. Local offices also differ from one another in the sentencing results they obtain. Thus, the North Carolina experience demonstrates the relatively weak influence of substantive criminal law, sentencing law, and other formal legal structures in the face of demographic differences, local political constraints, office size, and organizational culture. In a democratic society, residents expect prosecutors to make choices consistent with their own values and priorities. Yet in North Carolina, voters also recognize that the state is not culturally homogeneous: Charlotte is not like Shallotte. Localism is a natural consequence of tight popular control over criminal justice in a pluralistic democracy.

Ronald Wright is professor of law at Wake Forest University. I am grateful to the district attorneys in North Carolina who spoke with me during the research for this essay: Phil Berger, Ricky Bowman, Ben David, Jon David, Garry Frank, Peter Gilchrist, Doug Henderson, Maureen Krueger, Andrew Murray, Kristy Newton, Jim O'Neill, Colon Willoughby, and Jim Woodall. I also appreciate the help I received from Peg Dorer and Kim Overton of the North Carolina Conference of District Attorneys, from Patricia Brooks and Gail Adams in the Administrative Office of the Courts, and from Mary Winstead in the North Carolina Attorney General's office. In addition, I offer thanks to Kaitlyn Girard and Ramie Shalabi for terrific research assistance.

There is no single prosecutorial service in the state courts of North Carolina. It would be closer to the truth to say that there are 44 distinct prosecutor services in the state. Each district attorney's office in North Carolina sets its own priorities, pursues its own hiring, develops its own culture, and answers to its own voter constituency.

The local flavor of each prosecutor's office is a common phenomenon across many state court systems of the United States. What makes North Carolina remarkable is that localism persists despite unusually strong efforts—consistent with North Carolina's rationalistic, "good government" traditions—to centralize and unify the prosecution function across the entire state. The 44 offices share a common legal framework, including structured sentencing rules that channel the available punishments in predictable directions. Almost all the operating funds for the prosecutors derive from the state rather than from local government. Prosecutors operate within extraordinarily tight budget and personnel policies set at the state level and rely on support services from a common group of governmental and private organizations.

Nevertheless, the ties that bind the offices together do not create for them a single organizational identity. Each office pursues a unique mix of criminal charges, responsive to the priorities of local voters. Some emphasize property offenses, whereas others prioritize drug crimes. Some resort to trials more quickly than others; some rely more heavily on deferred prosecution programs. The local offices also differ in the results they obtain. Each district draws on state correctional resources without any central coordination from the state bureaucracy. Finally, the 44 districts provide distinct professional experiences for the attorneys who join the service. Prosecutors who work in different offices hold differing conceptions of their roles and follow different career paths. In short, even in a jurisdiction with particularly strong central institutions and funding structures, prosecutors in each district develop distinctive work environments and produce notably different results.

North Carolina prosecutors offer a case study in the limits of law. The North Carolina experience demonstrates the relatively weak influence of substantive criminal law, sentencing law, and other formal legal structures in the face of demographic differences, local political constraints, office size, and organizational culture. These differences among offices fall into an urban and rural pattern. The population size of each district, together with the divergent values and priorities of voters in larger and smaller districts, create distinct styles of prosecution. A visitor to the district attorney's office in a major North Carolina city such as Charlotte or Raleigh would observe that those prosecutors have much in common with the prosecutors in midsize cities in other states with roughly similar political cultures—say, Nashville or St. Louis or Cincinnati. They have far less in common with the smallest North Carolina prosecutors' offices, such as the eight-lawyer office that serves Stokes and Surry Counties in the western mountains.

This essay explores the connections between the structures of the 44 prosecutorial districts in North Carolina and the results they produce. Section I reviews the organizational basics of the prosecutorial districts in the state, details some of their divergent outcomes, and attempts to explain the differences. Section II reviews the budgetary, operational, and legal frameworks that prosecutor offices in North Carolina share. Section III surveys centrifugal forces that overwhelm the influence of those shared frameworks to produce distinctive prosecutorial cultures and distinctive results. These forces include diverse political environments, distinctive relationships with law enforcement agencies and judges, and the size of each office. Finally, Section IV describes the effects of these characteristics on the career paths and role conceptions of individual attorneys who choose to work as prosecutors.

My sources include statutes and other sources of positive law, state personnel statistics, case processing statistics from the courts, and interviews with representative state actors. Thirteen elected district attorneys spoke with me for approximately 1 hour apiece, most on condition that I not quote them directly. These interviews covered urban and rural districts, including the full range of small, medium, and large offices, spread geographically across the western, central, and eastern thirds of the state. I also interviewed actors in several supporting institutions for prosecutors, most of the assistant district attorneys in one larger district, and selected assistant public defenders. Together, these interviews, laws, and statistics portray a group of extraordinarily idealistic attorneys who select and prosecute criminal cases with a keen awareness of their obligations to their own communities—and who define their communities in local rather than statewide terms.

In North Carolina, as in most states, residents expect prosecutors to make choices consistent with their own values and priorities. Yet they also recognize that the state is not culturally homogeneous. Charlotte is not like Shallotte. Localism, therefore, is a natural consequence of tight popular control over criminal justice in a pluralistic democracy. In such a setting, statewide budgetary and organizational measures that push district attorneys to produce more consistent results make a great deal of sense as a counterbalance to local traditions.

I. Organizations and Outcomes

American prosecutors work in offices built around local constituencies, with each office applying state law and spending state revenue to address local priorities (Perry 2006). State law in North Carolina creates 44 prosecutorial districts, by and large following boundaries of judicial districts. The elected district attorney is the highest authority within that district concerning prosecutions in the state courts for violations of the state criminal code and criminal ordinances (Barkow 2011). Three US attorneys—for the eastern, middle, and western districts of North Carolina—prosecute federal crimes.

A. Historical Changes to Prosecutorial Districts and Court Structure

North Carolina prosecutors work in prosecutorial districts with boundaries that shift frequently to accommodate changes in local political alliances. There are 100 counties in the state and 44 prosecutorial districts. Some counties with larger populations now constitute separate prosecutorial districts. Other districts combine several smaller counties. There is, however, only a loose connection between county population and the number of counties in a district. Some counties with a relatively small population, such as Moore County, constitute a stand-alone district, whereas some counties with larger populations, such as New Hanover County, share a district with other counties. All prosecutorial authority in the state courts rests in the hands of these district attorneys, who are elected by the voters within the district.

The prosecutorial districts largely overlap with judicial districts. The judicial system is now designed to deliver uniform results across all districts. Before 1966, the state relied on municipal and county recorders' courts (funded and administered at the local level) to handle some misdemeanors, while state-funded superior courts had jurisdiction over felony prosecutions. A major restructuring grew out of a 1962 constitutional amendment and took effect incrementally during the late 1960s and early 1970s (Brannon 2000; NCGS secs. 7A-2–7A-4). The reform, now codified in the North Carolina General Statutes (NCGS), created a unified court system, funded and administered at the state level and known as the General Court of Justice, with an Appellate Division, a Superior Court Division, and a District Court Division.

Under this constitutional structure, the District Court Division has authority to try and sentence defendants for lesser crimes—misdemeanors and infractions. In felony cases, the district court may conduct preliminary hearings to determine whether probable cause exists to bind the defendant over to stand trial in superior court. The Superior Court Division provides the upper-level trial courts and has jurisdiction over the disposition of all felonies, along with jurisdiction over "misdemeanor appeals," a distinctive feature of North Carolina procedure that allows a misdemeanor defendant, after a conviction before a district court judge, to "appeal" the case to superior court and receive a de novo trial before a jury. As a matter of state constitutional law, all superior court criminal matters are tried before a jury rather than before a judge; this is a distinctive feature of North Carolina law, compared to many other state codes that allow defendants in some circumstances to waive a jury trial in favor of a bench trial (North Carolina Constitution, art. I, sec. 24; NCGS sec. 15A-1201).

The 1960s court reorganization prompted a restructuring of prosecution in North Carolina. Before the judicial system was unified, city attorneys and county attorneys prosecuted misdemeanors in the local recorders' courts, and solicitors prosecuted felonies in the superior courts (Spindel 1981, pp. 144–45). All solicitors were paid with state funds, and many worked part-time while maintaining a private law practice. The legislature periodically redrew district lines for the solicitors and from time to time added new positions: there were 20 solicitor districts in the state in 1955, less than half the current number of prosecutorial districts (North Carolina Courts Commission 1967). A few of the larger solicitor districts employed a small number of assistant solicitors, paid with city or county funds. In most districts no assistants were necessary. The workloads varied greatly between districts, with the annual number of court days ranging from 52 to 260 (North Carolina Courts Commission 1967, pp. 40–45). Amazingly, all solicitors—full-time and part-time, with assistants and without—received the same salary from the state.

As part of the court system unification, the legislature reassigned the prosecutorial authority from the city and county attorneys to a newly formed office, known as the district court prosecutor, to handle misdemeanors and infractions in the new statewide district courts. The solicitors continued to exercise all prosecutorial functions in the superior courts (Hinsdale 1972, pp. 7–8). After only 5 years of operating this dual statewide system, the legislature abolished the district court prosecutors and consolidated all criminal prosecutions within the solicitors' offices. In 1974, the solicitors were renamed district attorneys (NCGS sec. 7A-66.1). The boundaries of prosecutorial districts continued to shift over the years to reflect the preferences of local politicians for electoral control over district attorneys, but the statutory structure of prosecution in North Carolina has remained unchanged.

B. Outcomes at the Office Level

Some parts of the prosecution enterprise operate consistently throughout the state. Like criminal justice systems throughout the United States, the courts in North Carolina rely heavily on guilty pleas to obtain convictions. Trials have become rare for every category of crime except homicide.

Every district treats violent crimes that produce serious personal injuries or death as its top priority. The charges in such cases are dismissed or reduced only when prosecutors face serious evidentiary problems or when reduced charges will result in a credible punishment while shielding the crime victim or the victim's family from the traumatic and uncertain experience of a trial. Defendants with multiple convictions for prior serious crimes also invariably get the full attention of the office.

Local differences in prosecutorial environments do, however, produce different outcomes in some areas. These differences express themselves in the treatment of property and drug crimes, which some offices deemphasize to free up resources for other crimes or reflect local priorities (O'Neill 2004). Each office pursues a distinctive mix of charges, responsive to the priorities of local voters and the cases that local law enforcement agencies (whose leaders are also democratically selected by election or appointment by other elected officials) develop for prosecution. The local districts also seek different levels of punishment for the convictions they obtain. Each draws on state correctional resources at its own pace, without any central coordination.

1. *Selection of Crimes for Prosecution.* Prosecutors have only indirect control over the cases filed in their districts. Under state law, police

officers have the unusual authority to file charges, with or without the agreement of the prosecutor. The prosecutor, in turn, has complete authority to dismiss the cases after filing or to amend the charges. As a result, the police over time may adjust their filing practices in light of priorities and practices in the prosecutor's office.

As table 1 indicates, there is some variation in the prominence of some crimes in the dockets of different prosecutorial districts. Some of the differences are associated with the size of the prosecutor's office, but most reflect the different incidence of reported crimes in different regions.

The "typical range" is calculated by selecting points one standard deviation above and below the average percentage of felony filings in the prosecutorial districts. "Association with office size" is calculated on the basis of the correlation between the percentage of felony filings and the number of authorized assistant district attorneys (ADAs) in a district; table 1 reports any correlations with an absolute value greater than 0.2.

Some of the interdistrict differences are noteworthy. For example, robbery charges in typical districts range anywhere from 1.8 to 6.8 percent of the felony docket: the high-percentage districts give robbery charges more than three times as much docket space as the low-percentage districts. Similarly high ratios operate for homicide and sex offenses, and the absolute values of the differences between high and low districts for drug crimes and burglary are also striking.

What explains these differences? For the most serious violent crimes, the levels of reported crime explain much of the difference. Most of the high-percentage filing districts for the crimes of homicide, robbery, and sexual assault (i.e., those with a filing percentage more than one standard deviation from the mean) also reported higher rates for those crimes than the statewide averages in the 2009 FBI Uniform Crime Reports (Federal Bureau of Investigation 2009). Similarly, a majority of the low-percentage outlier districts reported homicide, robbery, and sexual assault rates below the state averages.

For property crimes, by contrast, the connections between reported crimes and felony filings are weaker. For burglary and larceny, the low-percentage outlier districts showed no tendency toward lower reported crime rates. For these lower-level crimes, which appear in greater volume in each district, the public allows the prosecutor more leeway to

TABLE 1
Variations in Felony Filings among Prosecutorial Districts, Fiscal Year 2009–10, Percentage of Total Felony Caseload

Crime Type	Low District (%)	High District (%)	Typical Range (%)	Association with Office Size
Homicide (murder and manslaughter)	.1	2.4	.3–1.1	None
Rape and sex offenses	1.0	10.6	1.2–5.4	None
Robbery	.6	10.9	1.8–6.8	Larger offices more likely to have higher percentage
Assault	.6	6.2	1.4–3.8	None
Burglary (including breaking and entering)	8.1	26.7	12.3–23.5	None
Larceny	3.4	14.0	5.6–10.8	Larger offices slightly more likely to have higher percentage
Fraud (including forgery)	1.0	16.8	5.0–12.7	Smaller offices slightly more likely to have higher percentage
Controlled substances	15.8	53.4	20.4–35.8	None

SOURCE.—North Carolina Administrative Office of the Courts (2010).

choose which cases to file. The more serious violent crimes leave the prosecutor with fewer viable choices.

State law in North Carolina gives law enforcement agencies authority to file initial charges with no input from the prosecutor. As a result, filing statistics reflect the varying relationships that prosecutors develop with different police and sheriffs' departments. In some places, the prosecutor may work more closely with law enforcement to influence their filing decisions. These relationships combine with the underlying crime rates to shape the filing differences among districts. Thus, the variety in the cases filed across districts says more about the raw materials presented to the prosecutors than about their discretionary choices.

2. *Processing Cases.* How a prosecutor disposes of a case tells us something about its relative importance. Categories of cases that result more often in convictions to the original charges filed (whether after trial or a plea of guilty) reflect the strongest commitments of the office. In those cases, the prosecutors devote the extra investigation resources needed to shore up evidentiary problems, clear aside other cases to make room on a limited trial calendar, and signal a willingness to pay the price for a conviction. High dismissal rates for particular crimes sometimes reveal that the office places greater emphasis on other crimes, although some dismissals may simply reflect evidentiary problems that cannot be remedied with more investigation (Fairfax 2011; Turner 2012).

Table 2 highlights some differences among prosecutorial districts in North Carolina in methods of disposition. Smaller offices appear to treat misdemeanors as higher priorities than do larger offices; they are more likely to take misdemeanors to trial in district court and are less likely to dismiss them outright. Larger offices, by contrast, are slightly more likely to go to trial in felony cases and slightly less likely to reduce felony charges in order to obtain a conviction.

Violent crimes such as homicide, rape, sex offenses, robbery, and felony assault all result in more trials than the average rate for felonies. However, rates of guilty pleas based on lesser charges are higher for violent crimes than for felonies as a whole. The violent crimes tend to have many lesser-included offenses built into the criminal code, and some prosecutors may be risk averse in these high-stakes cases, leading to compromise offers.

The dispositions for property crimes and drug crimes closely track

TABLE 2

Variations in Disposition Methods among Prosecutorial Districts, 2010, Percentage of Dispositions

	Low (%)	High (%)	Typical Range (%)	Association with Office Size
All felonies, by trial	.2	6	1–3	Larger offices slightly more likely to have higher percentage
All felonies, by plea of guilty as charged	23	67	35–57	None
All felonies, plea after reduced charges	6	22	7–15	Smaller offices slightly more likely to have higher percentage
All felonies, by deferred prosecution	0	4	0–2	None
All felonies, by dismissal	12	59	21–45	None
All misdemeanors, by trial	.7	17	1–8	Smaller offices more likely to have higher percentage
All misdemeanors, by guilty or nolo plea	13	42	19–34	None
All misdemeanors, by dismissal	21	57	31–50	Larger offices slightly more likely to have higher percentage

SOURCE.—North Carolina Administrative Office of the Courts (2010).

the rates for all felonies. The most notable exception is burglary: original charges more often result in guilty pleas than for felonies generally and are dismissed outright less often. These patterns characterize both larger and smaller offices.

Although offices vary in their dispositions of violent crimes, those differences (with one exception) do not correlate with the size of the office. The exception concerns felony assaults. Smaller offices are a bit more likely than large offices to dispose of those cases by offering to reduce the charge to a lesser form of assault (felony or misdemeanor) in exchange for a guilty plea. Large offices are more likely to dismiss felony assaults outright, suggesting a choice to give higher priority to other cases—possibly other violent crimes.

3. *Prosecutorial Influence on Punishment.* The punishments that prosecutors recommend to the court after conviction also demonstrate the influence of local policy choices (Simons 2009; Berman 2010). Some districts use more nonprison punishments—both "community" and "intermediate" sanctions—than others. Prosecutors who can realistically trigger use of a punishment more serious than simple probation tend to be more open to nonprison sanctions. Programs that offer such punishments are not equally available throughout the state. Although the most widespread nonprison punishments are funded by the state Department of Correction, a number of smaller experimental community programs are funded and operated by local nonprofit organizations or by city or county governments. The ongoing monitoring and treatment regime of a "drug court" is also more available in some jurisdictions than in others. Recent budget cuts at the state level have pushed the financial burden more decisively onto local governments.

The use of habitual felon laws that specify lengthier sentences for repeat offenders gives the prosecutor more direct control over punishments. State law creates a sentencing structure (described in more detail in Sec. II) that encourages judges to select a sentence within the "presumptive" range for a particular combination of offense severity and criminal history. The code does not provide for "mandatory minimum" penalties for high-volume crimes. The habitual felon provision, however, allows prosecutors to request higher levels of punishment for defendants convicted of a felony after accumulating enough prior felony convictions. These severe punishments attach even if the current offense is a low-level felony.

District attorneys make conscious policy choices about how often they file habitual felon charges. Some prosecutors—particularly in the smaller offices—charge defendants with the habitual felon crime whenever their prior record satisfies the statutory criteria. They explain that such a policy produces consistent results and best expresses the legislature's intent in passing the law. In jurisdictions in which the habitual felon indictment is automatic, some offices will use it as leverage to obtain more favorable sentencing terms in plea negotiations. For instance, a prosecutor might forgo a potential habitual felon charge if the defendant agrees to plead guilty and accept a sentence at the upper end of the presumptive range in the guidelines grid or a sentence in the "aggravated" range.

Other district attorneys use the habitual felon law more selectively, trying to reserve it for defendants whose current charges and past convictions represent the most serious threats to public safety. For these prosecutors, a prison term ranging between 44 and 92 months based on current charges for a minor felony plus three prior convictions for minor felonies is disproportionate. In the words of one district attorney, that is "a chicken scratch thing to do."

Every district puts some effort into monitoring habitual felon charges for internal consistency, even though they recognize that other districts use the charge in a variety of ways. In some larger offices, habitual felon charges are filed and tried by a specialized unit; many smaller offices funnel all defendants with qualifying prior records to a single attorney for evaluation.

While district attorneys must live with sharply limited courtroom time and authorized salary slots for ADAs, their access to state-funded prisons is not so strictly budgeted. Each district attorney can recommend sentences that consume more or less than the district's per capita share of the prison budget (Gershowitz 2008; Ball 2011; Gold 2011). This creates a theoretical incentive for local prosecutors to overspend state correctional resources, but prosecutors do recognize and discuss among themselves the need to be responsible stewards of taxpayer resources. Table 3 indicates some of the variation in the use of state corrections resources among prosecutorial districts.

Larger offices are somewhat more likely to obtain higher percentages of prison sentences compared with community or intermediate punishments. This is likely a result of the mix of crimes that make up the dockets in those districts.

TABLE 3

Use of State Correctional Resources among Prosecutorial Districts,
Fiscal Year 2009–10

	Low District	High District	State Average
Percentage of felons sentenced to prison terms	28.6	49.9	39.8
Percentage of felons sentenced within presumptive range	38.8	90.7	68.7
Percentage of felons sentenced within aggravated range	0	12.5	4.4
Percentage of felons sentenced within mitigated range	7.5	55.7	26.9
Average length of prison term (months)	25.2	57.6	40.3

SOURCE.—North Carolina Sentencing and Policy Advisory Commission (2011).

Some offices obtain high percentages of active prison sentences based on a deliberate policy to achieve the maximum available punishment for eligible defendants. By contrast, Jim Woodall of District 15B obtains prison sentences in a large percentage of felony cases (49.9 percent) as part of an effort to economize on the use of prison (North Carolina Sentencing and Policy Advisory Commission 2011). Voters in District 15B, a relatively progressive district that includes the university community at Chapel Hill, prefer that he use misdemeanor convictions and deferred prosecutions as the first responses to crime. By the time the office pursues felony charges, the defendant typically has a more extensive prior criminal record that merits a prison term under the statutory sentencing structure.

Such variations in the local use of state corrections resources remain underrecognized, both in public debate and among policy makers. A periodic report from the Administrative Office of the Courts (AOC) informs district attorneys of the percentages of felony convictions from each district that result in active prison terms. The AOC could promote more deliberation about the local use of state correctional resources by creating more detailed district-level reporting that sorts out the different strategies at work.

II. Shared Legal and Institutional Framework

It is common for prosecutors in different offices within a single American state to achieve different outcomes (Barkow 2011; Boerner, in this volume; Miller and Caplinger, in this volume). In that sense, North Carolina resembles other states. North Carolina is distinctive, however, in the range and extent of centralized legal tools, financial controls, personnel controls, administrative practices, and support institutions in operation. These arrangements are designed to produce more consistent prosecutorial services in the state.

The ideal of a unified prosecutorial service grows out of a long governmental tradition in North Carolina of openness to expertise and rational policy making. In criminal justice, the ideal of statewide uniformity starts with the state constitution, which calls for criminal prosecution to proceed "in such manner as the General Assembly may prescribe by general law uniformly applicable in every local court district of the state" (North Carolina Constitution, art. IV, sec. 16[2]).

Despite the difference between offices surveyed in Section I, it would be a mistake to assume that these centralizing devices are failures; they probably do promote consistency to some degree. When compared to the pre-1974 conglomeration of state-level solicitors, city attorneys, and county attorneys—with a mix of full-timers and part-timers and a variety of funding sources—the structure today does promote more consistent quality.

The current system, however, still leaves a remarkable amount of room for prosecutors in each district to develop their own cultures and priorities. The statutory framework offers comparable authority and roughly equal per capita resources to chief prosecutors in each district, but it provides for no hierarchical control over office policies or case-level decisions. The elected district attorneys use their authority to create distinctive styles of prosecution and relationships with other criminal justice actors. Efforts at statewide consistency swim against a strong current in North Carolina.

A. State and County Funding

State control of prosecutors in North Carolina centers on funding. County governments must pay for office space and furnishings. The state government funds almost all the salaries and operating costs.

The state legislature designates the amount of salary funding available in each district for ADAs and even specifies the number of ADAs to be funded with state revenue (NCGS sec. 7A-60). Districts employ as few as five ADAs and as many as 81. The legislature also designates the average amount that the district attorney is allowed to pay per attorney slot (for instance, the average salary for ADAs is set at $72,000 as this is written) and the minimum salary that an ADA can earn.

State law also provides for a minimum number of support staff for each office, including at least one administrative assistant and one victim-witness/legal assistant (NCGS secs. 7A-68, 7A-69; North Carolina Administrative Office of the Courts 2007, p. 19). State law specifies the minimum salary that a district attorney can offer to an employee in each employment category in the office.

The state money for prosecutors, who are officials within the executive branch, is administered through the AOC, which also provides logistical support and budgetary structure for judicial branch activities. The AOC sets limits on the total pool and average salary per slot that apply to support staff in each office. The AOC also restricts the amount of salary increase that a district attorney can award to an ADA or support staffer in a given year: raises are generally limited to 10 percent per year.

During lean budget years, the AOC supplements its other budgetary controls with a hiring freeze, which usually prevents the district attorney from promptly replacing an ADA or staff member who leaves. The district attorney can fill the open position only when it percolates to the top of the freeze list, which can take many months. An open position in an especially busy office—as measured under the most recent "workload study" commissioned by the AOC—is approved for rehiring more quickly, whereas an opening in a district that faces lower workloads might remain frozen indefinitely.

Some district attorneys, particularly those in smaller districts with relatively busy dockets, chafe at this budgetary restriction. They note that it severely restricts their authority to replace weaker employees. In effect, they say, the AOC operates a "firing freeze." They also observe that a hiring freeze affects the professional development of ADAs, making it difficult for an ADA in one county to transfer to another county for personal or professional reasons.

Budgetary controls at the state level are not limited to salaries. The AOC and one of its subunits, the Conference of District Attorneys, decide on the legal publications to be purchased for the district attorney law libraries. The Conference of District Attorneys also administers the state appropriations for the training of prosecutors. District attorneys must request permission to spend money for training ADAs or support staff, and the budget allows for only a handful of prosecutors each year to attend training events out-of-state, such as those sponsored by the National District Attorneys Association (a private professional association) or other national providers. Travel for other purposes, such as interviewing prospective witnesses, is also funded at the state level. Travel within the state receives routine approval; travel outside the state normally does not.

These various spending boundaries are more confining than the financial guidelines prosecutors face in many other states. In most states, the legislature authorizes a budget for each chief prosecutor at the local level, who then decides how to spend it. For instance, state law in Arizona and Washington gives more budgetary authority to the elected chief prosecutor (Boerner, in this volume; Miller and Caplinger, in this volume). It is also common in other state systems for city and county governments to pay the salaries of the ADAs, while state funds cover only the salaries of chief prosecutors. Half of all state prosecutors' offices in the United States receive more than three-quarters of their operating funds from county government, and about one-third are supported exclusively by county funding (Perry 2006, p. 4). The use of local taxes to fund salaries and other operations allows for full expression of local priorities in criminal law enforcement. The chief prosecutor must stay alert to the concerns and ideas of county commissioners and other influential local figures.

Funding is a powerful force in shaping prosecutorial choices, but state and county appropriations allow for enormous variety among the offices. A district attorney in North Carolina remains able to make meaningful choices even within the tight fiscal boundaries of state law. The district attorney, for example, can increase salaries for individual employees, as long as total salaries remain within the office allotment and the increases do not exceed AOC guidelines. Consequently, the district attorney is free to implement a merit-based salary structure, a seniority-based structure, or some combination of those strategies.

More important, the district attorney decides whom to hire. Employees of the district attorney's office, including the ADAs, are employees at will and serve at the pleasure of the chief prosecutor. In practice, mass firings seldom happen when a new district attorney wins an election, but turnover among the ADAs does increase during such transitional years. For instance, when a new district attorney took office in District 13 in 2011, within 6 months he hired seven new ADAs in an office with a total of 15.

The district attorney is entirely responsible for determining what the employees in his or her office will do. The legislature does not earmark funds for prosecutors to enforce particular criminal statutes (Richman 1999; Levine 2005).

District attorneys sometimes add to the number of positions in their offices by obtaining funds from county government or from grants from the federal government or other sources. For instance, the district attorney in Mecklenburg County persuaded the county government to fund several salaries in his office by pointing out that additional staff members could process cases more quickly for defendants housed in the county jail, thus saving the county the cost of operating extra beds. The prosecutor in Durham County also receives significant salary funds from local government. Other district attorneys in the state, however, believe that prosecutors who seek out local funding are "courting trouble," because the financial arrangements could compromise their independence when the time comes to enforce public corruption or other criminal laws against local power brokers.

It is common for a prosecutor's office to obtain federal grant money or private grant funds to pay the salaries of ADAs or support staff who are devoted to particular enforcement efforts. Federal highway safety grants fund prosecutions for driving while under the influence. Organizations concerned about domestic violence offer grants to prosecute intrafamily violence cases. While these grants typically add one or two positions to an office only for a limited period of years, in the smaller offices one additional prosecutor or staff member can make an enormous difference. Other district attorneys believe that the "emotional toll" of hiring an attorney for a year or two and then sending him or her away is too great and therefore do not apply for grant funds. This is a striking example of the long-term professional needs of the office staff taking priority over short-term gains in productive measures.

B. State Attorney General's Role

While budgetary control of the district attorneys in North Carolina is vigorous, the institutions that could promote statewide policies or practices in the 44 district attorneys' offices remain underused. State law grants them relatively limited authority. For instance, the North Carolina attorney general's office does not hold any supervisory authority over the district attorneys and cannot overrule their decisions to investigate, prosecute, or dismiss charges (NCGS sec. 7A-61). In

1959, the legislature rejected a proposal to give the attorney general supervisory authority over the solicitors in the performance of all their duties, including the prosecution of criminal cases in the superior courts (Sanders 1959, p. 17). The state constitution, even after its revision in 1962, continued to rely on local district attorneys rather than placing them under the control of the attorney general. The drafters must have envisioned the need for some local input.

The attorney general's office can provide support in particular cases, but only when district attorneys formally request assistance. The Special Prosecutors Division within the attorney general's office assumes full responsibility for prosecutions following a formal request by a district attorney and approval by the attorney general (NCGS sec. 114–11.6; *State v. Camacho*, 329 N.C. 589, 594–95, 406 S.E.2d 868, 871 [1991]). The most common situation involves interest between members of the district attorney's staff and individuals involved in a prosecution. In addition, the Special Prosecutors Division takes on some complicated, multijurisdictional prosecutions in order to coordinate efforts across the state. District attorneys commonly ask for support in capital murder trials, so the attorney general's staff develops expertise in such cases. The state attorney general's office and district attorneys interact primarily through case assistance (Mary Winstead interview with Kaitlyn Girard, February 1, 2011).

The infamous "Duke Lacrosse" case offers an example of an interaction between the state attorney general and a district attorney. In 2006, the police investigated allegations that members of Duke University's lacrosse team had sexually assaulted an exotic dancer during a party. The district attorney's office in Durham obtained grand jury indictments against several players. In an environment of intense media coverage, district attorney Mike Nifong made improper statements to news reporters about the case, prompting the North Carolina State Bar to file ethics charges against him in December 2006. At that point, Nifong requested that attorney general Roy Cooper take charge of the case. By April 2007, Cooper announced that his office would dismiss all charges and expressed his opinion that the students were innocent.

This case illustrates the extraordinary nature of the matters that district attorneys transfer to the attorney general. Prosecutors in some districts go years without requesting any assistance from the attorney general. Concerning handling of high-volume crimes or development of law enforcement priorities, the attorney general has no influence over the independent choices of 44 district attorneys.

The one circumstance in which the attorney general has authority with the potential to promote uniform statewide policy concerns criminal appeals. The state constitution instructs the district attorneys to "perform such duties relating to appeals . . . as the Attorney General may require" (North Carolina Constitution, art. IV, sec. 16[1]; NCGS sec. 7A-61). While defendants initiate the appeals for most cases on the appellate docket, the government can appeal pretrial judicial dismissals or pretrial evidentiary rulings that lead to a prosecutorial dismissal (*Ball v. United States*, 163 US 662 [1896]; Poulin 2008). The attorney general controls appellate work in criminal cases, and attorneys from that office have authority to decide which cases to appeal or to defend.

The power to control appeals could have a substantial impact on policy, as it does in the federal system (Devins 1994). The North Carolina attorney general, however, has not employed this tool to coordinate prosecution policy concerning high-volume questions of criminal law enforcement. In practice, the district attorneys themselves identify the trial judge rulings they would like to see overturned. The district attorneys "feel passionately" about some cases and file appeals without consulting the attorney general. For the other cases, the district attorneys flag a potential precedent-setting case but let the appellate lawyers in the attorney general's office decide whether to file. The appellate lawyers generally defer to those requests and call on the district attorney's office to provide the necessary background on trial court proceedings. In short, the attorney general takes a passive role in the selection of cases. The appellate attorneys operate as advocates for the district attorneys, allowing the "client" to choose the objectives of the representation, while zealously representing the state's interest on the cases that the local prosecutors choose.

The attorney general's passivity in the use of appellate practice is remarkable given the political prominence of this electoral position. The attorney general is elected to serve a 4-year term. Many attorneys general have had statewide political aspirations (several have gone on to become governors and lieutenant governors). They have every incentive to assert control over criminal justice policy in the state. Although budgetary and institutional tools are available that might allow the attorney general to claim a larger coordinating role, tradition and the difficulties of monitoring conditions across widely disparate districts have kept the effective policy control at the local level. Other states such as Arizona also place control of criminal appeals in the local office, despite a legal structure that would allow for more centralized control (Miller and Caplinger, in this volume).

C. Other Connecting Institutions

The North Carolina Conference of District Attorneys (NCCDA) is a statutory entity, created in 1983 as a unit within the AOC (NCGS sec. 7A-411). In governance terms, the staff serves at the pleasure of the board of directors, which is selected from among the elected district attorneys.

The NCCDA has a legislative lobbying function, a professional training function, and a resource function (North Carolina Conference of District Attorneys 2008). On the lobbying side, the district attorneys rely on NCCDA staff to advocate for changes in the substantive criminal law, criminal procedure rules, and sentencing statutes. They also represent the prosecutors on appropriations questions.

One useful tool in the lobbying effort is the periodic commissioning of workload studies by entities such as the National Center for State Courts (Kleiman and Lee 2010). The workload studies often determine which districts will receive new resources first or which will bear the heaviest budget cuts or the longest hiring freezes.

The NCCDA also supports local prosecution offices through on-site demonstrations of innovative techniques. It employs "resource prosecutors"—fewer than a half dozen—who carry active caseloads as specially designated ADAs who work by invitation of the local district attorney. They handle cases throughout the state. Typically these concern specialized subjects: for instance, when a resource prosecutor funded by a federal Violence Against Women grant takes domestic violence cases. The NCCDA staff attorneys also try to prosecute cases of first impression (again, at the request of a district attorney), such as a current case to test the admissibility of "recovered memory" evidence.

The NCCDA also sponsors the major training functions for prosecutors. The major training events each year are the summer and fall association meetings and the "new prosecutors school" or "baby DA school." Overall, the conference trains over 600 prosecutors and support staff each year. The NCCDA also produces manuals and other technical support materials in specialized areas.

The state also funds the North Carolina School of Government (SOG), an institute affiliated with the University of North Carolina, devoted to training public servants in a "nonpartisan, policy-neutral, and responsive" manner (http://www.sog.unc.edu/node/257). The SOG faculty jointly sponsors the new prosecutors school. It also supports the state's prosecutors throughout the year by dedicating one faculty member to work on legal issues of special interest to prosecutors, along with a handful of other faculty members who specialize in related fields such as motor vehicle law, forfeiture, and criminal procedure. The SOG faculty answer inquiries from individual prosecutors and from judges; they also create publications and maintain a public Internet blog about criminal law issues (http://www.sogweb.sog.unc.edu/blogs/ncclaw/).

D. Criminal Code

The district attorneys, in addition to operating under a common statewide budget authority and interacting in similar ways with the attorney general, enforce a single criminal code and statewide sentencing laws and policies. These shared legal tools, however, create only remote outer boundaries for the prosecutors' work.

The criminal code is a mess (Robinson, Cahill, and Mohammad 2000). Soon after the 1962 approval of the *Model Penal Code* by the American Law Institute, North Carolina—like many other states—explored the possibility of revising its criminal code (Governor's Committee on Law and Order 1969). An advisory commission recommended changes to the criminal procedure code and to the substantive criminal code; the legislature adopted the former but not the latter (Ad Hoc Criminal Code Revision Committee 1970). Proposed changes concerning topics such as the insanity defense proved more politically volatile than did proposed procedural changes.

Many crime elements do not appear in the statutes themselves, and a number of code sections simply state that the crime consists of its common-law elements. For instance, the code declares that "voluntary manslaughter shall be punishable as a Class D felony, and involuntary manslaughter shall be punishable as a Class F felony," but it never defines the elements of those two crimes (NCGS sec. 14-18). Common-law robbery, left undefined in statutory text, is still a high-volume offense in the state (NCGS sec. 14-87.1).

As a result of this ungainly criminal code, criminal practice depends on the esoteric knowledge of experienced attorneys, producing results that are difficult to evaluate or compare from district to district. Equally important, the building of the criminal code through the accretion of individual crimes over the years, with no effort to view the code as a coherent whole, leaves prosecutors with multiple charging options in many common factual scenarios (Brown 2010). The code also creates inconsistent bargaining options for attorneys involved in plea negotiations. In some areas, such as assault crimes, the code offers a large number of sections that could express the parties' agreement about the seriousness of the offense. A prosecutor might charge an assault as a felony at a number of different levels of seriousness, depending on the nature of the injury, the nature of the intended injury, or the identity of the parties (domestic partners, law enforcement officers, etc.). In other areas, such as kidnapping, the code offers fewer options, leaving the parties less likely to reach a charge bargain (Wright and Engen 2006, 2007).

E. Structured Sentencing

Although the substantive criminal code in North Carolina promotes nontransparent and inconsistent prosecutorial practices, the sentencing laws press in the opposite direction. The "structured sentencing" laws adopt many of the features of presumptive guideline sentencing in states such as Minnesota, Pennsylvania, and Kansas (Frase 2005). The charge of conviction, combined with the criminal history of the offender, determines a box within a grid that indicates for the judge a presumptive disposition (an active prison term or a nonprison punishment) and a presumptive sentence length. If legally sufficient aggravating or mitigating circumstances are present in the case, the judge may instead select a disposition or duration from the aggravated or mitigated range as indicated in the relevant grid box (Wright 2002). The judge has no authority, however, to "depart" from the three designated ranges or from the disposition (prison, intermediate, or community) designated in the grid box.

The state legislature amended structured sentencing in 2011 to reinstate the possibility of release from prison before the completion of the minimum sentence in some cases. For eligible offenders convicted of less serious felonies and with less serious prior criminal records, the court "may, in its discretion and without objection from the prosecutor" authorize "advanced supervised release" (NCGS sec. 15A-

1340.18). This disposition allows the corrections authorities to release inmates after they complete 80 percent of the minimum sentence if they successfully complete any "risk reduction incentives" that the corrections officials establish. This cost-saving measure is potentially the most important change to structured sentencing since its inception in 1995, but the prosecutor still controls access to this new-found flexibility.

Although the sentencing laws impose some rational order on the disjointed criminal code, the sentencing structure preserves sufficient legal tools for prosecutors to shape distinctive sentences in each district. The prosecutor's selection of the charge determines the largest portion of the sentence actually served (although the parties have no power to negotiate a sentence outside the ranges designated in the grid). In addition, the law leaves untouched the judge's discretion to select consecutive or concurrent sentences for a defendant who faces multiple charges (NCGS sec. 15A-1340.15). As a result, the prosecutor's decision about multiple counts can dramatically influence the defendant's exposure at sentencing. Relatively broad ranges within the designated sentencing ranges also leave a large zone of influence for the sentencing recommendations of the prosecutor.

The "habitual felon" provision of the structured sentencing laws has become one of the most important sources of prosecutor power and of divergent practices among the prosecutor districts. In effect, this is the only "mandatory minimum" sentencing provision under the North Carolina code. Under this habitual felon section, any defendant who commits a new felony after prior convictions for three other felonies can be charged with a Class C felony (the third most serious of the nine available offense classes), resulting in substantially higher penalties (NCGS secs. 14-7.1–14-7.12). A related provision, the "violent habitual felony" law, is a "three strikes" law that provides for a mandatory sentence of life in prison without the possibility of parole for a defendant who commits a violent felony after being convicted of two prior violent felonies (NCGS secs. 14-7.6, 7.7).

The habitual felon laws predate the enactment of structured sentencing in 1993. Although the sentencing commission noted the inconsistency between these laws and the treatment of prior criminal record elsewhere in the structured sentencing system, prosecutors successfully lobbied to keep the habitual felon laws intact. While habitual felon charges were relatively rare at the time, they subsequently became increasingly common (Wright 1994, 1995). These laws now produce some of the most striking differences in practice among various prosecutorial districts (Bjerk 2005). Such differences are difficult to track, however, because the standard reports of the sentencing commission do not show habitual felon prosecutions by district.

The state legislature amended the habitual felon provision in 2011 as part of a package of cost-saving measures. Instead of a potential increase of six offense class levels, the new habitual felon provision allows a maximum increase of only four offense class levels. While the district attorneys are generally critical of this change, some believe that prosecutors "brought it on themselves" through overuse of the statute in relatively minor cases.

F. Prosecutor Influence on the Legal Environment

The legal structure establishing the district attorneys' offices and the sentencing laws exert a common influence on the work of prosecutors across the state; it is also true that the prosecutors influence the terms of those laws. District attorneys, both individually and through the staff of the NCCDA, lobby the General Assembly and other decision-making bodies to obtain changes they want in the legal framework. In particular, prosecutors tend to advocate for laws that preserve the greatest possible room for diversity of practices among different districts.

The North Carolina Sentencing and Policy Advisory Commission (NCSPAC) is one forum for prosecutors to express their views on crime policy. The NCCDA appoints one voting member of the NCSPAC. The district attorney member on the commission is one of the most influential voices in setting sentencing policy, partly because of the prosecutors' technical expertise. In addition, several other voting members (those appointed by constituencies that approach issues from a law enforcement perspective) tend to take their lead from the district attorney commissioner (Wright and Ellis 1993).

The NCSPAC commissioners and staff closely track the views of the district attorney commissioner, because if that commissioner does not agree with the commission's recommendations, the NCCDA will sometimes lobby against the proposal when it reaches the General Assembly. On occasion, the district attorneys have traveled to Raleigh en masse to persuade legislators to reject proposed changes in the sentencing laws. They helped defeat several NCSPAC proposals, such as reductions in sentence lengths for the least serious felonies (rather than additional prison construction) as the preferred response to a forecast shortage of prison beds (Wright 1994, 1995, 1998*a*, 1998*b*, 1999, 2005).

Prosecutors also hold a seat on the North Carolina Governor's Crime Commission (GCC), the chief advisory body to the governor and the secretary of the Department of Crime Control and Public Safety on crime and justice issues. A district attorney is the current chair (North Carolina Department of Crime Control and Public Safety, http://www.nccrimecontrol.org). The commission lobbies the General Assembly for funds to enhance corrections and enforcement programs. It also offers technical support to law enforcement agencies and reviews applications for the state's federal block grants for criminal and juvenile justice. The GCC administers the grant money that prosecutors in the state receive.

The district attorneys do not always succeed in their lobbying efforts. One source of frustration for the prosecutors in recent years has been the amendment of the laws relating to discovery in criminal proceedings. The most recent changes grew out of the wrongful conviction in a capital case. A retrial and acquittal occurred after it came to light that defense attorneys in the first trial did not receive exculpatory and impeachment evidence as required by law. The state bar later brought disciplinary proceedings against two deputy attorneys general involved (Mosteller 2007). In the aftermath, the legislature enacted a new discovery law in 2004, broadening the scope of material that prosecutors must disclose to the defense attorney (NCGS secs. 15A-501, 15A-902–15A-910, 15A-959). In effect, this law imposed on prosecutors throughout the state an "open-file" policy close to the traditional practice in the state's larger cities before the passage of the new statute. Since the passage of the law, prosecutors have periodically lobbied the General Assembly to revise it. A recent amendment reduced the prosecutors' burden to seek out discovery material in the files of law enforcement agencies and clarified the obligation of the officers to produce such information (General Assembly of North Carolina, 2011 House Bill 408; Neff and Locke 2011).

Another legislative sore point for prosecutors involves legislative restrictions on the use of capital punishment, particularly under the Racial Justice Act of 2009. This legislation allows defendants convicted of capital murder to introduce statistical evidence on potential racial discrimination in the statewide application of the death penalty as a basis for postconviction invalidation of the individual defendant's death sentence (NCGS secs. 15A-2010–2012). The conference made repeal of the act a legislative priority in 2011 and the legislature voted for repeal, but the governor vetoed the bill. The ultimate effects of this legislation remain unclear, but in the short run, despite strong public support for capital punishment, it has produced a de facto moratorium (North Carolina Coalition for a Moratorium, http://www.nc moratorium.org).

III. Centrifugal Forces

North Carolina prosecutors operate under a common legal structure and employ a common set of legal tools. The funding system also plays a centralizing role, limiting some of the local prosecutor's power to allocate resources to fit local problems. These legal and institutional frameworks have evolved over time toward more uniformity.

The statutory structure for criminal prosecution in the state nonetheless leaves enormous room for prosecution to play out in different ways in local districts. In this section, I review the social and political forces that encourage prosecutors to approach their work differently from district to district. Those centrifugal forces include the different priorities of local voters, the relationships that each office develops with law enforcement and other partner organizations, and the divergent organizational needs that develop within offices of different sizes.

A. State Demographic Trends

North Carolina's prosecutors have changed their operations over time to serve the evolving needs of a state that is becoming more urban and more mobile. District attorneys serve over 9.5 million residents—the tenth-largest population in the United States according to the Census Bureau (http://www.census.gov). The state is unusual in its number of midsized cities, with no single dominant population center: nine cities have more than 100,000 residents, as table 4 shows. The two largest metropolitan areas, Charlotte and Raleigh, each have populations between 1.5 and 2 million.

The population has shifted over the last few decades from rural to urban and suburban areas (US Census Bureau 1995; *Raleigh News and Observer* 2011). The racial and ethnic composition of the state population has also changed. As table 5 indicates, while the black population

TABLE 4

North Carolina Cities with
Populations Greater Than
100,000 within City Limits

City	Population
Charlotte	731,424
Raleigh	403,892
Greensboro	269,666
Winston-Salem	229,617
Durham	228,330
Fayetteville	200,564
Cary	135,234
Wilmington	106,476
High Point	104,371

SOURCE.—US Census Bureau,
http://www.census.gov.

remained steady over the years, the Latino population grew from almost no population at all in 1960 to about 8 percent in 2010.

The change in Latino population affects some parts of the state more
than others. In general, cities have received a larger influx. For instance, in 2010 the Latino population in Durham County (an urban
and suburban county in the center of the state) was 13.5 percent, and
it was 4.8 percent in Ashe County, a rural county in the western mountains (North Carolina Rural Economic Development Center 2005).

The population has also become more fluid. Since 1990, more than
two-thirds of the population increase in the state is attributable to in-
migration (North Carolina Rural Economic Development Center
2005). This pattern has profoundly affected North Carolina politics,
particularly in the metropolitan areas in the central third of the state.

TABLE 5

Demographic Trends in North Carolina, 1980–2010 (%)

Racial-Ethnic Group	1980	1990	2000	2010
Asian	.4	.8	1.4	2.2
Black	22.4	22.0	21.6	21.5
Latino	1.0	1.2	4.7	8.4
White	75.3	75.0	72.1	68.5
Total population	5,882,000	6,629,000	8,049,000	9,535,000

SOURCE.—US Census Bureau, http://www.census.gov.

TABLE 6

Opposition to Incumbents in Prosecutor General Elections,
2000–2010

	North Carolina	National Sample
All races	127	1,788
Incumbent runs	92 (72% of all races)	77% of all races
Incumbent unopposed	81 (88% of incumbent races)	84% of incumbent races
Incumbent wins	92 (100% of incumbent races)	96% of incumbent races
Incumbent wins when opposed	11 (100% of opposed incumbent races)	73% of opposed incumbent races

SOURCE.—Wright (2010).

In these jurisdictions, the traditional aversion of southern voters—even very conservative voters—to the Republican Party has faded away, and the state has become genuinely competitive for both major political parties. The arrival of residents from other regions has also shifted traditional views of jurors and voters about the relative importance of crimes such as domestic violence, driving while intoxicated (DWI), and firearms violations (Sundt 1999).

B. Voter Priorities and the Electoral Connection

District attorneys are elected to 4-year terms. Because all ADAs hold their positions at the pleasure of the district attorney (in common parlance, "the elected"), local voters control the entire prosecutorial staff in their districts. In practice, however, this results in little turnover.

1. *Few Challenges to Incumbents.* Incumbent prosecutors who run for reelection in the United States can count on winning. In all likelihood, they will run unopposed and will never have to debate their policies or the quality of the work being done in their offices. The same is even more emphatically true for incumbents in North Carolina than for prosecutors elsewhere in the country.

As table 6 indicates, the incumbent district attorney was a candidate in 72 percent of all general elections between 2000 and 2010 in North Carolina, compared to 77 percent of a national sample of prosecutor elections (Wright 2010, p. 803 n. 18). When incumbents run, they win. In North Carolina, this held true without exception in general elections; on a national basis, 96 percent of the incumbents won reelection. The outcomes for primary elections closely track the outcomes for general elections. Only two incumbent district attorneys in North Carolina lost primary elections during the period 2000–2010.

Although incumbents in larger cities in the United States tend to face challengers and lose elections more often than incumbents in smaller jurisdictions, the same trend did not appear in North Carolina. Incumbent district attorneys were equally successful in larger and smaller jurisdictions.

Incumbent prosecutors in North Carolina faced opposition in only 12 percent of their races. Although state legislators also enjoy an incumbency advantage, they face opposition far more often. Typically when a new prosecutor takes office in the state, it happens because an incumbent decided to retire.

Incumbent prosecutors who do not attract opponents will not have to pass through the traditional campaign gauntlet. In that sense, they are not obliged to offer a public defense of their policy choices or prosecution outcomes (Green and Zacharias 2004; Wright 2009).

One result of this electoral system is a cohort of elected prosecutors in North Carolina with substantial experience in the position. Among the 44 district attorneys in office in 2011, 14 had more than 10 years of experience as the chief prosecutor, 14 had held the position for more than 4 years, and only 16 had less than 4 years of experience. Many among the newcomers, such as Jim O'Neill of Forsyth County or Jon David of District 13, could point to years of experience as an ADA.

It is tempting to conclude that district attorneys have little to fear from voters and need not and do not consider public views during the ordinary course of prosecuting crimes. That is not the North Carolina reality. District attorneys are highly aware of local media coverage and of the high-visibility cases that shape voters' views about their offices (Bandyopadhyay and McCannon 2010a, 2010b). They set internal office policies in light of the need to monitor sensitive areas especially closely. For instance, district attorneys in North Carolina say that they "audit" the files periodically to learn in more detail about charging and resolution of charges on sensitive subjects such as DWI or breaking and entering (Working Groups on Best Practices 2010, pp. 1995–2010). The elected district attorney also typically tries some cases personally; these cases include capital murder and public corruption crimes, offenses (known as "heaters") that attract the most public attention.

The responsiveness of prosecutors to the views of voters works as a centrifugal force among the offices (Bibas 2006). District attorneys try to reflect the values and priorities of very different electorates around the state. In broad brush strokes, Republican voters predominate in the western half of the state and Democratic voters predominate in the eastern half of the state. The elected district attorneys reflect this pattern: Republicans tend to win in the west and Democrats in the east.

The party affiliation of a district attorney does not normally predict his or her behavior as it might predict the behavior of a state legislator. The conference lobbies for much the same legislation, whether its officers happen to be Democrats or Republicans in a given year. In that sense, criminal prosecution is relatively nonpartisan. Some of the differences in the outputs among prosecutor offices create an appearance of distinctive Democratic and Republican approaches to criminal prosecution. That appearance, however, is misleading. Voters in larger urban areas more frequently elect Democrats, and charging and disposition patterns in urban offices are typically different from those in rural offices. For instance, offices led by Democratic district attorneys (dominated by the larger offices in the state) are slightly more likely to obtain prison sentences rather than alternative punishments. After one controls for the size of a prosecutor's office as an independent variable, however, the correlation disappears between political parties and types of charges filed or penalties obtained.

Differences between urban and rural voters are more salient than political party identifications. Voters in urban areas more clearly prioritize the prosecution of serious violent offenses, whereas rural voters expect heavier punishments to apply to both person and property offenses. Urban voters show more tolerance for drug crimes and less tolerance for firearms offenses than do voters in rural areas.

2. *Community Input Techniques.*   Local prosecutors must develop their own political bases and develop their own information about what voters prefer (Gordon and Huber 2009). When district attorneys in North Carolina are asked how they keep informed about the public safety priorities of the community and how they communicate with the public about the work of their office, they typically reply, "I don't do as much as I should." District attorneys in all types of jurisdictions rely on informal and spontaneous methods to stay in touch with their constituents. Particularly in larger jurisdictions, they have begun to explore more structured methods to obtain input from the public and to communicate office priorities to the voters. For instance, the district at-

torney in Charlotte has a "community liaison team" of about two dozen experienced ADAs who attend meetings of neighborhood associations and civic groups to explain office operations and priorities and to listen for critiques and suggestions.

Prosecutors monitor the local news media—including print, broadcast, and online sources—as a primary window into local voter views. Local reporters write stories about serious felony cases such as homicides and sexual assaults and cases involving public officials or other local leaders. They generally do not write about long-term trends in prosecution policy or changes in case dispositions or sentences from year to year (Miller and Wright 2008; Wright 2009).

The elected district attorneys give speeches and make other public appearances with various civic groups, professional associations, church groups, and others. Many of these take place at the invitation of the groups, but sometimes the district attorney takes the initiative. A few district attorneys regularly address students in the public schools. For instance, the district attorney in Wilmington speaks each year to student assemblies in every middle school and high school in the district.

The district attorneys do not typically place their initiatives under the banner of "community prosecution." The community prosecution philosophy draws on many of the same principles as the older and more broadly embraced model of community policing (Bureau of Justice Assistance 1994). Offices that embrace this model—prosecutors in Portland, Oregon, and Milwaukee, Wisconsin, offer two leading examples—decentralize prosecutors' work and adjust the priorities of the office to take account of local community views (Levine 2005; Klingele, Scott, and Dickey 2010; Milwaukee County District Attorney's Office 2012). Although North Carolina prosecutors tend not to embrace the community prosecution model explicitly, some pursue the basic objectives of such a model. For instance, some prosecutors decentralize their resources when they assign permanent staff to each of the counties of a multicounty jurisdiction. Some urban offices (such as in Wilmington) solicit the views of community leaders on committees that meet periodically to monitor neighborhood crime generally and crimes of particular emphasis, such as gang activity.

Internet web pages offer an area for potential growth in community input into the North Carolina prosecutors' offices (Miller and Wright 2012). A survey showed that 18 of the 44 district attorney offices maintain only a one-page website listing mailing addresses, with no further information about the office or the criminal justice system. The remaining 26 offices offer a standard palette of background information: a brief professional biography of the elected district attorney; information about victim rights and responsibilities under state law and statewide resources for crime victims; a generic description of the criminal process; a glossary of criminal justice terminology; links to the state court system's online court calendar system; and links to websites for the attorney general's office and other criminal justice agencies.

A few of the websites for larger jurisdictions, such as Doug Henderson's in Guilford County, contain information specific to the prosecutorial district, such as the locations of state courtrooms that handle traffic citations (http://www.ncdistrictattorney.org/18/traffic admin.html). The pages for Ben David in Wilmington describe office priorities, focusing on prosecution of violent crimes and discussing the importance of plea negotiations alongside trial outcomes (http://www .nccourts.org/county/newhanover/staff/da/default.asp). Not surprisingly, the two largest offices—Raleigh and Charlotte—offer a bit more office-specific information. Raleigh describes its office structure, its general mission statement, the victim services available in the office, and programs of special emphasis such as juvenile prosecutions and a domestic violence unit (http://web.co.wake.nc.us/districtattorney/). The Charlotte website describes office structure and includes a "community connections" page asking viewers to subscribe to an office newsletter or submit a request for an office representative to address a meeting of a community group (http://charmeckda.com/). With the exception of one rural office, the district attorneys do not currently publish annual reports or other assessments of office performance.

Victim and witness services programs illustrate the diversity in district attorney offices across the state. While state law provides for at least some victim support services in each office (an outgrowth of 1998 legislation and a new victim rights amendment to the state constitution), the larger support staffs in the urban offices can afford to offer services. More urban counties also operate a greater variety of victim support services outside the prosecutors' office and to offer more community corrections programs for defendants. The bulk of the spending on community corrections and deferred prosecution in North Carolina is funded at the state level, but local governments and private nonprofit organizations supplement the state budget for such services. The urban areas tend to attract such supplemental funding and to offer a wider range of programs for crime victims and for defendants. The support staff in the district attorneys' offices often take a leading role in connecting crime victims and potential defendants with local support programs.

C. Relationships within Working Groups

The sociolegal literature identifies the interests and priorities of the courtroom working group of the prosecutor, the defense attorney, the judge, and the other regular participants in criminal adjudication as a major driver of final outcomes in criminal cases (Eisenstein, Flemming, and Nardulli 1987; Flemming, Nardulli, and Eisenstein 1992; Johnson 2002; Levine 2006). The relationships between the prosecutors and the other actors in the local working group illustrate important differences among prosecutorial offices in North Carolina.

1. *Law Enforcement Relationships.*   One major difference among the prosecutors' offices is in their relations with law enforcement agencies (Richman 2003; Harris 2012). Prosecutors in each district interact with multiple law enforcement agencies. A typical district will be home to at least one sheriff's department and several city police departments. Some also include campus police forces for the state university system and enforcement officers for various regulatory agencies.

Some of the larger law enforcement agencies in North Carolina employ their own "police attorneys" or "public safety attorneys" who train police officers on criminal procedure and other legal matters relevant to criminal investigations. The smaller agencies rely on the district attorney's office for training and for legal advice as needed during criminal investigations. This advisory function has a constitutional foundation: "The District Attorney shall advise the officers of justice in his district" (North Carolina Constitution, art. IV, sec. 18[1]). Advice to law enforcement is an important part of the workload in some districts, but this varies widely and shapes profoundly different relationships with law enforcement from place to place.

In those districts that actively advise the police during their investigations, the district attorney usually designates particular ADAs with expertise in particular types of crime investigation and distributes contact information for those prosecutors to all officers investigating cases of that sort. Access to this legal advice is often available 24 hours a day, 7 days per week.

The more proactive district attorneys—particularly those recently elected to office—view themselves as the leader of the local criminal justice community and take it upon themselves to try to coordinate the work of different police departments. Their most common technique is to sponsor a monthly lunch for the leaders of all the departments. There they compare notes about current criminal suspects and community complaints and explain any new practices of the district attorney that will affect classes of cases. Other district attorneys—typically those who have held office for a longer time—meet with law enforcement leaders more sporadically, usually when particular issues prompt a meeting.

Although cooperative relationships are the norm, potential conflicts are built into the relationship with law enforcement officers. Most district attorneys view independence from law enforcement as a key component of their role. The prosecutor evaluates the file assembled by a police officer and sometimes decides to file less serious charges than the investigating officer would prefer or declines to file charges at all. Routines for sharing information between the different bureaucracies also generate conflict. For instance, prosecutors are responsible under state law for disclosing broad categories of relevant information to the defense, even if the information exists in police files and the police failed to transfer it to the prosecutor.

In some jurisdictions, tensions between the prosecutor and law enforcement agencies devolve into media wars. For one example, after the appointment of Police Chief Rodney Monroe in Charlotte in 2008, he began to make critical statements about the district attorney's office and the number of cases it refused to prosecute. District attorney Peter Gilchrist considered it unseemly to respond in the media. More recently, Gilchrist's successor Andrew Murray made a series of changes in office practices that appear to have calmed the relationship. An ADA now appears at the crime scene in every potential homicide case. The office also invites senior investigators from the police department to regular meetings to discuss plea offers in homicide cases, in light of proof problems and resource constraints.

2. Judicial Relationships.   Each prosecutor's office inevitably develops a distinctive set of relationships with the superior and district court judges in the district. The dynamics vary with the office structure. In some districts, each ADA cycles through the same courtroom and tries cases before the same small group of judges. As repeat players, they develop an individualized relationship with the presiding judge. Elsewhere, particularly in the larger jurisdictions, a larger number of judges cycle through the courtrooms and less frequently preside over the trials of any given ADA.

The relationship with the district court judges—the misdemeanor level court—is central to processing cases because the judge serves as the fact finder in all misdemeanor trials, at least initially. A small number of defendants appeal their misdemeanor convictions and obtain a fresh jury trial in superior court, but for the most part the district court judges dispose of all misdemeanors.

The elected district attorney often relies on judges for feedback about the quality of the courtroom work of the ADAs in the office. While the district attorney routinely circulates through courtrooms to monitor the proceedings (particularly in smaller jurisdictions), that monitoring is necessarily selective. Judges help complete the picture by informing the district attorney about unusual performances by ADAs, both for good and for ill.

District attorneys necessarily find themselves in administrative partnerships with the senior judges in their districts who have responsibility for organizing the work of the courts and managing the criminal dockets. If a district attorney has an idea for more efficient processing of cases, it generally will not work without the cooperation of the senior judges. Such cooperation between prosecutors and judges is the norm rather than the exception.

At the state level, judges and prosecutors take independent positions on policy questions. Prosecutors address policy questions both as individuals and through the Conference of District Attorneys, but judges address policy questions only through their professional associations— the Conference of District Court Judges or the Conference of Superior Court Judges. While Canon 4A of the North Carolina Code of Judicial Conduct allows judges to speak about matters related to the "administration of justice," a tradition of restraint leads judges to address policy issues only collectively and not as individuals (North Carolina Code of Judicial Conduct, canon 4). The judges' organizations over the years have more often opposed structured sentencing laws than have prosecutors.

3. *Federal-State Relationships.* Each elected district attorney also develops a distinctive relationship with the federal prosecutor. There are three US attorney's districts, each dealing with roughly one-third of the district attorneys. Particularly concerning high-volume crimes of

overlapping jurisdiction—narcotics trafficking, weapons, and fraud—the federal prosecutors tend to take the largest and most complex cases, leaving the bulk of cases for state prosecution. The sorting of cases sometimes happens informally during telephone conversations among police investigators. In other cases, the sorting takes place during regularly scheduled or ad hoc meetings between state and federal prosecutors. Although dual prosecutions are possible, they are rare (*Bartkus v. Illinois*, 359 US 121 [1959]; US Department of Justice 2009, sec. 9-2.031).

Sometimes federal prosecutors or federal law enforcement agencies promote joint enforcement activities at the training conferences for state prosecutors. They find willing partners at the state level: some district attorneys will designate a few ADAs as special assistant US attorneys to prosecute crimes in federal court (approximately eight to 10 throughout the state at any given time). Federal funds pay their salaries.

4. *Defense Attorney Relationships.* One additional relationship helps to create distinctive working environments in each of the 44 prosecutorial districts: the relationships between ADAs and defense attorneys. Some districts are known for respectful and even amiable relationships between these full-time advocates and adversaries: the attorneys in Guilford County carry such a reputation. Others are noted for their relatively hostile interactions, both in the courtroom and in pretrial proceedings and negotiations. The prosecutors and public defenders in Durham are reputed to have such a relationship.

Public defenders in North Carolina operate in nine of the 44 districts—generally speaking, the largest and busiest. In other districts, judges appoint individual attorneys to represent indigent criminal defendants, drawing the attorneys from a list of attorneys who volunteer for the appointments. Funding of defense attorneys is always a problem, but North Carolina is better situated than most other states in the region (Green 2003; Backus and Marcus 2006; Marx 2008). Prosecutors point out as they lobby the state legislature that the state spends more on criminal defense attorneys than it does on prosecuting attorneys—at least according to some measures (North Carolina Office of Indigent Defense Services 2011). State law requires parity of salary for ADAs and assistant public defenders with comparable experience levels (Wright 2004; Wright and Logan 2006).

The presence of a public defender in a district affects the work of prosecutors there because it provides a defense organization that has an interest in systemwide issues of cost and efficiency and a negotiating partner for exploring changes in the process. Prosecutors and public defenders, for example, might agree that certain defendants will receive priority scheduling for bail hearings to economize on jail space. Consequently, the limited presence of public defenders in only nine busy districts contributes to functional differences among prosecutors' offices across the state.

D. Office Size and Organization

Perhaps the most important source of variation among prosecutors' offices in North Carolina is differences in their size. There is an enormous range in the populations served in different districts, the numbers of cases prosecuted, and the numbers of ADAs available to do the work. This sheer volume of cases to be processed in some offices leads to different organizational strategies, with larger offices relying more heavily on specialization of labor.

Table 7 indicates the population served by the largest and smallest district attorney's offices in North Carolina—the largest and smallest quartiles. It also provides two estimates of workload: the number of felony filings per ADA and the number of ADA positions identified as a personnel deficit in the weighted caseload study commissioned by the conference of district attorneys (Kleiman and Lee 2010). The number of ADAs employed in each office sometimes differs from the authorized number of positions because a few city or county governments fund additional ADA positions.

Several aspects of table 7 warrant mention. First, the distribution of ADAs matches the population reasonably well. The ratio of population to prosecutors stays within fairly narrow bounds, with only a few outliers such as District 10 (Raleigh). In those districts with the highest population ratios, the caseload per attorney (particularly as reflected in the weighted caseload study) appears to be lower, suggesting that these are districts with comparatively modest crime problems.

The number of residents served by each prosecutor is much lower in some states than in North Carolina. For instance, the district attorney's office in Milwaukee serves a population almost identical to Charlotte's but employs 125 ADAs, compared to 79 in Charlotte (http://county.milwaukee.gov/DistrictAttorney7715.htm; http://quick facts.census.gov/qfd/states/55/55079.html). In other states, cities the

TABLE 7

Population Served and Workload of Largest and Smallest North Carolina District Attorney Offices, 2010

District	Population	ADA Positions	Ratio of Population to ADAs	Felony Filings per ADA	Weighted Caseload, Implied Need
Largest:					
26 (Charlotte)	919,628	79	11,641	127	3
10 (Raleigh)	900,993	43	20,953	108	6
18 (Greensboro)	488,406	33	14,800	279	10
21 (Winston-Salem)	350,670	26	13,487	48	2
12 (Fayetteville)	319,431	24	13,310	165	0
11 (Harnett, Lee Counties)	344,763	20	17,238	90	6
25 (Burke, Caldwell Counties)	329,299	19	17,332	136	3
4 (Duplin, Jones, Onslow, Sampson Counties)	309,861	19	16,308	192	3
14 (Durham)	267,587	19	14,084	95	1

248

District	Population				
5 (Wilmington)	254,884	19	13,415	137	3
7 (Edgecombe, Nash, Wilson Counties)	233,914	19	12,311	177	5
Smallest:					
29B (Henderson, Polk, Transylvania)	153,127	9	17,014	82	2
23 (Alleghany, Ashe, Wilkes, Yadkin Counties)	141,044	9	15,672	165	1
19C (Rowan County)	140,798	9	15,644	148	2
17B (Stokes, Surry Counties)	121,074	9	13,453	168	0
2 (Beaufort)	95,709	9	10,634	187	0
24 (Avery, Madison, Mitchell, Watauga, Yancey Counties)	123,037	8	15,380	156	0
29A (McDowell, Rutherford Counties)	106,449	8	13,306	140	1
17A (Rockingham County)	93,963	8	11,745	139	0
16A (Hoke, Scotland Counties)	83,109	8	10,389	138	1
6B (Bertie, Hertford, Northampton Counties)	68,050	7	9,721	142	0
9A (Caswell, Person Counties)	63,183	7	9,026	95	0
19D (Moore County)	88,247	6	14,708	152	2
6A (Halifax County)	54,691	6	9,115	168	1

SOURCES.—Kleiman and Lee (2010); North Carolina Administrative Office of the Courts (2010); US Census Bureau, http://www.census.gov.

size of Raleigh typically employ more prosecutors than North Carolina is willing to fund (Bureau of Justice Statistics 2007).

Second, table 7 documents large differences in size between offices. The largest is more than 13 times larger than the smallest. The average size of an office in the top quartile (29) is more than three times larger than the average size in the lowest quartile (8).

Finally, table 7 indicates a wider need for additional attorneys in the larger offices. The weighted caseload estimates indicate more offices with zero personnel deficits among the smallest offices. The population ratios are only slightly larger for the larger offices (an average of 14,989 for the largest offices compared to 12,754 for the smaller ones), and the felony filings per prosecutors are comparable for the two groups (an average of 141 for the larger offices compared to 145 for the smaller ones). Felony filings in the larger districts are likely weighted toward more cases that take longer to prosecute.

Not surprisingly, district attorneys in the larger offices organize their work differently from their counterparts in the smaller offices. Specialized units devoted to particular types of crime operate in the larger offices. The Raleigh office, for instance, assigns ADAs to a Robbery Unit, a Drug Unit, a DWI Court Unit, a Juvenile Court Unit, a Domestic Violence Unit, and a Worthless Check Deferred Prosecution Unit. Other offices in larger cities also create special assignments for domestic violence, drug cases, and juvenile matters.

The prosecutors in smaller offices also develop specialty areas, but informally. In general terms, more experienced ADAs handle the more serious felonies, and newcomers usually begin with misdemeanors in district court. While new prosecutors move through a predictable progression of assignments in larger offices, the development of expertise occurs on a more ad hoc basis in smaller offices.

Vertical prosecution is the norm in the smaller offices. The prosecutor who assumes responsibility for a file when it first arrives from the police department handles the case through each stage of the criminal proceedings.

Vertical prosecution combines with horizontal organization in the larger offices. In the Winston-Salem office, for example, several attorneys are assigned to the "probable cause rotation" in superior court, where they represent the state at a preliminary hearing to test the adequacy of the evidence to go forward to trial. They pass the case file along to other attorneys once it clears the probable cause stage. Similarly, in Raleigh, Charlotte, Greensboro, Wilmington, and several other offices, some attorneys are assigned to handle "misdemeanor appeals" (de novo jury trials of misdemeanors). In Charlotte, the Drug Team processes all of its cases on a horizontal model, with different attorneys taking responsibility for the file at different stages. In addition, most of the other felony specialty units—the Property Team, the Persons Team, and the Homicide Team—assign an experienced ADA to serve as the "papering DA" who first reviews the file, interviews the investigating officer, and makes the initial charging decision for all cases entering the system.

The supervisory structure in the larger offices is more elaborate than in the smaller offices. The elected district attorneys designate a "first assistant" who shares in operational supervision of the work. They also select one member of each internal unit to supervise the work of the other attorneys on the team, to set policies that relate to the work of the team, to monitor implementation of office policy by other attorneys on the team, and to evaluate the professional development of the attorneys for purposes of advancement within the office. In the smaller offices, most of the supervisory duties remain in the hands of the elected district attorney.

The higher level of subject matter specialization, the presence of horizontal organizational features, and the distribution of supervisory duties to a larger leadership group all distinguish larger offices from smaller ones. These organizational distinctions combine with the political landscape in each district and the organizational relationships that develop with individual judges and law enforcement agencies. Together, these differences create an environment that shapes the professional development of individual prosecutors and produces distinctive adjudicative results.

IV. Personnel and Culture

The prosecutors who work in different office environments follow somewhat different career paths and tend to hold different conceptions of their roles. While there are common elements in the professional experiences of prosecutors throughout the state, the organizational setting shapes the experience for many.

A. Who Becomes a Prosecutor?

District attorneys in North Carolina all do their own hiring and create their own processes for identifying candidates and selecting among them. They speak routinely about the need to hire a demographically diverse group of attorneys, a selection strategy that serves a number of purposes. The ADAs must deal sympathetically with crime victims and their families, and they must persuade grand juries and trial juries drawn from the community. An understanding of criminal defendants also leads a prosecutor to select charges that, they believe, stand the best chance of rehabilitating the offender or preventing future crimes. ADAs commonly refer to rehabilitation of offenders, especially in juvenile matters and in misdemeanor cases, as a professional responsibility they take seriously (King 2012). Each of these tasks becomes more difficult if the prosecutors in the district share little in common with the residents of the district.

Until late in the twentieth century, almost all solicitors, district attorneys, and assistant prosecutors in North Carolina were white and male. A good deal of movement has occurred since then. Statistics from the AOC show that 33 of the 206 ADAs (16 percent) in North Carolina in 1982 were female and 13 ADAs (6 percent) were African American. By 2011, women were 46 percent of the ADAs in North Carolina: 285 of 624. Racial minorities accounted for 16 percent of positions in 2011 (response to a public records request from the AOC, December 5, 2011).

There is no difference between larger and smaller offices in the hiring of women. Offices above the median size (11 ADAs) employed essentially the same percentage of women as did the offices below the median. Larger offices were, however, more likely to hire members of racial minorities to serve as ADAs. In offices above the median, a weighted average of 18 percent of those hired to work as prosecutors were from racial minority groups; offices below the median hired 12 percent. Seven of the 20 smaller offices employed no minority attorneys at all. During informal conversations, district attorneys stress the need for greater racial diversity among their ADAs and other office staff.

The political affiliations of prosecutors loosely track statewide party affiliation trends. For example, on the basis of voter registration records in North Carolina, 38 percent of the prosecutors in the Charlotte office whose party affiliation was known (15 of 40) were registered as

Democrats, 30 percent were registered as Republicans, 30 percent were registered as "unaffiliated voters" (i.e., independents), and one was registered as a Libertarian. A Gallup poll in 2002 estimated that 49 percent of North Carolinians were Democratic or leaning Democratic, and 39 percent were Republican or leaning Republican (Jones 2010).

One experience that many prosecutors in the state share is that their work as prosecutors began entry in their careers. Attorneys who work as prosecutors in North Carolina are usually quite young when they start. Thus, the district attorney's office is a formative professional experience for the typical prosecutor.

When ADAs explain during interviews why they want to become prosecutors, their answers tend toward the idealistic. Even among the least experienced attorneys, ADAs do not point primarily to the development of trial skills or to manageable work hours. Instead, they typically point to their ability to perform public service, to contribute to their community. Some link their choice of profession to their religious values. They also frequently discuss their concern both for victims of crime and for the well-being of criminal defendants. The ADAs say that they can accomplish more for a defendant who deserves mercy than a defense attorney could accomplish because the prosecutor can reduce or dismiss charges without having to convince anyone to cooperate (Bowers 2010; Burke 2010).

Prosecutors place a high value on professional independence and value the job in part because it places enormous responsibility on them right away. They express satisfaction that the elected district attorney typically sets general guidelines on only a few matters and then trusts the line prosecutors to exercise sound judgment on the many questions not addressed by office policy. There appears to be a difference here between larger and smaller offices. Attorneys in the larger offices, more keenly aware of supervisory structures and routines, refer more often to their identification as a team member than as an individual attorney.

B. Selection

The most common route into a district attorney's office in North Carolina is to work as an unpaid office intern during a summer in between years in law school and then to apply for a full-time position after passing the bar exam in July following graduation from law school in May. Among the 26 attorneys on the Misdemeanor and Drug Teams in the Charlotte office (the teams staffed by the junior-most attorneys) in 2010, 12 had worked as interns in a prosecutor's office, and another four had worked full-time in another prosecutor's office before being hired in Charlotte.

Some prosecutors have prior professional experience before they become ADAs. It is not unusual for a law school graduate to work for a short while in a private law firm, specializing in litigation, while waiting for a position to open up in the district attorney's office. A few have more substantial experience as criminal defense attorneys. The hiring philosophy on this possibility differs from office to office. While most chief prosecutors treat criminal defense work as a positive and relevant experience, others treat prior defense work as a cause of concern, raising issues about the temperamental fit between the attorney and the work of a prosecutor.

The elected district attorney remains actively involved in hiring, regardless of the size of the office. The district attorneys also routinely look to advice from trusted senior prosecutors in the office to inform their hiring choices. In the larger offices, input on the hiring decision tends to draw on the views of a larger committee, whereas the smaller offices seem to place a bit more emphasis on the compatibility of the new hire with the existing members of a small working group.

C. Training

Each district attorney's office develops its own methods for training new attorneys (Bibas 2009; Working Groups on Best Practices 2010). All the offices assign their least experienced attorneys to misdemeanor cases in district court. In some offices, every attorney entering the office spends some time in district court regardless of prior experience; in other offices, new hires with prior defense or prosecutorial experience move directly into superior court felony work.

One common method of training is to assign the newcomer to shadow a more experienced partner through the district court routine for a few days or weeks (the period varies among districts). Once the initial training period passes, new attorneys consult their partners about unusual situations as they arise. The larger offices also tend to assign an experienced attorney to supervise the entire group of district court attorneys; the supervisor monitors compliance with office priorities and promotes professional development among the district court attorneys. Some offices ask junior attorneys to "second chair" felony trials on an ad hoc basis.

The district attorneys generally do not create a comprehensive written set of office policies (Podgor 2004; Luna and Wade 2010). A few high-priority policies are typically reduced to writing in the form of memoranda or e-mail messages. Other policies are articulated but not reduced to writing. For instance, in Charlotte the elected district attorney insisted for many years that felony breaking and entering charges be filed against any defendant who entered a residence, and no reduced charges were allowed. Some of the offices also create written materials that describe standard operating procedure for certain units, types of cases, or particular stages in the proceedings.

The training of prosecuting attorneys does not stop, of course, after the first few months on the job. The development of professional skills and values remains an objective for prosecutors throughout their careers. Prosecutors, like all licensed attorneys in the state, must complete at least 12 hours per year of "continuing legal education." Most complete the bulk of their CLE credits through attendance at conferences sponsored by the Conference of District Attorneys and the SOG at the University of North Carolina. Faculty members at the SOG create and distribute technical advisories about new legal developments, hold periodic training sessions, and answer inquiries from individual prosecutors around the state. (Other SOG faculty members provide comparable services for public defenders.)

Prosecutors generally do not receive their training from CLE programs sponsored by their local bar associations. Prosecutors in the larger offices tend not to be involved in the affairs of the local or state bar association. In these offices, perhaps because of a broad range of mentors in-house, less experienced attorneys look for role models internally rather than externally. Prosecutors in smaller offices, by contrast, are somewhat more involved in local bar association activity and are more likely to look to the broader profession for guidance.

Prosecutors aim to develop subject matter expertise in topics that relate to the effective trial of criminal charges rather than in topics related to the origins or incidence of crime. Prosecutors who work on complex technical cases such as arson or DWI become educated about the science supporting the investigation of such crimes. The study of criminology or criminal justice on the undergraduate level tends to carry little or no weight in the hiring process, nor do the continuing education opportunities for prosecutors focus on criminology topics. Two exceptions to this trend appear among prosecutors who prosecute juvenile cases and sex offenses. In this setting, some prosecutors do pursue further education on topics related to childhood development and the effectiveness of various criminal justice responses to offenses.

D. Career Paths

Only a minority of new prosecutors remain in the prosecutorial service for their entire careers. A larger number move into some other legal practice—typically private criminal defense—after a few years. Attorneys who leave the district attorney's office most often migrate into private criminal defense work in the same jurisdiction. A move to the public defender's office is rare. One of the appeals of criminal defense work is a higher income, which is typically available to attorneys in private practice. As a result, attorneys often leave prosecution work when the financial demands of family life increase. Others who leave for criminal defense work express an interest in a change of pace, the challenge of building a successful legal practice, or some unhappiness about the policies of a newly elected district attorney. In smaller jurisdictions, a number of prosecutors leave office to become judges.

District attorneys often ask new recruits to commit to a minimum term of, say, 2 or 3 years as a condition of the job offer. The period of training is most intensive and expensive for the first few years, and the elected district attorneys hope to receive some dividends on this investment.

Most prosecutors' offices have people with a mix of experience levels on the payroll. The typical arrangement is a group of "career" prosecutors (something less than a third of the legal staff) working with a group of junior prosecutors who will stay for a few years before moving on to other legal work. As table 8 indicates, the midsized district attorneys' offices tend to retain more experienced ADAs than do the smaller or the larger offices. Experience is measured here by number of months employed by the state.

The larger offices have the same percentage of inexperienced attorneys as other offices but lower percentages of attorneys with more than 5 or 10 years of experience. Prosecutors with extremely long tenures (more than 20 years) are concentrated in the largest offices.

The smaller offices might keep fewer experienced attorneys than the midsized offices because the smaller offices present fewer opportunities for midlevel management and specialization to give experienced attor-

TABLE 8

Tenure in Office for North Carolina Prosecutors, 2011

	Statewide	Large Offices (Top Quartile)	Small Offices (Low Quartile)	Midsize Offices
Average months of service	94	92	88	98
Median months of service	64	61	66	72
Attorneys with more than 20 years' service (%)	8	9	2	7
Attorneys with more than 10 years' service (%)	30	26	31	35
Attorneys with more than 5 years' service (%)	52	50	53	54
Attorneys with more than 2 years' service (%)	80	80	82	79

SOURCE.—Response to a public records request from the AOC (December 5, 2011).

neys a sense of professional development. Larger offices may lose more of their midseniority prosecutors because they are located in larger cities where the economic opportunities in private law firms are greater (Long and Boylan 2005).

Finally, there are reasons to believe that prosecutors in larger and smaller jurisdictions hold different conceptions of their role and of the reach of the criminal justice system. Prosecutors in smaller offices may expect more from the criminal justice system overall. They are less likely to dismiss low-level felonies such as drug crimes and property crimes and are less inclined to take felonies to trial. Instead, prosecutors in smaller offices more frequently accept guilty pleas to lesser charges, taking half a loaf in a larger range of cases.

Prosecutors in larger offices may have more modest expectations for the criminal courts. They appear to be more willing to prioritize cases, dismissing some defendants entirely and seeking more severe sentences against the remaining defendants. In larger urban districts, higher numbers of violent crimes crowd out the property and drug crimes. The presence of more social services in urban areas reinforces the idea that criminal courts represent only one piece of the public response to crime. In such an environment, the prosecutor's responsibility is to identify the defendants who present the greatest threats to public safety and to conserve criminal sanctions for those cases.

V. Conclusion

It is sometimes said that "biology is destiny." When it comes to prosecutor organizations, it appears that office size is destiny—or at last a part of destiny. The scale of the operation determines many aspects of the work in the office, including the priorities that drive the selection of charges, the choice of procedural methods used for adjudicating charges, and the punishments that the office seeks after obtaining convictions. The size and complexity of the prosecutor's office also help to determine the nature of the professional experience for the prosecutors who work there and their conceptions of the roles they should play within the larger criminal justice system.

It is not clear what mechanisms produce different results in smaller and larger organizations. Do larger bureaucracies necessarily bring along certain economies of scale? Or is the real driver the diverse natures of the surrounding communities rather than the size or structure of the prosecutorial service itself? Do people who choose life in smaller communities (or those who choose larger communities) hold attitudes and expectations about crime and public order that systematically differ and determine the shape of the local prosecutorial service?

Whether it is the preferences of the local community or the organizational features of the prosecutor's office that produce distinctive prosecutorial styles in different places, North Carolina makes it clear that statewide laws and institutions do not stamp out localism. State leaders are strongly committed to uniform resources and operations for prosecutors. They place extraordinarily tight restrictions on local choices about the number of positions to fill, the training and travel of attorneys, and the duties of staff members. A system of central state funding for most corrections and relatively strict legal guidelines on the available punishments make state-level policy choices about sentencing more important in North Carolina than in many other jurisdictions. And yet, despite the existence of this extensive statewide infrastructure devoted to uniformity, local variety persists.

Local variety in criminal prosecution is irrepressible in a pluralistic democracy. There are certain outcomes that all state residents expect, such as prompt and certain prosecution and punishment of serious violent offenses. Prosecutor districts look much the same in their dealings with these crimes. When it comes to lower-level assaults, property crimes such as burglary and larceny, and drug crimes, public views differ and leave room for prosecutors to respond differently. These views about crime and public safety play out as people choose their homes and communities. People tend to sort themselves into like-minded local groups. In states with relatively homogeneous populations, local differences may be harder to notice. But in a jurisdiction like North Carolina, where the population has become more mobile and diverse over the past few generations, differences among prosecutorial districts stand out.

In one sense, this irrepressible local variety is a good thing. It allows people with different public safety values to live and work in the same state, with criminal prosecutions that meet their different expectations. In another sense, the combination of a centralized legal and financial infrastructure with local prosecutorial styles is an invitation to trouble. When state taxpayers commit themselves to fund whatever criminal penalties the local prosecutor obtains on behalf of local voters, the incentives are all wrong. Local prosecutors are spending other people's money. The state therefore needs to track more closely the connection between local benefits and local burdens of criminal prosecution. State taxpayers should become aware of those times when they subsidize local priorities in crime control.

In a more general sense, the state needs to play more of an informational role and less of a regulatory role in its efforts to produce uniform criminal justice. For instance, rather than telling district attorneys that they can give their ADAs only a 10 percent salary raise in a given year, the state would add more value by reporting prosecutor salaries in a clear format that allows elected district attorneys (and potential challengers and voters) to understand local salary choices in light of other approaches at work in other districts. As long as the tax laws and state appropriations of public funds link local prosecutor choices to local tax burdens, looser controls and stronger disclosure can be an effective combination.

Criminal prosecution will keep its local flavor in a state as large and diverse as North Carolina. Tightening the administrative screws at the state level will produce more discontent than uniform justice. Better local deliberation and accountability are goals that are both more achievable and more worthwhile in a pluralistic democracy.

REFERENCES

Ad Hoc Criminal Code Revision Committee. 1970. *Final Report of the Ad Hoc Criminal Code Revision Committee*. Raleigh: North Carolina State Government.

Backus, Mary Sue, and Paul Marcus. 2006. "The Right to Counsel in Criminal Cases: A National Crisis." *Hastings Law Journal* 57:1031–1130.

Ball, W. David. 2011. "Tough on Crime (on the State's Dime): How Violent Crime Does Not Drive California Counties' Incarceration Rates—and Why It Should." Unpublished manuscript. Social Science Research Network. http://papers.ssrn.com/sol3/papers.cfm?abstract_id = 1871427.

Bandyopadhyay, Siddhartha, and Bryan C. McCannon. 2010*a*. "The Effect of Re-elections on Prosecutors." Unpublished manuscript. Social Science Research Network. http://papers.ssrn.com/sol3/papers.cfm?abstract_id = 1641345.

———. 2010*b*. "Prosecutorial Retention: Signaling by Trial." Unpublished manuscript. Social Science Research Network. http://papers.ssrn.com/sol3/papers.cfm?abstract_id = 1691800.

Barkow, Rachel E. 2011. "Federalism and Criminal Law: What the Feds Can Learn from the States." *Michigan Law Review* 109:519–80.

Berman, Douglas. 2010. "Encouraging (and Even Requiring) Prosecutors to Be Second-Look Sentencers." *Temple Political and Civil Rights Law Review* 19:429–42.

Bibas, Stephanos. 2006. "Transparency and Participation in Criminal Procedure." *New York University Law Review* 81:911–66.

———. 2009. "Prosecutorial Regulation versus Prosecutorial Accountability." *University of Pennsylvania Law Review* 157:959–1016.

Bjerk, David. 2005. "Making the Crime Fit the Penalty: The Role of Prosecutorial Discretion under Mandatory Minimum Sentencing." *Journal of Law and Economics* 48:591–625.

Boerner, David. In this volume. "Prosecution in Washington State."

Bowers, Josh. 2010. "Legal Guilt, Normative Innocence, and the Equitable Decision Not to Prosecute." *Columbia Law Review* 110:1655–1726.

Brannon, Joan C. 2000. *The Judicial System in North Carolina*. Raleigh: North Carolina Administrative Office of the Courts.

Brown, Darryl K. 2010. "Can Criminal Law Be Controlled?" *Michigan Law Review* 108:971–91.

Bureau of Justice Assistance. 1994. *Understanding Community Policing: A Framework for Action*. Washington, DC: US Department of Justice.

Bureau of Justice Statistics. 2007. *National Census of State Court Prosecutors*. Washington, DC: Government Printing Office.

Burke, Alafair S. 2010. "Prosecutorial Antagonism." *Ohio State Journal of Criminal Law* 8:79–100.

Devins, Neal. 1994. "Unitariness and Independence: Solicitor General Control over Independent Agency Litigation." *California Law Review* 82:255–327.

Eisenstein, James, Roy B. Flemming, and Peter F. Nardulli. 1987. *The Contours of Justice: Communities and Their Courts.* Philadelphia: University of Pennsylvania Press.

Fairfax, Roger. 2011. "Prosecutor Nullification." *Boston College Law Review* 52: 1243–81.

Federal Bureau of Investigation. 2009. *Crime in the United States.* Washington, DC: US Department of Justice. http://www.2fbi.gov/ucr/cius2009/index .html.

Flemming, Roy B., Peter F. Nardulli, and James Eisenstein. 1992. *The Craft of Justice: Communities and Their Courts.* Philadelphia: University of Pennsylvania Press.

Frase, Richard. 2005. "State Sentencing Guidelines: Diversity, Consensus, and Unresolved Policy Issues." *Columbia Law Review* 105:1190–1232.

Gershowitz, Adam M. 2008. "An Informational Approach to the Mass Imprisonment Problem." *Arizona State Law Journal* 40:47–84.

Gold, Russell. 2011. "Promoting Democracy in Prosecution." *Washington Law Review* 86:69–124.

Gordon, Sanford C., and Gregory Huber. 2009. "The Political Economy of Prosecution." *Annual Review of Law and Social Science* 5:135–56.

Governor's Committee on Law and Order. 1969. *Assessment of Crime and the Criminal Justice System in North Carolina.* Raleigh: North Carolina State Government.

Green, Bruce. 2003. "Criminal Neglect: Indigent Defense from a Legal Ethics Perspective." *Emory Law Journal* 52:1169–99.

Green, Bruce A., and Fred C. Zacharias. 2004. "Prosecutorial Neutrality." *Wisconsin Law Review* 2004:837–904.

Harris, David. 2012. "The Interaction and Relationship between Prosecutors and Police Officers in the US, and How This Affects Police Reform Efforts." In *The Prosecutor in Transnational Perspective*, edited by Erik Luna and Marianne Wade. New York: Oxford University Press.

Hinsdale, Charles Edwin. 1972. *North Carolina's General Court of Justice.* 2nd ed. Chapel Hill, NC: Institute of Government.

Johnson, David T. 2002. *The Japanese Way of Justice: Prosecuting Crime in Japan.* New York: Oxford University Press.

Jones, Jeffrey M. 2010. "Party ID: Despite DOP Gains, Most States Remain Blue." Washington, DC: Gallup. http://www.gallup.com/poll/125450/Party-Affiliation-Despite-GOP-States-Remain-Blue.aspx.

King, John D. 2012. "Procedural Justice, Collateral Consequences, and the Adjudication of Misdemeanors." In *The Prosecutor in Transnational Perspective*, edited by Erik Luna and Marianne Wade. New York: Oxford University Press.

Kleiman, Matthew, and Cynthia G. Lee. 2010. *North Carolina Assistant District Attorney/Victim Witness Legal Assistant Workload Assessment.* Williamsburg, VA: National Center for State Courts.

Klingele, Cecelia M., Michael Scott, and Walter Dickey. 2010. "Reimagining Criminal Justice." *Wisconsin Law Review* 2010:953–98.

Levine, Kay L. 2005. "The New Prosecution." *Wake Forest Law Review* 40: 1125–1214.

———. 2006. "The Intimacy Discount: Prosecutorial Constructions of Intimacy in Statutory Rape Cases." *Emory Law Journal* 55:691–748.

Long, Cheryl X., and Richard T. Boylan. 2005. "Salaries, Plea Rates, and the Career Objectives of Federal Prosecutors." *Journal of Law and Economics* 48: 627–51.

Luna, Erik, and Marianne Wade. 2010. "Prosecutors as Judges." *Washington and Lee Law Review* 67:1413–1532.

Marx, G. Paul. 2008. "Public Defender Reform Act of 2007: The Process of Reform." *Louisiana Bar Journal* 56:12–14.

Miller, Marc L., and Samantha Caplinger. In this volume. "Prosecution in Arizona: Practical Problems, Prosecutorial Accountability, and Local Solutions."

Miller, Marc L., and Ronald F. Wright. 2008. "The Black Box." *Iowa Law Review* 94:125–96.

———. 2012. "Reporting for Duty: The Universal Prosecutorial Accountability Puzzle and an Experimental Transparency Alternative." In *The Prosecutor in Transnational Perspective*, edited by Erik Luna and Marianne Wade. New York: Oxford University Press.

Milwaukee County District Attorney's Office. 2012. "Community Prosecution: Focused, Responsive, and Efficient Law Enforcement." Milwaukee: Milwaukee County District Attorney's Office. http://county.milwaukee.gov/Image Library/User/jkrueger/Electronic/cpu.pdf.

Mosteller, Robert P. 2007. "Exculpatory Evidence, Ethics, and the Road to the Disbarment of Mike Nifong: The Critical Importance of Full Open-File Discovery." *George Mason Law Review* 15:257–318.

Neff, Joseph, and Mandy Locke. 2011. "DA's Say Guilt of Suspects Affirmed." *Raleigh News and Observer*, March 23.

North Carolina Administrative Office of the Courts. 2007. *The Judicial System in North Carolina*. Raleigh: North Carolina State Government.

———. 2010. *North Carolina Trial Court Case Load Statistics*. Raleigh: North Carolina Administrative Office of the Courts. http://www.nccourts.org/Citizens/SRPlanning/Statistics/CaseLoad.asp.

North Carolina Conference of District Attorneys. 2008. *Continuation Review Report*. Report presented to the North Carolina House of Representatives and Senate Appropriations Committee, North Carolina Administrative Office of the Courts, Raleigh.

North Carolina Courts Commission. 1967. *Report of the Courts Commission to the North Carolina General Assembly*. Raleigh: North Carolina State Government.

North Carolina Office of Indigent Defense Services. 2011. *North Carolina's Criminal Justice System: A Comparison of Prosecution and Indigent Defense Resources*. Durham, NC: Office of Indigent Defense Services.

North Carolina Rural Economic Development Center. 2005. *Population in*

North Carolina. Raleigh: Rural Economic Development Center. http://www
.ncruralcenter.org/databank/trendpage_Population.php.

North Carolina Sentencing and Policy Advisory Commission. 2011. *Structured
Sentencing Statistical Report for Felonies and Misdemeanors—Fiscal Year 2009/
10 (July 1, 2009–June 30, 2010).* Raleigh: North Carolina State Government. http://www.nccourts.org/Courts/CRS/Councils/spac/Publication/
Statistical/Annual/Default.asp.

O'Neill, Michael Edmund. 2004. "Understanding Federal Prosecutorial Declinations: An Empirical Analysis of Predicative Factors." *American Criminal
Law Review* 41:1439–98.

Perry, Steven W. 2006. *Prosecutors in State Courts, 2005.* Washington, DC:
National Criminal Justice Research Service.

Podgor, Ellen S. 2004. "Department of Justice Guidelines: Balancing 'Discretionary Justice.'" *Cornell Journal of Law and Public Policy* 13:167–202.

Poulin, Anne Bowen. 2008. "Government Appeals in Criminal Cases: The
Myth of Asymmetry." *University of Cincinnati Law Review* 77:1–62.

Raleigh News and Observer. 2011. "Census: Suburban, Urban Counties Blossom;
Rural Counties Wilt." March 2.

Richman, Daniel C. 1999. "Criminal Law, Congressional Delegation, and Enforcement Discretion." *UCLA Law Review* 46:757–814.

———. 2003. "Prosecutors and Their Agents, Agents and Their Prosecutors."
Columbia Law Review 103:749–832.

Robinson, Paul H., Michael T. Cahill, and Usman Mohammad. 2000. "The
Five Worst (and Five Best) American Criminal Codes." *Northwestern University Law Review* 95:1–84.

Sanders, John L. 1959. *Constitutional Revision and Court Reform: A Legislative
History.* Chapel Hill, NC: Institute of Government.

Simons, Michael A. 2009. "Prosecutors as Punishment Theorists: Seeking Sentencing Justice." *George Mason Law Review* 16:303–55.

Spindel, Donna J. 1981. "The Administration of Criminal Justice in North
Carolina, 1720–1740." *American Journal of Legal History* 25:141–62.

Sundt, Jody L. 1999. "Is There Room for Change? A Review of Public Attitudes toward Crime Control and Alternatives to Incarceration." *Southern
Illinois University Law Journal* 23:519–37.

Turner, Jenia Iontcheva. 2012. "Prosecutors and Bargaining in Weak Cases: A
Comparative View." In *Transnational Perspectives on Prosecutorial Power,* edited
by Erik Luna and Marianne Wade. New York: Oxford University Press.

US Census Bureau. 1995. "Urban and Rural Population: 1900 to 1990." Washington, DC: Census Bureau. http://www.census.gov/population/censusdata/
urpop0090.txt.

US Department of Justice. 2009. *United States Attorneys' Manual: Dual and
Successive Prosecution Policy.* http://www.justice.gov/usao/eousa/foia_reading
_room/usam/title9/2mcrm.htm.

Working Groups on Best Practices. 2010. "New Perspectives on *Brady* and
Other Disclosure Obligations: Report of the Working Groups on Best Practices." *Cardozo Law Review* 31:1961–2036.

Wright, Ronald F. 1994. "North Carolina Prepares for Guideline Sentencing." *Overcrowded Times* 6(February). Reprinted in *Sentencing Reform in Overcrowded Times*, edited by Michael Tonry and Kathleen Hatlestad. New York: Oxford University Press, 2001.

———. 1995. "North Carolina Avoids Early Trouble with Guidelines." *Overcrowded Times* 6(February). Reprinted in *Sentencing Reform in Overcrowded Times*, edited by Michael Tonry and Kathleen Hatlestad. New York: Oxford University Press, 2001.

———. 1998*a*. "Flexibility in North Carolina Sentencing, 1995–1997." *Overcrowded Times* 9(6). Reprinted in *Penal Reform in Overcrowded Times*, edited by Michael Tonry and Kathleen Hatlestad. New York: Oxford University Press, 2001.

———. 1998*b*. *Managing Prison Growth in North Carolina through Structured Sentencing*. Washington, DC: National Institute of Justice, Program Focus. http://www.ncjrs.org/txtfiles/168944.txt.

———. 1999. "The Future of Responsive Sentencing in North Carolina." *Federal Sentencing Reporter* 11:215–18.

———. 2002. "Counting the Cost of Sentencing in North Carolina, 1980–2000." In *Crime and Justice: A Review of Research*, vol. 29, edited by Michael Tonry. Chicago: University of Chicago Press.

———. 2004. "Parity of Resources for Defense Counsel and the Reach of Public Choice Theory." *Iowa Law Review* 90:219–68.

———. 2005. "*Blakely* and the Centralizers in North Carolina." *Federal Sentencing Reporter* 18:19–22.

———. 2009. "How Prosecutor Elections Fail Us." *Ohio State Journal of Criminal Law* 6:581–610.

———. 2010. "Public Defender Elections and Popular Control over Criminal Justice." *Missouri Law Review* 75:803–29.

Wright, Ronald F., and Susan Ellis. 1993. "A Progress Report on the North Carolina Sentencing and Policy Advisory Commission." *Wake Forest Law Review* 28:421–61.

Wright, Ronald F., and Rodney L. Engen. 2006. "The Effects of Depth and Distance in a Criminal Code on Charging, Sentencing, and Prosecutor Power." *North Carolina Law Review* 84:1935–82.

———. 2007. "Charge Movement and Theories of Prosecution." *Marquette Law Review* 91:9–38.

Wright, Ronald F., and Wayne A. Logan. 2006. "The Political Economy of Up-Front Fees for Indigent Criminal Defense Counsel." *William and Mary Law Review* 47:2045–87.

Marc L. Miller and Samantha Caplinger

Prosecution in Arizona: Practical Problems, Prosecutorial Accountability, and Local Solutions

ABSTRACT

Arizona prosecutors focus on solving local crime problems and administrative challenges. Both workaday habits and provocative innovations emerge without much attention being paid to statewide or national concerns. Arizona prosecutors dramatically downplay their own power and discretion. They do not recognize the risk of disparity highlighted in the scholarly literature. They see themselves as operating within a context of established habits, office structures, and procedures including supervisory review. The local perspective is not a barrier to innovation, but innovations are largely restricted to the places where they take root. Institutions that invite statewide interaction and priority setting, such as the Arizona Prosecuting Attorneys Advisory Council, the Arizona Attorney General Office, and the Arizona Criminal Justice Commission, do not in practice facilitate statewide developments. Other collaborations, including various initiatives under the label "community prosecution," work toward local variation rather than toward statewide consistency.

Arizona prosecutors focus on solving crime problems and administrative challenges in their own counties or cities. Both workaday habits and some provocative innovations emerge without much attention be-

Marc L. Miller is vice dean, Ralph W. Bilby Professor at the University of Arizona College of Law, and codirector of the Arizona Law Program in Criminal Law and Policy. Samantha Caplinger is a doctor of law graduate of the University of Arizona College of Law. We thank Ronald Wright, Michael Tonry, Jack Chin, and Kathie Barnes for comments and Kaitlin Shaw for research assistance.

265

ing paid to statewide or national debates and concerns, whether the concerns are those of prosecutors in other places or those of scholars and other observers of the criminal justice system.

Statewide data are not available on basic aspects of how criminal cases are processed, such as the number of cases brought by law enforcement; the declination, charging, and plea bargaining decisions of prosecutors; and sentencing outcomes. This makes statewide quantitative comparisons and policy evaluation difficult to impossible.

In this essay, we describe prosecution in Arizona primarily on the basis of extensive in-person and telephone interviews with county and city chief prosecutors.[1] In several cases an office representative preferred to respond in writing, and some of the interview subjects sent additional written information or responded to additional questions. We interviewed lead county attorneys and senior staff in 14 of the 15 county attorney offices and heard from about the same number of leaders from among the largest of the many city attorney offices.

Prosecutors were asked about office structure, priorities and challenges, innovations, community prosecution, and hiring and training of new prosecutors. We asked about relationships with other prosecutorial agencies and about working with other actors in the criminal justice system including defense lawyers.

Several themes emerged. First, with regard to local political and administrative issues, Arizona prosecutors are largely uninterested in major issues discussed in the national media and by legal scholars. For example, Arizona was in the national news in 2010–11 because of new state criminal immigration laws, especially the highly controversial law known as Senate Bill (SB) 1070 (Chin et al. 2010; Chin and Miller

---

[1] We are deeply grateful to all of the county prosecutors, city prosecutors, and others who responded willingly and enthusiastically to our request for information. In particular, we thank John Belatti, Linda Brinwood, Kent Catanni, Jay Cairns, Brad Carlyon, Amelia Cramer, Steve Duplissis, Daisy Flores, Art Harding, Robert Hubbard, Vicki Hill, Barbara LaWall, Jose Machado, Dennis McGrane, Michael Mitchell, Elizabeth Ortiz, Jennifer Paetkau, Richard Platt, Mike Rankin, Derek Rapier, Edward Rheinheimer, Tobin Sidles, George Silva, Matthew Smith, Tami Suchowiejko, Alfred Urbina, Sam Vederman, James Walsh, and Michael Whiting. These county and city attorneys and chief criminal deputies responded in person, on the phone, and in writing, and often committed an hour or more, or involved multiple members of their staffs. Most interviews were with the chief prosecutor in the relevant jurisdiction. Some of these individuals also provided feedback on a draft of this essay. This openness reflects well on the confidence and public-mindedness of prosecutors in Arizona. Perhaps it also reflects western habits of neighborliness. But in any case, this essay could not have been written or would be very different if based solely on the limited public information, statistics, and literature.

2011). Yet our interviews with prosecutors revealed a surprising lack of attention to illegal immigration as a policy issue or problem.

The people we interviewed do not recognize some of the issues about prosecution systems discussed in legal scholarship or at least see those issues in fundamentally different lights. For decades legal scholars have been concerned about the substantial and unreviewable discretionary power of prosecutors in declination and charging; risks of disparity across cases, prosecutors, and counties; the hidden nature of plea bargaining; and the effects of mandatory minimum sentences on disparity and system resources. Arizona prosecutors dramatically downplay their own power and discretion. They do not see themselves operating within a wide discretionary range of decision making, and they do not recognize the risk of disparity highlighted in the scholarly literature.

The perspectives of scholars and on-the-ground prosecutors are related, but they are disjointed—more distant cousins than siblings. The second major theme in this essay helps to explain why. Prosecutors understand their own decisions in a subjective context of established habits, office structures, and procedures including supervisory review. They see themselves not as exercising broad unfettered discretion but as operating within well-established conventions, expectations, and local norms. The local perspective is not a barrier to innovation. We learned about provocative innovations that address some of the larger critiques of modern prosecution such as the hidden and unreviewable nature of plea negotiations. But these innovations have so far seldom migrated from the places where they take root. The lack of good statewide process data may explain why innovations have been slow to spread or to make a dent in national scholarly or practitioner conversations. Data would make possible more convincing assessment of reforms within the state and beyond.

American prosecution is highly localized. One prominent theme in the literature on how prosecutors and other criminal justice actors resolve individual cases and make the system function is the role of local "courtroom work groups" (Eisenstein and Jacob 1977; Heumann 1977; Nardulli 1978; Eisenstein, Flemming, and Nardulli 1988; Flemming, Nardulli, and Eisenstein 1992). One recurring element in this literature is the "legal pluralism" of American law and politics and how this plays out with special vigor in the "craft and court communities" of criminal justice systems built primarily at the county and city levels. Prosecutors have a distinctive and unequal role in the courtroom work group because of their political role as protector of law and order, the electoral process that gives them political legitimacy, and their functional ability to screen, charge, dismiss, and plea out cases (Flemming, Nardulli, and Eisensten 1992, p. 23).

Our interviews reinforce the importance of the localism of American criminal justice. We explored the power of localism in the context of collaborations and relationships with other actors in the local justice system and around the state. Several institutions potentially provide forums for statewide conversations and priority-setting; these include the Arizona Prosecuting Attorneys Advisory Council, the Arizona Attorney General, and the statutory Arizona Criminal Justice Commission. But these institutions do not have a strong generalizing effect. Other collaborations, including various initiatives under the umbrella label "community prosecution," work toward local variation rather than toward larger consistency.

Here is how this essay is organized. Section I describes Arizona and its prosecutorial systems. Section II discusses prosecutors' power and discretion and their lack of concern about disparity, sentencing reform, and mandatory minimum penalties. Section III examines transparency in plea bargaining and Section IV prosecutorial accountability and initiatives undertaken to obtain legitimacy and support. Section V explains the working relationships of prosecutors and other criminal justice actors in Arizona. Section VI compares theory and practice.

I. Geography, Demography, and General Institutional Design

Arizona is well known for its stunning geography—from the Grand Canyon, Petrified Forest, and the Four Corners region in the north; to the mountains of the Mogollon Rim and Sedona; and to the major deserts, basin and range, and the long border with Mexico. The political, social, and institutional geography are similarly varied.

Arizona is the sixth-largest state in the United States with an area of about 114,000 square miles. Arizona is a "public lands" state, and 45 percent of the land area is under federal jurisdiction. Tribal lands constitute over one-quarter of the state.

With a population of about 6.4 million in 2010, Arizona has the sixteenth-largest population but is ranked thirty-third by population density. Arizona is also relatively poor, with per capita income near the bottom in the United States, ranking forty-first in 2008. Yet Arizona has also been one of the fastest-growing states, growing almost 35 percent in population in the 1980s, 40 percent in the 1990s, and more than 28 percent in the first decade of the twenty-first century (US Department of Commerce 2012).

Arizona is made up of 15 counties and 91 incorporated cities. Phoenix and Tucson account for about 33 percent of the state's population. But that figure significantly understates the urban, small town, and rural divisions. Phoenix is located in Maricopa County, which alone constitutes about 63 percent of the state's population. Maricopa and Pima Counties, where Tucson is located, account for about 80 percent of the state's population.

The other 20 percent is spread across the state. The third-largest city, Yuma, has a population just under 100,000; Flagstaff is a university town with a population of 65,000. At the other end of the spectrum the historic town of Jerome has a population of 353.

A. Arizona Prosecutors

The fundamental organization of Arizona prosecutors is at the level of counties and incorporated cities and towns. County prosecutors handle felonies and some misdemeanors. City and town prosecutors handle misdemeanors.

Prosecutors function within the Arizona court system. The Arizona Supreme Court is the top of the hierarchy, followed by the Arizona Court of Appeals, which has offices in Phoenix and Tucson. Next are the superior courts, located in each county, which hear all felony cases occurring in that county. Superior courts try felonies. Each county has a justice court and each municipality has a municipal court; they hear misdemeanor cases, traffic violations, and preliminary hearings in felony cases.

After being convicted at the misdemeanor level, the defendant may appeal to the superior court and from there to the court of appeals and the Arizona Supreme Court. After being convicted on the felony level, the defendant can appeal to the court of appeals and then the Arizona Supreme Court. Some issues, such as the death penalty, require a mandatory appeal. Others are subject to discretionary review.

Section 11-532 of the Arizona Revised Statutes (ARS) provides that "the county attorney is the public prosecutor of the county and shall

. . . [a]ttend the superior and other courts within the county and conduct, on behalf of the state, all prosecutions for public offenses."

There are 15 county attorneys and a larger number of city and town prosecutors. The five largest county and prosecutors' offices are in Maricopa County (around 320 attorneys), Pima County (around 75), Phoenix (around 52 attorneys), Tucson (around 35 attorneys), and Pinal County (around 30 attorneys). These offices account for about a quarter of just over 800 prosecutors in the state system. There are five additional offices with more than 30 attorneys, around five with 15–30 attorneys, and about eight with 5–15 attorneys. The remainder—the largest number of offices but a minority of all prosecutors—have five or fewer attorneys.

Two other prosecution offices—the Arizona Attorney General's Office and the US attorney—and one other kind of prosecutor (tribal prosecutors) round out the picture.

The US Attorney's Office for the District of Arizona is the chief federal law enforcement officer in the state. The office is headquartered in Phoenix, with branches in Tucson, Flagstaff, and Yuma. Arizona and Mexico share a 389-mile border, and the US attorney has substantial interaction with some Arizona prosecutors due to immigration and drug cases.

The US Attorney's Office also has ongoing interactions with tribal prosecutors because of the complex nature of jurisdiction over crimes committed on tribal lands. The US Attorney's Office handles cases ranging from firearms trafficking to fraud relating to tribal gaming and from bank robberies to theft of artifacts, protected plants, wildlife, and cultural resources and also has jurisdiction over violent crime in Indian country and mortgage fraud.

Arizona has a large population of Native Americans. In 2000, Arizona had the third-largest total population of Native Americans; on the release of 2010 census data, it will almost certainly have moved to second after Alaska. Arizona has 24 recognized Native American reservations, each with its own jurisdiction, laws, and prosecuting authorities.

In Arizona most felony criminal acts are handled by the county attorney's office in the county in which the crime occurs. All misdemeanors that occur in incorporated municipalities are handled by a city attorney's office or town attorney's office. All misdemeanors in unincorporated areas are handled within the county attorney's offices.

County attorney's offices in Arizona also represent county government, including county boards and officials, in civil matters (ARS sec. 11-532[A][7], [9–10]). This can create conflicts because the county attorney's office is expected to investigate the offices which in the end it will be defending in the instance of a lawsuit. For example, Arizona law requires the county attorney to "receive, investigate, and resolve complaints about any member of the board of supervisors or county commissioner." This law makes the county attorney the lawyer for the county commissioners, which makes the task of investigating complaints a delicate one.

The attorney general serves as the chief legal officer of the state. The office is mandated by the Arizona Constitution, and the attorney general is elected for a 4-year term. The Attorney General's Office represents and provides legal advice to most Arizona agencies, enforces consumer protection and civil rights law, and prosecutes criminals charged with complex financial crimes and certain conspiracies involving illegal drugs.

The Attorney General's Office also handles all appeals from felony convictions throughout the state. The Attorney General's Office has jurisdiction over Arizona's Consumer Fraud Act, white-collar crime, organized crime, public corruption, environmental laws, civil rights laws, and crimes committed in more than one county. The attorney general has offices in Phoenix and Tucson.

B. Organization and Funding

The way cases are handled varies by the size of the office. The larger and midsized county attorney's offices have a horizontal prosecution system for the most part, whereas the city and town offices and the smaller county attorney's offices have vertical systems. In vertical prosecution, a case is handled by a single attorney at each major stage in the process such as bail, charging, trial, and sentencing: one attorney takes each case "up the ladder." In horizontal prosecution, different attorneys handle a case at each major stage, or at each rung on the ladder. Sometimes the difference between horizontal and vertical systems is analogized to "assembly line" versus "custom-made" systems, though the relative efficiencies and case-by-case specialization probably reflect a variety of staffing, funding, and management factors. In very small offices, the need for each attorney (including the county attorney) to be able to handle any case at any point effectively mandates a vertical system.

The larger offices often have vertical units for particular types of crime. These vary by office but typically include homicide, drug crimes, auto theft, sex crimes, domestic violence, and white-collar crime. At times the decision to establish a vertical structure is based on grant funding, for example, a grant in support of sex crime prosecution. At other times the vertical system is preferred because the crime calls for special expertise, such as for white-collar offenses.

Prosecution offices throughout Arizona show both variety and continuity, with similar structures and issues appearing mostly on the basis of size, but with different innovations and priority areas in each location. The two largest counties, Maricopa County and Pima County, are the most similar to urban prosecutors' offices commonly described in the scholarly literature. The largest city attorney offices in Phoenix and Tucson operate on a similar scale, although misdemeanor prosecution has largely been ignored by scholars (Feeley 1992). These two city attorney offices have more attorneys and staff than any other county attorney's office in the state other than Maricopa and Pima. But the smaller counties have interesting stories to tell in relation to creativity in prosecution approaches and the formation of strong norms when the work is shared among a handful of lawyers, including the lead prosecutor.

Jobs with the county and city attorney (and with public defender organizations) have traditionally been entry-level legal positions. It is not uncommon for 10 or even 20 percent of a graduating University of Arizona Law School class to take such positions. Often such jobs have gone to graduates who worked in the office as an extern or over one or more summers. Many young lawyers work in prosecutors' offices for several years and then move to private civil or criminal practice or to other government positions. Career prosecutors work their way up the ranks, especially in larger offices with more extensive organizational structures and divisions.

With the legal profession and the larger economy under strain, a government career path is increasingly desirable for many law graduates, and yet the opportunities for initial employment are becoming scarcer as a result of budget cutbacks and reduced turnover. When new positions open, county attorneys find that they can be more selective than in the past and that there is an opportunity to draw from a larger number and wider-ranging pool of applicants, including for positions in smaller towns and smaller offices. When the economy picks up steam, it will be interesting to see if the turnover rate within county attorney's offices increases. The increase in applicants during the downturn may mean that law graduates are increasingly becoming interested in criminal law or that law graduates are increasingly willing to take whatever job they can get.

The relevance of defense experience in hiring was a topic discussed with each county attorney and several city and town attorneys. Generally defense experience was seen as a positive factor. Some interviewees, however, question the loyalty of such an applicant and said that prior defense experience, even a summer job or externship, raises questions about whether the applicant really wants to be a prosecutor or just wants a job. Other offices greatly value defense experience and point to the additional value such candidates bring because of their ability to see both sides of cases. Several county attorneys remarked that they rarely receive applications from people with defense experience.

Some offices that in the past tended to hire recent law graduates are now looking for experienced attorneys. Experienced attorneys can carry a greater burden from the start and usually have demonstrated their desire for prosecution. This development, however, may be disadvantaging highly qualified candidates who have a deep passion and commitment to criminal law yet are fresh out of law school or coming from a judicial clerkship. Some counties have established 1-year experience requirements and say that they are finding applicants with such experience, especially in the civil realm. This change excludes applicants who have criminal clerking experience as they do not have a year of practice experience. Students with extensive experience as law clerks may actually have more criminal law experience than an attorney with a year of civil practice experience.

Smaller offices remark that they like to "steal" prosecutors from the larger offices. For some prosecutors there is a great appeal to being part of a smaller office where they have a larger voice on policy and more discretion in handling cases.

Funding for county and cities attorneys is mostly local—from county and city budgets—although county attorneys also receive some funds from state, federal, and sometimes private sources. The county boards of supervisors receive funds from the Arizona legislature that are added to the county general fund revenues, consisting of taxes, fines, and surcharges. Generally, the county attorney prepares a proposed budget for the county board of supervisors. Each county attorney presents the fiscal situation to the board at a public meeting.

So, for example, the Coconino County Attorney's Office has a total budget of approximately $4.9 million, of which $2.8 million comes from county general funds, and $2.1 million comes from a mix of "special revenue funds" including state appropriations, grants, and county Racketeer-Influenced Corrupt Organization funds. The Pima County Attorney's Office has a budget of around $32 million. Approximately 60 percent comes from the county general fund. For the much larger Maricopa County Attorney's Office, with a budget of around $60 million, around 78 percent comes from general fund sources, about 10 percent from special revenues, and about 9 percent from grants.

A small amount of funding comes directly from the Arizona legislature. The legislature created the Arizona Criminal Justice Commission to enhance the effectiveness and coordination of the criminal justice system. The commission is to identify needs and revisions in the system and make reports. The Arizona legislature created a special line item in the Arizona Justice Commission budget for State Aid to County Attorneys, which in fiscal year 2010–11 was $973,600. The commission is required to distribute these funds to each county on the basis of a composite index formula using superior court felony filings and county population.

Counties may also apply for federal and state grants, and many do. Grants are to be used for specific purposes, such as a federal border grant, which gives offices money to be used on border crimes only. Pima County has an entire unit, consisting of four attorneys and staff, paid for by this grant. Recently several significant federal grants to Arizona county attorney offices have been cut. The largest county offices have legislative liaisons whose primary responsibility is to advocate for legislation, including appropriations, on behalf of the county.

City attorney offices have a similar funding situation. The town or city they are in has a council that appropriates money to the office as part of its annual budget. The general fund income in cities and towns also comes from a variety of taxes. The Arizona legislature at times has appropriated funds directly to cities, and the cities also receive modest grants from the Arizona Prosecuting Attorneys Advisory Council (APAAC).

II. Power, Discretion, and Disparity

Scholars see prosecutors as the dominant actors in American criminal justice systems. That dominance is perceived to come from the power they wield, the discretion they exercise, and their political role as the representative of the people. Most scholars express concern with the extent of prosecutorial power and discretion, especially given the relatively few formal avenues for external regulation. For example, Kenneth Culp Davis, one of the academic godfathers of modern administrative law, wrote that "viewed in broad perspective, the American legal system seems to be shot through with many excessive and uncontrolled discretion powers but the one that stands out above all others is the power to prosecute or not to prosecute" (Davis 1969, p. 188).

More specific scholarly critiques of prosecutorial power stem from the starting point of the massive power and discretion vested in American prosecutors (Wright and Miller 2002; Davis 2007; Miller and Wright 2008). This discretion includes the decision not to charge individuals—the power to decline cases (Bowers 2010).

Three primary concerns about prosecutorial power and discretion include possibilities of unwarranted disparities within and across criminal justice systems, risks of racial and other invidious distinctions, and the enhanced powers accorded prosecutors by the proliferation of mandatory minimum sentence and career offender statutes (Miller 2004). Other critiques focus on the extent to which prosecutorial power and discretion undermine efforts to craft coherent, proportional, and resource-sensitive sentencing schemes and the effects of excessive power over preliminary stages of the criminal justice process such as bail (Ebbeson and Konecni 1975; Bibas 2009; Rehavi and Starr 2012).

We saw no signs of concerns about excessive prosecutorial power, the exercise of prosecutorial discretion, or risks of disparity among the Arizona prosecutors we interviewed. Not one expressed concern about potential disparate treatment of suspects or defendants. Across the state we found no concern or even substantial interest in topics that touch on disparity such as comparison of prosecutorial decisions across districts, the role of statewide prosecutorial policy discussions, the role of the attorney general, and the impact of mandatory minimum sentences.

A. Discretion

Perhaps the lack of interest in our questions about prosecutorial discretion and unwarranted disparities simply reflects that prosecutors like the power they have. Power to produce desired outcomes allows prosecutors to achieve what they perceive to be just outcomes across many cases. Another possibility, for which there was some confirmation during the interviews, is that prosecutorial power is viewed as a reflection of local, not statewide, concerns, and so disparity within a county attorney's office would be of greater concern than disparity between offices.

We concluded that most prosecutors, including the heads of offices and senior officials who were most of our interviewees, do not believe that they exercise substantial discretion; they see their powers as large but regulated by a combination of statutory law, judicial and adversary review, and local norms, and they believe that these constraints and norms minimize concerns about disparity. Ronald Wright and Marc Miller have discussed this widely held perspective of prosecutors—and also by judges and probation officers and other actors in the criminal justice system—as the difference between objective (scholarly) and subjective (practitioner) views of discretion (Miller and Wright 2008; Wright and Miller 2009).

Prosecutors do not deny the conceptual possibility that they might choose from among a wide range of potential charges in a particular case or that through declinations and plea bargains there might be a wide range of outcomes and sanctions in similar cases. But practitioners respond to the terms "power" and "discretion" as if they believe scholars assume that practitioners exercise random or varied power, something akin to throwing a dart to decide charges, acceptable pleas, and sentences. To the contrary, practitioners see their decision making as reasoned and following familiar and established patterns for familiar facts and settings. Thus their experience of the exercise of discretion is an experience of normality and rationality, and one that is inconsistent with the concerns of scholars.

A lack of concern for disparate treatment of defendants is a direct by-product of the belief that constrained discretionary choices are actually being made. If the subjective perception is that like cases are treated alike—that hard cases are closely examined and familiar cases are handled "in the usual way"—then the risk of disparity (or imagined disparity) is seen as minimal.

The emphatically local nature of prosecutorial power and policy also explains lack of interest in disparities between jurisdictions or around the state. At a gathering of lawyers in Tucson sponsored by the Pima

County Bar Association, the audience discussed whether disparities in prosecutorial decision making in Arizona should be a subject of concern. Pima County District Attorney Barbara LaWall mentioned a case in a neighboring county (Cochise) of an older family member who was prosecuted for aiding a younger family member who had committed a crime. In return, an audience member (almost certainly a defense attorney) observed that lesser charges and penalties attached to possession of 100 pounds of marijuana in Cochise County than in Pima County. These were treated by the participants as observations about the reality of differences across counties, but no one expressed concern about those differences.

B. Sentencing Guidelines

A confirmation of the lack of concern among prosecutors in Arizona about disparities can be seen in a lack of interest in (and even full awareness of) modern sentencing guideline reforms. Structured sentencing systems are a systemic national response to concerns about disparities (Frankel 1973; Parent 1988; Frase 2005). Since the early days of guidelines in Minnesota, Washington State, and the federal system, scholars and policy makers have been concerned that prosecutorial discretion can undermine achievement of the goals of more rational sentencing including reduction of unwarranted sentencing disparity and wiser allocation of punishment resources (Boerner 1995). But modern sentencing guidelines can also be seen as providing a framework that conceptually and institutionally allows for more attention to be paid to issues of proportionality and disparity between individual cases and across systems, including a framework for more structured decision making by prosecutors working within guideline systems (Wright 1999, 2005a, 2011).

When we asked several chief prosecutors about the possible relevance of sentencing guidelines to Arizona, several responded that Arizona already had sentencing guidelines and sometimes asserted that the existence of these guidelines produces similar sentences across the state. From a national standpoint, neither sentencing scholars nor the National Association of Sentencing Commissions considers Arizona to be part of the modern guideline sentencing reform movement (Reitz 1998; Frase 2005; http://thenasc.org/aboutnasc.html).

Arizona has a set of presumptive legislative sentence standards that are characterized as minimum, presumptive, and maximum sentences (and sometimes additional mitigated or aggravated sentences) by offense class and criminal record (Byrd 1994). These code provisions incorporate a variety of mandatory minimum sentences, repeat offender, and truth-in-sentencing provisions. The Arizona Supreme Court issues annual "guidelines" reflecting the most current code provisions, the 2011 version of which runs 10 pages.

Follow-up questions to prosecutors pointing out the difference between the Arizona legislative sentencing "guidelines" and sentencing guideline reforms in places such as North Carolina and Virginia were met with an emphatic lack of interest. That is in line with recent articles in the Arizona state bar publication, the *Arizona Attorney* magazine. In an article titled "Incomplete Sentence: No Traction for Reform in Arizona," editor Tim Eigo documented the deeply rooted hostility among prosecutors to the idea that guideline sentencing reforms might have any relevance to Arizona, despite a prison and jail population of 54,000; an imprisonment rate of 580 per 100,000, above the national state average of 502; and a corrections budget of more than $1 billion in a state experiencing extreme financial stress (Eigo 2012).

The lack of interest in sentencing reform was nicely captured by Eigo when he quoted a staff attorney at the APAAC: "'Sentencing reform' is a solution in search of a problem in Arizona. It is being driven by a misunderstanding of how our sentencing laws actually work and a flawed belief that releasing prisoners will somehow save the state money. The fact is the right people are in prison for the right reasons in Arizona, and the public is safer as a result" (Eigo 2012, p. 36). Our point is not the soundness of the assertions made by one attorney in the statewide prosecutor's organization, but that her lack of interest and basic understanding of guidelines sentencing reform probably reflect the collective view of prosecutors around the state. These same prosecutors are perfectly willing to innovate on other matters, but not one expressed interest in supporting guidelines sentencing reform.

In other states, prosecutors have played essential roles in proposing, developing, implementing, and promoting sentencing reforms, and prosecutors have generally had a major and often the decisive voice on sentencing commissions (Parent 1988; Wright 1999). Given the absence of any chief prosecutor willing even to consider guideline sentencing reforms, an interesting question is what kind of information about the inefficiency or inequality of the Arizona criminal justice system might lead to a different view. Later in this essay we explore the possibility that Arizona prosecutors might at least support better information systems to assess the effectiveness of the strategies and reforms they have pursued.

C. Mandatory Minimum Sentences

Mandatory minimum penalties provide one final example of the gap between scholarly concerns and their absence among Arizona prosecutors. The scholarly literature contains compelling critiques of the effects of mandatory minimum sentences including the transfer of additional power to prosecutors, who typically have the tools to trigger or avoid the application of mandatory sentences, the corresponding undermining of the ability of defendants to seriously challenge such charges (due to the threat of even greater plea/trial differentials), and the resulting sentencing disparities (Tonry 2009; US Sentencing Commission 2011). Researchers and system actors in many systems have shown that mandatory penalties produce more dramatic disparity—often hidden disparity—than occur in their absence. That disparity reflects both dramatically different treatment of like cases and similar treatment through the application of mandatory penalties to unalike cases (Alschuler 2005; Tonry 2009).

Prosecutors tend to highlight what they see as constructive uses of mandatory minimums. Matt Smith, the chief prosecutor in Mojave County, explained in some detail how mandatory penalties in Arizona for child sexual abuse cases have aided his office in its goal of prosecuting child sexual abuse. The threat of lengthy mandatory minimum sentences elicits guilty pleas, he said, and thereby spares young victims the stress of testifying, often against a parent or relative.

Few prosecutors have been willing to explain in writing that they view mandatory penalties as a benign part of a criminal justice system (Mueller 1992). Perhaps the reason is that prosecutors like the additional power and discretion that mandatory minimum sentences provide, yet they realize that such penalties are disliked by scholars and defense lawyers and so leave the political burden of enacting and defending them to legislators. But the difference between the objective and subjective perspectives of discretion noted earlier may also help to explain the prosecutorial perspective.

County attorney Matt Smith's observations suggest that, from a subjective perspective, the leverage created by mandatory penalties can be used to achieve both convictions and secondary goals such as protecting particularly vulnerable victims who frequently would be necessary witnesses and would be called to testify if a case went to trial. Because prosecutors perceive their decisions about each case, and across cases, to be bounded by consistent judgments about the strength of evidence, the defendant's prior criminal record, and so forth, they see the benefits of their power but not the risks.

If good local and statewide data on police recommendations, prosecutorial decision making, and case outcomes were available, prosecutors, state agencies, scholars, defense lawyers, reporters, or citizens could assess the extent to which like and unalike cases were handled in a similar fashion, both within jurisdictions and across the state. While data systems alone cannot fully reveal the extent to which mandatory penalties create inequality, the absence of such data makes critical examination and self-examination virtually impossible. This is a theme to which we return.

III. Plea Bargaining and Transparency

A second predominant theme in the scholarly literature on prosecutors concerns the lack of transparency and potential for disparity that arises from the dominant use of plea bargains to resolve guilt and innocence and to shape sentences (Miller 2004; Bibas 2009, 2011). Scholars have highlighted the virtual elimination of the criminal trial and especially the jury trial as a result of the prosecutor's ability to force guilty pleas and plea bargains (Wright 2005*b*).

While plea bargaining is central to the administration of prosecutorial systems throughout Arizona, some Arizona prosecutors have shown an interest in addressing the hidden and individualized nature of the process. Several county attorneys identified unusual methods of creating more open and collective discussions about plea offers than traditional approaches afford.

One striking innovation occurred in Yavapai County. For the more populous portion of the county, and for many cases, plea bargaining takes place during what defense attorneys and the county attorney refer to colloquially as "Sharkfest" and more formally as the "Case Resolution Conference." Yavapai is small enough that prosecutors, defense attorneys, judges, and court personnel not only know each other well professionally but also interact outside of the workplace.

On the same day at the same time each week, deputy county attorneys and deputy public defenders, and occasionally some private defense attorneys, gather in one large room with their open files and discuss plea bargains. The goal from the standpoint of the prosecutor is not to make plea bargains more transparent but to reach as many plea bargains as possible in a short amount of time. Nonetheless, Sharkfest raises the question whether it is possible to inform plea negotiations with larger group norms from both prosecutors and defense attorneys by discussing cases in a group setting.

From the perspective of the county attorney, the defense attorneys at Sharkfest generally have more discretion than the line prosecutors to enter plea agreements because they answer only to their clients. Consistent with the subjective view of discretion, the deputy county attorneys claim to have relatively little discretion. According to the county attorney, the deputy county attorneys at Sharkfest are generally bound by the plea offers outlined by their charging departments, with relatively little room left for them to make changes according to the facts of the case or information supplied by the deputy public defender.

This view certainly does not fit with the general understanding among nonprosecutors of which party can exercise greater discretion in plea negotiations, and we suspect that both private and public defense attorneys in Yavapai would contest this characterization. At Sharkfest the defense attorneys pull out one of their cases, find the appropriate deputy county attorney, argue over the facts and the legal issues, and try to reach agreement on a possible bargain.

It is not the group gathering alone but the process that makes Sharkfest fascinating. While a prosecutor and a defense attorney are talking to each other, their colleagues in the same room may or may not be listening. If another lawyer—a prosecutor or a defense attorney—is listening, she may chime in with additional thoughts. She may comment on the facts, note a similar case she had in the past and the resolution to that case, or mention applicable case law. While other lawyers are not required to listen to each other's cases and are not required to interject comments, they often do. The defense attorneys generally rely on the input of their colleagues more often than do the prosecutors.

After a potential plea agreement is reached but before the defense attorney can take that plea offer to her client, the prosecutor is required to take the proposed deal to the chief deputy county attorney for approval. The chief answers to the county attorney, and the county attorney answers to the voters, so "tough on crime" is the motto (but not necessarily the reality) of Sharkfest.

According to the county attorney, defense attorneys agree that Sharkfest can be a positive phenomenon. True bargaining often takes place because defense attorneys know that once they have made their case and reached an agreement, the prosecutor will be on their side when they go together to argue to the chief. Many agreements are reached during Sharkfest, though sometimes a "happy medium" is simply not achievable.

Group settings for resolving plea bargains are not discussed in the scholarly literature. The courtroom work group literature reflects strong work group norms, but the implementation of those norms is typically left to negotiations between one prosecutor and one defense attorney (subject to occasional review and even participation from judges and magistrates). Sharkfest, by contrast, is the product of the local work group's conception of what is efficient and is not apparently an innovation to respond to the lack of transparency in typical plea bargaining processes. If the reform were grounded on deeper principles of transparency, presumably a similar process would be applied throughout Yavapai County rather than only in its more populous part.

Perhaps the outcomes from group discussion of plea negotiations are no different than would occur in hidden one-on-one negotiations. Also group discussions risk violating the attorney-client privilege, for both the prosecutor and the defense lawyer. The group setting might create even more compelling pressures to plead guilty if a particular plea offer finds approval from other defense attorneys who have handled similar cases. All of these questions are worth further analysis. That such a strikingly different plea bargaining procedure has remained unknown around the state, must less among researchers and beyond the borders of Arizona, testifies to the emphatically local focus of both the operation and assessment of Arizona criminal justice.

Other Arizona counties use innovative procedures to attempt to achieve fairness in plea offers. For example, Coconino County uses a "case review panel" to explore the appropriateness of pleas with defense attorneys in some cases. In this system a plea offer is made by the prosecutor. When the defense believes that there are factors in mitigation, equitable considerations, or additional facts that should be considered or has a counteroffer, the defense attorney requests a case review panel. The panel is composed of the county attorney, the chief deputy, a senior trial attorney, a senior charging attorney, and the assigned attorney. Defense counsel presents information to the panel, which is followed by an open discussion.

In a substantial proportion of cases—the Coconino county attorney thought that it was as much as 65–70 percent—the panel ends up adjusting the plea offer. This surprising level of adjustment no doubt requires some strong social norms on both sides; if defense attorneys raise weak cases, their own adjustment rates, and the overall rate, would no doubt decrease. At the same time, a defense attorney must satisfy the ethical obligations to individual clients to represent them diligently.

As with Sharkfest, whether a case review panel is a valuable procedural innovation in terms of transparency, fairness, equality of outcomes, or any other measure cannot be assessed from a simple description. However, lack of transparency in plea negotiations is a major critique of prosecution by criminal justice scholars, and both of these initiatives have the potential to respond to that critique.

IV. Paths to Accountability

Scholars have often commented on the extraordinary autonomy of the American prosecutor given the lack of judicial or other external review of prosecutorial decision making and especially of declination, charging, plea negotiations, and sentencing decisions (Bowers 2010; Miller and Wright 2012). Some scholars have called for more judicial oversight, notwithstanding the absence of any indication that US courts or justice systems would welcome such review. Other scholars look to internal self-regulation; still other scholars have focused on the political accountability of prosecutors.

Accountability from the perspective of Arizona prosecutors comes from their status as locally elected officials. Their priorities and policies, they say, are attentive to the needs of their local communities.

All Arizona county attorneys are elected and have to run for office every 4 years. City and town attorneys are appointed by city or town councils and the mayor. All of the county attorneys run on a partisan ticket. In 2011, the county attorneys in Arizona were equally politically balanced: about half were Republicans and half Democrats. This may surprise both in-state and out-of-state observers as Arizona is often perceived as strongly Republican, with party dominance in the state legislature, the governor's office, and the state's federal congressional delegation (both senators are Republican, as are five of eight representatives). Most representatives and senators come from the Phoenix area, which is predominantly Republican. Yet, across the state, Democrats also get elected.

The equal split should not be a surprise, as party label does not appear to shape particular prosecutor policies or priorities. County attorneys' positions in Arizona, or elsewhere, appear to be highly stable, with most running without opposition; those who run with opposition are overwhelmingly reelected (Wright 2009).

The security in office of Arizona prosecutors raises questions about the meaningfulness of accountability through local elections. It may, however, have benefits for administrative decision making and efforts at reform. Innovations in prosecutorial practice in Arizona seem to come from more senior chief prosecutors who are secure in their jobs. The same security that invites (or at least allows) innovation may provide a political shield for hard declination, charging, bargaining, or sentencing choices in controversial and high-profile cases. A politically exposed prosecutor, in contrast, may be too tempted to make decisions that are popular at the polls but are not necessarily a wise expenditure of state power or resources.

Arizona prosecutors in our interviews often referred to their accountability to the electorate. They also pointed to a variety of approaches to connect with and build accountability and support in the local community. One common theme, though attached to a wide range of policies and programs, was that they were engaged in developing "community prosecution" and were regularly interacting and communicating with citizens through speeches, community meetings, and office websites.

A. Community Prosecution

Several county, city, and town attorneys mentioned their adoption of what they call the "broken windows theory" of prosecution in discussing the responsiveness of their offices to the local community. It is not clear what they thought the broken windows theory implies. After mentioning it, prosecutors were more likely to discuss their efforts to involve the community in decisions and educating the public about the criminal justice system rather than aggressive controls on loitering, antigraffiti efforts, or enforcement of other low-level offenses (Kelling and Wilson 1982; Harcourt 2001).

Some neighborhood efforts are designed to build public support for law enforcement agencies, including provision of information about possible offenses. For example, the Community Outreach Program in Coconino County provides public education about the criminal justice system and encourages citizen action in support of public safety and justice agencies. Activities include attorney and staff participation in community meetings, neighborhood block watches, and chapter house meetings.

Other community efforts aimed more at seeking assistance in law enforcement and prosecution than in building general community (and political) support. One example is the Anti-Slum Project in Maricopa County, which focuses on "crime properties" that prosecutors and police believe attract illegal activity and contribute to the deterioration of communities. The program is chaired by a member of the county attorney's staff and is a collaboration between city and county agencies trying to clean up or remove slum properties.

The Anti-Slum Project supported legislation that requires residential property owners who rent in Arizona to register their name, address, and phone number with the county assessor's office. According to the Maricopa County Attorney's Office, this legislation has proved helpful in locating out-of-state renters who own slum properties. This project also helped to enact a criminal abatement law that put responsibility on property owners to take reasonable steps to deter repeated crime on their properties. The criteria used to determine which properties should be the focus of antislum activity include the number of police calls on the properties and past and present building and health code violations. According to the Maricopa County Attorney's Office, since 1998 the program has coordinated the successful rehabilitation of over 50 slum properties.

The Phoenix City Attorney Office has a unit labeled the Community Prosecution Bureau, which appears to combine public education with some effort to solicit advice on local enforcement and social disorder priorities. An example provided was a desire of the bureau to respond to complaints about things like graffiti, which would produce both noncriminal (cleaning up the area, new lighting, public education) and prosecutorial (prosecuting offenders) responses.

Another example of a self-identified "problem-solving approach" from the Phoenix City Attorney is called the Prostitution Diversion Program. A neighborhood asked the Phoenix City Attorney to help respond to prostitution in its area. The Prostitution Diversion Program allows prostitutes to accept diversion to a program run by a Catholic charity. If the prostitute completes the program, her charges are dismissed. The Prostitution Diversion Program is offered only one time to any individual, and the Phoenix City Attorney made no specific claims about its success rate.

Other community-based initiatives appear to be aimed at a mix of building legitimacy and support, responding to community needs, and responding to crime and disorder. For example, community justice boards started in Pima County in 1998 with the goal of reducing juvenile crime. The Pima County Attorney's Office envisioned a partnership with local neighborhoods and volunteers balanced on principles of restorative justice. The program is made up of volunteers from the community who received special training from the county attorney. The community justice boards give juvenile offenders two choices: they can volunteer to work with their community or face prosecution. Only offenders 8–17 years old and who are accused of minor offenses such as criminal trespass, property damage, simple assault, disturbing the peace, truancy, shoplifting, possession of alcohol or illegal substances, and graffiti are eligible. In 2011 there were 140 volunteers and 19 boards. The Pima County Attorney's Office claims that juveniles who participate have about a 90 percent graduation rate. The office also asserts that of those 90 percent, there is a complete lack of recidivism within 1 year of the crime being committed.

Other community efforts appear to be aimed at public education as a vehicle for obtaining greater legitimacy and support. Several larger counties—Pima, Maricopa, and Coconino—have implemented a citizen's prosecution academy. These academies are taught by attorneys within each county office, as well as by medical examiners, a crime lab specialist, and local police. Citizens are taught how criminal cases are handled from intake to grand jury review, trial, and appeals. The academy seeks to make citizens aware of public policy, social issues, and crime trends and to provide a general introduction to the criminal justice system as a whole. Several counties also have a speaker's bureau that pursues the same goals as the prosecution academies through events set up by other organizations. County attorney staff and representatives of other justice agencies speak to elementary schools, high schools, colleges, civil organizations, and other business and professional associations.

While many Arizona prosecutors discussed community-focused programs, there does not seem to be a consistent theoretical or practical goal. Community prosecution (like community policing) has become a familiar theme for prosecutors throughout the United States over the past decade (Wright, in this volume). But like innovations in case processing, prioritization of prosecutorial resources, plea bargaining, and sentencing, and diversion and prevention more generally, there do not appear to be clear articulations of the aims, costs, and benefits of the programs or data to demonstrate their success.

Several county attorneys said they would welcome better information on "what works," and several county attorneys provided examples of their own efforts to assess day-to-day booking and charges as a way of keeping track of emerging trends and making rough subjective determinations about program effects. The absence of more clearly articulated statements of purpose, measures of success, and data about operations and outcomes undermines the prospects for adoption of innovations by other counties and other states.

B. Priority Areas

Another path to increasing community outreach and support comes from crime-specific initiatives, some oriented toward prosecution and others toward diversion or civil solutions. Many of the county attorneys identified drugs, domestic violence, and, to a decreasing extent, "bad checks" as priority areas.

1. *Drugs.* Prosecutors in several counties worked with citizens and other criminal justice system actors on multiagency and public-focused responses to drug crimes. Drug issues are prominent in Arizona. This is hardly surprising given the long border with Mexico, the large amount of rural and remote land, and the poverty of the state. Many prosecutors say that they are concerned with getting help for drug users and fully prosecuting drug manufacturers and dealers.

Anti-meth coalitions exist in several counties. Members of the rehabilitation community focus on preventative measures and public education. Yavapai County started a Methamphetamine Advisory Task Force. It aims to reduce the market for methamphetamine in Yavapai County by educating the public. The task force also aims to improve the effectiveness of intervention with meth users by building a partnership between the criminal justice system and treatment and social services professionals. The meth task force is a good example of how a statewide issue is being addressed with local solutions while making use of the authority of state criminal statutes and, sometimes, additional state and federal funds.

County and city prosecutors have adopted a mix of prosecutorial, diversion, preventive, and educational strategies for drug problems. While the distinction between addicts and low-level dealers may not always be clear, one structural sorting device is a substance abuse court. These courts focus on defendants who are failing on probation primarily because of substance abuse issues, including alcohol. Several counties, both large and small, have such courts. County attorneys say that they have statistics showing that substance abuse courts lower recidivism rates and are successful in helping defendants make lifestyle changes. These statistics do not appear to be available to the public and were not provided to us, so there is no way to test or examine these claims.

2. *Domestic Violence.*   Another effort to adopt community outreach was to create a domestic violence court, modeled on the Navajo County drug court. Another response was organizational: prosecution is handled vertically within these courts. One judge handles misdemeanor cases and some felonies. The prosecution will almost always try to take the case to a preliminary hearing and not a grand jury so that the prosecution can create usable victim testimony.

Other offices have established domestic violence diversion programs. These programs usually involve monitored probation. They include a Department of Health Services–approved domestic violence education course of 26 classes. Other offices send staff to attend public events, participate in local and regional domestic violence task forces and councils, provide training on domestic violence issues, and attend training on domestic violence responses. The APAAC has also helped to send prosecutors to a national domestic violence conference in Washington, DC.

3. *Bad Checks.*   Another typical crime-specific initiative around the state was a bad check program created to decrease the use of fraudulent checks. When a bad check is received by a business, it must first send it back to the check writer, who is offered a chance to make full restitution, and the business can charge a fee. If the defendant will not make restitution, the prosecutor can turn the check over to the county bad check program, which can prosecute and seek full restitution. The

shift away from checks and toward electronic payments has reduced the importance of bad check programs in many counties.

4. *Immigration.* We were surprised that none of the Arizona prosecutors discussed immigration and capital punishment as priorities. These are areas for which Arizona has been the focus of national public attention, extensive litigation, and scholarly commentary.

Surprisingly, given the controversy over Arizona SB 1070 and other state efforts to enforce immigration laws, county attorneys said little about undocumented immigrants or the general problem of immigration enforcement as they described the function, priorities, and challenges of their offices. Of course traditionally immigration crimes are the sole province of federal prosecutors (Chin and Miller 2011). But the aim of SB 1070 is to increase state involvement in the enforcement of immigration laws. With the exception of a few prominent county attorneys, it does not appear that most Arizona county attorneys have internalized this policy shift.

Other than from the Attorney General's Office and the Maricopa County Attorney's Office, we heard a general dislike for SB 1070. The Attorney General's Office is committed to enforcing SB 1070, which creates state criminal statutes that expand on federal immigration law. Representatives of the Maricopa County Attorney's Office noted that if SB 1070 is upheld, they will enforce it. No other office said they would not enforce the law, but illegal immigrants were emphatically not a priority concern or issue for the prosecutors we interviewed, even in counties near the border.

5. *Capital Punishment.* The death penalty is available in Arizona only for first-degree murder cases. In 2002 in *Ring v. Arizona*, 536 U.S. 584 (2002), the US Supreme Court declared Arizona's then-existing judge-based death scheme unconstitutional. Some prosecutors, including capital prosecutors, believed that this was a window for abolition and would have supported the change. But the state legislature had no interest in abolition, and after *Ring*, the Arizona Supreme Court established a Capital Case Commission to consider and propose next steps.

The commission directed the state legislature and courts to change from a system dominated by judicial discretion to one defined by jury discretion. This shift led to several policy changes within county attorney's offices. The Pima County Attorney's Office formed a panel to decide which cases should be capital cases. The panel looks for aggravators such as multiple murders, child victims, and the grue-someness of the crime. Under the post-*Ring* procedures, Pima County decreased its filings of capital charges from 35 percent of capital-eligible cases to 7–8 percent.

Ring also led to an increase in Pima County in the percentage of capital cases in which death was being imposed. One explanation is that the increase is the product of better case selection through the capital panel; juries are seeing a smaller number of typically more serious cases. Another is that judges hear these cases regularly and can identify the most egregious, but jurors are probably being exposed to these kinds of cases and may be shocked by often-gruesome facts. According to the chief trial counsel, when a capital case is presented to a jury in Pima County, the defendant receives the death penalty 60 percent of the time, compared with 20 percent of the time under the prior regime.

While Pima County was decreasing its total number of capital cases, after *Ring*, Maricopa went from filing capital charges in 40 percent of capital-eligible cases to 50 percent. The Maricopa County Attorney's Office also has a capital review committee made up of division chiefs and experienced homicide prosecutors.

C. Public Communication and Transparency

All county attorneys and many city and town attorneys have websites. Many are simply a single web page with the local street address or other contact information. But some provide far more information. Each office makes decisions on what to publicize.

Several county attorney websites stand out. Yuma County alone places declination policies and data online. Pima County includes budget information. When asked why they chose to make this information available, senior personnel commented that they believed the public and policy makers overestimated how much money was being spent on prosecution and the criminal justice system in general, and they wanted to show that the prosecution system does not eat up the bulk of the criminal justice budget.

Maricopa and Pima Counties published and posted annual reports. Coconino County published a report to citizens. The value of annual or other reports depends, of course, on their content and purpose (Miller and Wright 2012). In general, annual and other public reports reflect a desire by a county attorney to inform the public about the prosecutorial function. Even reports focused less on data and more on high-profile cases, individuals, or office functions provide useful information.

Arizona prosecutors might build a more consistent practice of public communication through websites by taking the best of current practices already in the state, including annual reports (as in Maricopa); annual budgets (as in Pima); declination rates (as in Yuma); declination, charging, plea, and sentencing policies; and careful descriptions of the function and structure of each office, including special units and programs.

Accountability in smaller jurisdictions relies heavily on local relationships with other actors in the criminal justice system. The handful of large urban county and city attorney's offices in Arizona resemble large prosecutors' offices in other parts of the country. The details of relationships and decision making are highly local, but if viewed from 30,000 feet the larger offices like those in other large urban districts have horizontal structures, priority crimes, and a mix of career and short-term prosecutors. The big urban offices are where multiple projects and initiatives appear, such as the community prosecution initiatives and boards.

Small offices with five or seven attorneys look very different from the large urban offices described in the scholarly literature. They tend to operate in highly collaborative work groups, and typically the chief prosecutor carries a substantial caseload. Sometimes the chief prosecutor handles especially high-profile cases—murders and sexual assaults.

But there is innovation in small offices also. It emerges from close working relationships within the office and within smaller criminal justice systems. For example, in Apache County with a population of 70,000, the county attorney's office has about seven attorneys, and chief prosecutor Michael Whiting handles cases. When asked about the structure of the office—who handles what—Whiting replied, "Everyone handles everything." The only filtering for felonies is that the most serious cases are handled by the more senior attorneys and the county attorney himself.

The small size of the Apache County Attorney's Office parallels the size of local law enforcement and the structure of the defense function. Prosecutors have the cell phone numbers for local police and sheriff's officers and make use of them. The leaders of the various law enforcement, prosecutorial, and court agencies meet regularly and value friendly working relationships.

The public defense function in Apache County is handled by four contract defenders. Since they are contract attorneys, scheduling for hearings and discovery is more difficult than with a full-time public defender's office. But this small courtroom work group also makes accommodation and personal relationships more central, and the county attorney explained that he and his staff try hard to work effectively and smoothly with the small defense bar.

Even small counties implement some special programs and initiatives, but the number and range are small compared with the large counties and notably smaller even than midsized jurisdictions. So, for example, Apache County has a diversion program for first-time offenders, including a 26-week domestic violence program. The county attorney and other actors would like a driving under the influence drug court, and a local work group is searching for grant funding to support such an effort.

But even Apache County has a large prosecutorial presence compared to some Arizona counties. Greenlee County, population 8,041, has a county attorney with three lawyers. Graham County, population 37,045, has only one—the county attorney, Kenny Angle.

V. Working Relationships

The local focus of Arizona prosecutors was especially apparent when we discussed their working relationships with other criminal justice actors. In each jurisdiction, the primary relationships were with local law enforcement, courts, and defense counsel and then with various other entities that interacted with the criminal justice system. This local perspective is consistent with the courtroom work group literature. It is also consistent with a separate literature that focuses on prosecutors as part of an administrative system that, especially in urban jurisdictions, must respond to and process huge numbers of cases (Lynch 1998).

The emphatically local and primarily administrative perspective of the prosecutors we spoke with was mediated to a modest extent by two institutions with a statewide perspective: the Arizona Attorney General's Office and the statewide APAAC. While both the Attorney General's Office and the APAAC have the potential to provide statewide leadership and to try to pursue greater uniformity in county and city attorneys' offices, they do not.

A. The Arizona Attorney General

The Arizona Attorney General's Office has broad concurrent jurisdiction with the county and city attorneys, meaning that its lawyers generally can prosecute Arizona crimes. Exceptions include homicide and domestic violence, although the attorney general can "receive" jurisdiction if the county attorney transfers such cases to his office. In practice the Attorney General's Office focuses its criminal prosecutorial workload on white-collar crimes, on specific areas such as mortgage fraud, and on crimes occurring on state property. The attorney general handles criminal appeals for the entire state.

Section 41-193 of the Arizona Revised Statutes gives the attorney general authority for criminal cases by providing that "the department of law shall be composed of the attorney general and the subdivisions of the department as created." The attorney general should operate when deemed necessary or at the direction of the governor to "prosecute and defend any proceeding in a state court other than the supreme court in which the state or an officer thereof has an interest." The attorney general is also directed to "assist the county attorney of any county in the discharge of the county attorney's duties." The attorney general has taken "assist the county attorney" to mean aiding with complex cases, conflict cases, and cases in which the attorney general has a particular expertise, such as white-collar crime.

The attorney general is granted authority to handle appeals in ARS 11-352(B), which states, in pertinent part, "Upon receipt of an appellant's brief in a criminal appeal, the county attorney shall furnish the attorney general with a true statement of the facts in the case." County attorneys handle some appeals directly through common "special actions"—interim appeals, often on evidentiary issues and including challenges to the admissibility of expert testimony. If the constitutionality of a statute is at issue in an interim appeal, judges will ask the attorney general to file an amicus brief, though such issues are quite uncommon as part of special actions. In a modest proportion of special actions in which substantial legal issues are at stake, or in areas where the law is changing, the attorney general will work with county attorneys as part of a special action. The closest working relationships are between the attorney general and the larger and nearby county attorneys—especially Maricopa, but also Pinal, Yavapai, and sometimes Coconino Counties.

No county prosecutor we spoke with expressed any concerns about the appellate role of the attorney general. They described turning over cases on appeal to the attorney general and then sometimes reviewing briefs for or responding to questions from the attorney general's appellate staff.

Although the attorney general has authority to file charges throughout the state, most county attorneys we spoke with indicated that the Attorney General's Office generally did not intrude into local prosecutorial affairs. Only Pinal County, whose county attorney is a former assistant attorney general, expressed any hesitation about giving cases to the attorney general (other than appeals).

The attorney general also serves as a principal contact with state legislators on matters of policy. However, the county and city attorneys speaking individually and through the APAAC (in which the attorney general is also a voting member) can and do take positions on potential legislation.

While county and city attorneys have authority to participate in national organizations or work with prosecutors in other states, the attorney general has taken a more direct role in national policy developments. For example, in part on the basis of highly controversial cases including cases before the US Supreme Court, along with a series of local reports and state legislative leadership, the attorney general has taken a prominent national role concerning the handling and preservation of, and trial and postconviction access to, DNA evidence. Arizona policies include a particular postconviction focus on cases in which there are claims of innocence. Another area of research and national policy involvement for the attorney general, working with individual county attorneys, concerns eyewitness identification procedures and recording of confessions. More recently the attorney general has taken a forceful position trying to clarify the intersection of new state laws legalizing medical marijuana and federal laws that continue to make possession and distribution of marijuana a federal crime.

B. APAAC

The attorney general's lack of effort to guide and direct county and city attorneys, and the substantial lack of interest we found throughout Arizona in seeking uniform practices and data collection, might suggest a lack of interest among prosecutors in working together at all. Yet there is a steady and surprising amount of communication, especially among county attorneys, going well beyond communications about specific cases.

The APAAC brings prosecutors from around the state together through training, policy representation in the state legislature, and communication with all prosecution offices and prosecutors and with individual offices (http://apaac.az.gov/). Scholars have done little work on the organizations that represent and work with prosecutors in multiple jurisdictions. (The legal and political science literature has begun to take account of these "translocal" organizations of government actors under the colorful acronym TOGAs; Resnik, Civin, and Freuh 2011.)

APAAC began in 1973 as the Arizona County Attorney's Association. It grew and in its modern form was created by the state legislature in 1977 (ARS sec. 41-1830). The members of the organization, its powers and duties, and funding options are specified by this statute.

The organization receives no state general fund revenues. It gets an appropriation from the Arizona Criminal Justice Enhancement Fund (CJEF). The CJEF is supported by a surcharge on criminal and civil traffic fines. Thus, despite legislative authorization for CJEF, subjects of the Arizona civil and criminal justice system, and not Arizona taxpayers, fund APAAC. The revenue stream varies with the collections of fines and penalties; the agency typically receives over $100,000 a month, or about $1.5 million annually.

The Prosecuting Attorney's Advisory Council training fund, codified at ARS section 41-1830.03, is APAAC's other funding source. Under this statute, APAAC is allowed to accept contributions, grants, gifts, donations, services, or other financial assistance from any individual, association, corporation, or other organization having an interest in prosecution training and from the federal government. All funds in the account are appropriated to the Attorney General's Office.

The primary mission of APAAC is to coordinate and provide training and education. Currently the organization serves over 819 full-time state, county, and municipal prosecutors. APAAC assists prosecutors' offices in the preparation of trial briefs, forms, and instructions. It provides research memoranda accessible to the general public on new federal and state cases and emerging issues. The organization prepares statements on proposed rule changes from the Arizona Supreme Court, which individual prosecution offices can decide not to follow. APAAC coordinates amicus briefs to the state appellate courts on issues of statewide concern and serves as liaison with agencies of all branches of government, including the legislature. APAAC also provides case-specific advice. Local prosecutors' offices contact APAAC with specific requests for advice or training.

APAAC has a council of 22 members consisting of the Arizona attorney general, the 15 elected county attorneys, four municipal prosecutors, a representative from the Supreme Court of Arizona, and, in theory, a dean of one of the state's law colleges. (No Arizona law dean is listed on the current council.) All members are ex officio, and one of the municipal prosecutors and the dean of the law school are appointed by the governor.

APAAC conducts several seminars each year (http://apaac.az.gov/training). Examples include a basic introduction to prosecution course, which all new prosecutors are encouraged to attend; a professionalism seminar; a capital litigation seminar; a grand jury seminar; a misdemeanor issue seminar; an intermediate advocacy course; a disclosure and ethics seminar; and a charging seminar. An annual criminal year seminar is held in the largest cities. Chief prosecutors throughout the state said they encouraged their staff members to attend these meetings.

APAAC also provides annual meetings for high-level criminal deputies and training for prosecutors specializing in particular areas. APAAC also holds meetings throughout the year for specialized members of each office, for example, a chief deputy meeting. These meetings encourage the chief deputies from each office to discuss current issues.

While APAAC is active and important, our interviews suggest that there are few pressures to normalize local decision making or to implement statewide policies. APAAC appears to be an effective way to train lawyers in particular prosecutorial and trial practice skills and to speak for statewide prosecutors on particular policy and budgeting issues. But the organization does not appear to be a mechanism for exchanging innovations, promoting data and research, or otherwise seeking a more consistent set of local practices.

The emphatically local prosecutorial perspective focused on the local work group and local issues remains largely unaffected by the general powers granted by state law to the attorney general or by the existence of the active and statutorily funded APAAC organization.

C. Coordination and Planning

The courtroom work group literature emphasizes that local procedures and decision making are importantly influenced by the relationships among key actors—the judiciary, prosecutors, defense lawyers, and probation officers (e.g., Eisenstein and Jacob 1977). Had the courtroom work group literature emerged in the last decade rather than in the 1970s and 1980s, it might have included victim advocates as well, at least for some cases.

We have no systematic way to assess relationships between Arizona prosecutors and other actors in the criminal justice system. We heard about some dramatic conflicts within counties and across the state. Nonetheless, many county attorneys described particular strategies for planning and cooperating with other prosecuting and investigative agencies and some striking innovations for engaging defense attorneys.

The Gila County Attorney's Office holds a meeting every 2 months with the local police chief, the sheriff, the presiding superior court judge, the presiding justice of the peace, the head clerk of the court, the head of the probation department, and a representative of the local jail. They discuss emerging issues and work together to identify changes and connections throughout the system. The county attorney always invites tribal leaders, but we were told that no representative attends from the tribal authority. The county attorney suggested that the reason might be that there is less overlap between state and tribal jurisdiction. The absence of tribal prosecutors may undermine the goal of full communication throughout the Gila criminal justice system.

The Pinal County Attorney's Office participates in the training of all local police officers, focusing on criminal procedure and constitutional law. This training is offered on a voluntary basis, and the county attorney believes that it assists effective prosecution in the long run because the police are the source of most cases received by the office and the prosecutors rely on the police for evidence and testimony. The Pinal County Attorney's Office also conducts ad hoc training for law enforcement when requested. It often sends an attorney to the police office to discuss common issues such as search and seizure law and provide case law updates. The Pinal County Attorney's Office reported that it has open communication lines with the local police chiefs and line officers.

Most county, city, and town attorneys' offices described ongoing procedures in which they work with other local and nearby prosecuting agencies to decide who should charge misdemeanors that may ultimately become felonies and decide how to handle conflict cases. The goal is to avoid charging a defendant in two different jurisdictions.

D. Shoot-Out 2.0 at the O.K. Corral

Not all relationships among local criminal justice actors in Arizona have been so happy. A striking conflict occurred 5 years ago between the Cochise county attorney and local police chiefs. This conflict and its resolution reinforce the theme of localism but also suggest the capacity of local work groups to learn and evolve.

In 2006 the newly appointed county attorney, Ed Rheinheimer, a career lawyer in the office, sent a letter to the six police chiefs in the county proposing fundamental changes in how cases were filed. Cochise was one of the few counties in Arizona in which the police departments filed felony complaints directly with the local courts, without preliminary review by the County Attorney's Office. Rheinheimer wrote:

> We all know that a high number of cases forwarded to the County Attorney's Office each week end up being dismissed, without prejudice, because, either they cannot be fit into the grand jury's schedule for that week, or the case, in the opinion of the reviewing prosecutor, requires further investigation and/or additional evidence. . . . I would estimate that of the cases which are submitted to this office after a felony complaint has been filed, virtually half are dismissed without prejudice for one or more of the reasons cited above. . . .
>
> Even though I have spoken in the past about moving toward a system where all cases are reviewed by a prosecutor before a felony complaint is filed, I have hesitated to do so for several reasons. First and foremost, I don't want anyone in the field of law enforcement to perceive the change as being, in any way, a criticism of law enforcement procedures. Police officers are not lawyers. . . . In having police officers file felony complaints, it puts them in a position of having to arrive at conclusions that they are, simply, not trained, or experienced enough to draw. They should not have to handle this burden. (Miller and Wright 2011, p. 891)

The police chiefs responded:

> We certainly understand the timeliness requirements surrounding felony complaints, but your letter does not give sufficient information on the problems encountered by your office that would encourage us to support your proposals. . . . We are extremely concerned with the dismissal of cases and your inability to take them to a grand jury. . . .
>
> Police officers are not lawyers and thank goodness for that! If lawyers had to make decisions in the split seconds our police officers have, people would be needlessly injured! There is a strong argument that the police officers need to know the law better than the lawyers, because of the need to apply it in immediate situations. . . .
>
> Our police officers are risking their lives to protect the community they serve. We don't believe they will sit back and listen to someone who insults their intelligence and minimizes the importance of their duty. (Miller and Wright 2011, pp. 892–93)

Personalities matter. There was prior tension between one or two of the police chiefs and the County Attorney's Office. But the more important story is how the conflict was resolved. Part of the problem was the inherent tension between the different standards used by police and prosecutors to assess cases. Probable cause and trial sufficiency are not the same, and it is the latter, not the former, that the County Attorney's Office uses in filing charges. When the police hear that a case has led to an indictment, they generally believe their work is done, other than appearing to testify at any trial. When the county attorney indicts, it is just the beginning of his case. For prosecutors the decision to pursue an indictment requires more information and a different and higher standard of evidence than police feel they need to file an indictment.

In Cochise the county attorney was dismissing 50 percent of the cases the police filed, and the police were very unhappy. The difference in standards can be worked out when the prosecutor screens cases; it cannot, without cost, when the police file felonies directly. Bad relations between actors in the criminal justice system, however, like those between individuals, rarely are limited to one issue. The practice before the 2006 (legal) shoot-out was for little personal interaction between prosecutors and police, with police dropping off paperwork at the County Attorney's Office and then walking out the door. This led to paperwork being misplaced and accusations about lost documents and lost cases. The documentation issue coupled with high amounts of turnover led to the exchange of letters quoted above. It has become famous in the Arizona criminal justice community.

Resolution came through a mechanism suggested by the police chiefs: a special statewide panel. The three-person panel strongly endorsed the basic framework suggested by the county attorney. As of 2012 the county attorney reports that the prosecutors and law enforcement are working together much better, partly as a result of the implementation of a new system for receiving and filing documents. When police want to file a case, they bring the case to the office and get a receipt. There is also a way to file the information online and receive an electronic receipt. The history of conflict with the local police chiefs may have some lingering effect: the county attorney commented that he thinks the system works best when prosecutors and the police are at arm's length because he believes this creates a system of checks and balances.

E. Early Disposition Courts

Several counties have developed speedy plea systems, primarily in response to caseload pressures on the local court and pretrial detention systems. One example is the Early Disposition Court (EDC) in Yavapai County. This system accepts mostly first-time defendants. The prosecution will provide discovery and make an early plea offer. The EDC in Yavapai County is administered within the Justice Court by a superior court judge who has a special calendar set aside for this process. If the defendant rejects the offer, he is indicted the following week.

Early plea offers are generally not available for defendants with prior offenses or egregious current crimes. However, it is not unheard of for a murder conviction to be solved under this system. The Yavapai county attorney explained that a defendant knows whether he committed the crime and knows his criminal history, and that most defendants do not want to deal with a full adjudicatory process.

The Yavapai early disposition system has provided huge cost savings. A jail was closed down after its initiation, saving millions of dollars. Six attorneys and four support staff run the Yavapai EDC, but these costs are easily covered through the savings on jail expenses and the reduced costs of full adjudication.

In Cochise County the system is called the Early Resolution Court

(ERC). The system was created in response to a backlog of about 700 cases. The County Attorney's Office was receiving between 35 and 40 felony submittals a day, and the grand jury was able to indict at most 20 cases a day. An increasing backlog was creating the kind of tension between police and prosecutors that had been seen earlier in the direct police filing dispute. But with better relations among the key local actors, they created the ERC. According to the Cochise county attorney, the ERC has led to a complete clearing of the backlog. Between 50 and 60 percent of cases are disposed of before indictment, and the county attorney is now indicting only eight to 10 cases a week.

After a complaint is filed, the accused is summoned to the Cochise County Justice Court and receives an initial appearance. These are never cases requiring arrest or custody. The accused is then ordered to appear before the ERC the following Wednesday morning. The accused must agree to waive a grand jury indictment or a preliminary hearing. He or she then receives an offer from the prosecutor at the ERC hearing and has a minimum of 7 and a maximum of 10 days (depending on when he or she was arrested) to consider the plea offer.

According to the county attorney, defendants receive full evidentiary disclosure—an open file policy—to encourage a quick decision. About 10 percent of the time the prosecution has only probable cause to indict. Critical information such as lab reports on blood work or DNA evidence is generally not available. In this minority of cases the county attorney takes the view that the accused knows whether he is guilty and can decide to take or reject the plea offer.

As an example of how the ERC works, in a methamphetamine case a defendant faces the possibility of 10 years in the Department of Corrections under Arizona's presumptive sentencing scheme. Under an early resolution agreement, the defendant would be offered a plea agreement to an offense with a 3-year sentence. In a typical (post-charge) case, the defendant would be offered a 5-year plea agreement.

In Pinal County, the EDC was developed in cooperation with the public defender's office and the superior court as a way to help clear up caseloads. A complaint is filed with the superior court instead of an indictment. If the accused does not accept the plea, he or she will be indicted; if he has waived a preliminary hearing, he goes to the regular docket with the understanding that he will never see the early disposition offer again. Pinal County resolves 70–80 cases a week through its EDC.

Fast-track plea bargaining procedures such as the EDCs in Cochise, Yavapai, and Pinal Counties raise significant questions about the balance of power between prosecutors and defendants. These programs illuminate precisely the dynamic that leads scholars to wonder whether American prosecutors in many settings, and making use of messy criminal codes and rigid and punitive sentencing schemes, can create such a great differential between a guilty plea and sentencing after trial that virtually every offer seems to follow the instructions of Vito Corleone: "make him an offer he can't refuse."

F. State-Federal Relations and Tribal Prosecutors

The US Attorney's Office handles only federal issues. Several county attorneys reported an especially good relationship with the current US attorney. Under an earlier US attorney, there was some tension with Pima County over drug cases. The US attorney declined to take any marijuana case under 500 pounds because of a lack of resources. This burden fell directly on the county. County attorney Barbara LaWall indicated that she would take all of the declined cases and did not want to see them go unprosecuted. Under the subsequent US attorney the thresholds disappeared, and Pima County prosecutors say the relationship has greatly improved. An example of this improvement can be seen in the handling of the shooting of Arizona Congresswoman Gabrielle Giffords and 18 other people in Tucson on January 8, 2011. The two offices coordinated before arrival on the crime scene, upon arrival at the scene, the evening after, and thereafter with daily communication. They also coordinated the provision of victim advocates.

According to the county attorneys, there is little interaction with tribal authorities. However, according to at least one tribal authority, there are several areas of overlap where coordination is needed. There is a lot of federal and tribal interaction given the critical jurisdictional framework. One county attorney says that invitations to tribal prosecutors to participate in county-level and state policy discussions are generally declined.

Some county attorneys' offices have worked to become licensed or cross-designated to prosecute on native lands and help with conflicted out-cases or those involving transportation of drugs within county lines.

A particular problem noted by county attorneys is a high level of public intoxication among Native Americans. Historically, local law enforcement officials would respond by placing many severe drunks in a "drunk tank." The Navajo County Attorney's Office is currently setting up community meetings with municipal leaders, tribal leaders, counselors, health care professionals, and members of the faith-based community to develop alternative responses.

The Navajo county attorney has negotiated intergovernmental agreements between the county, state, cities and towns, tribal authorities, and federal agencies such as the Bureau of Indian Affairs. These agreements foster working partnerships among the participants and, from the standpoint of the country, often benefit tribal lands by providing for the creation and maintenance of roads, ensuring a coordinated approach to critical activities such as homeland security and public health, and enhancing law enforcement and emergency preparedness.

VI. Theory and Practice

Part of the disjunction between the way scholars and practitioners assess prosecutorial power and discretionary decision making is a difference between objective and subjective views of discretion. Legal scholars have not adequately explored the implications of this difference. Judges (e.g., Edwards 1992) have complained about the irrelevance to practitioners of much of legal scholarship. The problem appears to be that the concerns of scholars are simply not the concerns of judges, lawyers, and legislators. Legal scholars have echoed these complaints more than answered them, with the suggestion that legal scholarship seek to be more relevant. But whether scholars and practitioners are talking with each other, or reading each other's written work, is different from the question whether they recognize the same issues or prioritize issues in the same way.

Some legal scholars have been attentive to the ways practitioners actually work, using interview and observational methods that humanize, contextualize, and inform more theoretical or purely quantitative studies. The classic political science literature on criminal courts portrays prosecutors as focused on local concerns and resolving problems on an ongoing basis as part of local work groups. That literature resonates in the county- and city-specific procedures and reforms described by Arizona prosecutors. But understanding that practitioners have a local focus and make decisions in the context of views and capacities of other system actors is not the same as recognizing that the problems they see and seek to resolve through local and regularized processes and relationships may not be the same problems scholars see.

Scholars in other fields, and especially in business and management, have focused attention on the different perspectives of scholars and practitioners. Andrew Van de Ven and Paul Johnson noted that the idea that scholars and practitioners view the world very differently has deep philosophical foundations:

> The recognition that research and practice produce distinct forms of knowledge has been long-standing in the literature. In *The Nicomachean Ethics*, Aristotle made distinctions between techne (applied technical knowledge of instrumental or means-ends rationality), episteme (basic knowledge in the pursuit of theoretical or analytical questions), and phronesis (practical knowledge of how to act prudently and correctly in a given immediate and ambiguous social or political situation). Habermas made explicit distinctions between technical and practical knowledge, which overlap Aristotle's distinctions. He viewed practical knowledge as tacit and embodied in action and technical knowledge as formal, explicit, propositional, and discursive. (Van de Ven and Johnson 2006, p. 805)

Van de Ven and Johnson continue:

> Scholarly work and managerial work differ . . . in the context, processes, and purposes of their practices. The context of the practitioner is situated in particular problems encountered in everyday activities. As such, managers develop a deep understanding of the problems and tasks that arise in particular situations and of means-ends activities that make up their solutions. Knowledge of management practice is typically customized, connected to experience, and directed to the structure and dynamics of particular situations. In contrast, scholarship is committed to building generalizations and theories that often take the form of formal logical principles or rules involving causal relationships. Scientific knowledge involves the quest for generality in the form of "covering" laws and principles that describe the fundamental nature of things. The more context free, the more general and stronger the theory.
>
> Both forms of knowledge are valid; each represents the world in a different context and for a different purpose. The purpose of practical knowledge is knowing how to deal with the specific situations encountered in a particular case. The purpose of scientific and scholarly knowledge is knowing how to see specific situations

as instances of a more general case that can be used to explain how what is done works or can be understood. (P. 806)

Others have tried to articulate in more detail the kinds of information and issues of relevance to practitioners instead of scholars. Judith Myers-Walls, writing about challenges to collaboration between researchers and practitioners in family studies and child development, emphasizes the different cultures of researchers and practitioners as reflected in such factors as different "temporal orientation," with practitioners focused more on short-term challenges, and in different "ways of knowing," with practitioners focused on "intuition, instinct, [and] direct experience" while researchers focus on "logic, statistics, systematic gathering of information, prediction . . . and empiricism" (Myers-Walls 2000, pp. 342–43; Ospina and Dodge 2005).

Commenting on a related issue—the disjunction between the views of researchers on business and management and actual managers, and the disinterest of managers in insights from scholarship—Sara Rynes, Jean Bartunek, and Richard Daft noted, "A substantial body of evidence suggests that executives typically do not turn to academics or academic research findings in developing management strategies and practices. Similarly, researchers rarely turn to practitioners for inspiration in setting their research questions or for insight in interpreting their results. Given this state of affairs, it is hardly surprising that considerable gaps often exist between the normative recommendations of organizational researchers and actual management practices in organizations" (2001, p. 340).

This literature helps to illuminate the gap between scholars and practitioners in thinking about prosecutorial power and discretion, and the potential for disparities or abuses of power that may result. Works by Wright and Miller on the difference between objective (scholarly) and subjective (practitioner) perspectives on discretion, power, and disparity are consistent with the views of these scholars from other disciplines. Information and analysis might ultimately resolve differences in objective and subjective views, but the different priorities of practitioners seem grounded in the responsibility of day-to-day problem solving and management and in the political and social contexts in which they operate.

Scholars who have highlighted the practitioner-researcher divide have for the most part directed their advice toward encouraging better collaboration. Myers-Wall encourages researchers and practitioners to "understand and manage" the conflict (Myers-Wall 2000, p. 346; Rynes, Bartunek, and Daft 2001, p. 349). Ospina and Dodge write that "as preconditions of successful collaboration, researchers need to appreciate the knowledge base that practitioners bring as insiders; trust practitioners' ability to be reflexive and sophisticated about their practice and to locate practice within a broader context or 'big story'" (2005, p. 420). Rynes and her colleagues suggest strategies for better communication aimed at the larger goal of "knowledge creation" (2001, pp. 346–51). The scholarly literature on "research utilization" described by Michael Tonry focuses on the kind of issues and circumstances concerning which policy makers and practitioners are most likely to be interested in and receptive to research-based evidence (Tonry 2010).

The implications we draw are more modest: better data systems are a precondition to better interaction between scholars and prosecutors and others in the criminal justice system. Throughout our interviews, chief and senior county attorneys and city attorneys made strong claims about the effectiveness of various initiatives, whether they were aimed at reducing criminality, making the processing of cases more efficient, making the process of plea bargaining more transparent and hence more fair, or involving the community in setting prosecutorial priorities. Yet none of these claims can be tested in the absence of more detailed and reliable data on case processing and outcomes.

Data on the operation and outcomes of justice systems should be collected and reported statewide with reasonable uniformity and address concerns of diverse actors including the state legislature and the executive branch. Currently crime data are collected and reported by the Arizona Criminal Justice Commission (http://www.azcjc.gov/ACJC .Web/Default.aspx). The commission is mandated by statute (ARS secs. 41-2401–2420) to "facilitate research among criminal justice agencies and maintain criminal justice system information" and to "facilitate coordinated statewide efforts to improve criminal justice information and data sharing." The commission is tasked with providing each year "an overall review of the entire criminal justice system including crime prevention, criminal apprehension, prosecution, court administration, and incarceration at the state and local levels as well as funding needs for the system" (ARS 41-2405, 41-2405[A][4][d]). Currently the commission, with the support of its statistical analysis center, produces reports focused entirely on crime trends rather than "criminal justice system information." But it does not appear that any additional statutory authority would be required for the commission to collect process data as well (ARS 2405[B][1]).

The prosecutors we spoke with uniformly said that they would welcome more state support for data collection and analysis about prosecutorial decision making and outcomes. Though it may sound like an academic's lament, prosecutors in other jurisdictions have found that access to better data can improve management and provide public information and that costs in creating data systems have a payoff in the more effective use of public resources and the pursuit of public safety. Similarly, prosecutors in Arizona express a desire and demonstrate efforts in both large and smaller jurisdictions to be responsive to local communities.

VII. Conclusion

We found considerable stability throughout the systems of prosecution in Arizona. We also found that the stability is grounded in local relationships and priorities within each county, each city, each office, and each set of local institutional and personal relationships. All county attorneys in Arizona seem comfortable allowing local variation—and therefore statewide variation—in such choices.

Common training and communication among prosecutors, largely through APAAC, do not appear to lead to uniform procedures or to concern for more uniform exercise of prosecutors' powers. Arizona prosecutors large and small have been innovative, yet despite the existence of a healthy communication and training institution in APAAC, innovations have been slow to spread.

The lesson for scholars and policy makers is that efforts at reform must recognize local perspectives and local power. It is important for scholars to understand how prosecutors view their own power, discretion, and prosecution priorities.

Better data systems, supported by state or federal funding, might allow for more systematic assessment of innovations. A system of prosecutors more focused on the articulation of prosecutorial and program goals and the collection of empirical evidence to test these goals would provide a more compelling basis in efficiency, public safety, health, and other values for innovations to be shared.

REFERENCES

Alschuler, Albert. 2005. "Disparity: The Normative and Empirical Failure of the Federal Guidelines." *Stanford Law Review* 58:85–117.

Bibas, Stephanos. 2009. "Prosecutorial Regulation versus Prosecutorial Accountability." *University of Pennsylvania Law Review* 157:959–1016.

———. 2011. "Regulating the Plea Bargaining Market: From Caveat Emptor to Consumer Protection." *California Law Review* 99:1117–61.

Boerner, David. 1995. "Sentencing Guidelines and Prosecutorial Discretion." *Judicature* 78:196–200.

Bowers, Josh. 2010. "Legal Guilt, Normative Innocence, and the Equitable Decision Not to Prosecute." *Columbia Law Review* 110:1655–1726.

Byrd, Cami. 1994. "Criminal Code Revision." *Arizona State Law Journal* 26: 341–43.

Chin, Gabriel (Jack), Toni Massaro, Carissa Hessick, and Marc Miller. 2010. "A Legal Labyrinth: Issues Raised by Arizona Senate Bill 1070." *Georgetown Immigration Law Journal* 25:47–92.

Chin, Gabriel (Jack), and Marc Miller. 2011. "The Unconstitutionality of State Regulation of Immigration through Criminal Law." *Duke Law Journal* 62: 251–314.

Davis, Angela. 2007. *Arbitrary Justice: The Power of the American Prosecutor.* New York: Oxford University Press.

Davis, Kenneth Culp. 1969. *Discretionary Justice: A Preliminary Inquiry.* Baton Rouge: Louisiana State University Press.

Ebbeson, James, and Vladimir Konecni. 1975. "Decision Making and Information Integration in the Courts: The Setting of Bail." *Journal of Personal and Social Psychology* 32:805–21.

Edwards, Harry. 1992. "The Growing Disjunction between Legal Education and the Legal Profession." *Michigan Law Review* 91:34–78.

Eigo, Tim. 2012. "Incomplete Sentence: No Traction for Reform in Arizona." *Arizona Attorney* (January): 36–44. http://www.azattorneymag-digital.com/azattorneymag/201201/#pg1.

Eisenstein, James, Roy Flemming, and Peter Nardulli. 1988. *The Contours of Justice: Communities and Their Courts.* Boston: Little, Brown.

Eisenstein, James, and Herbert Jacob. 1977. *Felony Justice: An Organizational Analysis of Criminal Courts.* Boston: Little, Brown.

Feeley, Malcolm. 1992. *The Process Is the Punishment: Handling Cases in a Lower Criminal Court.* New York: Sage.

Flemming, Roy, Peter Nardulli, and James Eisenstein. 1992. *The Craft of Justice: Politics and Work in Criminal Court Communities.* Philadelphia: University of Pennsylvania Press.

Frankel, Marvin. 1973. *Criminal Sentences: Law without Order.* New York: Hill and Wang.

Frase, Richard. 2005. "State Sentencing Guidelines: Diversity, Consensus, and Unresolved Policy Issues." *Columbia Law Review* 105:1190–1232.

Harcourt, Bernard. 2001. *Illusion of Order: The False Promise of Broken Windows Policing.* Cambridge, MA: Harvard University Press.

Heumann, Milton. 1977. *Plea Bargaining: The Experiences of Prosecutors, Judges, and Defense Attorneys*. Chicago: University of Chicago Press.

Kelling, George, and James Q. Wilson. 1982. "Broken Windows: The Police and Neighborhood Safety." *Atlantic Monthly* 249(3):29–38.

Lynch, Jerry. 1998. "Our Administrative System of Criminal Justice." *Fordham Law Review* 66:2117–52.

Myers-Walls, Judith A. 2000. "An Odd Couple with Promise: Researchers and Practitioners in Evaluation Settings." *Family Relations* 49:341–47.

Miller, Marc. 2004. "Domination and Dissatisfaction: Prosecutors as Sentencers." *Stanford Law Review* 56:1211–69.

Miller, Marc, and Ronald Wright. 2008. "The Black Box." *Iowa Law Review* 94:125. http://www.law.uiowa.edu/documents/ilr/miller-wright.pdf.

———. 2011. *Criminal Procedures: Cases, Statutes and Executive Materials*. New York: Wolters Kluwer Law and Business.

———. 2012. "Reporting for Duty: The Prosecutorial Accountability Puzzle and an Experimental Transparency Alternative." In *Transnational Perspectives on Prosecutorial Power*, edited by Erik Luna and Marianne Wade. New York: Oxford University Press.

Mueller, Robert. 1992. "Mandatory Minimum Sentencing." *Federal Sentencing Reporter* 4:230–33.

Nardulli, Peter. 1978. *The Courtroom Elite: An Organizational Perspective on Criminal Justice*. Cambridge, MA: Ballinger.

Ospina, Sonia, and Jennifer Dodge. 2005. "Narrative Inquiry and the Search for Connectedness: Practitioners and Academics Developing Public Administration Scholarship." *Public Administration Review* 65:409–23.

Parent, Dale. 1988. *Structuring Criminal Sentences: The Evolution of Minnesota's Sentencing Guidelines*. Stoneham, MA: Butterworth Legal.

Rehavi, M. Marit, and Sonja Starr. 2012. "Racial Disparity in Federal Criminal Charging and Its Sentencing Consequences." Law and Economics Empirical Legal Studies Center Paper. University of Michigan. http://papers.ssrn.com/sol3/papers.cfm?abstract_id=1985377.

Reitz, Kevin. 1998. "Modeling Discretion in American Sentencing Systems." *Law and Policy* 20:389–428.

Resnik, Judith, Joshua Civin, and Joseph Frueh. 2011. "Changing the Climate: The Role of Translocal Organizations of Government Actors (TOGAs) in American Federalism(s)." In *Navigating Climate Change Policy: The Opportunities of Federalism*, edited by Edella Schlager, Kirsten Engel, and Sally Rider. Tucson: University of Arizona Press.

Rynes, Sara, Jean Bartunek, and Richard Daft. 2001. "Across the Great Divide: Knowledge Creation and Transfer between Practitioners and Academics." *Academy of Management Journal* 44:340–55.

Tonry, Michael. 2009. "The Mostly Unintended Effects of Mandatory Penalties: Two Centuries of Consistent Findings." In *Crime and Justice: A Review of Research*, vol. 38, edited by Michael Tonry. Chicago: University of Chicago Press.

———. 2010. "'Public Criminology' and Evidence-Based Policy." *Criminology and Public Policy* 9:783–97.

US Department of Commerce. 2012. "State Rankings: Statistical Abstract of the United States." http://www.census.gov/compendia/statab/2011/ranks/rank29.html.

US Sentencing Commission. 2011. *Report to Congress: Mandatory Minimum Penalties in the Federal System.* Washington, DC: US Sentencing Commission.

Van de Ven, Andrew, and Paul Johnson. 2006. "Knowledge for Theory and Practice." *Academy of Management Review* 31:802–21.

Wright, Ronald. 1999. "The Future of Responsive Sentencing in North Carolina." *Federal Sentencing Reporter* 11:215–18.

———. 2005a. "Sentencing Commissions as Provocateurs of Prosecutorial Self-Regulation." *Columbia Law Review* 105:1010–47.

———. 2005b. "Trial Distortion and the End of Innocence in Federal Criminal Justice." *University of Pennsylvania Law Review* 154:79–156.

———. 2009. "How Prosecutor Elections Fail Us." *Ohio State Journal of Criminal Law* 6:581–610. http://ssrn.com/abstract=1339939.

———. 2011. "Charging and Plea Bargaining as Forms of Sentencing Discretion." In *Oxford Handbook on Sentencing and Corrections*, edited by Kevin Reitz and Joan Petersilia. New York: Oxford University Press.

———. In this volume. "Persistent Localism in the Prosecutor Services of North Carolina."

Wright, Ronald, and Marc Miller. 2002. "The Screening/Bargaining Tradeoff." *Stanford Law Review* 55:29–118.

———. 2009. "Subjective and Objective Discretion of Prosecutors." In *Criminal Law Conversations*, edited by Paul Robinson, Kimberly Ferzan, and Steven Garvey. New York: Oxford University Press.

Author Index—Volumes 1–41

The number in parentheses indicates the volume in which the essay is published.

Subject Index—Volumes 1–41

The number in parentheses indicates the volume in which the essay is published.

Title Index—Volumes 1–41

Volume Index—Volumes 1–41

Crime and Justice: An Annual Review of Research, edited by
Michael Tonry and Norval Morris, Volume 6 (1985):

Prediction and Classification: Criminal Justice Decision Making, edited by Don M. Gottfredson and Michael Tonry. Volume 9 of *Crime and Justice: A Review of Research*, edited by Michael Tonry and Norval Morris (1987):

Crime and Justice: A Review of Research, edited by Michael Tonry and Norval Morris, Volume 10 (1988):

Family Violence, edited by Lloyd Ohlin and Michael Tonry. Volume 11 of *Crime and Justice: A Review of Research*, edited by Michael Tonry and Norval Morris (1989):

Crime and Justice: A Review of Research, edited by Michael Tonry and Norval Morris, Volume 12 (1990):

Crime and Justice: A Review of Research, edited by Michael Tonry, Volume 16 (1992):

Crime and Justice: A Review of Research, edited by Michael
Tonry, Volume 22 (1997):

Crime and Justice: A Review of Research, edited by Michael Tonry, Volume 25 (1999):

Prisons, edited by Michael Tonry and Joan Petersilia. Volume 26 of *Crime and Justice: A Review of Research*, edited by Michael Tonry (1999):

Crime and Justice: A Review of Research, edited by Michael
Tonry, Volume 27 (2000):

Crime and Justice: A Review of Research, edited by Michael Tonry, Volume 30 (2003):

Youth Crime and Youth Justice: Comparative and Cross-National Perspectives, edited by Michael Tonry and Anthony N. Doob. Volume 31 of *Crime and Justice: A Review of Research*, edited by Michael Tonry (2004):

Crime and Justice: A Review of Research, edited by Michael Tonry, Volume 32 (2005):

Crime and Justice: A Review of Research, edited by Michael
Tonry, Volume 39 (2010):